Domination and Mobilization

Examining the miraculous rise of the Chinese Communist Party (CCP) and the surprising downfall of the Kuomintang (KMT) in the early twentieth century, Xiaobo Lü reveals that domination and mobilization are key for revolutionary parties to seize state power, challenging the prevailing wisdom on power-sharing in authoritarian parties and emphasizing the importance of dominant party leaders for organizational strength and resource mobilization. Lü further demonstrates that the CCP's mass mobilization infrastructure, initially seen as a disadvantage before the Sino-Japanese War, became a powerful asset during the war and led to its victory. The KMT's elite mobilization infrastructure, conversely, was decimated by the war, and its lack of a strong leader prevented a successful shift in party-building strategy. Party building subsequently played a pivotal role in shaping the successes and failures of resource mobilization for both parties. The book sheds new light on the origins of the CCP and the inner workings of revolutionary parties, making in a landmark study in Chinese politics.

Xiaobo Lü is Associate Professor at the Department of Political Science at the University of California, Berkeley. His research centers on distributive politics of fiscal policies and party building in authoritarian regimes, with a focus on China. Lü is particularly interested in how fiscal extraction shapes state–society relations and its implications on the evolution and functioning of authoritarian parties.

Domination and Mobilization

The Rise and Fall of Political Parties in China's Republican Era

XIAOBO LÜ
University of California, Berkeley

CAMBRIDGE
UNIVERSITY PRESS

Shaftesbury Road, Cambridge CB2 8EA, United Kingdom

One Liberty Plaza, 20th Floor, New York, NY 10006, USA

477 Williamstown Road, Port Melbourne, VIC 3207, Australia

314–321, 3rd Floor, Plot 3, Splendor Forum, Jasola District Centre, New Delhi – 110025, India

103 Penang Road, #05–06/07, Visioncrest Commercial, Singapore 238467

Cambridge University Press is part of Cambridge University Press & Assessment, a department of the University of Cambridge.

We share the University's mission to contribute to society through the pursuit of education, learning and research at the highest international levels of excellence.

www.cambridge.org
Information on this title: www.cambridge.org/9781009588874

DOI: 10.1017/9781009588867

© Xiaobo Lü 2025

This publication is in copyright. Subject to statutory exception and to the provisions of relevant collective licensing agreements, no reproduction of any part may take place without the written permission of Cambridge University Press & Assessment.

When citing this work, please include a reference to the DOI 10.1017/9781009588867

First published 2025

A catalogue record for this publication is available from the British Library

A Cataloging-in-Publication data record for this book is available from the Library of Congress

ISBN 978-1-009-58887-4 Hardback
ISBN 978-1-009-58884-3 Paperback

Cambridge University Press & Assessment has no responsibility for the persistence or accuracy of URLs for external or third-party internet websites referred to in this publication and does not guarantee that any content on such websites is, or will remain, accurate or appropriate.

To BBD

Contents

List of Figures	page ix
List of Tables	xi
Acknowledgments	xiii

1 The Reversal of Fortune of Revolutionary Parties 1
   1.1 Argument in Brief 4
   1.2 Why Study China in the Republican Era? 12
   1.3 What's New? 21
   1.4 Looking Ahead 28

2 A Theory of Party Building by Revolutionary Parties 31
   2.1 Resource Mobilization & Party Strength 32
   2.2 Domination Rules: Elite Incentives & Party Building 34
   2.3 The Equilibria of Party Mobilization Infrastructure 43
   2.4 From Dominant Leadership to Resource Mobilization 45
   2.5 Summary and Scope Conditions 51

3 Prewar Resource Mobilization (1921–1937) 55
   3.1 Resource Mobilization Challenges at Inception (1921–1927) 56
   3.2 The Triumph of Elite Resource Mobilization (1928–1937) 61
   3.3 Summary 73

4 Reversal of Fortune: Wartime Resource Mobilization (1937–1945) 75
   4.1 The Initial War Shock (1937–1940) 76
   4.2 The Liability of KMT's Elite Mobilization 81
   4.3 The Rise of CCP's Mobilized Compliance 86
   4.4 The Divergence of Grain Mobilization (1941–1945) 96
   4.5 Summary 107

5	The CCP: Elite Conflict & Party Struggle (1921–1934)	109
	5.1 A Tepid Communist Movement (1921–1927)	111
	5.2 CCP Elite Conflict and Party Fragility (1927–1935)	119
	5.3 Summary	135
6	Mao's Rise and the Birth of a Strong Party (1935–1945)	137
	6.1 From Contested Leadership to Dominant Leadership	138
	6.2 Unifying Party-Building Strategies	144
	6.3 The Emergence of Rural Mobilization Infrastructure	148
	6.4 Summary	151
7	The KMT: Revolutionary Party Aborted	152
	7.1 The KMT under a Dominant Leader (1921–1925)	153
	7.2 The Age of Ambition & Leadership Contestation (1925–1937)	160
	7.3 Quasi-Dominant Leader & Party Reform (1938–1945)	176
	7.4 Summary	186
8	The Legacies of Party Building in China and Beyond	188
	8.1 The CCP: *Victim of Its Own Success*	189
	8.2 The KMT: *Old Wine in a New Bottle*	195
	8.3 Dominant Leader, Mobilization Infrastructure, and Contingencies	202

Appendices	207
References	233
Index	253

Figures

1.1	Membership of the CCP and the KMT (1921–1949)	page 2
1.2	The origins of revolutionary party strength	4
1.3	CCP Central Committee class backgrounds (1921–1945)	17
1.4	KMT Central Committee factions (1924–1945)	18
2.1	Party ideology and types of mobilization infrastructure	36
2.2	Intraparty power struggle and party-building strategy	41
2.3	The equilibria of party mobilization infrastructure	44
2.4	A dynamic model of revolutionary party strength	50
3.1	Comintern aid to the CCP (1922–1927)	59
3.2	Comintern aid to the KMT and the CCP (1922–1927)	60
3.3	Comintern aid to the CCP (1927–1931)	63
3.4	Comintern aid vis-à-vis expropriation (1927–1932)	66
3.5	Sources of KMT fiscal revenue (1929–1937)	71
3.6	Prewar distribution of customs and salt production	72
3.7	Prewar distribution of KMT national government revenue by province	73
4.1	Wartime fiscal demand and supply shock to the KMT	78
4.2	Share of opium revenue in Shaan-Gan-Ning and Jin-Sui	81
4.3	Evolution of KMT response to the wartime fiscal shock	85
4.4	Evolution of CCP response to the wartime fiscal shock	96
4.5	Degree of grain extraction by the CCP and KMT	98
4.6	Sources of resource mobilization by the CCP and KMT (1939–1945)	100
4.7	Distribution of grain burden across classes of rural residents (1941–1945)	103
4.8	Statistical analyses of grain levy and party size	105
5.1	CCP membership (1921–1927)	117
5.2	Class backgrounds of party membership	118

5.3	CCP grassroots party cells and county committees (1921–1927)	118
5.4	CCP membership and party cells by province (1921–1927)	119
5.5	The policy cascade on the rise of worker	127
5.6	The policy cascade on the demise of rich peasants	128
5.7	CCP membership (1927–1937)	132
5.8	CCP grassroots party cells and county party committees (1927–1935)	132
6.1	CCP membership (1937–1945)	148
6.2	CCP membership class backgrounds in Shaan-Gan-Ning and Shandong base areas (1927–1945)	150
6.3	CCP grassroots party cells and county party committees (1935–1945)	150
7.1	KMT membership (1924–1926)	159
7.2	KMT membership (1926–1937)	171
7.3	KMT rank-and-file and military membership (1926–1935)	172
7.4	Occupational backgrounds of KMT rank-and-file members (1926–1933)	173
7.5	Geographic concentration of KMT rank-and-file members (1926–1929)	174
7.6	KMT grassroots county party committees and district cells (1926–1937)	176
7.7	KMT membership (1937–1945)	183
7.8	Education of newly recruited KMT rank-and-file members (1939–1945)	184
7.9	Occupational backgrounds of KMT rank-and-file members (1939–1945)	185
7.10	KMT grassroots county party committees and district cells (1937–1945)	186

Tables

1.1 Equilibria of elite conflict and party building	page 9
1.2 Observable indicators of key concepts	14
4.1 Outside assistance and CCP fiscal revenue	79
5.1 CCP resolutions and internal reports on party building (1921–1926)	115
7.1 Military background of KMT provincial party committee chairmen (1928–1949)	179
A.1 CCP and KMT party membership and grassroots organizations	208
A.2 CCP party membership class backgrounds (%)	209
A.3 KMT rank-and-file and military membership	209
A.4 KMT party membership occupational background (%)	210
C.1 Shaan-Gan-Ning itemized fiscal revenue (in local currency)	216
C.2 Shaan-Gan-Ning itemized fiscal revenue (in grain (*shi*))	218
C.3 Shaan-Gan-Ning itemized fiscal revenue as share of total revenue	220
C.4 Jin-Sui itemized fiscal revenue (in local currency)	221
C.5 Jin-Sui itemized fiscal revenue (in grain (*shi*))	222
C.6 Jin-Sui itemized fiscal revenue as share of total revenue	223
C.7 KMT central government itemized fiscal revenue (in millions of *fabi*)	224
C.8 KMT itemized fiscal revenue as share of total revenue	225
C.9 Degree of grain extraction by the CCP and KMT	225
C.10 Distribution of grain burden across classes of rural resident (1941–1945)	226
D.1 Regression analysis of CCP grain extraction and party size (1940–1945)	229

D.2 Regression analysis of KMT grain extraction
and party size (1941–1945)   230
D.3 Regression analysis of CCP grain extraction
and party size (controlling for informal institution)   231

Acknowledgments

"Serendipity!" This was one word a senior scholar once described his experience in academic research when I was contemplating a career in academia. During our conversation, he shared his wisdom on identifying good research projects with this single word. At the time, I did not fully grasp his meaning, but throughout the research process of this book, I have come to appreciate the unexpected and delightful surprises that define the journey of academic research.

This was not the book I originally set out to write. My initial interest lay in studying state-building under the Chinese Communist Party (CCP) in mainland China and the Kuomintang (KMT) in Taiwan after 1949. During the early stage of my research of the original topic, I cannot escape the lingering questions concerning the political development experienced by these two parties prior to 1949. It soon became clear that the reversal of fortunes between these two parties during the pre-1949 era was a far more fundamental and intriguing topic. After all, this is perhaps the only time in history when the CCP faced intense political competition from another political party. Unlike its dominance today, the CCP was the underdog in its struggle with the KMT, and the reversal of fortune between these two parties took everyone by surprise.

The deeper I ventured into this research, the more captivating it became, despite the challenges of navigating unfamiliar territory in both subject matter and research methodologies. I had to immerse myself in party histories through archival research and employ qualitative methods to uncover key empirical insights. Ultimately, the research process for this book became a highly rewarding journey, as I learned far more than I had anticipated. Most importantly, it provided me with new perspectives on the formation and evolution of political parties operating outside electoral institutions, as well as on the logic of CCP rule in contemporary China and political development under the KMT in Taiwan.

As the saying goes, "It takes a village to raise a child." I have been incredibly fortunate to receive support from countless scholars and institutions throughout the research and writing process. Writing a book based on the histories of the CCP and the KMT was a humbling experience, revealing just how much I had yet to learn. This book would not have come to fruition without the insights, encouragement, and inspiration by so many along the way. In particular, this project underwent significant transformations during two critical periods.

The first pivotal period occurred during my sabbatical leave as a National Fellow at the Hoover Institution, Stanford University, from September 2019 to May 2020. The Hoover National Fellowship provided me with invaluable time, free from teaching and administrative responsibilities, to dive deeply into the extensive literature and gain crucial insights for this book project. The exceptional library system at Stanford University offered essential resources for my early research. Although my stay at Stanford was cut short by the COVID-19 pandemic, it was during this time that the main ideas of this book began to take shape. Importantly, I was fortunate to engage in enriching conversations with many scholars at Stanford. Jean Oi and Andy Walder warmly welcomed me into the China studies community, inviting me to various events and offering the opportunity to present my preliminary work at their China Studies workshop. Jean Oi, in particular, provided detailed feedback on several early drafts of the manuscript, for which I am deeply grateful. I also greatly appreciate the discussions and insights shared by Anna Grzymala-Busse, Jen Pan, Ken Scheve, and Yiqing Xu, which offered me numerous perspectives and encouragement for this project. My heartfelt thanks go to the Hoover Institution for their hospitality and support, with special recognition to Kathy Campitelli, the fellowship program manager, who went out of her way to assist me both during and after my visit.

The second pivotal moment occurred during the book workshop I organized in December 2022. I was incredibly fortunate to have Bruce Dickson, Liz Perry, Dan Slater, and Milan Svolik as the discussants. The insights and expertise shared by these leading scholars significantly contributed to the development of my book. Their feedback helped me reformulate my arguments, highlight supporting evidence, and refine the central "hook" of the book. I owe a special debt of gratitude to Liz, who consistently supported my work throughout the research process. Despite her demanding schedule, Liz always found time to offer timely and thoughtful feedback on various drafts, from the early drafts of the manuscript to the revised chapters following the workshop. Bruce's kind encouragement and support also had a profound impact, as this book draws inspiration from his pioneering work comparing party-building by the CCP and the KMT after 1949. Dan and Milan were instrumental in helping me engage more deeply with key arguments in comparative politics. Despite an unexpected delay the day before the book workshop, Dan managed to travel to Austin for even half a day. His ability to distill the essence of my arguments and articulate the unique contribution of

Acknowledgments   xv

the book was remarkable. He also provided additional insights on the revised manuscript after the workshop and suggested the book's title – *Domination and Mobilization*, which perfectly captures the core themes of my work. Although Milan couldn't attend the workshop in person due to an unforeseen event, he read the entire manuscript and met with me over Zoom afterward. Together, these four scholars elevated my book to a new level, and it was only after this workshop that I truly began to see the light at the end of the tunnel!

I would like to extend my heartfelt thanks to my wonderful colleagues at the University of Texas at Austin. Since my arrival in Austin in 2014, I have been fortunate to be part of such a stimulating and supportive academic community. I owe a particular debt of gratitude to my wonderful colleagues Jason Brownlee, Dan Brinks, John Gerring, Wendy Hunter, Connor Jerzak, Patti Maclachlan, Raul Madrid, Kate Weaver, and Kurt Weyland, all of whom provided detailed feedback on various drafts of this book project at different stages. John, Jason, and Kurt had the challenging task of reading the preliminary drafts during the various stages of the project, yet their encouragement and enthusiasm never wavered. In addition, Wendy, Jason, and I organized a support group for each other's research projects during the summer of 2023, which was instrumental in helping me cross the finish line. Our monthly meetings were not only a source of invaluable feedback but also provided much-needed guidance in navigating the book publishing process.

I have also been fortunate to receive invaluable assistance, insightful comments and suggestions, and unwavering encouragement from numerous scholars across mainland China, Taiwan, and the United States. I thank Lisa Blaydes, Yu-tzung Chang, Yung-fa Chen, Yun-han Chu, Debbie Davis, Martin Dimitrov, Shitao Fan, Joe Fewsmith, Jessica Gottlieb, Gang Han, Haifeng Huang, Shixin Huang, Daniel Koss, Jason Kuo, Tai-chun Kuo, Ruixue Jia, Junyan Jiang, Ning Leng, Lianjiang Li, Hsiao-ting Lin, May-li Lin, Lizhi Liu, Mingxing Liu, Kevin Luo, Dan Mattingly, Anne Meng, Hsin-hsin Pan, Peng Peng, Tom Pepinsky, Jiwei Qian, David Stasavage, Scott Rozelle, Paul Schuler, Victor Shih, Tuan Hwee Sng, Ming Sun, Yuhua Wang, Wen-chin Wu, Yu-shan Wu, Kuisong Yang, Wangan Ye, Juwei Zeng, Changdong Zhang, Yang Zhang, Nuo Zhao, Zonghong Zhuo, and seminar participants at Columbia University, Harvard University, Hong Kong Baptist University, Johns Hopkins University, Georgetown University, Peking University, Renmin University, Stanford University, Tsinghua University, University of California at Berkeley, as well as the 2021 APSA Conference and 2023 AAS Conference for comments and suggestions at various stages of this project.

This book project would not have been possible without the generous financial support I received from the Center for East Asian Studies Faculty Grant, the Faculty Research Assignment (FRA), the Humanities Research Award, the Littlefield Faculty Fellowship, the Provost's Authors Fellowship, and the VPR Research & Creative Grant, all from the University of Texas at Austin. I also received the Glenn Campbell and Rita Ricardo-Campbell National Fellowship from Hoover Institution, Stanford University, which supported my sabbatical leave from Fall 2019 to Summer 2020.

I am deeply grateful to the many talented and hardworking research assistants who assisted with data collection and cleaning. My heartfelt thanks go to Liyan Chen, Yuanqing Chen, Matthew Delaguila, Andrew Garza, Zhenze Huang, Siyun Jiang, Mickey, Li, Shengqiao Lin, Kenny Miao, Jie Min, Xin Nong, Daniel Porter, Benjamin Reynolds, Hsu Yumin Wang, Daisy Ward, Byron Xu, Wenhui Yang, and Hong Zeng for their exceptional research support. I also owe much to the invaluable resources that I accessed at Academia Historia, the Hoover Institution Library & Archives, Shanghai City Archives, as well as the university libraries at Stanford University and the University of Texas at Austin, which were instrumental to my research.

I am profoundly grateful to Rachel Blaifeder, the Cambridge University Press editor, for her unwavering support of this book project from the very beginning. I also deeply appreciate the insightful comments provided by the two anonymous reviewers, whose feedback has immensely enriched the manuscript. Finally, I owe special thanks to Linda Meixner, who meticulously copyedited the entire manuscript multiple times, addressing everything from major issues to minor details, for which I am profoundly thankful.

I extend my deepest gratitude to my family, whose unwavering support has been the cornerstone of my journey. My parents, Chengxian Lü and Qinghui Wang; my sister, Xiaodan Lü; my brother-in-law, Jiaheng He; and my in-laws, Bifang Sun and Jiabiao Wang, have provided countless forms of support, allowing me to fully concentrate on this book. I also want to thank my daughters, Elena and Eleanor, who have grown alongside this book. They have filled my life with joy and have been remarkably patient even at very young age, waiting for me to complete what they affectionately called this "boring manuscript."

Last but certainly not least, my deepest thanks go to my wife, Wendy (Di) Wang, who has stood by me through the highs and lows of this journey and beyond. She is the one and only one who has always believed in me no matter the challenges, lifting my spirits during the difficult moments, and celebrating each step forward with me. Her unconditional love and support as my lifelong partner have been the bedrock of my strength, and I know I couldn't have brought this manuscript to its fullest potential without her by my side. It is to her that I dedicate this book.

1

The Reversal of Fortune of Revolutionary Parties

Was the triumph of the communist revolution in China during the early twentieth century a foregone conclusion? The Chinese Communist Party (CCP) certainly believes it was: In a fiercely held narrative, the CCP maintains that the social, economic, and political conditions of the time destined it to be the one chosen by the Chinese people, once and for all. Nonetheless, the CCP in 1935 bore little resemblance to the dominant political party it is today; its membership had dwindled to 40,000, and its remaining military forces were besieged by the Kuomintang's (KMT) troops in Shaanxi. Few could have foreseen the CCP's swift victory over the KMT in the 1946–1949 Civil War, and even the CCP leaders were surprised by the rapid collapse of the KMT.[1]

The reversal of fortune between the CCP and the KMT was arguably among the most astonishing developments in the history of revolutionary movements. Throughout much of the Republican Era, most domestic and international observers anticipated the KMT's domination as China's ruling party. Their judgment seemed indisputable because KMT membership consistently outpaced that of the CCP in the Republican Era (Figure 1.1); in fact, the KMT drove the CCP to the brink of extinction twice – in 1927 and 1935.[2] The Sino-Japanese War (1937–1945) was widely considered a critical juncture that gave rise to communism in China (Johnson 1962; Koss 2018). Although the CCP membership grew from 40,000 in 1937 to 1.2 million in 1945, the growth of KMT membership dwarfed CCP achievement, increasing from 1.5 million to

---

[1] The CCP leaders had anticipated prolonged warfare with the KMT at the time. See Chen (1998), Pepper (1999), and Coble (2023) for the collapse of the KMT government during the period of 1946–1948.
[2] The CCP membership shrank by 75 percent in 1927 during the aftermath of the anti-Communist purge and declined by another 90 percent by the end of the Long March in 1935.

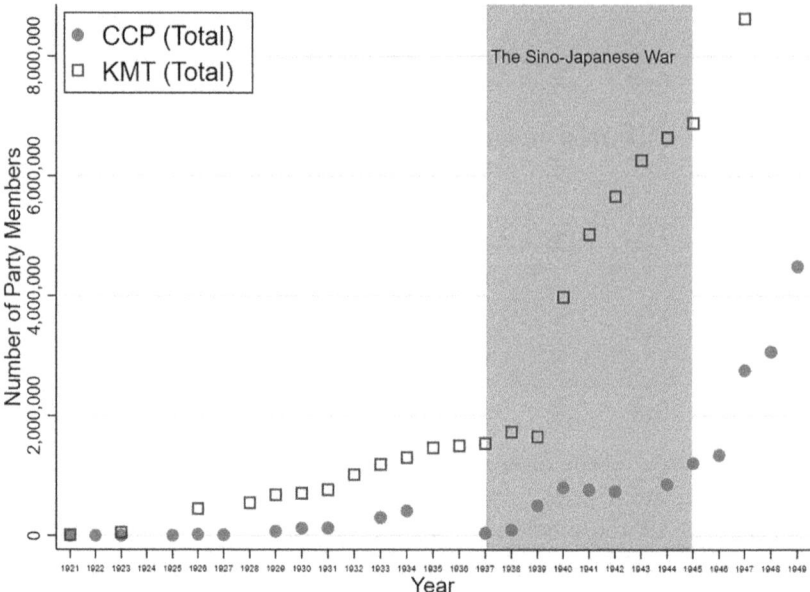

FIGURE 1.1 Membership of the CCP and the KMT (1921–1949)
Note: Author's data. See Appendix A for detailed data and their sources. The shaded area indicates the period of the Sino-Japanese War (1937–1945).

6.8 million during the same period. Even the Soviet Union placed its bets on the KMT, not once but twice, supplying greater financial and military support to the KMT than to the CCP during the First United Front (1924–1927) and the Sino-Japanese War (1937–1945).[3]

The reversal of fortune of the CCP and the KMT serves as a reminder that outcomes are far from certain for those living through revolutionary movements; most of which involve violent repression that brings them to their knees. The revolutionary movements in Algeria, Eritrea, and Bolivia were beset with internal factional division amid external repression, and existential threats failed to unify party elites and engender a resilient political party. The revolutionary movement in Vietnam was all but dead from 1930 to 1941, when the Indochinese Communist Party (ICP) repeatedly fell victim to external repression. Most revolutionary movements were born weak, and even the successful ones often caught both domestic and international observers off guard (Levitsky and Way 2022).

Earlier scholarship on revolutions highlights broader political, societal, and international contexts as well as historical, preexisting social ties and

---

[3] For Soviet aid to the CCP and the KMT, see Yang (2011), Wan (2005), and Zhu (2007). Figure 3.2 offers some comparison of Soviet aid to the CCP and the KMT from 1922 to 1927.

organizations;[4] but little is dedicated to understanding the organizational development of revolutionary entities amid violent struggles.[5] Although the collapse of old regimes and foreign intervention are crucial for creating political openings for revolutionary movements, not all such organizations manage to seize the opportunity: Behind every successful revolution lie countless failed insurrections. Anarchy and failed states are the more common outcomes following regime collapse. If the outcomes of revolutions are at the mercy of the agents involved, one cannot fully grasp the dynamics of revolutions without understanding the sources of the organizational strength of these entities. Indeed, the Chinese communist revolution would not have succeeded without the CCP's transformation from a frail and marginalized party into a disciplined and effective one, an observation shared even by Chiang Kai-shek, the leader of the KMT, in his own reflections (Eastman 1981).

Upon closer examination, the organizational changes occurring within the CCP and the KMT appear paradoxical because they contradict the conventional wisdoms surrounding authoritarian politics and revolutions. A prominent view of authoritarian politics emphasizes power sharing through institutions such as political parties and legislatures as the cornerstone of regime resilience. Key to this line of reasoning is that power sharing among political elites allows them to access the spoils of office and engenders elite cohesion.[6] Nonetheless, the downfall of the KMT followed closely on the heels of repeatedly faltering power-sharing arrangements and elite cooptation. Furthermore, the revival of the CCP was preceded by Mao Zedong's emergence as a dominant party leader, a marked contrast to the earlier period when the CCP experienced contested leadership and fragile party organization. In fact, the emergence of strong authoritarian regimes, such as China, Cuba, Eritrea, and Vietnam, has frequently been characterized by a strong political party with a dominant leader.

How can we explain the reversal of fortune of the CCP and the KMT, where a dominant leader led to successful transformation of the CCP's organization while power sharing among party elites resulted in an ineffective party organization and eventually undermined the KMT's dominance? More generally, why do some political parties succeed in overcoming adversity and

---

[4] See, for example, Eisenstadt (1978), Goodwin (2001), Moore (1966), Paige (1975), Skocpol (1979), Trimberger, (1978), and Wolf (1969). Goldstone (1980) offers an excellent review of this third generation of scholarship on revolutions.

[5] In studies of social movements, scholars have uncovered the importance of formal and informal mass mobilization through *preexisting* social ties and organizations but less about how these organizations evolve during the process of revolutionary struggle. See Gould (1995), Magagna (1991), Parsa (2000), Stokes (1993), Van Vugt (1991), and Wickham-Crowley (1992).

[6] Scholars of authoritarian politics have offered some compelling theoretical arguments and empirical evidence for this line of argument. See, for example, Blayde (2010), Brownlee (2007), Gandhi (2008), Geddes (1999), Geddes, Wright, and Frantz (2018), Magaloni (2006, 2008), Pepinsky (2007), and Svolik (2009).

transforming into robust political organizations that seize state power while others fail? These are the central inquiries that I aim to answer by examining through the lens of the organizational transformation of the CCP and the KMT in China's Republican Era.

1.1 ARGUMENT IN BRIEF

My central argument is that *domination* and *mobilization* are pivotal for the triumph of revolutionary parties. To become dominant, revolutionary parties must develop the infrastructure to mobilize not only committed individuals but also financial resources; and to mobilize effectively, the party must have a dominant leader who resolves intraparty elite conflict and facilitates building party mobilization infrastructure.

The theoretical framework centers on three claims. First, power consolidation by a party leader rather than power sharing among party elites strengthens party organization. In weak institutional environments, the emergence of a dominant party leader alleviates conflicts stemming from contested party leadership. Second, the success of a revolutionary party lies in its ability to mobilize crucial financial resources, not merely its ability to recruit committed activists. Resource mobilization plays a foundational yet often overlooked role in party strength during a protracted violent struggle. Finally, contingent events could shift the balance of power among party elites and alter the comparative advantage of party mobilization infrastructure, which in turn disrupt the equilibria of elite conflict and party strength. Viewed through this lens, the rise of the CCP and the downfall of the KMT were not preordained; instead, the reversal of fortune of these two parties arose from evolving dynamics in intraparty elite power struggles and the shifting comparative advantage of their respective mobilization infrastructures, both shaped by contingent events and unforeseen circumstances.

Figure 1.2 encapsulates the essence of my argument. In what follows, I first define the primary subject of interest in this book and then elaborate on the logic behind this theoretical framework.

1.1.1 Definition of Revolutionary Party

The primary interest of this book revolves around political entities seeking to capture state power through protracted, violent struggle, rather than through

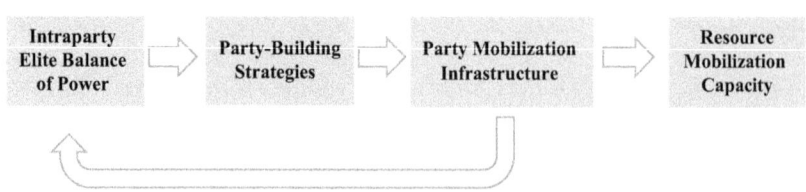

FIGURE 1.2 The origins of revolutionary party strength

electoral competition. Such entities often operate in environments where traditional political processes are either absent or ineffective. Understanding the strategies and structures these groups employ reveal the dynamics of power acquisition and state formation in contexts where conventional electoral mechanisms are not the primary means of political engagement. For the sake of simplicity, I call them revolutionary parties throughout this book[7] and adopt the following general definition based on earlier studies of revolutions and social movements: Political entities organizing formal and informal mobilization intended to overthrow a political regime through noninstitutional means, including demonstration, protest, and violence (Goldstone 2001: 142; Goodwin 2001: 9).

This minimalist definition offers two advantages by avoiding the selection of the dependent variable – investigating successful revolutions exclusively or only certain types of revolutions could result in incomplete or even misleading conclusions. Specifically, this definition embraces a wide spectrum of revolutionary entities, whose organizational forms are shaped by the strategic decisions of those driving the movement. Skocpol (1978) has distinguished two types of revolutions, suggesting that in social revolution "basic changes in social structure and in political structure occur together in a mutually reinforcing fashion, [whereas] political revolutions transform state structures but not social structures" (4–5). Social and political revolutions are, however, often intertwined. Some political revolutions originated as social revolutions, but political entities later adopted an accommodationist path without significantly restructuring the society (Levitsky and Way 2022). The exclusive focus on either social or political revolutions overlooks the strategic decisions on revolutionary strategies by political actors over the course of the political and social movements.

Second, this broad definition includes political organizations that instigate "revolutions from above" led by elites who directly control the mobilization movement and who may not always pursue radical social transformation (Trimberger 1978). The process of revolutions rarely follows a blueprint or a script fulfilling a specific purpose. Instead, revolutionary parties improvise distinct strategies when facing opportunities and constraints at various points in time. Skocpol (1979) maintained that "a purposive image is just as misleading about the processes and outcomes of historical revolutions as it is about their causes" (17). Depicted in this book, the evolution of the organizational structure of revolutionary parties arises from strategic calculations improvised by party leaders in response to internal and external pressures. These considerations change the course of party-building strategies targeting certain segments of the population for the development of their mobilization infrastructure.

---

[7] See Chapter 2 on the scope conditions of this conceptualization relative to other political entities, stemming from independence movements and insurgencies.

1.1.2 Argument 1: The Curse of Power Sharing and the Blessing of a Dominant Party Leader

When does a revolutionary party succeed in building an effective mobilization infrastructure? I argue that power consolidation by a dominant party leader, but not power sharing among a group of party elites under contested leadership, strengthens party building. At the heart of my argument lies the notion that party elites are constantly confronted with three concerns stemming from any party-building endeavor: a free-rider problem, distributional conflict, and ex ante uncertainty about party-building outcomes. Consequently, party elites under contested party leadership often pursue strategies benefiting their own power even if the party faces existential threats. The emergence of a dominant party leader, however, mitigates these concerns, thereby facilitating intraparty elite cohesion that strengthens party mobilization infrastructure.

My argument roots in two premises. First, party elites inherently yearn to reach the pinnacle of party hierarchy. Their desire is not only driven by personal ambition, but also by the belief that power accumulation is necessary to advance their preferred policies. This is true even for revolutionaries motivated by ideological orientation rather than personal ambition. Second, party elites are endowed with a variety of sources of power, which manifest in their de facto power within the party. For instance, some party elites' endowed source of power originates from their ability to raise financial resources; for others, it stems from their roles as power brokers to mobilize groups of actors through their personal networks and prestige. Some party elites even command the coercive apparatus that bolsters their de facto power.

Any party-building endeavors generating distinct benefits to each individual party elite in turn shape the elite's incentive to adopt specific party-building strategies. First, the total benefit of any party-building strategy – a stronger party – creates a free-rider problem, as party elites prefer to benefit from a stronger party without bearing personal costs. Thus, party elites would rather see others commit their vital resources to engage in labor-intensive party-building endeavors. Second, some party elites may disproportionately obtain more benefits from a party-building strategy than others, therefore altering the balance of power among party elites. Hence distributive conflict emerges because party elites become acutely sensitive to any potential power shifts resulted from a specific party-building strategy. Last, the party-building outcomes are often uncertain ex ante, undermining party elites' commitment to pursue party-building strategies, given that they operate in a rapidly changing revolutionary movement.

With these characteristics, the relative balance of power among party elites shapes their preferences for party-building strategies. On the one hand, party elites under contested party leadership are motivated to pursue party-building strategies that strengthen their individual source of power. That is, they prefer a party-building strategy expanding their share of benefit over a strategy that benefits the whole because the distributional conflict overshadows the free-rider problem. Such dynamics frequently culminate in conflicting and inconsistent party-building strategies, thereby compromising the integrity and quality of party mobilization infrastructure. On the other hand, the rise of a dominant party leader alleviates the distributional conflict and free-rider problem, resulting in a coherent set of party-building strategies that strengthen the overall party mobilization infrastructure.

1.1.3 Argument 2: The Primacy of Resource Mobilization as Party Strength

Irrespective of which party-building strategy is chosen, the goal is to enhance the party mobilization infrastructure that is essential for party strength. Building on studies of social movement[8] and state capacity,[9] I define party mobilization infrastructure as collective vehicles that enable a revolutionary party to project its power onto the political system. The party mobilization infrastructure extends beyond merely soliciting political support from key sectors of society; rather, assistance from party members is sought to leverage their formal and informal networks to ensure policy compliance from the targeted population, willingly or unwillingly. Simply put, party members act as conduits to achieve the party's objectives under an effective party mobilization infrastructure.

What then is the primary objective of a revolutionary party's mobilization efforts? Earlier scholars have examined mobilization of *human resources*, that is, attracting and recruiting committed activists and fighters willing to make personal sacrifices and undertake risky actions when facing repression from existing power holders. Few, however, have emphasized the mobilization of *financial resources* despite their pivotal role in funding the operation of revolutionary parties. The need to secure stable financial resources is particularly crucial during protracted violent and nonviolent struggle against the state. Scholars have recently turned their attention to rebel taxation and governance[10] as key aspects of civil conflict beyond the greed and grievance framework developed by Collier and Hoeffler (2004).

How can party mobilization infrastructure facilitate resource mobilization? For the sake of simplicity, I conceptualize two ideal types of party mobilization infrastructure for resource mobilization. The first type entails a mass mobilization infrastructure aiming to overthrow existing elites and state

---

[8] I follow McAdam, McCarthy, and Zald (1996), who define mobilizing structures as "those collective vehicles, informal as well as formal, through which people mobilize and engage in collective action" (3).

[9] See Mann (1984). Slater (2010) has extended this line of logic by emphasizing the importance of state infrastructural power in his studies of contentious politics in Southeast Asia.

[10] For rebel taxation, see, for instance, Breslawski and Tucker (2022), Mampilly (2021), Mampilly and Thakur (2025), and Revkin (2020).

apparatus. This is a common type of revolutionary party, in which the establishment of grassroots organizations is prioritized, and the core party members are the powerless masses occupying the lower strata of the socioeconomic hierarchy in the society (e.g., teachers, blue-collar workers, and farmers). Communist parties in Russia, China, Cuba, and Vietnam are examples of revolutionary parties with a mass mobilization infrastructure.

The second type is an elite-centric mobilization infrastructure, in which cooperation is solicited from progressive political and economic elites who serve as power brokers on behalf of the party. Revolutionary parties with an elite mobilization infrastructure prioritize building party organizations to coopt existing national and local elites, positioning them the core party members. This type of revolutionary party often manifests in revolutions from above but it could also emerge from mass social movements when party elites recalibrate their revolutionary strategies. Many of these parties originate from independence and nationalist movements, seeking liberation from the old regime occupied or sponsored by imperial powers. The KMT, the Revolutionary Nationalist Movement (MNR) in Bolivia, the Sandinista National Liberation Front (FSLN) in Nicaragua, and the Congress Party in India share many characteristics of a revolutionary party with an elite mobilization infrastructure.

Notably, elite mobilization and mass mobilization infrastructures are characterized by distinct comparative advantages and trade-offs. On one hand, building an elite mobilization infrastructure is often a pragmatic strategy because the party can quickly access financial resources with the help of existing elites serving as conduits. Nonetheless, party elites face potential rebellion risks from those elites who facilitate the party's resource mobilization: The assimilation of strong economic and political elites into a party inevitably increases the difficulty in maintaining elite cohesion. Parties with elite mobilization infrastructure under contested leadership, therefore, often exhibit a mixed capacity in resource mobilization. Although they excel in extracting resources from economic elites, this approach tends to be a leaky bucket when it comes to contributing to overall party strength. Consequently, dominant leaders rarely emerge in elite-mobilization parties with coherent party-building strategies sustained over long periods.

On the other hand, building a mass mobilization infrastructure mitigates the risk of intraparty elite rebellion, but it is a labor- and resource-intensive endeavor, requiring unwavering commitment and tremendous effort by party elites. Although the initial cost of building a mass mobilization infrastructure is staggeringly high, it allows the party to better penetrate society with grassroots organizations and to replace the power structure occupied by existing elites. Nonetheless, contested leadership exacerbates the start-up challenges in the mass mobilization infrastructure, resulting in a much weaker capacity for resource mobilization than elite parties under similar circumstances.

Although the strategic calculation of party leaders may steer the direction of party-building strategies, the type of party mobilization is bound by party

1.1 Argument in Brief

TABLE 1.1 *Equilibria of elite conflict and party building*

Mobilization infrastructure	Intraparty elite conflict	Party-building strategy	Resource mobilization capacity	Examples
Elite-centric	Contested leadership	Conflictual party-building strategy	Mixed resource mobilization capacity	KMT (1928–1945) FLN in Algeria
	Dominant leadership	Coherent party-building strategy	Strong resource mobilization capacity	
Mass-centric	Contested leadership	Conflictual party-building strategy	Weak resource mobilization capacity	CCP (1927–1935) MNR in Bolivia ELF in Eritrea ICP in Vietnam
	Dominant leadership	Coherent party-building strategy	Strong resource mobilization capacity	CCP (1938–1945) EPLF in Eritrea Viet Minh in Vietnam

Note: As discussed earlier, few dominant leaders emerged in parties with an elite mobilization infrastructure.

ideologies and external political environments. Traditionally, party ideology is viewed as a signaling device that shapes the belief system for revolutionaries and promotes multigroup and cross-class coalitions.[11] Another important function of party ideology, I contend, is serving as a constraining device that ties the hands of party elites. The interparty competition from the external political environment implies that once a revolutionary party commits to a specific type of mobilization infrastructure, it falls into a state of self-reinforcing equilibrium. Any deviation from their adopted mobilization infrastructure dilutes the party brand and identity, undermining its credibility to the core constituency and generating more harm than benefit. To this end, revolutionary parties cannot pursue mixed strategies to build a broad coalition because such efforts engender internal conflict and factionalism, resulting in incoherent party-building strategies and weak mobilization infrastructure.

Table 1.1 illustrates the implications of intraparty elite conflict and diverging mobilization infrastructure for revolutionary parties' resource mobilization capacity, along with some comparative examples. Specifically, contested leadership engenders conflictual party-building strategies, crippling the party's mobilization capacity for human and financial resources, regardless of the

---

[11] See Goldstone (2001) for a summary of studies on the role of ideology in revolutionary movements.

type of mobilization infrastructure. As illustrated in Chapter 7, the KMT's apparent domination over the CCP from 1928 to 1945 cannot conceal the relentless intraparty conflicts among its elites, resulting in a party flush with some strength in elite resource mobilization but weak penetration into the society. The revolutionary movement of the National Liberation Front (FLN) in Algeria consisted of political elites with diverse preferences, their coalition weakly linked by a nationalistic sentiment. The party was constantly mired in conflict among these elites over party-building strategies, and its attempt to implement a collegial leadership between interior and exterior broke down (Jackson 1977).

For revolutionary parties with a mass mobilization infrastructure, persistent intraparty conflict is a luxury they cannot afford. Before the seizure of state power, mass-mobilization parties lack the direct access to state and societal resources that parties with elite mobilization infrastructures enjoy. Although the fragility of these political organizations, such as the CCP from 1927 to 1935, the MNR in Bolivia, the Eritrean Liberation Front (ELF) in Eritrea, and the ICP in Vietnam, can be attributed to a variety of domestic and international factors, the failure to resolve intraparty elite conflicts was a hallmark common to all these parties.

Once a dominant leader emerges, however, these political organizations often experience a transformation leading to resilient parties. As shown in Chapter 6, Mao Zedong's power ascendancy from 1935 to 1938 fundamentally shifted the CCP away from earlier discriminatory and self-defeating party-building strategies. This crucial transformation into a peasant-centric mobilization infrastructure became a timely preparation for the CCP's expansion in grain extraction after 1941 during the Sino-Japanese War. Meanwhile, the EPLF in Eritrea broke away from the ELF in 1977, ending the earlier efforts of the ELF to divide its mass organizations on the basis of class status. The rise of Isaias Afwerki as a dominant leader turned the party into an effective mass mobilization organization that later dominated the Eritrean political system after achieving independence in 1991 (Pool 2001; Plaut 2016). Similarly, Nguyen Ai Quoc (i.e., Ho Chi Minh) has been credited for holding the Vietnamese communist movement together (Huỳnh 1982).

1.1.4 Argument 3: Contingencies as Equilibrium Disruptor

Importantly, Figure 1.2 highlights that dominant and contested party leadership must be recognized as self-perpetuating equilibria, resulting in divergent paths for party-building strategies and ultimately impacting party strength. Contested leadership breeds conflictual party-building strategies in which elites seek to bolster their own power sources while undermining their intraparty rivals, only further intensifying intraparty elite conflicts. Conversely, dominant leadership mitigates elite conflict and paves the way for the development of mobilization infrastructure that solidifies the party leader's power base.

1.1 *Argument in Brief*

The equilibrium outcome is not destined, however. Despite the best efforts of party elites, the fortunes of revolutionary parties could be subject to the changing winds of external political and economic environments. Specifically, I conceptualize contingent events as external shocks that disrupt the equilibria of intraparty elite politics and comparative advantage of party mobilization infrastructure. First, although the equilibria of the power dynamics among party elites and party-building strategies are self-enforcing, the balance of power among party elites could be upset by external contingent events, leading to a departure from the state of equilibrium. For instance, counterrevolutionary repression by France generated significant discontinuity in leadership within revolutionary organizations in Algeria and in Vietnam, reshaping factional dynamics within these two revolutionary parties.[12] Stalin initially faced stiff resistance to his power consolidation after Lenin's death. The assassination of Sergei Kirov in 1934, a member of the Bolshevik faction and friend of Stalin, became a pretext for Stalin to initiate the Great Purge that facilitated his ascent to dominant leader (Kotkin 2017; Levitsky and Way 2022). For the equilibrium of dominant leadership, the sudden departure of a dominant leader can trigger fierce power struggles among a group of equally powered party elites. This occurs because the leader had insufficient time to groom a strong successor.[13]

Second, contingent events may alter broader social, political, and economic environments, reshaping the comparative (dis)advantage of party mobilization infrastructure. Ultimately, the comparative advantage of elite-mobilization infrastructure rests on the strength of the very elites whom the party relies on. Exogenous shocks such as interstate wars, foreign invasions, and natural and economic crises could significantly weaken the de facto power of existing elites in the society and, by extension cripple those political entities relying on an elite mobilization infrastructure. Scholars have presented evidence that colonization challenged – if not dismantled – the de facto power of local elites (Acemoglu, Johnson, and Robinson 2002; Mahoney 2010). Meanwhile, economic shocks and the depletion of natural resources rattle the very foundation that dominant parties monopolize in the current political system (Greene 2007; Pepinsky 2009). Fundamentally, the success of revolutions in many societies follows on the heels of the decline of existing elites and the weakening of the old regime suffering from political and economic shocks not of their own making.[14]

---

[12] See Jackson (1977) for FLN leadership turnover in Algeria and Duiker (2000) for the ICP in Vietnam.

[13] Shih (2022) highlights the coalitions of weak political elites around strong leaders, and Egorov and Sonin (2011) develop a formal model offering important insights on the loyalty-competence trade-off facing dictators.

[14] The structural perspective of revolutions by Skocpol (1979) emphasizes how interstate wars weaken the old regime and give rise to revolutions. Studies of revolutionary parties in Levitsky and Way (2022) provide copious examples of the crucial role powerful neighboring countries and foreign support play in the fate of old regime. See Levitsky and Way (2022), Moore (1966), and Skocpol (1979).

The weakening of existing elites creates a political vacuum that parties with mass-mobilization infrastructure could fill.

1.2 WHY STUDY CHINA IN THE REPUBLICAN ERA?

The proposed theoretical framework is most applicable within a specific type of revolutionary party: Those that face intense competition to seize state power but not those that have already seized and consolidated power. In addition, electoral institutions are not the primary arena for political competition. To this end, studying the power struggle between the CCP and the KMT in China during the Republican Era, particularly the period of 1921–1945, is ideal for evaluating the theoretical arguments.

China was embroiled in wars and revolutions in the early twentieth century. The 1911 Chinese Revolution, orchestrated by the forerunners of the KMT, toppled the Qing Dynasty, ushering in the Republican Era. Subsequently, the CCP triumphed in the Chinese Communist Revolution, culminating in the establishment of the People's Republic of China in 1949. Despite being a case for scholarly inquiry of revolutions, a notable lack of comparative studies on the organizational development of the CCP and the KMT during this crucial period is apparent.

Importantly, the reversal of fortune experienced by the CCP and the KMT during China's Republican Era serves as an exemplary case for examining the intricate consequences resulting from intraparty elite power struggle, mobilization infrastructure, and unforeseen contingencies. In the remainder of this section, I first discuss the research design, detailing the ways I employ process tracing and statistical analysis to assess the principal arguments in a historical examination of the CCP and KMT spanning 1921–1945. I then summarize the key insights stemming from my case study, offering a fresh perspective on the monumental political evolution in early twentieth-century China.

1.2.1 Research Design

Case Selection. The organizational evolution of both the CCP and the KMT during the Republican Era illustrates vital variations in the explanatory and outcome variables within and between these two parties. To start, the CCP and the KMT were steered by distinct ideological orientations, resulting in the adoption of different types of mobilization infrastructures. The party ideologies were not merely theoretical guides but also actively shaped the paths that each party pursued. In addition, both parties encountered intense intraparty conflicts throughout this period, often marked by violent conflicts among party elites. The outcomes of these intraparty power struggles led to radical shifts in party-building strategies within these two parties. Finally, this tumultuous era saw various contingent events sparked by both domestic and international sources, significantly shaping the balance of power among party elites and

1.2 Why Study China in the Republican Era?

the comparative advantage of party mobilization infrastructure within and between these two parties.

Noting that the fates of the CCP and KMT were intertwined throughout this period is crucial. This distinctive feature of the within-country research design provides a holistic approach to studying the evolution of revolutionary parties, emphasizing that both internal dynamics and interactions with political adversaries within the same country are consequential drivers behind party strength. After all, the success or failure of revolutionary parties and that of their political rivals are two sides of the same coin. Examining the intra and interparty struggles between the CCP and KMT offers a holistic understanding of the drivers and outcomes of party-building strategies pursued by revolutionary parties.

A Mixed-Methods Approach. I integrate both qualitative and quantitative evidence drawn from a historical examination of the CCP and the KMT from 1921 to 1945. Specifically, I employ process tracing at critical junctures during which exogenous events shift the balance of power among party elites, resulting in radical departures in party-building strategies. I also explore the effects of exogenous shocks stemming from two types of warfare, that is, domestic conflicts vis-à-vis interstate conflicts, on the comparative advantage of party mobilization infrastructure held by the CCP and KMT, respectively. To complement the qualitative evidence, I offer quantitative analysis derived from a novel dataset constructed from party and government archives. This dataset comprises party membership size, the socioeconomic background of party members, grassroots party organizations, and importantly, both the sources and levels of financial resources mobilized by these two parties over time. The quantitative evidence underscores the pivotal role of party mobilization infrastructure in resource mobilization, particularly within the context of party-building strategies and wartime conditions.

Observable Indicators of Key Variables. To operationalize the key variables of interest, I adopt several approaches to identify the observable indicators for both explanatory and outcome variables. Some concepts present challenges in pinpointing these indicators because of their multifaceted nature and varying contexts, difficulties compounded by the scarcity of data available for this turbulent historical period. Consequently, I rely on several sets of observable indicators to measure important concepts in the theoretical framework. Table 1.2 summarizes the important indicators for these crucial concepts in the theoretical framework: intraparty elite balance of power, party-building strategy, party mobilization infrastructure, and finally, and resource mobilization.

1.2.1.1 Intraparty Elite Balance of Power

Measuring the degree of power possessed by a political actor poses an acute challenge. Not only are interpersonal power dynamics difficult to observe, but they are also fluid, changing over time. This issue is particularly pronounced in non-democracies, where electoral support and public opinion

TABLE 1.2 *Observable indicators of key concepts*

Intraparty elite balance of power	Party-building strategy	Mobilization infrastructure	Resource mobilization capacity
(1) Party leadership turnover (2) The composition of members serving on party committees (3) Opinions adopted in party decision-making	(1) Types of individuals that the party prioritizes in recruiting and holding leadership positions (2) Priority in building organizations for elite power sharing or grassroots mobilization	(1) Number of party members (2) Attributes of party members (3) Strength of grassroots organizations	(1) Sources of resource mobilization (2) Levels of resource mobilization

fail to reflect the genuine degree of power. To overcome these challenges, I employ three observable indicators to evaluate the degree of intraparty elite balance of power between dominant leadership vis-à-vis contested leadership.

Following the studies of institutional analysis, where formal structures and rules define political power in any given position, I rely on *changes* in party leadership to evaluate intraparty elite balance of power. Specifically, a party experiencing contested leadership is characterized by frequent turnover in leadership and a relatively equal share of factions in party committees. Conversely, a party under dominant leadership exhibits stable leadership and a dominant faction aligning with the leader within the committees. Meanwhile, I gauge the de facto power of party elites by examining the extent to which their preferences are reflected in decisions and policies and the allocation of resources. Specifically, I scrutinize the connection between the opinions voiced by specific party elites and the content articulated in party policy documents.

1.2.1.2 *Party-Building Strategy*

To measure the shifts in party-building strategies, I focus on the *timing* and *content* of party resolutions, announcements, and internal communications on party recruitment, internal promotion, and organizational reforms issued by both the Party Center and local party organizations. For instance, internal party documents, particularly CCP sources, contain rich information on CCP party resolutions mandating which groups of individuals the Party should recruit or exclude and who should hold leadership positions. The KMT archives reveal the important debates among party elites on the abolition of mass mobilization strategies after the purge of the CCP.

1.2 Why Study China in the Republican Era?

1.2.1.3 Mobilization Infrastructure

I use three indicators to capture the characteristics of party mobilization infrastructure: (1) size of party membership, (2) attributes of party members, and (3) strength of grassroots organizations. The size of party membership reflects a raw measure of party strength; however, the quantity of party membership does not always match the quality. Hence, I employ the second indicator – the attributes of party members – that reflects the very nature of party mobilization infrastructure. For instance, tracing the attributes of CCP party members reveals a tension in recruiting intellectuals, workers, and peasants, reflecting an urban-centric mass mobilization infrastructure vis-à-vis a rural one. The attributes of KMT members, by contrast, demonstrate the elite nature of its mobilization infrastructure despite a mass membership; moreover, the characteristics of party members reveal the nuanced strategies of party elites, each leveraging their unique sources of power with aims to bolster their influence while undercutting their adversaries. Finally, the strength of grassroots party organization, manifested in the total number of members and organizational effectiveness, is a key indicator of party grassroots mobilization capacity.

1.2.1.4 Resource Mobilization Capacity

For resource mobilization capacity, not only do I evaluate the level of financial resources mobilized by the party and its governing bodies, but I also investigate the methods and sources of revenue mobilization that reflect the very nature of mobilization infrastructure. An elite-mobilization infrastructure, for example, depends on the collaboration of economic elites, who make financial contributions through donation and taxation. A mass-mobilization infrastructure, however, relies on grassroots organizations and party members to address the complexities of taxation and fiscal extraction, ensuring widespread participation and compliance.

Data Sources. Garnering evidence on elite conflicts and party building in China during the Republican Era is challenging because violent warfare and radical party reforms undermined systematic record-keeping for both parties. Thus, I assembled the empirical evidence from scattered primary and secondary archives of party and government records. For the CCP, I rely on a wide range of compendiums containing archived political and economic records for central and local CCP activities during the period before 1949, especially in those revolutionary base areas before and during the Sino-Japanese War. As for the KMT, I rely on both internal government and party records as well as secondary sources. Specifically, the compendiums of KMT organization archives, produced by both Chinese and Taiwanese scholars, offer critical information on party building by the KMT during the Republican Era. Appendix A–C highlight the sources of CCP and KMT party and government archives used in my empirical investigation.

Some maintain that party archives may not reliably portray reality because they tend to paint an optimistic picture of party affairs without mentioning challenges and internal turmoil. This sentiment rings true for many authoritarian regimes. Nevertheless, party archives also reveal critical insights about party elite dynamics and party-building efforts, portraying surprisingly vivid information about the challenges and setbacks confronted by the CCP and the KMT. If anything, challenges and setbacks depicted in party archives are only the tip of iceberg in terms of the harsh reality both parties faced.

1.2.2 A Fresh Lens: Understanding the Reversal of Fortune of the CCP and KMT

The investigation of intraparty elite competition, resource mobilization, and contingent events shed new light on the puzzling reversal of fortune between the CCP and KMT during the Republican Era. These new perspectives bridge an important gap between the fragility of the CCP prior to 1935 and its transformation during the Sino-Japanese War. Together, these fresh perspectives call into question conventional wisdom about the ascent of the CCP and the decline of the KMT.

Power Consolidation of Party Leadership and Party Building. Although external repressive circumstances hindered the CCP's efforts to expand its mass mobilization infrastructure from 1921 to 1935, the presence of contested leadership and lack of a dominant leader were equally pivotal in exacerbating its vulnerability in the early days. The intense intraparty power struggle generated conflictual party-building strategies (Chapter 5). The CCP was, therefore, far from the disciplined Leninist party that it claimed to be,[15] suffering from leadership defection and self-defeating party-building strategies. Although the CCP achieved significant expansion during the Sino-Japanese War (1937–1945), this achievement is inextricably linked to Mao's resurgence and power consolidation from 1935 to 1938 (Chapter 6). The transformation of the CCP organization would not have happened had Mao not become a dominant party leader. Importantly, the resurgence of the CCP was driven more by the resolution of contested leadership than by his vision and tactics alone.

Figure 1.3 vividly illustrates the evolving balance of power among CCP elites, revealing two radically different pictures under contested leadership and dominant leadership from 1921 to 1945. Using data from different cohorts of CCP Central Committee (中央委员会), I trace the shares of Central Committee (CC) members stemming from different social backgrounds, a proxy for the balance of power among party elites. Under contested leadership, we observe frequent and pronounced changes in the social backgrounds of CC members

---

[15] Van de Ven's (1992) careful study of early activities of the CCP from 1921 to 1927 reveals that it lacked a centralized leadership with ideological authority and that party mobilization primarily relied on interpersonal networks instead of party mobilization infrastructure.

1.2 Why Study China in the Republican Era?

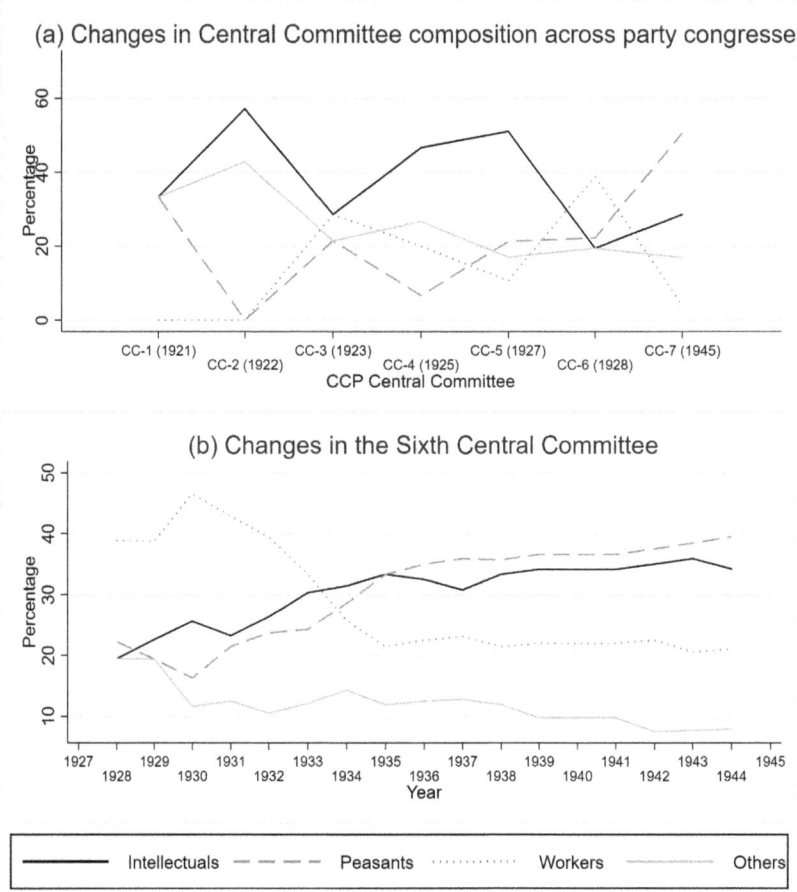

FIGURE 1.3 CCP Central Committee class backgrounds (1921–1945)
Note: The data derive from the author's database, which includes both full and alternate members of CCP Central Committee (CC). The social class of CCP CC members was coded based on family background. See Appendix B for more details on the coding rule.

from the first CC in 1921 to the Sixth CC in 1928 (Figure 1.3a), subsequently leading to radical shifts in party-building strategies. By contrast, Mao's return to the CCP's highest leadership circle after 1935 led to a striking stability in the social-class composition of the Central Committee. Mao's power consolidation accompanied a gradual but steady rise of CC members from the peasant class and the decline of members from the worker class from 1935 onward in the Sixth CC (Figure 1.3b). Mao's power consolidation put an end to the self-inflicted damage caused by the CCP's discriminatory practices in recruiting

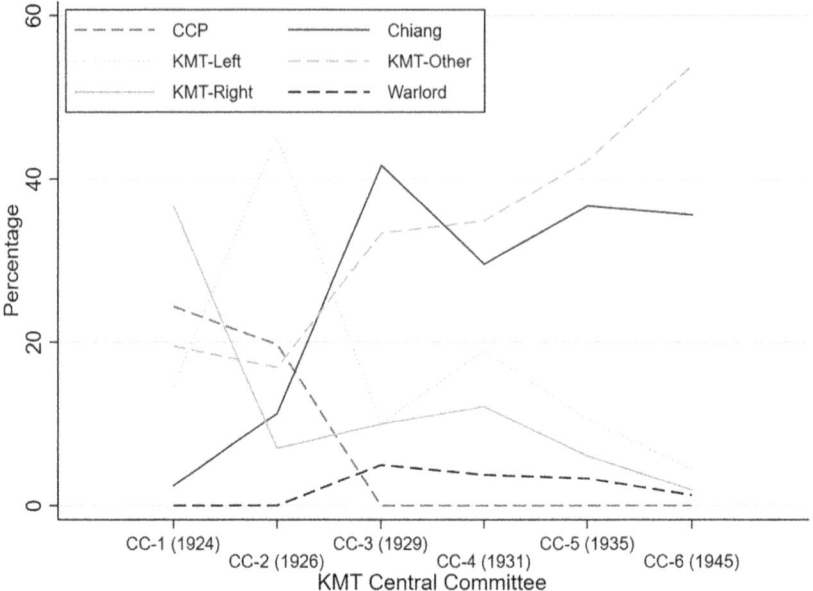

FIGURE 1.4 KMT Central Committee factions (1924–1945)
Note: The data derive from the author's database, which includes both full and alternate members of the KMT Central Committee. The coding of factions was based on these individuals' biographies, which indicate the political factions to which they belonged when they were elected to the KMT Central Committee. See Appendix B for more details on the coding rule.

and promoting party membership and facilitated building the foundation for a robust rural mass mobilization infrastructure during wartime.

In contrast, the unrelenting elite conflicts within the KMT crippled its party building, rendering an elite mobilization infrastructure with mixed quality (Chapter 7). The intraparty elite power struggle had been a constant theme in party politics, which significantly intensified after the death of Sun Yat-sen in 1925. The succession battle was fought mainly among Chiang Kai-shek, Wang Ching-wei (KMT Left Faction), and Hu Han-min (KMT Right Faction). For the purpose of comparison with the CCP, I use the faction classification of the KMT Central Committee (中央执行委员会) members to illustrate the evolution of power struggles among KMT elites (Figure 1.4). As shown, the evolution of the power struggle among KMT elites led to the radical changes in faction composition of the KMT Central Committee. Chiang's opportunistic alliance with the KMT-Left and the KMT-Right throughout this period reveals the fragile nature of any formal and informal power-sharing arrangement under contested leadership. Although the balance of power gradually shifted in favor of Chiang, he continually faced challenges from elder KMT party elites and regional military strongmen. Elite power struggles persisted even within Chiang's inner circle.[16] Consequently, the subsequent KMT Central Committees (1935–1945) primarily consisted of a quasi-dominant Chiang faction and a large number of smaller factions (KMT-Other) that were unable to unite and challenge Chiang.

Resource Mobilization and Party Strength. Tracing the level and source of fiscal extraction by both parties, I demonstrate that resource mobilization is a genuine source of party strength. As demonstrated below, this alternative perspective reflects party strength better than the size of the membership of the CCP and the KMT depicted in Figure 1.1.

First, the KMT's early domination over the CCP was rooted in its superior resource mobilization capacity (Chapter 3). Before the CCP fully developed its mass mobilization infrastructure, the fragility of the CCP from 1921 to 1935 can be exhibited in its weak capacity for resource mobilization. At its inception the CCP largely relied on windfall revenue, that is, financial assistance from the Comintern and the Soviet Union, which was hardly sufficient for party expansion. When the CCP was forced to instigate urban and rural insurgencies after 1927, the establishment of Soviet revolutionary bases offered a new revenue source – expropriation of rural elites – which replaced meager Comintern aid as a major source of revenue for the CCP. Despite the success of the CCP in expanding its military strength manifested in the Red Army, resource mobilization through coercion and expropriation was not a sustainable strategy. The CCP finally lost its Jiangxi Soviet base to the KMT's Fifth Encirclement military campaign in 1935 after exhausting the human and financial resources in its base.

By contrast, the KMT's early domination over the CCP was linked to its success relying on its elite mobilization infrastructure, which allowed the KMT to assimilate existing elites into the party and build fiscal institutions targeting business elites prior to the Sino-Japanese War. Hence, the KMT achieved remarkable success in building fiscal capacity through indirect taxation of urban business activities. The KMT's robust capacity in resource mobilization played a pivotal role in its dominance over the CCP despite constant internal elite conflicts.

Nonetheless, extant studies have insufficiently emphasized the devastating impact of the Sino-Japanese War on the KMT's extractive capacity.[17] The Sino-Japanese War exposed the weakness of the KMT's urban-centric elite mobilization structure concentrated in coastal and northern China, turning its comparative advantage into disadvantage. When both parties were forced to extract grain from rural China to finance the war, the CCP's rural mobilization infrastructure began to shine (Chapter 4).

---

[16] See excellent studies of the KMT party elite power struggle by Cui (2013), Eastman (1974), and Q. Wang (2010).

[17] One exception is Boecking (2017), but he studies only the customs revenue, which accounts for around one third of the KMT revenue (1929–1937). See Chapter 3 for a comprehensive picture of KMT central government's prewar revenue sources, such as customs, the salt monopoly, consolidated taxes, and borrowing.

In contrast to conventional wisdom, internal party archives reveal that the CCP imposed a more onerous fiscal burden on the peasantry than the KMT central government did during the Sino-Japanese War. On the one hand, the CCP was able to levy grain from approximately 70–90 percent of rural households in their base areas, and its progressive grain levies extracted from 10 to 20 percent of local grain output across major base areas from 1941 to 1945. Relying on its mass mobilization infrastructure, the CCP employed a technique I call "mobilized compliance," the essence of which is twofold: (1) mobilize ordinary citizens to become the eyes and ears of the party and (2) reshape the focal point of conflicts stemming from grain extraction. The CCP was, therefore, able to secure compliance in grain extraction from rural China without stirring mass resentment. Notably, the CCP's success in employing mobilized compliance through its grassroots organizations after 1941 was preceded by Mao's power consolidation from 1935 to 1938, which enabled the CCP to build an effective mass mobilization infrastructure in rural China. This transformation stood in stark contrast to the earlier period of contested leadership when the CCP failed to build an effective mass mobilization infrastructure.

On the other hand, the KMT suffered a deadly revenue shock because the invading Japanese seized control of a significant portion of northern and coastal provinces, which contributed to nearly 75 percent of the KMT's prewar revenue. Facing twin crises in fiscal revenue and spending, the KMT intensified its tax reform, including the expansion of direct taxation, but to no avail. When the KMT centralized the land tax through the grain levy in kind in 1941, its regressive grain extraction strategies led to inefficient and inequitable fiscal extraction in rural China because of the KMT's reliance on local elites for assessment and compliance. On average, the KMT central government was able to extract only 6.62 percent from local grain production, far less than the degree of grain extraction by the CCP during the same period. Furthermore, the KMT's inability to effectively control ad hoc grain extraction by both military and local governments is a clear manifestation of the failure to achieve fiscal centralization, a hallmark of its weak fiscal capacity. The failures of KMT fiscal extraction in turn gave rise to reliance on monetary expansion to finance the war, which planted the seeds of the KMT's later downfall.

The Role of Contingent Events. As much as the CCP may have wanted to emphasize its predestinated triumph, one must recognize the significant influence of contingent events in shaping both its internal party-building endeavors and the dynamics of interparty competition. Specifically, contingent events shifted the balance of power among party elites, leading to a major departure in party-building strategies. For instance, although some attribute the rise of Mao to his strategic maneuvers, specifically during the 1942–1944 Yan'an Rectification Campaign (Gao 2000), he would have been unable to launch this campaign had his main political rivals – Zhang Guotao and Wang Ming – not been weakened by a disastrous military debacle and a shift in Stalin's support, respectively.

By the same token, the sudden death in 1925 of Sun Yat-sen, the preeminent KMT leader, generated constant factional struggle within the KMT in the ensuing succession battle. A fierce power struggle among party elites resulted in Chiang Kai-shek's 1927 anti-Communist purge, marking the collapse of the First United Front and the end of Sun's aspirations to integrate Leninist principles into the KMT organization. In his quest for power consolidation, Chiang encountered formidable opposition from KMT elites and regional powerholders. Chiang finally neutralized major intraparty rivals Hu Han-min and Wang Ching-wei, who eventually succumbed to health issues and assassination, respectively, in 1935.

The reversal of fortune of the CCP and the KMT during the Sino-Japanese War (1937–1945) captures another critical role played by contingencies in shaping external political and economic environments. By the time the CCP's First Red Army reached northern Shaanxi in 1935, it was an exhausted and demoralized group of men and women. They were immediately besieged by the Northwestern Army under General Yang Hucheng and the Northeastern Army under General Zhang Xueliang. As Chiang Kai-shek arrived in Xi'an to personally orchestrate the final assault, Yang and Zhang staged the shocking Xi'an incident on December 12, 1936, putting Chiang on house arrest, and forced him to end the civil war against the CCP. The Xi'an incident single-handedly altered the course of history, affording the CCP the crucial breathing room needed to recuperate and revive.

Furthermore, the war's most consequential impact was the decimation of the KMT's elite mobilization infrastructure. The outbreak of the Sino-Japanese War dealt a serious blow to the comparative advantage of KMT's elite-mobilization infrastructure in urban China. The Japanese invasion in coastal and northern regions of China forced major business elites and the KMT central government to retreat. Because the KMT was unable to "tax the rich" as a war mobilization strategy, it turned to local elites as power brokers for grain extraction, thus generating vast inequity and resentment. By contrast, the rural mobilization infrastructure developed by the CCP from 1937 to 1940 became a comparative advantage, allowing the CCP to intensify its rural extraction without generating mass resentment after 1941. Ultimately, the Sino-Japanese War propelled the rise of the CCP, but its impact centered on weakening the elite mobilization infrastructure of the KMT while bolstering the strength of the CCP's mass mobilization infrastructure.

1.3 WHAT'S NEW?

This book offers three unique perspectives contributing to major scholarly debates about authoritarian politics, political parties, and Chinese politics. At the outset, I join recent scholar in examining the origins of authoritarian parties; however, I diverge from the current emphasis concerning the violent origins of political parties in enhancing regime durability *after* they seized state power. Instead, I delve into the turbulent moments *before* revolutionary parties seize state power, examining why and how they make pivotal decisions concerning organizational development in their struggles with their political rivals. I challenge the established narrative of power sharing, calling attention to the surprising role of dominant party leadership in facilitating successful organizational transformation of revolutionary parties. One major takeaway from this new insight is that the mechanisms sustaining the durability of authoritarian parties are not the same as those allowing them to conquer the state in the first place.

In addition, I address a crucial omission in the scholarship on political parties. Prominent research on political parties primarily centers on mobilizing voters as the chief function of political parties and explains the ways institutional rule and societal cleavages shape the development of political parties. Focusing on revolutionary parties, I emphasize that the value of their mobilization infrastructure extends beyond rallying dedicated supporters; instead, party mobilization infrastructure plays a pivotal role in aiding the parties to implement difficult and sometimes unpopular policies. Crucially, I view the organizational form of revolutionary parties as an outcome shaped by intraparty elite conflicts but not predetermined by initial structural factors such as social ties and resource endowment.

Finally, this book offers a unified framework to explain both the ascent of the CCP and the decline of the KMT during China's Republican Era. I fill an important gap in existing studies that inadequately explain the miraculous resurgence of the CCP from a fragile and marginalized organization prior to 1935 into a strong party after 1945. My answer lies in pivotal rise of Mao in CCP leadership circle from 1935 to 1938. In addition, I concur with existing scholarship that the Sino-Japanese War was truly a catalyst for the rise of the CCP, but not for the reason that conventional wisdom suggests. The most consequential effect of the war was the devastation of KMT's elite mobilization infrastructure; otherwise, the CCP's rural mobilization infrastructure would not have succeeded.

1.3.1 Party Building amid Violent Struggle: The Blessing of Power Consolidation and the Perils of Power Sharing

Extant studies of authoritarian parties center on their role in managing elite conflict and controlling the masses, two fundamental challenges facing any authoritarian regime (Svolik 2012). Nonetheless, few focus on the vital organizational development of revolutionary organizations before they seize state power. This oversight may obscure the complex dynamics underpinning leadership dynamics, party cohesion, and party strength during the revolutionary movement. After all, not all authoritarian parties were created by the ruling elites for the purpose of maintaining regime stability; in fact, less

1.3 What's New?

than 40 percent of authoritarian ruling parties were established by autocratic leaders.[18] Importantly, not all authoritarian parties succeeded in seizing state power. If parties created by dictators and the military juntas are excluded, only 19 percent of authoritarian ruling parties seized power during the first two years; and the average year of power seizure is sixteen years.[19]

Although some scholars have recently turned their attention to the origins of authoritarian parties, the predominant focus remains on the long-term impact of violent struggles experienced by these parties on regime longevity.[20] The conjecture underlying this research enterprise is that violent struggles during political parties' inceptions prolong regime resilience because they foster partisan identities, territorial organizations, and elite cohesion.[21] Regarding the fateful decisions concerning the revolutionary strategies and the organizational development of these political entities prior to the seizure of state power, scholars fall short in elucidating reasons why some revolutionary parties triumph in their quest for power while others falter. Instead, scholars posit a host of idiosyncratic factors, such as leadership traits, ideological commitment, foreign support, size of the country, and powerful neighbors (Levitsky and Way 2022). If the origins of authoritarian parties play a crucial role in their durability, both those parties that survived and deceased require study because the legacies of revolutionary struggle – successes and failures – have a profound impact on their later resilience and governing style (Schenoni 2021).

This book marks a significant departure from conventional wisdom by focusing on the early period of revolutionary parties prior to their seizure of state power. In this context, I challenge the primacy of the power-sharing arguments by emphasizing the link between dominant leadership and party strength. This alternative explanation illuminates reasons that some political parties but not others managed to bolster their organizational prowess and ultimately clinch state power. During the critical moments when these political parties fought for survival, I demonstrate that the function of political parties is not necessarily a constraining device for political elites but serve as vehicles for resource mobilization. I show that power sharing among party elites weakens party mobilization infrastructure more than power consolidation because the former undermines party elites' commitment in party building and

---

[18] These statistics are calculated based on the *Autocratic Ruling Party Dataset* constructed by Miller (2020).

[19] For all authoritarian parties, only 44 percent of them successfully seized power during the first two years of their creation; on average, authoritarian parties take 10 years to become the ruling party.

[20] The conflict-centric view could be traced back to a classic work by Huntington (1968). Levitsky and Way (2012, 2022) build on this idea by contending that the experience of revolution strengthens the unity among the elite, resulting in the creation of robust political parties.

[21] For case study evidence, see the edited volume by Levitsky, Loxton, Van Dyck, and Domínguez (2016) as well as Loxton (2021), Smith (2005), and Van Dyck (2017). For cross-national evidence, see Lachapelle, Levitsky, Way, and Casey (2020).

weakens the party's capacity to extract financial resources. By contrast, power consolidation by a party leader mitigates the collective action problem and engenders coherent party-building strategies. Crucially, my arguments do not center on the impact of leadership traits on political movements and revolutions (Aminzade et al. 2001; Robnett 1997; Selbin 1993; Tavits 2013); instead I underscore how balance of power among party elites alters their strategic approaches to party-building.

This perspective on the costs of power-sharing resulted from intraparty competition reinforces the insights of thinkers like James Madison and V. O. Key.[22] Specifically, factionalism and intraparty conflict generate distorted and biased information undermining party decision-making, leading to policymaking divorced from reality. Although some scholars have suggested that factional politics and intraparty democracy could benefit the party at the aggregate because they facilitate information flow for better policymaking and broaden the appeal to voters, their studies primarily situate the argument in functioning democracies.[23] Revolutionary parties, nevertheless, aim to mobilize committed agents and financial resources instead of voters. Thus, broadening the appeal to voters is irrelevant.

1.3.2 The Emergence of Dominant Parties: Resource Mobilization Is as Important as Human Mobilization

The canonical models of political parties aim to explain the mobilization techniques through which parties compete to garner support from voters (see Cox 2015 for a review). Scholars often regard political parties that seize power through nonelectoral means, such as revolutionary parties, as outliers or nonparty organizations.[24] Many political parties, including revolutionary parties, independence parties, and even rebel organizations, engage in intense power struggles outside the electoral arena. This book fills an important void in the studies of these political organizations by offering a new theoretical account to elucidate why some of them succeed in accumulating power outside electoral institutions but not others.

This book departs from recent scholarship on party building in Africa (Lebas 2011; Riedl 2014), Europe (Grzymala-Busse 2002; Kernell 2024; Reuter 2017; Tavits 2013; Ziblatt 2017), and Latin America (Lupu 2016). Notably, Ziblatt (2017) differentiates conservative political parties into "hierarchical mass

---

[22] See Madison's (1787) discussion in the *Federalist 10*. Key (1949) attributes favoritism and graft to factions. See Boucek (2009) for a review on factionalism in political parties.

[23] Dewan and Squintani (2015) offer a formal model to illustrate that factionalism facilitates information sharing. Boucek (2009) contends that factionalism promotes cooperation at times through a case study of the Christian Democratic Party in Italy.

[24] See Duverger (1954) as well as Gunther and Diamond (2003) on the typology of political parties. Friedrich and Brzezinski (1965) contend that political parties in autocracies and totalitarian societies bear little resemblance to political parties in democracies.

parties" and "contracting-out parties," and Riedl (2014) introduces the concept of "incorporation" versus "state substitution" as a power accumulation strategy by authoritarian leaders in her study of party systems in Africa. These conceptualizations bear some resemblance to the ideas about elite and mass mobilization infrastructures set forth in this book. Nonetheless, these studies situate party building in environments where vote mobilization serves as the ultimate objective of the parties.

In contrast, I highlight the crucial role of resource mobilization in the construct of party-building by political parties that operate in an environment where resource mobilization – but not just vote mobilization – is the principal goal for their survival.[25] One key distinction between democratic and revolutionary parties is that the mobilization infrastructure of the former aims to maximize votes, but the goal of the latter is to maximize crucial resources for party power. This distinction means that revolutionary parties do not necessarily pursue the pivotal "median voter," but instead radical and committed individuals who are critical to revolutionary parties' resource mobilization. To this end, the success of building party mobilization infrastructure resembles state building to a large extent, requiring strong commitment from party elites to build infrastructural power that penetrates civil society and logistically implements political decisions (Mann 1984).

Notably, this book departs from the prevailing notion that the sources of organizational development by revolutionary parties and rebel organizations stem from preexisting social networks and natural resource endowment.[26] This book emphasize the role of agency, demonstrating the ways intraparty elite conflicts shape party mobilization infrastructure as well as the trials and errors that occur in seeking alternative revenue when political parties experienced exogenous shocks to their revenue intake and spending.

1.3.3 The Rise of Communism and the Demise of the KMT during the Republican Era

How did the CCP, which ran on an exclusive platform emphasizing conflicts among social classes, transform itself from a fragile and marginalized party into a ruling party with strong mobilization capacity? Why did the KMT, which seemed to embody a more inclusive ideology aiming to liberate China from imperialism, once dominated China's political system, and consistently had a larger party membership than the CCP, collapse so quickly after the Sino-Japanese War? The stark contrast in the strength of these two parties

---

[25] Tilly (1978) is one of the early seminal works on resource mobilization theory. See Jenkins (1983) and Goldstone (2001) for a review of this strand of literature.
[26] Weinstein (2006) offers perhaps the most prominent work emphasizing the role of resource endowment in rebel organizations. Staniland (2014) contends the endowment of social ties is crucial for the organizational structure of insurgent groups.

before and after the Sino-Japanese War is perhaps one of the most enduring puzzles in the twentieth century.

Studies of the KMT have largely attributed its collapse to factional politics and mismanagement of economic policies after 1945[27] despite some recent historical revisionist accounts highlighting a hostile economic environment and its war efforts.[28] Importantly, scholars investigated factional politics within the CCP and the KMT in insolation,[29] but they have yet to compare the elite politics of the CCP and the KMT. Why the KMT was prone to factional politics and why elite power struggle did not plunge the CCP into fragility remain unexplained.

Specifically, existing scholarship on the CCP tends either primarily to emphasize its fragility from 1921 to 1935 or to examine its rise during the period from 1937 to 1945. For instance, scholars have attributed the rise of the CCP to nationalism, political ideology, party discipline, land inequality, cadre training, and class representation.[30] The regional variation in party expansion during the Sino-Japanese War that paved the way for the CCP to penetrate the society during the post-1949 era has also been emphasized (Koss 2018). Nonetheless, these accounts cannot explain why the CCP was so fragile prior to the Sino-Japanese War if it embodied superior party ideology and popular support. Indeed, scholars have documented the earlier struggle by the CCP to attract popular support from the working class and peasantry (Huang 2011; Saich 2021; Van de Ven 1992). These struggles persisted even in CCP base areas during the Sino-Japanese War.[31] This striking struggle reveals that the CCP did not embody intrinsic ideological appeal to peasants, nor did the War naturally push peasants into the arms of the CCP. Moreover, the internal party archives of the CCP disclose many incidents of graft, embezzlement, and extortion committed by local CCP cadres and armed forces, suggesting that the CCP was not so disciplined as it claimed to be.[32]

---

[27] For studies of KMT factional politics, see Eastman (1984, 1991) and Q. Wang (2010). See Pepper (1999) and Coble (2023) for the KMT's disastrous economic and domestic policies during the period of 1946–1948.

[28] See Mitter (2020) on the battle of historical narratives on the roles of the CCP and KMT during the Sino-Japanese War. Boecking (2017) suggests that the KMT suffered a fiscal shock due to the loss of customs revenue during the Sino-Japanese War.

[29] For the elite politics of the CCP during this period, see Chen (1998), Gao (2000), and Teiwes (1994).

[30] For the rise of the CCP, see, for example, Bianco (1971), Hofheinz (1977), Johnson (1962), Opper (2020), Schurmann (1966), Selden (1971), and Saich (2021). For the demise of the KMT, see, for example, Eastman (1984), Pepper (2004), and Young (1947). Huang (2024) offered a detailed study examining CCP cadre training tactics during the Sino-Japanese War.

[31] Vibrant scholarship on CCP activities in revolutionary base areas during the pre-1949 period has yielded similar conclusions (Dorris 1976, Gillin 1964, Huang 2011, Kataoka 1974, Hartford 1980, Perry 1980, Saich 1994, Thaxton 1983, Wou 1994). Saich and Yang (1996) and Esherick (1995) provide excellent summaries of the key findings in the studies of base areas.

[32] *Kang ri zhan zheng shi qi shaan gan ning bian qu cai zheng jing ji shi liao zhai bian (Shaan-Gan-Ning Border Region Finance and Economic Selective Historical Record during the Sino-Japanese War)* (1981, V6: 92).

1.3 What's New?

Other strands of recent scholarship have turned attention to the role of local actors and contingent events. The contention in one such strand is that the CCP organization was largely dismantled after the purge by the KMT in 1927, saved only by local activists and educated youth, who leverage their social networks to revive the communist movement, setting the stage for the later establishment of CCP base areas (Fewsmith 2022). Another strand traces the development of the Shaan-Gan-Ning base area, which later became the refuge of the CCP revival, and proposes that peasant mobilization was hardly inevitable, that multiple contingent events shaped the fates of the CCP and the KMT, and that very little was predestined (Esherick 2022). Indeed, a long line of scholars suggests that socioeconomic inequality varied vastly across China prior to the rise of communism; therefore, China was hardly a hotbed ripe for peasant revolt (Averill 2006; Bianco 2001; Galbiati 1985; Hofheinz 1977; Perry 1980). The bottom-up approach in this scholarship, however, cannot explain why the CCP turned into a disciplined and effective party organization during the Sino-Japanese War.

I offer a unified framework, shedding new light on the reversal of fortune of the two parties. First, the CCP was not immune to factional politics, so much so that it crippled its party organization, similar to what happened in the KMT. The intense intraparty elite power struggle occurring from 1927 to 1934 helps explain the weakness of the CCP. Mao's ascent to CCP leadership and the weakening of his main rivals *prior* to the Sino-Japanese War were key to the CCP's transformation but not to the War as a transforming event by itself.

Second, resource mobilization is a crucial currency for the strength of the CCP and the KMT. As demonstrated in this book, the weakness of the CCP during the early stages of party formation could be attributed to its inadequate resource mobilization, which relied largely on foreign assistance and expropriation. Meanwhile, the KMT was a stronger party because its elite mobilization infrastructure allowed it to tap into state resources. Unfortunately, the foundation of KMT extractive capacity crumbled during the Japanese invasion in areas populated by the very economic elites upon whom it had relied.[33] Hence, wars matter, but not the way that existing bellicist theories suggest.[34] The impact of the Sino-Japanese War is more about its detrimental impact on the fiscal foundation of the KMT than about its beneficial impacts on that of the CCP.

---

[33] Boecking (2017) reaches a similar conclusion, but his work exclusively focuses on KMT's custom revenues.

[34] The bellicist theory of state formation highlights interstate wars as the critical juncture putting states onto diverging paths of political and economic development. Some states took advantage of the fiscal demand shock driven by the war and succeeded in expanding fiscal capacity. See, for example, Brewer (1990), Dincecco (2011; 2017), Ertman (1997), Levi (1989), Scheve and Stasavage (2010), and Tilly (1990).

1.4 LOOKING AHEAD

The remainder of this manuscript is organized as follows. I detail a theoretical framework in Chapter 2, underscoring the way strategic interactions among party elites shape the party's strategies to develop its mobilization infrastructure, which in turn facilitates resource mobilization. The key insights of the theoretical framework are threefold. First, party ideology serves as a constraining device determining the types of party mobilization infrastructure – elite-centric vis-à-vis mass-centric – which embody distinct comparative advantages. Second, domination by a party leader mitigates the collective action problem faced by party elites, leading to the implementation of coherent party-building strategies that improve the effectiveness of mobilization infrastructure. In contrast, when party elites engage in contentious leadership struggles, the quality of mobilization infrastructure suffers because of conflicting party-building strategies. Finally, I integrate the concept of contingent events into the theoretical framework, positing that the balance of intraparty elite power and the comparative advantage of mobilization infrastructure act as mediators through which these events influence party strength. Specifically, I illustrate the function of such contingencies as exogenous shocks disrupting the equilibrium of party-building strategies and the comparative advantages of various forms of mobilization infrastructure. The disruptions in turn have a profound and often transformative impact on the robustness and resilience of the party.

Following Chapter 2's theoretical framework, Chapters 3 and 4 demonstrate the crucial role of resource mobilization for the CCP and the KMT from 1921 to 1945. Using a diverse range of party and government archives, I constructed a novel dataset tracking the scale and sources of financial revenues mobilized by these two parties. These novel data provide a comprehensive fiscal portrait of the financial undertakings of both parties throughout this epoch.

I reveal in Chapter 3 that the KMT benefited from its elite mobilization infrastructure and consistently maintained a more robust resource mobilization than the CCP in the early days, thus establishing dominance in China's political landscape prior to the Sino-Japanese War. On the contrary, the CCP relied on meager financial support from the Comintern and ad hoc expropriation of rural elites, struggling to develop a consistent flow of financial resources.

Chapter 4 illustrates that the outbreak of the Sino-Japanese War fundamentally shifted the comparative advantages of party mobilization infrastructures of the CCP and the KMT. Specifically, the Japanese occupation in coastal and northern China significantly weakened the KMT by undermining the economic elites upon whom its elite mobilization infrastructure relied. Meanwhile, the CCP was able to take advantage of its mass mobilization infrastructure to respond to fiscal shocks from the war. At the point when both parties were forced to extract grains-in-kind after 1941 as a remedy to rising fiscal demand, my novel dataset uncovers a surprising pattern: The CCP developed a significantly stronger fiscal capacity for grain extraction than the KMT. I further

1.4 Looking Ahead

demonstrate that the CCP used its grassroots party organization to mobilize compliance in the peasantry. Alongside progressive grain extraction, the party was able to maintain popular support even in the face of a significantly higher degree of extraction. The KMT, by contrast, employed a form of indirect rule relying on local elites for grain extraction, which generated regressive taxation and corruption, stirring mass resentment despite a lower grain burden. Using grain extraction as a point of illustration and data from a wide range of party and government archives, I present qualitative and quantitative evidence to shed light on the source of the party strength of the CCP and the KMT.

Chapters 5, 6, and 7 offer detailed process tracing of the organizational evolution of the CCP and the KMT, pinpointing the cascades from intraparty elite power struggles to party-building strategies and subsequently, the development of party mobilization infrastructure. In these case studies I pay close attention to contingencies, showing that they shifted the balance of power among party elites and generated a ripple effect on party-building strategies and party mobilization infrastructure. Specifically, Chapter 5 documents the intense intraparty power struggle occurring within the CCP after the sudden downfall of CCP leader Chen Duxiu in 1927 following intervention by the Comintern and the Soviet Union. From 1927 to 1934, the intense elite contestation under the shadow of the Comintern led CCP elites to follow Leninist doctrine, strictly pursuing radical urban insurgencies and worker-centric party-building strategies despite China's predominance as an agrarian society.

Chapter 6 shows that Mao Zedong's return to the CCP highest leadership circle after the Zunyi Conference in January 1935 was indeed a pivotal event, after which the CCP changed its party-building strategies. Mao would not have been able to consolidate his power without the help of contingent events undermining his main political rivals, Zhang Guotao and Wang Ming, who were weakened by a military debacle and the shift in Stalin's support, respectively. By tracing CCP party-building strategies, I illustrate that the CCP's departure away from conflictual and discriminatory party-building strategies and the embrace of intellectuals and peasants into its mobilization infrastructure after Mao consolidated his power. By late 1938 the CCP had completely abandoned its previous discriminatory practice of emphasizing social classes as the primary criteria for the party-building strategies, resulting in a party mobilization infrastructure ripe for rural fiscal extraction starting in 1941.

Chapter 7 traces the unrelenting intraparty power struggle within the KMT from 1921 to 1945. After the sudden death of Sun Yat-sen, the party founder, Chiang Kai-shek quickly ascended the KMT ranks by exploiting ideological conflicts between the KMT-Left and KMT-Right factions, but he constantly faced challenges from his intraparty rivals, who coalesced around regional military strongmen. Similar to the rise of Mao, Chiang benefited from contingent events and finally eliminated threats from Hu Han-min and Wang Ching-wei, two main rivals who suffered from medical problems. Chiang, however, was only a quasi-dominant party leader, and regional strongmen remained defiant in the face of his reform efforts. Importantly, the KMT remained a party deeply entrenched in an elite mobilization infrastructure, heavily reliant on the cooperation of regional strongmen and local elites for policy implementation. The lack of infrastructure for mass mobilization became an impediment later when the power of those elites upon which the KMT relied was weakened during the Japanese invasion, as shown in its failures in grain extraction detailed in Chapter 4.

In Chapter 8 I briefly discuss the legacies of the revolutionary struggle for both the CCP and the KMT after 1949. I then offer some concluding reflections as well as major takeaways beyond China for understanding how political parties operate in a weak institutional environment and seek to accumulate power outside of the electoral institutions. Specifically, I show that the party-building experience of the CCP and the KMT during their revolutionary struggles cast a long shadow on political development in mainland China and Taiwan after 1949, respectively. I illustrate the enduring emphasis on leadership dominance for party unity and mobilized compliance for policy implementation in the CCP's post-1949 governance style. Conversely, KMT leaders recognized the superior organization of the CCP as a decisive factor in its downfall. As a result, the KMT shifted its focus toward fostering elite cohesion and grassroots party structures in Taiwan. Although this strategy initially bore fruit for the KMT's power consolidation in Taiwan, the party still relied on elite mobilization infrastructure for societal penetration. The KMT's clientelistic machine eventually broke down when Taiwan democratized, losing its monopoly to the Democratic Progressive Party. Finally, I revisit the puzzling reversal of fortune among the CCP and the KMT, highlighting both leadership domination and resource mobilization as the key foundations of powerful revolutionary parties. I further underscore the significance of contingencies in comprehending the evolution of revolutionary parties.

2

A Theory of Party Building by Revolutionary Parties

Revolutionary parties comprise committed and radical political actors with the audacity to challenge and seize state power. The ideological and psychological underpinnings of these highly motivated revolutionaries to engage in radical and seemingly irrational behaviors have attracted considerable scholarly attention.[1] Motivation alone, however, is insufficient for revolutionary parties to prevail. Although some revolutions swiftly conquer the old regime overnight, most of them encounter prolonged violent conflicts and counterrevolutionary suppression. The organizational strength of revolutionary parties then becomes pivotal for their survival and ultimate triumph during the protracted struggle.

I develop a theoretical framework in this chapter to elucidate the variation in the organizational strength of revolutionary parties. A major departure in my framework is the emphasis on *resource mobilization* as the outcome of interests because of its crucial role in determining the strength of revolutionary parties. The variation in resource mobilization, in turn, was shaped by the nature, type, and quality of party mobilization infrastructure. The crucial question, then, is why revolutionary parties develop distinct types of mobilization infrastructure with varying quality. Some scholars have attributed the organizational structure of revolutionary parties and rebel organizations to preexisting social, political, and economic endowments, but this line of argument falls short of accounting for the dynamic organizational changes over time.[2] In this theoretical framework, I trace the organizational development

---

[1] For instance, Gurr (1970) was among the first to propose the theory of relative deprivation for rebel movements in his seminal work *Why Men Rebel*. In *Revolutionary Change*, Johnson (1966) suggests that revolutions take place in response to ideological movement and disrupt the equilibrium in social and system values.

[2] Weinstein (2006) suggests that initial economic endowment shapes the strategies of rebel groups. Kalyvas (2007) points out that path-dependent arguments fail to recognize the dynamic and

of revolutionary parties by investigating the strategic choices of party elites. Specifically, I contend that the dynamics of intraparty power struggle shape party elites' commitment and preferences in their endeavors of building party mobilization infrastructure.

The theoretical framework offers three core arguments. First, mobilizing financial resources is integral to the strength of revolutionary parties during prolonged struggles with their external adversaries. Second, domination by a party leader mitigates the collective action problem faced by party elites during the party-building process, leading to cohesive party-building strategies that enhance the effectiveness of the party mobilization infrastructure. In contrast, when party elites engage in contentious power struggles without a dominant leader, the quality of mobilization infrastructure suffers because of conflicting and self-defeating party-building strategies. Finally, contingent events are equilibrium disruptors, shifting the balance of power among intraparty elites and altering the comparative advantages of mobilization infrastructure. These disruptions subsequently have a transformative impact on the course of party building and ultimately on party strength.

2.1 RESOURCE MOBILIZATION & PARTY STRENGTH

What makes resource mobilization a pivotal source of party strength? Mobilization lies at the core of any political party's existence and success, apart from power sharing among ambitious political actors. Canonical theories of political parties have primarily focused on explaining the success or failure of *voter mobilization* in electoral competitions.[3] Revolutionary parties, however, operate in a chaotic environment, where electoral institutions are either absent or inconsequential to the distribution of de facto power.[4] Mobilizing voters is, therefore, not the most crucial lifeline for these parties.

For revolutionary parties operating outside the confines of electoral politics, their mobilization efforts revolve around recruiting dedicated political actors and raising necessary financial resources. Much of the existing discourse centers on rallying committed individuals to answer the call of revolutions, but few scholars recognize that resource mobilization plays an equally crucial role in determining the fate of revolutionary organizations. Ultimately, even die-hard revolutionaries cannot fight with empty hands and stomachs.

---

endogenous interactions among rebels, civilians, and the state. Staniland (2014) conducts a comprehensive study of insurgency groups, arguing that the nature of insurgency organizations is determined by the prewar social networks in which insurgent leaders are embedded. Organizational changes among insurgency groups, Staniland argues, hinge on endogenous or exogenous changes to the social ties.

[3] See, for example, Bartels (1998) and Shively (1972). Table 1.1 in Tavits (2013) offers an excellent summary of theories of party building and party strength in a democratic context.

[4] In Pakistan, for example, political parties often engaged in political violence to weaken rival parties prior to elections. See Jones (2003) and Siddiqui (2022).

2.1 Resource Mobilization & Party Strength

The task of building and expanding revolutionary organizations requires substantial financial resources, a challenge that both revolutionary parties and rebel organizations must confront. In the seminal *From Mobilization to Revolution*, Tilly (1978) stresses the importance of resource mobilization for revolutionary movements, maintaining that "the analysis of mobilization deals with the ways that groups acquire resources and make them available for collective action (7)."[5]

Notably, the targeted population of a revolutionary party's resource mobilization extends beyond its own members – membership dues alone are insufficient to finance the operations of any revolutionary movement. Hence, the purpose of mobilization infrastructure by revolutionary parties differs from Etzioni's model of organizational effectiveness[6] that focuses on compliance from members of the organization (1975). Instead, the objective of mobilization infrastructure by revolutionary parties aligns with Mann's notion of state capacity, which emphasizes the extent to which the party permeates civil society and effectively implements political decisions at various levels (1984).

Broadly speaking, party mobilization infrastructure enhances various party capacities, including the bureaucratic, the extractive, and the coercive. Bureaucratic capacity entails the proficiency of party organizations in formulating effective policies and implementing them through the active involvement of rank-and-file party members. Extractive capacity refers to the party's capability to mobilize financial resources, not only for its own operations but also for the governance of the territory under its control. Finally, coercive capacity encompasses the party's control over armed forces, allowing it to exert authority and enforce its policies through violence or threat of violence.

Of these three types of capacity, extractive capacity for resource mobilization is often the precursor to establishing effective bureaucratic and coercive apparatus. Building effective bureaucratic capacity for party operations requires significant financial investment because ideology and coercion alone cannot sustain party members' loyalty in the long run. Resources are the lifeblood of any political activity, enabling revolutionary parties to finance campaigns, organize events, and engage in insurrection. The employment of propaganda and normative suasion among the public cannot succeed without adequate resources to spread an idea in print or over the air; moreover, building bureaucratic capacity entails the establishment of national and grassroots party organizations, which cannot function without sufficient financial resources.

Meanwhile, extractive capacity is essential for revolutionary parties to establish an effective coercive apparatus for their armed struggle. Although success in building extractive capacity does not always lead to an effective coercive

---

[5] In the same work, Tilly (1978) defines resources as "labor power, goods, weapons, votes, and any number of other things, just so long as they are usable in acting on shared interests" (7).
[6] Etzioni proposes a typology on the type of power organizations use to direct the behavior of their members: coercive, utilitarian, and normative.

apparatus, failure in developing such capacity consistently spells its demise.[7] By contrast, relying solely on coercive apparatus to facilitate extractive capacity ultimately undermines the sustainability of resource mobilization: Rebel and insurgent organizations that depend predominantly on windfall revenues, such as natural resources, foreign support, and drug trafficking, remain highly susceptible to external shocks that disrupt these income streams.[8] Importantly, the ineffective extractive capacity forces rebel organizations to employ coercive tactics for resource mobilization, which subsequently alienate the local population and lose the crucial support that they need to survive. In a comparative study of guerrilla and revolutionary movements in Latin America, Wickham-Crowley (1992: 51–55) emphasizes the degree of peasant support as a crucial determinant of their failure or success. These supports are not limited to goods and services for guerrillas; they also include the cooperation and intelligence sharing critical to guerrilla warfare.

2.2 DOMINATION RULES: ELITE INCENTIVES & PARTY BUILDING

In the unforgiving landscape of revolutionary struggle, organizational strength stands as a cornerstone of survival for revolutionary parties. If organizational strength is pivotal for their existence, why do some party elites commit wholeheartedly to bolster party mobilization infrastructure, while others exhibit only lackluster efforts? What accounts for their varying strategies and efforts to shape party mobilization infrastructure? In the remainder of Section 2.2, I offer a theoretical framework by first specifying key parameters concerning the objective function, strategy choices, and payoff associated with party-building strategies in the eyes of party elites. I then delve into the ways through which the balance of power among party elites shapes their preferences in building party mobilization infrastructure. One key implication of this theoretical framework is that dominant party leadership fosters coherent party-building strategies, which in turn enhance the effectiveness of party mobilization infrastructure.

2.2.1 Party Ideology as a Sorting and Constraining Device

If organization structure is the skeleton of a political party, ideology is its heart and soul. Conventional wisdom suggests that party ideology is conceived as a signaling device defining what the party stands for and whose interests

---

[7] Mampilly and Thakur (2025) discuss the ways military control contributes to better rebel taxation; however, Ellis (1999) suggests the opposite mechanism, contending that limited resource mobilization is the culprit for undisciplined military tactics.
[8] See Collier (2000), Giustozzi (2022), Mansfield (2017), Sánchez de la Sierra (2020), and Weinstein (2006).

2.2 Elite Incentives & Party Building

it represents. Ideology also serves as a persuasive device designed to shape the belief system of its members as well as the targeted population,[9] motivating fervent followers and supporters to make sacrifices for the greater good. A strong ideology resembles a "spiritual optimum" to some extent, providing solace to followers in challenging and even perilous environments. Finally, a strong ideology is a bonding device that connects members domestically and internationally and fosters a cohesive organization.[10] Absent a strong party ideology, party building by revolutionary parties often falters. The National Liberation Front (FLN) in Algeria is a classic example of what happens when nationalism alone is insufficient to cultivate a successful revolutionary party organization through a board coalition.[11]

These benefits of party ideology overshadow one important aspect: Political ideology limits the strategies and options available to party leaders involved in party building. Specifically, party ideology forces party leaders to build an *exclusive* mobilization infrastructure targeting a particular population; those who deviate from party ideology would encounter an impossible task in maintaining a broad coalition without factional conflicts.

To illustrate the logic of the binding power of ideology on party elites' preference for strategies, I consider two types of revolutionary parties, each rooted in different principles of mobilization because of their ideology. For the sake of simplicity, I posit one party embodying a political ideology and following an elite-mobilization principle, which entails prioritizing the incorporation of existing economic and political elites (e.g., businessmen, landowners, intellectuals, gentry, church leaders, and ethnic chiefs) as the core constituents of the party. I call it an "elite mobilization party." By contrast, the second party's political ideology pursues a mass-mobilization principle, which emphasizes assimilating the powerless masses who occupy the lower strata of socioeconomic hierarchy in the society (e.g., teachers, blue-collar workers, farmers). I call it a "mass mobilization party."

Because of distinct party ideologies, these two parties appeal to different types of political actors, each endowed with distinct sources of power. Those whose source of power stems from mobilizing existing political and economic elites choose to join the elite mobilization party. Conversely, political actors whose source of power stems from mobilizing the masses would join the mass mobilization party. Figure 2.1 illustrates the self-selection of political actors into these two parties due to their distinct party ideologies.

---

[9] The notion of party ideology as a device to shape individual beliefs has roots in studies of political parties in the United States (Campbell, Converse, Miller, and Stokes 1964; Converse 1964). See Carmines and D'Amico (2015) for a review.

[10] Vu (2016) emphasizes this role of ideology in his investigation of the Vietnamese revolution.

[11] Both Jackson (1977) and Quandt (1969) observe that lack of coherent party ideology undermined party building by the FLN during its wartime struggle with France, resulting in a less stable regime after the revolution.

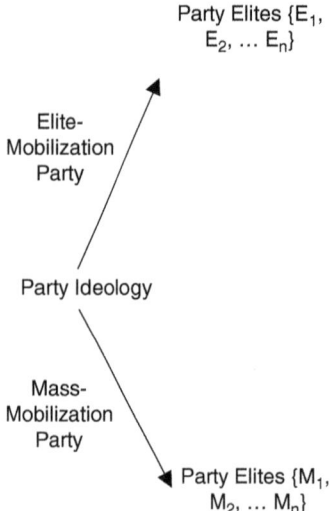

FIGURE 2.1 Party ideology and types of mobilization infrastructure

Once these two parties are populated with political actors endowed with different sources of power, party ideology then resembles self-perpetuating constraints on the *type* of mobilization infrastructure that a party could pursue for several reasons. First, party elites are likely to prefer a mobilization infrastructure that closely aligns with their individual sources of power: Investing in a mobilization infrastructure that could potentially weaken party elites' source of power is irrational and illogical. Leaders in an elite mobilization party are, therefore, unlikely to invest in building the infrastructure to mobilize the masses. Conversely, leaders in mass mobilization parties must distance themselves from existing elites to preserve their power.

Second, the process of party leadership reproduction naturally prevents those who do not fully subscribe to the party ideology from rising in the party ranks, possibly altering the course of the development of party mobilization capacity. Note that the initial cohort of party members typically comprises radical revolutionaries with fervent convictions. The early cohort of party leaders controls the recruitment and promotion of party cadres, favoring individuals who share similar ideological orientation. For instance, the old guard and radical party members prevented opposition parties from adjusting the party platform during the Institutional Revolutionary Party's domination in Mexico (Greene 2007).

Third, one could argue that a party could pursue a mixed strategy by mobilizing both elites and the masses. Scholars have found similar strategies adopted by conservative parties in Great Britain (Ziblatt 2017) and in the Bharatiya Janata Party in India (Thachil 2014). Unlike parties in electoral democracies, revolutionary parties often have little motivation to deviate from party ideology and appeal to median voters because they operate in an environment where elections are not the primary means for power contestation. This is the key distinction between revolutionary parties operating in an environment of weak institutions and political parties operating in a functioning electoral system.

Note that the mixed strategy of building mobilization infrastructure imposes significant risks for political parties in democracies and nondemocracies alike. Lupu (2016) pinpoints party elites' deviation from traditional positions in policy implementation as a cause of the dilution of the party brand, leading to the collapse of dominant parties in Latin America. In the case of revolutionary parties, adopting the mixed strategy and accommodationist approach results in an incoherent party ideology and undermines its appeal to radicals, thereby engendering more harms than benefits. For example, armed groups deviating from their ideological precepts often lose fighters as a result.[12] More importantly, the accommodationist approach tends to expand the size of the coalition at the expense of creating conflictual ideological differences within the party; therefore, revolutionary parties with a broad coalition constantly confront intraparty factional conflicts in both party-building strategies and revolutionary tactics.

The failed revolution in Bolivia is a telling example. The Revolutionary Nationalist Movement (MNR) was initially a small and relatively well-knit organization attracting support from the middle class. Following its suppression in 1946, the MNR made a fatal decision to adopt an accommodationist stance, absorbing groups across the political spectrum – from reformists to labor unions and peasantry – who sympathized with its goals.[13] Although the MNR was able to seize state power in 1952, the ensuing postrevolutionary government was built on a shaky coalition. Eventually, serious conflicts emerged within the MNR coalition despite President Siles' efforts to centralize power and mitigate factional politics with the MNR and the government. Thus the MNR remained a weak party, later overthrown by a coup in 1964.[14]

2.2.2 Party Elites

The Premise. Besides ideological orientation, what are the crucial characteristics of party elites in revolutionary parties? I consider party elites to be political actors driven by self-interest and aiming to maximize their own political power. One may argue that elites in revolutionary parties are ideological and policy-driven, often willing to prioritize the greater societal good over personal

---

[12] See Horgan (2009), Oppenheim et al. (2015), and Revkin and Mhidi (2016).
[13] See Malloy (1970) for a detailed study of MNR party evolution in Bolivia.
[14] Mitchell (1977) traces the political development in Bolivia from a revolutionary movement to military rule. Anria and Cyr (2017) compare the coalition-building and maintenance strategies by the MNR and the Movement for Socialism in Bolivia.

gain. Even for these policy-driven party elites, however, they still have a strong interest in expanding their personal power within the organization. The desire for power stems from the inherent conflict among party strategies – party elites harbor diverse preferences for revolutionary tactics and direction even as they share the same objective to fortify the party against existential threats. To this end, party elites seek to maximize their personal power for the sake of implementing their preferred policies because resolving intraparty conflict in policy-making ultimately rests on their personal power within the party.

The Choices. I specify that party elites face a menu of difficult choices stipulating a variety of party-building strategies for the party mobilization infrastructure. For the sake of simplicity, I assume that each party elite has only one crucial decision to make – whether to endorse or sabotage a specific party-building strategy.

The Payoffs. The payoffs of party-building strategies for each party elite can be conceptualized in two dimensions: first, the *total* benefit to the party as a whole; and second, the *individual share* of the total benefit. Stated differently, each party elite's payoff hinges on the size of the pie (i.e., party strength) and the individual's portion of it. These two dimensions of benefits imply that party elites face the free-rider problem, distributional conflict, and ex ante uncertainty arising from any party-building strategy.

First, the total benefit stemming from a party-building strategy is a public good to all party elites because the fortunes of party elites are closely tied to party strength. A resilient revolutionary party is better equipped to ward off competition from rival organizations and generate political and economic benefits for party elites. When the revolutionary party seizes power from the state, party elites are the first in line to access valuable state resources. Notably, the public-good nature of a strong party mobilization infrastructure also means that party elites may be tempted to free ride the coattails of other party elites who invest their crucial resources in party building.

Second, the individual share of the total benefit from a party-building strategy is a *private good* to each party elite, implying that distributional conflict is inevitable. When revolutionary parties capture any rewards during the power struggle, it is highly unlikely, often impossible, to distribute the rewards in an egalitarian manner. In the end, the distribution of the total benefit is likely determined by the relative power among party elites: Powerful party elites capture greater rewards. Therefore, party elites become wary when a particular party-building strategy could shift the balance of power within the party leadership circle, benefiting some at the expense of others. Consider the following scenario: If a party invests in mobilization infrastructure to extend its reach into a specific geographic region or a targeted population where a party elite holds leadership, the benefits are likely to be disproportionately advantageous to this elite compared to others whose power originates from different sources. The distributional conflict of party-building strategies might give some party elites pause before endorsing them.

Third, both the total benefit and individual share are *uncertain* ex ante. Despite a party's efforts to invest in building a party mobilization infrastructure, such efforts could be thwarted by rival political organizations. The "early deaths" of many revolutionary parties due to the counterrevolutionary forces is hardly a surprise (Levitsky and Way 2022). Furthermore, party-building often entails the transformation of horizontal and vertical party organizational structure and reshuffling personnel. These transformations cannot occur overnight because of institutional inertia and resistance to change from existing power holders; therefore, the uncertainty in the payoff from a party-building strategy is compounded by the time delay between implementation and tangible outcomes.

The discussion above highlights the conundrum facing party elites in their strategic calculation of whether to endorse a particular party-building strategy. The public-good attribute means that all party elites benefit from a stronger party mobilization infrastructure even though they are confronted with a collective action problem due to a temptation to free ride. The private-good nature of the unequal distribution of benefits from a strong party exacerbates the collective-action problem. Party elites become anxious when a party-building strategy could shift the balance of power within the party, favoring their intraparty rivals. The issue of unequal distribution is further made worse by the uncertainty in party-building outcomes, thus generating a status quo bias, a classic problem for resistance to reform.[15] Finally, party elites with short time horizons, a common trait in violative political environments, may be reluctant to invest in time-consuming party-building efforts because of their high discount rate on delayed rewards.

2.2.3 Balance of Power and Incentives in Party Building

Having outlined the actors, strategies, and payoffs associated with party-building strategies, I now turn to the following question: Why are some party elites more eager to invest in party building but not others? Below, I reveal that the decisions of party elites are strongly shaped by their sources of power and intraparty elite conflicts.

The Source of Power of Party Elites. If a party elite's source of de facto power does not rely on party strength from the outset, then expanding party mobilization infrastructure pays little dividend. The reason is that party elites prefer bolstering their extraparty power over enhancing the party's mobilization infrastructure because the latter mostly benefits their intraparty rivals. The lack of interest by some party elites to strengthen their own party is widely observed in many political systems. The emergence of "party substitutes," such as regional political machines and "oligarchic" financial–industrial groups,

---

[15] Fernandez and Rodrik (1991) develop a formal model specifying the logic of the status quo bias and resistance to liberalization reforms.

undercut the development of the party system after the collapse of the Soviet Union (Hale 2006). Similarly, politicians in Peru developed alternative strategies to win elections in the post-Fujimori era, weakening their incentives for party building (Levitsky and Zavaleta 2016). In nondemocracies, political elites in military regimes rely on their coercive apparatus (e.g., military, secret police) to maintain rule, making political parties obsolete (Geddes 1999; Geddes, Wright, and Frantz 2018).

Party elites have an inherent interest in expanding a party mobilization infrastructure that transcends their personal power only when their authority is rooted in the strength of the party itself. Therefore, party elites would be careful to consider how a particular party-building strategy may strengthen or weaken their source of power within the party. This consideration is heavily influenced by the balance of power among party elites.

Balance of Power Among Party Elites. I conceptualize the balance of power among party elites as a continuum, where contested leadership occupies one end; and dominant leadership, the other.[16] Contested leadership implies relatively equal balance of power among a small group of party elites, and no party elite, including the party leader, can unilaterally dictate party policies. Under dominant leadership, by contrast, the party leader obtains supreme status over other party elites and faces little resistance from them in policy-making. I should note that dominant leadership differs from personalistic leadership: The latter centers on building a personal cult and often disregards the strengthening of party institutions. Broadly speaking, contested leadership is far more common than dominant leadership in revolutionary parties – only in a handful of revolutionary organizations is the emergence of dominant leaders observed, for example, the Chinese Communist Party (CCP) under Mao Zedong in China after 1942, the Eritrean People's Liberation Front (EPLF) under Isaias Afwerki in Eritrea after the mid-1980s, and Nguyen Ai Quoc (Ho Chi Minh) in Vietnam after 1945.

Although the balance of power is a dynamic and fluid process stemming from strategic maneuvering among party elites, my focus is on the pivotal moment when party elites must decide whether to endorse a specific party-building strategy. At this critical juncture of decision-making, the balance of power becomes an exogenous, static factor imposed upon party elites. Figure 2.2 illustrates the ways through which these two stages shape party-building strategies. Perhaps counterintuitively, I argue that power consolidation by one party elite under dominant leadership but not power sharing among a group of elites under contested leadership mitigates distributional concerns and ex ante uncertainty, thus leading to coherent party-building strategies.

---

[16] The definition of leadership type shares some similarity with contested and established dictatorships proposed and developed by Svolik (2012). The key difference is that Svolik aims to explain regime outcomes in his conceptualization, whereas this framework focuses solely on party strength.

2.2 Elite Incentives & Party Building

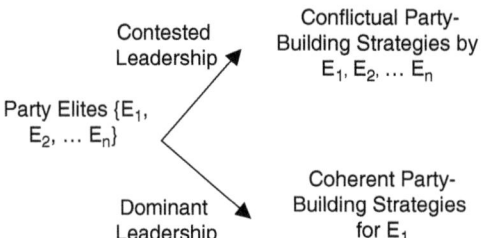

FIGURE 2.2 Intraparty power struggle and party-building strategy
Note: This figure illustrates only the self-enforcing equilibria for revolutionary parties with elite mobilization infrastructure. Revolutionary parties with mass mobilization infrastructure share the same equilibrium dynamics.

The Curse of Power Sharing. When party elites enjoy relatively equal balance of power under contested leadership, for example, they are highly sensitive to any potential shift in balance of power. Because the expansion of party mobilization infrastructure involves the recruitment and promotion of party members, it provides opportunities for some party elites to cultivate personal patronage networks. Consequently, party elites prefer strategies that increase their individual share of the total benefit stemming from a party-building strategy.

On the surface, the detrimental impact of power contestation seems to be at odds with the prevalent argument that the coexistence of a relative equal balance of power and a weak leader leads to institutionalized power-sharing, which is crucial to the longevity of authoritarian regimes.[17] Nonetheless, Meng, Paine, and Powell (2023) detail the double-edged sword of power sharing. Using a formal model, Powell (2021) further illuminates that weak institutions can undermine power sharing because tying their hands and giving up power could spell the downfall of powerful elites in the long run.[18] For revolutionary parties that have yet to seize state power and operate in a weak institution environment, power sharing becomes exceedingly difficult to maintain amidst contested party leadership. Factional struggle is often the norm rather than the exception among revolutionary organizations. In fact, the fragility of revolutionary parties not only stems from external repression, but also coincides with internal intraparty turmoil. For instance, internal elite factions doomed the organizational strength of Malayan Communist Party, making it vulnerable to British crackdown in the early 1950s (Staniland 2014). Elite conflict within the Hungarian Communist Party cut short the Hungarian revolution (Levitsky and Way 2022). Not all authoritarian parties can resolve elite conflict during early regime formation, leading to divergence in regime durability (Brownlee 2007).

---

[17] See, for example, Meng (2020), Reuter (2017), and Svolik (2012).
[18] Powell (2021).

Notably, revolutionary parties constantly face counterrevolutionary forces, and one could argue that these external existential threats force party elites to set aside their differences and unite in their efforts to strengthen the party.[19] Nonetheless, existential threats alone are insufficient to foster collegial leadership and power sharing within revolutionary parties. Precisely because the party is in a vulnerable position, party elites prioritize their personal survival over that of the party. In Algeria, for example, the interior and exterior leaders of FLN persistently clashed over revolutionary strategies and leadership arrangement throughout a seven-year independence struggle with France's counterinsurgency (Jackson 1977; Quandt 1969). When Mohammed Khider, the first secretary general of the Political Bureau, attempted to build FLN as an institutionalized mass party by integrating or coopting popular constituent groups, Ahmed Ben Bella became deeply wary that these party-building efforts could undermine his personal power. Ben Bella later forced Khider out and built a coalition with military leader Houari Boumédiène. Ultimately, protracted intraparty elite conflict exacerbated the FLN's institutional weakness, undermining its potential to become a cohesive party. Ben Bella was ousted by a coup merely three years after Algeria gained independence.

The Blessing of Power Consolidation. While contested leadership undermines incentives to engage in party building, power consolidation by a single party elite mitigates the uncertainty and distributional conflict of such efforts. Specifically, the strategy calculation by party elites transcends survival *within* the party to survival *with* the party when a dominant party leader emerges.

From the perspective of the dominant party leader, not only does a strong party present little threat to his own power, but it also extends his power by strengthening the party's ability to compete with external rivals. From the perspective of party elites, expanding party mobilization capacity is less likely to be used by their intraparty rivals to undermine their political power. In essence, dominant party leadership shares the spirit of strong parties, defined as "synchroniz[ing] individual career goals with the party's quest for political power" (Gerring and Thacker 2008: 36–37).

The importance of dominant leadership is not unique in revolutionary parties. Michels (1915) has coined the term "iron law of oligarchy," arguing that effective organization is rooted in the concentration of power by the leaders. Some could argue that this observation is at odds with the notion that internal democracy could be beneficial to mediate between government and society (Scarrow 1999; Sartori 1976). However, the latter arguments are built in the context of electoral democracies. For revolutionary parties operating mostly in an environment with weak electoral institutions, party organizations do not necessarily serve as checks and balances on party leaders but instead as vehicles to help them gain access to power. Regarding contemporary politics in

---

[19] In the context of electoral democracies, scholars have noted an inverse relationship between intraparty and interparty competition (Invernizzi 2023; Persico, Pueblita, and Silverman 2011).

Southeast Asian countries, "the raison d'etre of authoritarian institutions is not to constrain 'despotic power' but to supply a regime with the 'infrastructural power' necessary to implement its command over potential opposition in civil society and within the multiple layers of the state apparatus itself" (Slater 2003: 82).

Across revolutionary movements, the emergence of a dominant party leader is often conducive to building stronger insurgency organizations and reviving revolutionary struggles. In Eritrea, for instance, the power consolidation by Afwerki within the EPLF helped pave the way for building a stronger party by shifting away from previous discriminatory practice in party recruitment (Connell 2001; Pool 2001). The party-building efforts by the EPLF under the dominant leadership of Afwerki were a stark contrast with the earlier period before the EPLF split from the Eritrean Liberation Front (ELF) because the latter was weakened by patronage and contested leadership (Iyob 1995). Similarly, Ho has been credited for singlehandedly restoring unity among party elites and reviving the struggle when the Vietnamese communist movement succumbed to external repression (Huỳnh 1982). Importantly, most dominant revolutionary leaders are highly ideological, thus fostering the bonding within revolutionary organizations (Levitsky and Way 2022: 15).

2.3 THE EQUILIBRIA OF PARTY MOBILIZATION INFRASTRUCTURE

The discussion above illustrates that dominant party leadership and contested party leadership incentivize party elites to pursue distinct choices on party-building strategies, thus leading to two equilibrium outcomes for the quality of the party mobilization infrastructure. On one hand, contested leadership motivates party elites to pursue tactics aiming to strengthen their own power. Consequently, the party frequently adopts conflicting party-building strategies and undergoes radical shifts, leading to a mixed quality of party mobilization infrastructure and wavering party strength. While the party may effectively mobilize certain segments of the population, internal conflicts among party elites often result in counterproductive policies that undermine the party's mobilization capacity at times. On the other hand, when a dominant party leader consolidates power, a cohesive set of party-building strategies emerges, aligning with the source of power wielded by the leader.

Importantly, the divergence of party-building strategies reinforces the balance of power among party elites, perceptualizing the equilibrium of party mobilization infrastructure. Under dominant leadership, party-building would enhance party mobilization infrastructure by benefiting the dominant leader's own power exclusively. Party mobilization infrastructure under consolidated party leadership, therefore, buttresses only the domination of the party leader. Conversely, conflicting party-building strategies under contested leadership suggest a mixed quality of party mobilization

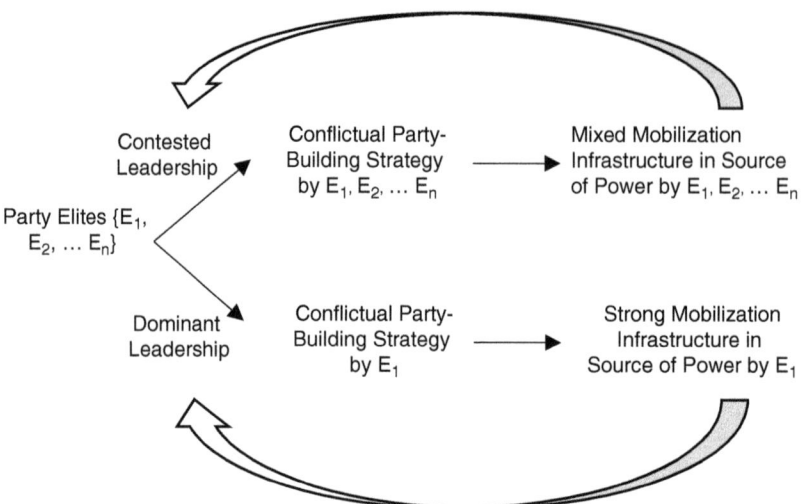

FIGURE 2.3 The equilibria of party mobilization infrastructure
Note: This figure illustrates only the self-enforcing equilibria for revolutionary parties with elite mobilization infrastructure. Revolutionary parties with mass mobilization infrastructure share the same equilibrium dynamics.

capacity among party elites, further perpetuating their relatively equal balance of power. Figure 2.3 illustrates the equilibria of elite party mobilization infrastructure.

One should not view these equilibria as static outcomes – the departure from one equilibrium to another could be driven by contingencies – exogenously change the balance of power among party elites, which in turn generates cascading impacts on party-building strategies and the quality of mobilization infrastructure. External repression not only generates negative repercussions on the party, but it could also disproportionately weaken some party elites over others. For instance, France's counterrevolution strategy created discontinuity in FLN leadership in Algeria (Jackson 1977: 47) because the repression wiped out some party elites in a region and shifted the balance of power among party elites to the survivors. Furthermore, the fatal misstep committed by the Provisional Government of the Algerian Republic (GPRA) leaders attempting to dismantle the military influence led to the rise of Ben Bella, who seized the opportunity to build an alliance with military leader Boumédiène (Jackson 1977: 68). Crucially, the outcomes of these external repressions are beyond the control of party elites, thus serving as an exogenous shock that changes the internal dynamics of intraparty elite competition.

The revival of Ho exemplifies the importance of external shock in shifting the balance of power among party elites. Before he became the dominant leader in the Vietnamese Communist movement, Ho was marginalized within the Indochinese Communist Party, which was dominated by Moscow-trained factions supported by the Comintern (Huỳnh 1982: 179). For nearly a decade between 1933 and 1941, Ho was forced to remain in Moscow to receive further training mandated by the Comintern, sharing a similar fate with CCP leaders Qu Qiubai and Li Lisan in the early 1930s. Nonetheless, the France's Sûreté had systematically eliminated most of his potential rivals, including Tran Phu, Ha Huy Tap, and Le Hong Phong, paving the way for his claim to the hegemony of the Party when he later returned from Moscow (Duiker 2000; Marr 2013: 442–498).

Notably the departure of a dominant party leader is another source of equilibrium disruption, leading to a rupture in balance of power among party elites and a shift from dominant to contested party leadership. The demise of a dominant leader, whether through natural causes or unforeseen events, often triggers an intense struggle among party elites during the succession process. In such cases the likelihood of the succession of a dominant leader by another dominant leader is low because dominant leaders are less inclined to groom competent subordinates as potential successors.[20] This succession struggle invariably gives rise to conflicting party-building strategies and the deterioration of party mobilization infrastructure.

2.4 FROM DOMINANT LEADERSHIP TO RESOURCE MOBILIZATION

Extant research often treats the financial resources of revolutionary parties and rebel organization as an exogenous endowment. Few recognize that these organizations must constantly explore new opportunities in mobilizing financial resources. In an environment with weak institutions, the effectiveness of resource mobilization does not solely rely on the establishment of formal fiscal institutions but employing its party mobilization infrastructure to secure quasi-voluntary compliance from the targeted population. To this end, elite mobilization and mass mobilization infrastructure exhibit distinct comparative advantages in resource mobilization but also suffer from some limitations, as the discussion below illustrates.

2.4.1 Challenges in Resource Mobilization

Taxation is a fundamental form of resource mobilization for any modern state, which has to develop the capacity for income assessment and tax compliance. Ideally, the state seeks cooperation from taxpayers to reveal their

---

[20] Egorov and Sonin (2011) develop a formal model explaining the loyalty and competence trade-offs when autocrats select subordinates. Shih (2022) offers a detailed study of post-1949 elite politics in China.

income truthfully and pay taxes diligently on time. To achieve voluntary or quasi-voluntary tax compliance,[21] prevailing wisdom highlights various strategies such as investing in bureaucratic capacity for monitoring and sanctioning capability[22] or enhancing tax morale by offering political concessions and economic benefits to taxpayers.[23]

Nonetheless, these strategies are not viable options for revolutionary parties. First, many revolutionary parties have yet to seize power from the state; hence they cannot credibly offer power-sharing and state sources in return for tax compliance. In the context of weak institutionalization and the absence of possessing state power, it is impractical for revolutionary parties to follow the path of the taxation–representation exchange as highlighted in canonical theories of fiscal bargaining and representative governments in early modern Europe.[24]

Importantly, the expansion of bureaucratic capacity requires financial and human resources, which are often in short supply for revolutionary parties in the first place, especially those at the early stages of party formation. By the same token, offering economic benefits to entice tax compliance may not be feasible either because some revolutionary parties have limited economic resources to begin with, and they face paramount pressure to prioritize financing their own operation to assure their survival. Unsurprisingly, many revolutionary parties rely on windfall revenues and external sources but not on developing domestic fiscal capacity for taxation for war finance.

2.4.2 The Comparative Advantage of Elite Mobilization Infrastructure

An elite mobilization infrastructure has an inherent comparative advantage allowing the targeting of the economic assets from existing economic elites for resource mobilization. "Taxing the rich" does not necessarily involve expropriation and redistribution levied against economic elites. Instead, revolutionary

---

[21] See Kirchler (2007) and Kirchler, Hoelzl, and Wahlfor (2008) for the framework of tax compliance.
[22] See, for example, Beramendi, Dincecco, and Rogers (2019), Besley and Person (2009), Garfias (2018), and Queralt (2019).
[23] See Luttmer and Singhal (2014) for a review of mechanisms critical to tax morale. For canonical models of taxation and the rise of representative institutions, see Bates and Lien (1985), Dincecco (2011), Levi (1989), North and Weingast (1989), and Tilly (1990). In terms of the relationship between tax compliance and public goods provision, see Ross (2004) and Timmons (2010).
[24] Canonical studies such as Bates and Lien (1985) and North and Weingast (1989) place the origins of constitutional government in an explicit fiscal contract between rulers and taxpayers: The latter agree to comply with higher tax rates in return for constitutional provisions granting them leverage over policymaking. The quest for revenue compels rulers to share power with taxpayers, clearing the path to a limited government. See also related work by Dincecco (2009), Levi (1989), Stasavage (2011), and Tilly (1990).

2.4 From Dominant Leadership to Resource Mobilization

parties aim to establish a sustainable revenue stream from existing elites and seek their help in raising financial revenues from society.

For instance, parties with an elite mobilization infrastructure offer economic elites protection for their assets or diffuse redistribution pressure in return for financial resources, especially those parties that have established a coercive apparatus. The incentive to cooperate does not necessarily derive from economic elites' desire for power sharing: They are driven by seeking protection for their business assets, which are at risk in a fragile political system. In addition, economic elites are deeply concerned about potential redistributive pressure from rival political organizations. In times of political turbulence, economic elites consider parties with elite mobilization infrastructure a safer harbor compared to revolutionary forces aiming to overturn existing political and economic order.

Another comparative advantage of elite mobilization infrastructure is access to some state resources through the assimilation of existing political and economic elites into the party. Consequently, the party shares the "spoils of office" with these elites in return for their financial contribution and cooperation. These maneuvers carry some credibility because capturing state resources allows revolutionary parties to offer concrete benefits instead of empty promises to the elites. Indeed, seeking elite cooperation is a pragmatic strategy many rulers face; "incorporation" is a strategy superior to "state substitution" for power accumulation by authoritarian leaders (Riedl 2014); furthermore, strong opposition parties in Africa are likely to be those borrowing resources and organization from preexisting institutional structures (LeBas 2011).

2.4.3 The Comparative Advantage of Mass Mobilization Infrastructure

By contrast, parties with mass mobilization infrastructure lack the ability to offer political concessions or economic benefits to facilitate resource mobilization. Because of their party ideology, existing political and economic elites are unlikely to be the allies of mass mobilization parties, nor does this type of party have easy access to state resources. The parties, therefore, turn to their most valuable asset – mass mobilization infrastructure – allowing them to collect information and achieve compliance from targeted population for resource mobilization.

I introduce the concept of *mobilized compliance* that captures the ways by which mass-mobilization parties mobilize ordinary citizens to secure quasi-voluntary compliance in fiscal extraction. The essence of mobilized compliance is twofold: (1) mobilize ordinary citizens to become the eyes and ears of the party and (2) reshape the focal point of conflicts stemming from tax extraction.

First, mobilizing the masses is necessary to alleviate the informational deficiency resulting from weak bureaucratic capacity: Legibility is the foundation for strong state capacity (Scott 1998). Mass mobilization infrastructure allows the party to exploit a web of grassroots organizations and solicit party members to serve as its eyes and ears. For instance, socially embedded party members help reveal critical information like the income and wealth of members of their community to the tax agencies, particularly in a rural setting, where the village is a tight-knit community. Hence, mobilizing the masses fills the important information gap caused by weak bureaucratic capacity for monitoring and assessment.

Second, mass mobilization infrastructure empowers the party to leverage its robust grassroots organization in shaping political attitudes and boost the morale of targeted taxpayers for compliance. This is especially significant in rural areas where access to media is limited, thus highlighting the importance of local mobilization efforts. Party members, who are often local activists and opinion leaders, can assist the party in carrying out information campaigns to influence public discourse. The information campaigns could shift the focal point of conflict arising from fiscal extraction and persuade taxpayers to participate in voluntary tax assessment and compliance.

Finally, in rural areas where formal institutions are weak, party members with embedded social networks could use their interpersonal interactions to persuade or even pressure taxpayers to comply with fiscal extraction. Recent scholarship has shown that informal institutions, such as social networks and religious affiliations, play a vital role in attracting voters and even engaging in violent uprising.[25] In rural China, for example, informal institutions are key to reward and sanction both villagers and their leaders (Duara 1988; Tsai 2007).

In fact, scholars studying insurgency and rebel organizations have emphasized the critical role of seeking cooperation from civilians for resource mobilization when these organizations do not have access to natural resources or foreign support.[26] FLN cadres in Algeria used their connection to obtain intelligence from Algerians in countryside villages and urban areas, and the FLN local cells shouldered the burden of tax collection on behalf of the larger organization (Jackson 1977: 45–46). For the Communist Party of Kampuchea (CPK) in Cambodia, rural cooperatives helped to bolster the food supply for CPK armed forces (Etcheson 1984: 124). The EPLF in Eritrea organized elected village committee to facilitate the provision of public services while collecting taxes (Pool 2001: 108–119).

---

[25] For the interplay between political parties and religious organizations, see Kalyvas (1996), Mainwaring and Scully (2003). Van de Ven (1992) highlights the reliance of informal institutions to mobilize by the CCP during the early stage of party formation. Tsai (2007) discusses the role of informal institutions in facilitating public goods provision in rural China during the contemporary era.

[26] See Weinstein (2006) for the discussion of the National Resistance Army in Uganda and Shining Path in Peru.

2.4.4 From Equilibria of Party Mobilization Infrastructure to Equilibria of Resource Mobilization

Having specified the equilibrium of party-building strategies under dominant and contested leadership as well as the comparative advantage of various mobilization infrastructure types, a question arises: How do these factors influence the variations in resource mobilization? Figure 2.4 illustrates the rippling effects from intraparty balance of power to resource mobilization. On one hand, the absence of a dominant party leader leads to an equilibrium of conflicting party-building strategies, which in turn generate a party mobilization infrastructure with mixed quality. This lack of coherence impedes the party's ability to establish a robust and sustainable capacity for resource mobilization.

For instance, parties with an elite mobilization infrastructure may initially benefit from elite cooption and gain access to state and societal resources, but the process of revenue mobilization often becomes ineffective as local elites divert economic resources for their own power consolidation. By relying on political and economic elites for resource mobilization, revolutionary parties inadvertently provide them with leverage to attain political power within the party and resist party directives. This dynamic perpetuates intraparty power contestation and hampers elite cohesion. By the same token, mass mobilization parties with conflicting party-building strategies face the same challenges in effectively using their grassroots organizations for revenue mobilization. This limitation in resource mobilization reinforces the challenges in the expansion of mass mobilization infrastructure, creating a vicious cycle of weak party mobilization infrastructure and limited extractive capacity.

On the other hand, power consolidation by a dominant party leader engenders a stronger capacity for resource mobilization because party elites overcome the collective action problem and are willing to pursue coherent strategies to expand party mobilization infrastructure. In the case of parties with elite mobilization infrastructure, existing elites become conduits to fulfill party objectives without actively seeking power sharing from the party; in fact, many developmental states, such as Taiwan and South Korea have achieved prosperous economic growth under a strong leader.[27] Meanwhile, mass-mobilization parties exploit their robust grassroots organizations to penetrate the society and achieve policy compliance in resource mobilization.

It is tempting to compare the relative strength of revolutionary parties with either strong elite or mass mobilization infrastructure. Such comparison is futile without considering the external political and economic environments under which the revolutionary parties operate. Exogenous shocks like interstate wars and foreign invasions could change the fortunes of revolutionary parties with varying mobilization infrastructure. Specifically, interstate

---

[27] See a review in Haggard (2018).

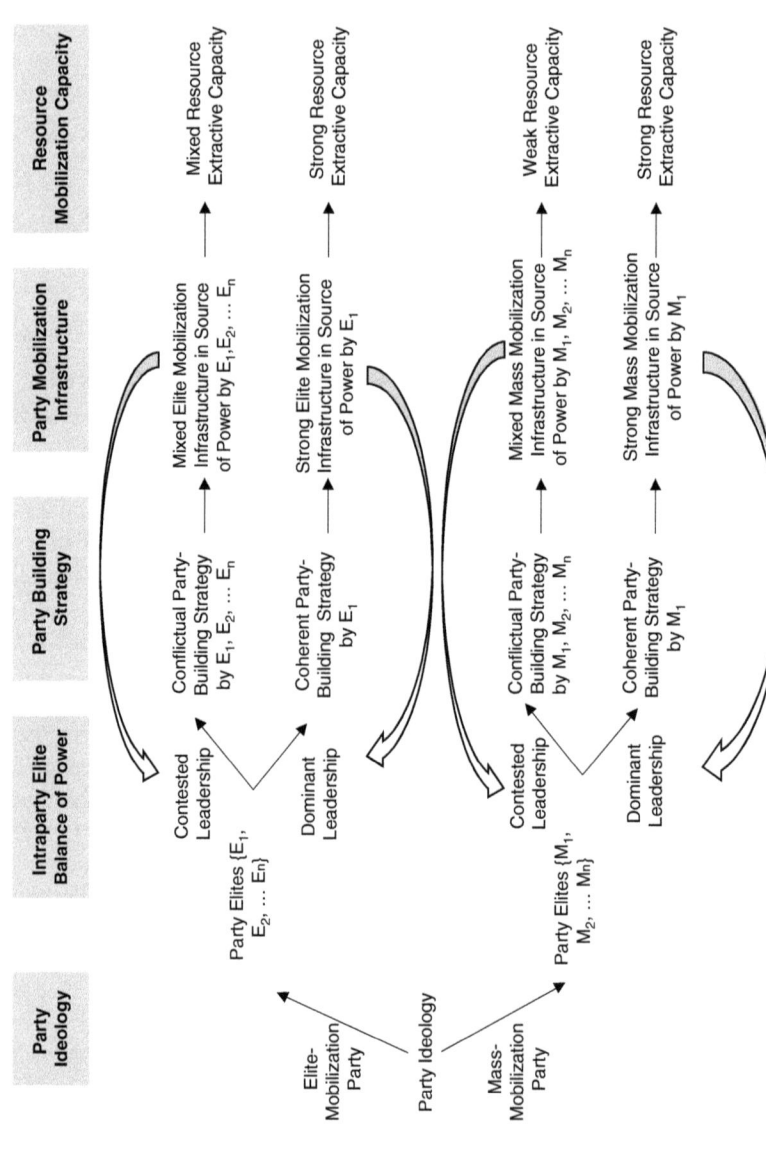

FIGURE 2.4 A dynamic model of revolutionary party strength

wars may create conditions favoring mass mobilization parties over elite mobilization parties.

For instance, elite mobilization parties face several challenges to cope with sharp fiscal uptick that occurs during wartime. Although canonical bellicist theories of state building emphasize the fiscal bargaining between the state and economic elites, this phenomenon is unique to societies where rulers are relatively weak vis-à-vis economic elites and the parliamentary system has some binding power.[28] War mobilization often leads to power centralization, but revolutionary parties cannot make credible promises to economic elites about their political concessions, thus undermining the willingness of those elites to cooperate.

Importantly, interstate wars – but not civil wars – are one of the most important income and power equalizers because they destroy the stock of wealth and political power accumulated by existing elites on which elite-mobilization parties rely. Scholars have systematically documented how countries lost their capital stock during wars (Atkinson and Piketty 2007; Scheidel 2018). Although wars facilitate taxing the rich or the formation of protection pacts between the state and the elites (Scheve and Stasavage 2010; Slater 2010), this option becomes less effective when the wealth of economic elites is decimated by war. The depletion of existing elites' wealth and power undermines the very foundation of revolutionary parties relying on the elite mobilization infrastructure.

By contrast, revolutionary parties with a mass mobilization infrastructure could prevail during the external war shock. Wars weaken existing elites and lead to a political vacuum that mass mobilization parties could fill: The success of revolutions in many societies, in fact, follows on the heels of the decline of existing elites in the society after crises (Levitsky and Way 2022; Moore 1966; Skocpol 1979). Building on their grassroots party organizations, revolutionary parties with mass mobilization infrastructures are better equipped with wartime mobilization.

2.5 SUMMARY AND SCOPE CONDITIONS

In this chapter I present a theoretical model detailing the motivation and outcome of party building by revolutionary parties. I contend that resource mobilization, beyond merely human mobilization, is a crucial objective for revolutionary parties that compete for power aside from electoral realm. The success of resource mobilization lies in the strength of party mobilization infrastructure, which is determined by the balance of power among party elites, who play a pivotal role in shaping party-building strategies. Finally, contingencies could tilt the balance of power among party elites and reshape the comparative

---

[28] Stasavage (2016) highlights the peculiar scope conditions of bellicist theories specific to premodern European states.

advantage of various types of party mobilization infrastructure. In the remainder of this book, I offer both qualitative and quantitative evidence through a study of the CCP and the KMT during the period from 1921 to 1945 to shed light on this theoretical model.

I should note that revolutionary parties do not stand alone as the only instigators of radical political and social changes; they are among myriad political organizations that challenge state power, operating outside the conventional realm of electoral competition. Specifically, two types of political entities – rebel organizations and independence parties – bear certain resemblances to revolutionary parties in their aspirations and tactics. Do the principal catalysts that fortify revolutionary parties – dominant leadership and resource mobilization – extend their applicability to these two types of organizations?

Notably, rebel organizations and revolutionary parties share a multitude of characteristics, with the former frequently serving as the predecessor of the latter. For instance, Saich (2021) even called the CCP a rebel organization during its inception in his recent book *From Rebel to Ruler*, an overview of the history of the CCP from 1921 to 2021. In a study of rebel organizations, Staniland (2014) uses the Communist Parties in the Philippines, French Indochina, and Malaya as empirical cases to illuminate his arguments on organizational changes in rebel groups. Indeed, both rebel groups and revolutionary parties strive to mobilize the masses, and they often engage in violent insurrection challenging the state.

Despite the blurred line between revolutionary organizations and rebel organizations, one must also note the key distinctions between the two. Revolutionary parties, in essence, are political organizations that aim to exert legal authority over the state, but they sometimes resort to violence to achieve their goals;[29] by contrast, insurgency groups are often formed with the primary objective of employing violent tactics without an intention to claim legal authority over the state: The transformation of some insurgency groups into political parties following a peace settlement is only an afterthought.[30]

Similarly, independence parties bear resemblance to revolutionary parties in that they too strive to assert legal authority over the state, wresting power from the colonial power. These parties frequently endeavor to rally the masses and progressive elites, orchestrating a nationalist movement to fulfill their objectives. For instance, the Congress Party in India, the People's Action Party in Singapore, and the African National Congress in South Africa are

---

[29] Scholars have documented the use of violence by political parties in Africa, Asia, and Latin America. See Birch, Daxecker, and Höglund (2020), de la Calle and Sanchez-Cuenca (2013), Hafner-Burton, Hyde, and Jablonski (2013), LeBas (2013), Siddiqui (2022), Staniland (2014), and Reno (2011).

[30] For the transformation of rebel groups into political parties, see de Zeeuw (2008), Lyons (2016), Manning (2007), Ishiyama and Batta (2011). Ishiyama (2016) offers numerous detailed case studies.

2.5 Summary and Scope Conditions

typical independence parties. The key distinctions between revolutionary and independence parties are their means of power contestation. Independence parties commonly follow a nonviolent trajectory, choosing to engage in electoral competition as opposed to resorting to armed insurrection.

The foregoing discussion highlights the scope conditions of the core arguments – leadership domination and mobilization infrastructure – in studying political organizations during their struggle to seize state power. First, the theoretical framework chiefly pertains to understanding the organizational strength of political entities *during* their endeavors to usurp state control rather than *after* their transformation into authoritarian ruling parties. Upon ascending to this ruling status – with domestic competition significantly diminished – the incentive structures of the party leader may well change: The urgency for maintaining a robust party structure to govern may no longer prevail. Instead, the power of these dominant leaders could stem from their control of the military, party substitutes, or a cult of personality, which then undermines party building (Dikötter 2019; Hale 2006). Mao Zedong and Joseph Stalin were widely considered such leaders who stood above the party and the state, who even initiated purges and campaigns that dismantled their own party organizations (Fainsod 1963; Suny 1998; Torigian 2022). Comparatively, scholars have found a negative correlation between personalistic party leaders and the state's bureaucratic capacity (Li and Wright 2023).

Second, the power contestation outside of electoral institution is another key scope condition of the theoretical framework. If the path to power through electoral competition is a legitimate and realistic option, even in only semicompetitive elections with limited suffrage, opposition political parties may pursue an alternative strategy by strengthening the electoral institution so that it competes with the existing ruling elites or parties through elections. In fact, one prominent school of thought on the rise of representative government emphasizes the causal pathway of fiscal bargaining between the rulers and economic elites in regimes with limited (elite) political participation (see, for example, Bates and Lien 1985; Levi 1989; North and Weingast 1989). Ultimately, if vote mobilization is crucial for party strength, resource mobilization may not play such an imperative role as emphasized in the theoretical framework.

Third, the theoretical framework does not include an investigation of the role of the military and party–military relations. Some may argue that the superiority of the CCP over the KMT is rooted in its command of the military. Although this observation has merit, it does not explain why the CCP was vulnerable prior to 1935 despite its tight command of the military or why the KMT collapsed despite Chiang Kai-shek's source of power stemming from his supreme control of the military. Nonetheless, if the military is independent of political parties and plays a decisive role in the political system, it may impede any party-building efforts by revolutionary parties. The arguments put forth in this book, therefore, may not be applicable in regimes where the military is the most dominant force, towering over all other political organizations.

Taken together, these scope conditions delineate the boundaries and the potential for applying the theoretical framework to study the organizational development of political entities other than revolutionary parties. Particularly in a protracted struggle to challenge existing holders of state power, resource mobilization proves as vital as human mobilization to sustain the movement. Without it, political organizations may cease to function because even the most committed political agents cannot wage war on empty stomachs and with bare hands in the long run. Meanwhile, the presence of a strong leader is crucial for holding these organizations together in the face of existential threats. That successful independence movements and robust rebel organizations are often helmed by prominent leaders is hardly surprising. Although some may attribute the strength of these organizations to particular leadership styles, recognizing the *existence* of a dominant leader can mitigate collective action problems and maintain elite cohesion within the organization is equally vital.

Perhaps counterintuitively, the pivotal role contingencies play in shaping the fate of political organizations must be recognized despite the significance attached to leadership domination and resource mobilization. "Even an event as momentous as the Chinese Revolution must be understood as the result of a long process of multiple contingent events" (Esherick 2022: xxiv). Outside of China, exogenous events, such as depressions, riots, assassinations, and wars, created openings that altered American political development (Mayhew 2007); furthermore, political actors can sometimes be the victims of contingent events that they neither understand nor control (Hochschild and Burch 2007). After all, once any radical changes in a society are imminent, political leaders often find themselves subject to the whims of whoever is running that "big casino in the sky."

3

Prewar Resource Mobilization (1921–1937)

To fully assess the strength of revolutionary parties, we must recognize that their power lies not only in their ability to rally committed individuals but also in their capacity to mobilize financial resources. The success of raising financial resources rests on the party's capacity to inspire and incentivize its members to serve as conduits during the process of resource mobilization. In democracies, campaign finance is crucial for political parties' electoral success.[1] In weak states and autocracies, financial resources are key for political parties to control the masses and coopt elites.[2] Ultimately, resource mobilization is the lifeline enabling political parties to outmaneuver their rivals; otherwise, the party's organizational structure disintegrates and collapses.

Examining party strength through the lens of resource mobilization complements previous indicators of authoritarian party strength, such as party institutionalization, organizational structure, or party longevity (Keefer 2007; Miller 2020; Tavits 2013; Ziblatt 2017). For instance, although the institutionalization of party rules codifies power distribution within a party, they reflect de jure, but not de facto, party strength; after all, organizational rules are effective only when party elites follow them. In other words, the institutionalization of party rules may not reflect the strength of the party if it has no binding power. Meanwhile, organizational structure is a relatively static measure of party strength that fails to capture its dynamic changes across space and time. Finally, conceptualizing party strength through its longevity reflects a retrospective measure because it cannot capture the decline of a longstanding political party over time. The collapse of the Communist Party of the Soviet

---

[1] For the role of party finance in democracies, see, for example, Fisher and Eisenstadt (2004) and Scarrow (2004).
[2] See discussion in Dimitrov (2022), Hunter (2010), Magaloni (2006), and Kitschelt and Wilkinson (2007).

Union caught many scholars and observers by surprise because few expected the seventy-four-year-old party to dissolve in a matter of months (Beissinger 2002; Suny 1993).

To this end, I investigate the extractive capacities of the CCP and KMT from 1921 to 1945 as a reflection of their genuine party strength. I rely on primary and secondary party and government archival resources to construct a holistic picture of these two parties' resource mobilization during this contentious period. I demonstrate that resource mobilization offers a revealing depiction to capture fluctuations in party strength experienced by these two parties. In the remainder of Chapter 3, I trace the resource mobilization of the CCP and the KMT prior to the Sino-Japanese War (1921–1937). In Chapter 4, I turn to wartime resource mobilization to uncover the reversal in their extractive capacity during the Sino-Japanese War (1937–1945).

3.1 RESOURCE MOBILIZATION CHALLENGES AT INCEPTION (1921–1927)

Some may argue that it is unfair to compare the extractive capacity of the CCP and the KMT because they were not founded on equal ground. The KMT was a successor party to secret societies and revolutionary parties founded as early as 1894, aiming to topple the Qing Dynasty. At the helm of these organizations was Sun Yat-sen, a prominent figure who played a pivotal role in spearheading China's revolution.[3] In contrast, the CCP began as a small political organization established by a group of intellectuals inspired by the Russian Revolution. They aimed to adopt the Russian model to liberate China from imperialism and warlordism.[4] The KMT, therefore, inherited a stronger party mobilization infrastructure and better national recognition than the CCP in 1921.

Despite the KMT's stronger origins, both the CCP and KMT faced severe financial constraints at the outset of party formation, a common plight for many nascent revolutionary parties. Subsequently, the KMT proved more adept than the CCP in overcoming these challenges. The disparity in the initial resource mobilization among these two parties can be attributed primarily to the contrasting nature of their party mobilization infrastructures – one centered around elite mobilization and the other around mass mobilization. Specifically, the KMT's elite mobilization infrastructure possessed a comparative advantage over the CCP's mass mobilization during the early phase of party formation, enabling the KMT to swiftly acquire crucial financial resources.

---

[3] The predecessors of the KMT included Xingzhonghui (1894~1905), Tongmenghui (1905~1912), the Kuomingtang (1912~1914), and the Zhonghua Gemin Dang (1914~1919). These organizations were commonly considered a form of anti-Qing secret societies (会党).

[4] See Chapter 5 for the sociopolitical context during both parties' founding moments in 1921.

3.1 Resource Mobilization Challenges at Inception

As demonstrated in this chapter, although both parties initially relied heavily on external financial assistance, the KMT secured a solid financial footing by consolidating territorial control in Guangdong and establishing the National Government in Guangzhou. Consequently, the KMT obtained vital access to financial resources by levying taxes on business activities. The success of the KMT in generating fiscal revenue in Guangdong was instrumental in its victory over regional warlords during the Northern Expedition (Li 2018).

In contrast, the CCP had to exclusively rely on the Comintern for meager financial support and achieved little access to alternative financial resources during the early days. Because of the relatively unknown nature of Communism as a foreign ideology in China, the CCP faced strong headwind in utilizing ideological propaganda for mass mobilization. The inability to expand a mass mobilization infrastructure generated a vicious circle in the CCP's extractive capacity – weak mass mobilization infrastructure failed to mobilize financial resources, in turn further constraining the expansion of mass mobilization infrastructure. The CCP's weak extractive capacity coincides with its haphazard organization during its early days (Van de Ven 1992), an observation is concurred by Yang (2011) who maintains that the CCP operated under the shadow of the Comintern during this period because of its weak resource mobilization capacity.

3.1.1 The CCP: A Fragile Fiscal Foundation

From its inception, the CCP began as a peripheral political entity, struggling to establish its mass mobilization infrastructure. From 1921 to 1927, party membership numbered only in the hundreds, and party cells were sporadic. Even when the CCP achieved significant expansion after forming the First United Front with the KMT, party operation was far from that of a disciplined and centralized Leninist organization. Consequently, weak mass mobilization infrastructure undermines its extractive capacity for resource mobilization: Neither its rural mobilization infrastructure nor its urban counterpart actively engaged in resource mobilization, and the party had to rely primarily on financial assistance from the Comintern and the Soviet Union to fund basic operations.

A close examination of the CCP's funding sources during this period highlights the reasons behind its weak resource mobilization. To begin, the CCP party bylaws stipulated membership dues as the primary source of revenue.[5] Relying solely on membership dues, however, proved insufficient for the CCP, given its small membership base primarily comprising individuals from lower socioeconomic backgrounds. In a letter to the Comintern in 1923, Maring shared his concern about the sustainability of CCP finances: Of 420 party members at the time, fewer than 10 percent of them paid membership dues, and most party members were unemployed (Yang 2011: 75). Maring further

---

[5] "中国共产党章程 [The CCP Party Constitution]," July 1922 in *Zhong gong zhong yang wen jian xuan ji* (*CCP Party Center Selected Documents*) (1989, VI: 93–98).

revealed that the CCP lacked transparency in financial management, with party operation relying almost entirely on foreign funding. The inability to mobilize financial resources imposed a severe constraint on CCP operations, and the nature of mass mobilization infrastructure prevented it from raising any financial resources from business and landed elites. Party cadres from both provincial headquarters and regional branches repeatedly lamented that the lack of financial resources severely hampered their ability to implement strategies aimed at attracting a critical mass in Chinese society.[6]

Given the CCP's failures to mobilize financial resources on its own, external assistance from the Comintern and other international pro-Communist organizations became its indispensable source of revenue. As early as 1920, the Comintern offered various types of financial assistance to the CCP, including monthly stipends, targeted grants for the labor movement, and small loans.[7] Figure 3.1 illustrates the meager financial assistance from the Comintern, which increased slowly from 1921 to 1926. Only after the bloody April 12 Shanghai Massacre by the KMT in 1927 did the Comintern substantially expand its financial assistance to the CCP, surpassing the initially planned budget of 144,000 Chinese yuan (Li 2020: 42).

3.1.2 The KMT: A Head Start Benefited from Elite Mobilization

When the KMT rebranded itself in 1919, fundraising from overseas party members and business elites was its primary source of revenue, largely because Sun Yat-sen had extensive connections with overseas Chinese communities.[8] Revenue from these sources was, nonetheless, inadequate to finance the growing military expenses needed to confront regional warlords. The disparity in financial resources forced the KMT to cooperate with Chen Jiongming, the governor of Guangdong, who later turned his back against Sun Yat-sen.

The establishment of the First United Front was a major turning point that facilitated the KMT's elite mobilization of financial resources. In March 1923, two months after Sun formally endorsed the First United Front, the Soviet Union immediately offered two million rubles and a team of five military advisors to the KMT Guangzhou Government (Li 2020; Yang 2011; Zhu 2007). With financial and military assistance from the Soviet Union, the KMT established

---

[6] "中共中央执行委员会书记陈独秀给共产国际的报告 [Report to the Comintern by the CCP Central Executive Committee Secretary Chen Duxiu]," June 30, 1922 in *Zhong gong zhong yang wen jian xuan ji* (*CCP Party Center Selected Documents*) (1989, V1: 47–55); "陈独秀在中共共产党第三次全国代表大会上的报告 [The Report by Chen Duxiu at the CCP Third Party Congress]," June 1923 in *Zhong gong zhong yang wen jian xuan ji* (*CCP Party Center Selected Documents*) (1989, V1: 167–173); "山东报告 [Report of Shandong]," June 1, 1924 in *Zhong gong zhong yang wen jian xuan ji* (*CCP Party Center Selected Documents*) (1989, V1: 277–281).
[7] See detailed discussion in Yang (2011) and Li (2020).
[8] See Cui (2013) for a discussion of fundraising for these revolutionary organizations under Sun.

3.1 Resource Mobilization Challenges at Inception

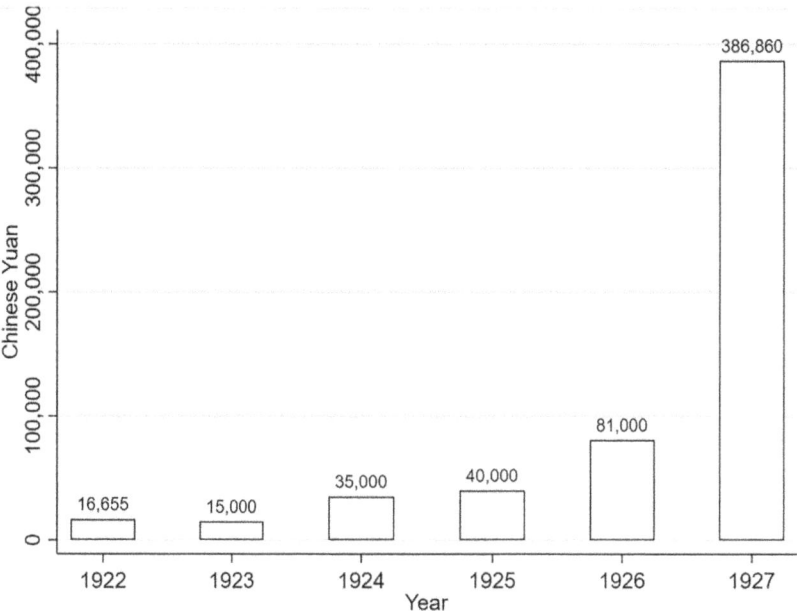

FIGURE 3.1 Comintern aid to the CCP (1922–1927)
Note: Most Comintern aid data derive from Yang (2011), and some are supplemented by data from Li (2020).

the Whampoa Military Academy in 1924.[9] Subsequently, the Soviet Union sent hundreds of military advisors and millions of rubles in financial aid to modernize the KMT military force (Cui 2013); with the Soviet aid, the KMT defeated Chen Jiongming and consolidated territorial control of Guangdong as its base.

Perhaps not too surprisingly, Soviet financial assistance to the KMT during this period far exceeded that given to the CCP, as the latter was considered a peripheral party despite sharing the same ideology with the Communist Party of the Soviet Union. The stronger position of the KMT led the Soviets to view it as having greater potential to become the ruling party in China than the CCP. This perspective sheds light on why the Soviets provided much more financial support to the KMT than the CCP following the establishment of the First United Front (Figure 3.2). By some calculations, the KMT received fourteen million rubles from the Soviets and the Comintern from June 1923 to July 1927, towering a total of approximately a quarter million rubles to the CCP during the same period.[10]

---

[9] For Soviet military aid to the Whampoa Military Academy, see Li (2020) and Yang (2011).
[10] The prioritization of assistance to the KMT over the CCP persisted even during the Sino-Japanese War, when the Soviets offered military and financial assistance to help the Chinese fight the Japanese. See Zhu (2007) and Wan (2005) for a comparison of Soviet aid to the CCP and the KMT.

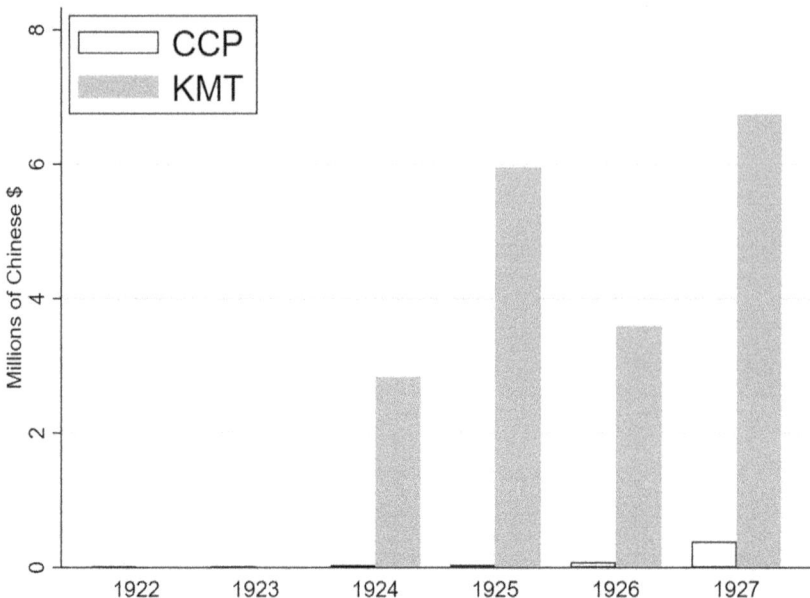

FIGURE 3.2 Comintern aid to the KMT and the CCP (1922–1927)
Note: The CCP data are from the same source as in Figure 3.1. The KMT data derive from Zhu (2007). The financial assistance includes both monetary and military aid, and I converted the value of the aid from ruble to Chinese yuan (one ruble was equal to 0.89 Chinese yuan).

Establishment of territorial control in Guangdong legitimized the KMT's efforts to institutionalize its extractive capacity, thereby enabling the financing of its national government and military expenditures. Led by Soong Tse-ven, the son of a Chinese businessman and a Harvard-educated financier, the KMT witnessed a stunning expansion of its government's extractive capacity during his tenure. From 1924 to 1926, the fiscal revenue of the Guangdong National Government rose from 8.6 million Chinese yuan to 69 million Chinese yuan, an astonishing 800 percent increase in a mere two-year span (Li 2018). By 1927 the tax revenue reached over 90 million Chinese yuan in Guangdong. This tax revenue offered a steady stream of money to the KMT, which overtook ad hoc overseas donations and Comintern financial assistance as the primary source of financial assets at the disposal of the KMT.

Crucially, the remarkable expansion of fiscal revenue in Guangdong benefitted from a series of financial reforms initiated by Soong, including the establishment of a Central Bank in 1924, the centralization of fiscal collection and spending, and the modernization of fiscal institutions in 1925. These reforms paved the way for the expansion of the tax base and the consolidation of various types of taxes during this period. Soong's fiscal expansion encountered little resistance from local business elites because of two key factors. First, most of the tax expansion was derived from regressive indirect taxes, enabling local businesses to shift the burden onto consumers. Second, Soong's implementation of fiscal centralization and favorable financial policies brought about economic stability, greatly appealing to the interests of business elites.

3.2 THE TRIUMPH OF ELITE RESOURCE MOBILIZATION (1928–1937)

The year 1928 proved to be a pivotal moment for the CCP and KMT, marking the divergence in their paths of resource mobilization. On the one hand, the KMT established the Nanjing Nationalist Government (南京国民政府), positioning itself as the ruling party in China after the triumph in the Northern Military Expedition. Despite periodic and intense power struggles among party elites, the KMT managed to expand its elite mobilization infrastructure and made notable progress in building institutions and mobilizing economic resources. In fact, some called 1928–1937 the "Ten Golden Years" of the Nanjing Government.

The CCP, on the other hand, suffered a major setback after the April 12 Shanghai Massacre by the KMT in 1927. The CCP urban operation went underground, and the party was forced to explore alternative opportunities in the countryside. Despite branding itself as a proletariat party serving the interest of the masses, CCP ideology did not naturally register with peasants in rural China at the time. Because of the absence of an effective mass mobilization infrastructure in rural China, the CCP's extractive capacity remained limited; therefore, the CCP had to turn to the expropriation of rural economic elites for resource mobilization, and this revenue source was ad hoc and hardly institutionalized. To expropriate rural elites, the CCP had primarily relied on its coercive apparatus – the Red Army – to facilitate resource mobilization. The limitation in resource mobilization spelled trouble for the CCP; eventually, the party lost all its Soviet base areas to the KMT's Fifth Encirclement Campaign in 1934, forcing it to undertake the Long March in order to escape the KMT's military campaign.

Although the CCP's fragile extractive capacity can be attributed to the hostile external environment, one cannot overlook the intense elite power struggle experienced by the CCP during the period of 1928–1934 after Chen Duxiu was forced out as the party leader following the August 7th Emergent Central Committee Meeting in 1927. In Chapter 5 I trace the cascading effects from high-level elite power struggle to low-level party building, revealing how these conflicts undermined the CCP's efforts to build a robust mass mobilization infrastructure.

While the KMT enjoyed success in the expansion of party mobilization infrastructure and extractive capacity during this period, its apparent achievements masked some crucial limitations. Importantly, the KMT's elite mobilization infrastructure was concentrated in urban China, particularly in coastal areas, while failing to penetrate rural areas. These shortcomings, although not immediately apparent, brought its demise during the subsequent Sino-Japanese War, laying bare the weaknesses within the KMT elite mobilization structure that Chapter 4 illustrates.

3.2.1 The CCP: Extracting Like a Roving Bandit

Although the CCP continued to seek financial support from the Comintern and the Soviet Union, external financial resources were neither sufficient nor reliable in sustaining the CCP's armed uprising. The establishment of Soviet base areas in rural China presented a new opportunity for the CCP to mobilize financial revenue. The CCP relied primarily on expropriation from affluent rural elites, such as those of landlords, rich peasants, and merchants, for its resource mobilization. Notably, the CCP's Soviet Government sought to establish a formalized tax collection system in rural China, but the lack of a robust mass mobilization infrastructure hindered its ability to effectively implement these policies.[11] Because the success of expropriation rests on the party's coercive capacity, the Red Army became the primary apparatus for the CCP's fiscal extraction. The indispensable role of the Red Army was on full display when the CCP Party Center briefly rescinded the Red Army's responsibility for resource mobilization in 1932 – the Party Center had to reverse its position a mere five months later. The CCP exhausted its brute-force resource mobilization in the Ruijin base area in myriad ways during this period, leading to its defeat to the KMT's military encirclement campaign in 1934 (Huang 2011).

Comintern Financial Assistance: When Supply Failed to Meet Demand. The collapse of the First United Front in 1927 intensified the urgency in the CCP to finance both urban and rural uprisings. By and large, financial assistance from the Comintern became increasingly unreliable and inadequate to meet the needs of the CCP after 1928. Financial support from the Comintern increased from approximately 386,860 Chinese yuan in 1927 to 522,472 Chinese yuan in 1928, but it stagnated at 400,000~450,000 Chinese yuan over the next four years even when the CCP urged the Comintern to help finance its military expenditure (Figure 3.3). Making matters worse, the Comintern leader who oversaw the Far East Bureau sometimes withheld or delayed payment to the CCP because of the leadership conflict between the CCP and the Far East Bureau.[12] The CCP had to appeal to Soviet leaders directly, including Stalin, hoping they would intervene and mediate the conflicts. Financial support from the Comintern eventually became sporadic and irrelevant after the CCP Party Center was forced to relocate from Shanghai to Soviet base areas after 1931.

---

[11] See Huang (2011), Wang (2017), and Zhou (2023) for insights into the strategies and constraints of CCP resource mobilization in Soviet bases.

[12] See the conflict between the CCP and the Comintern Far East Bureau; see Li (2020), Yang (1991), and Zhu (2007).

3.2 The Triumph of Elite Resource Mobilization

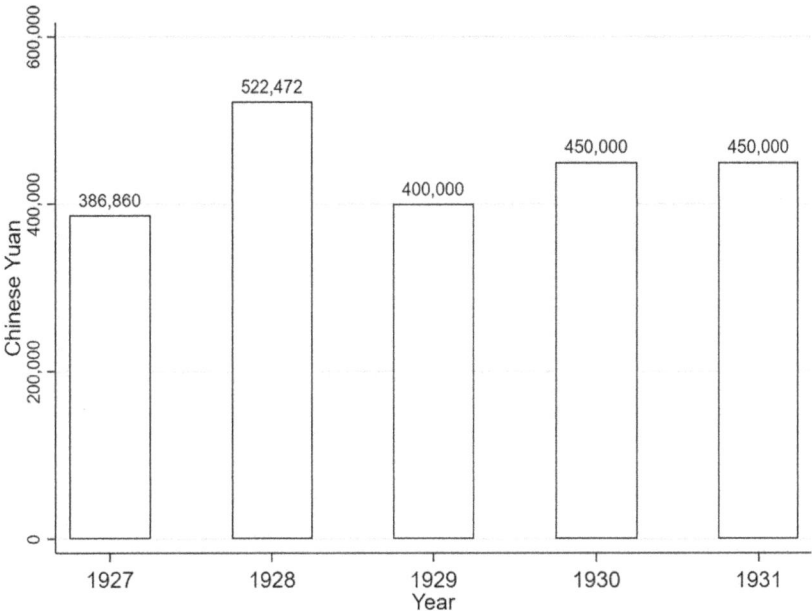

FIGURE 3.3 Comintern aid to the CCP (1927–1931)
Note: See Figure 3.1 for data source.

The Rise of Fiscal Extraction in Base Areas as a New Source of Revenue. Insufficient and unreliable financial support from the Comintern, coupled with an uptick in the fiscal demands of funding armed insurgencies, compelled the CCP to search for alternative revenue sources. The establishment of Soviet base areas offered a timely lifeline for its financial needs. Indeed, fiscal extraction in the base areas quickly emerged as the primary source of revenue – even the CCP headquarters in Shanghai requested remittance from the base areas to finance its operation (Sun 2019).

The CCP's weak mobilization infrastructure and extractive capacity become self-evident upon closer examination of the *sources* and the *instrument* of CCP resource mobilization during this period. The primary source of CCP revenue stemmed from the expropriation from wealthy rural households instead of the institutionalization of tax collection, with coercion the main instrument for resource mobilization. The CCP's failures in building taxation institution cannot be ascribed to a lack of trying. On the contrary, the CCP Soviet Government had attempted to transform the traditional tax system in rural China, for example, by introducing the consolidated progressive tax in 1931 (统一累进税), designed to replace the existing agricultural taxation system in China.

The challenge, however, lay in the implementation of these new progressive tax policies. Specifically, the CCP had not consolidated territorial control of these base areas, thus undermining its own attempt to formalize tax collection by establishing an alternative to the existing governing apparatus. For example, the CCP had to adopt a guerrilla warfare strategy in its armed struggle with the KMT. Roving the countryside to circumvent the constant military attacks by the KMT and regional warlords, the CCP-supported ruling entities lost their credibility as a government stable enough to collect taxes and carry out public spending and land reform because they resembled "roving bandits" instead of "stationary bandits" (Olson 1993). Compounding the issue, local CCP cadres largely disregarded the progressive tax collection mandated by the CCP Soviet Government because of the challenges in income assessments and tax compliance; in practice, most Soviet base areas relied on quota distribution and coercive measures targeting businesses and individuals.[13]

The failure of the institutionalization of tax collection resulted in expropriation from affluent rural elites (打土豪) as a pragmatic strategy for the CCP to raise fiscal revenue. Expropriation offered several advantages over taxation. First, expropriation from affluent rural households solidified its ideological appeal to peasants. The CCP often employed propaganda campaigns to highlight their expropriation from rural elites to garner local political support among peasants. Although most of the revenue from expropriation was not redistributed to peasants, the expropriation challenged the power of traditional elites, thereby strengthening peasants' support to the CCP. Second, expropriation was a far more effective revenue-raising tool than formal taxation to generate timely revenue in practice. A well-functioning taxation system requires accurate assessment of income and wealth as well as the strict enforcement of tax collection; the CCP had little bureaucratic capacity to achieve either goal. Expropriation, on the other hand, relied on coercion, a skill that the Red Army has mastered. Moreover, expropriation provided an immediate source of revenue, whereas taxation collection relied on a schedule that did not meet the urgent financial needs of the CCP in funding its military operations against the repeated military encirclement campaigns by the KMT.

Given that expropriation through coercion was the primary mechanism of resource mobilization, the Red Army shouldered most of the burden in resource mobilization is unsurprising. Although the Red Army was not initially responsible for fiscal extraction, the dire need for fiscal resources to finance armed uprisings quickly forced CCP military leaders to reconsider their role in facilitating resource mobilization. Specifically, the armed uprising led by Mao Zedong in 1927 became a turning point for the role of the Red Army in fiscal extraction. Mao recognized the need for a better resource mobilization for CCP uprisings in late 1927 and concluded that the Red Army should serve three core missions: (1) engaging in warfare, (2) expropriating from rural elites for fiscal extraction, and (3) mobilizing the masses through propaganda and establishing a new

---

[13] "关于湘鄂西具体情形的报告 [A Detailed Report on Xiang-er-xi]" in *Xiang-er-xi su qu ge ming li shi wen jian hui ji (Compendium of Historical Revolution Documents in the Xiang-er-xi Soviet Area)* (1985, VI: 266–355).

3.2 The Triumph of Elite Resource Mobilization

governing body.[14] From this point onward, expropriation for fiscal revenue became a primary political task for the Red Army throughout the base areas.

The indispensable role of the Red Army in the CCP's fiscal extraction became evident when it was temporarily relieved of its expropriation duties in late 1932. The CCP Soviet Central Bureau issued a resolution on June 27, 1932, in which Wang Ming maintained that the Red Army's sole responsibility should center on the battleground.[15] To remedy the shortfall in fiscal extraction, the resolution mandated the CCP Soviet governments to take over the responsibility for fiscal extraction; nevertheless, the CCP's limited rural mobilization capacity and extractive capacity were insufficient to generate the required financial resources. The timing of relieving the Red Army of its role in fiscal extraction could not have been worse. The CCP was forced to mobilize greater resources during the first wave of drastic expansion of the Red Army in the Soviet base areas, from March 1932 to February 1933, in response to KMT's military campaign. The shrinking revenue thus met with an urgent fiscal demand.[16]

This disastrous fiscal condition forced the CCP to reverse its policy directive a mere five months later in November 1932, restoring the Red Army's responsibility to raise fiscal revenue through expropriation. The Soviet government even institutionalized expropriation by budgeting the size of expropriation in both Jiangxi and Fujian in 1933.[17] For instance, the Soviet Government set a quota targeting 870,000 yuan from expropriation revenue for the final quarter of 1933 but a quota of only 256,500 yuan from taxation. Adding the revenue (225,000 yuan) from the auction of previously confiscated goods to the revenue of expropriation results in the total budgeted revenue from expropriation amounting to 1.1 million yuan, four times that of the tax revenues.[18]

---

[14] See discussion of the process in which the CCP decided to make use of the Red Army to raise fiscal revenue in Xu (1982 V2: 414–419).

[15] "苏区中央局关于争取和完成江西及其邻近省区革命首先胜利的决议 [Resolution on Attempting to Achieve the First Revolutionary Success in Jiangxi and Nearby Provinces by the Soviet Central Bureau]," June 17, 1932 in *Zhong gong zhong yang wen jian xuan ji* (*CCP Party Center Selected Documents*) (1989, V8: 240–261).

[16] In order to counter the KMT's military campaign, the CCP initiated three waves of expansion of the Red Army. The first wave from March 1932 to February 1933 added 87,600 soldiers to the Red Army. The second wave from May to August 1933 registered approximately 50,000 service members. Finally, the third wave from August 1933 to July 1934 added 112,105 to the Red Army. See Table 2 in Xie and Xiao (2019).

[17] "江西省苏维埃政府财政部三个月财政经济计划（摘录）[Jiangxi Province Soviet Government Ministry of Finance's Fiscal and Economic Plan for the Next Three Months]," January 29, 1933 in *Zhong yang ge ming gen ju di gong shang shui shou shi liao xuan bian 1929.1–1934.2* (*Selected Documents on Industry, Commerce, and Taxation in the Party Central Revolutionary Base Areas 1929.1–1934.2*) (1985: 177–181).

[18] "闽赣省财政部七、八、九三个月工作和八、九、十、十一、十二、一、二七个月筹款计划 [Report on July through September Work and Fundraising Plans for August through February]," August 8, 1933 in *Zhong yang ge ming gen ju di gong shang shui shou shi liao xuan bian 1929.1–1934.2* (*Selected Documents on Industry, Commence, and Taxation in Party Central Revolutionary Base Areas 1929.1–1934.2*) (1985: 224–233).

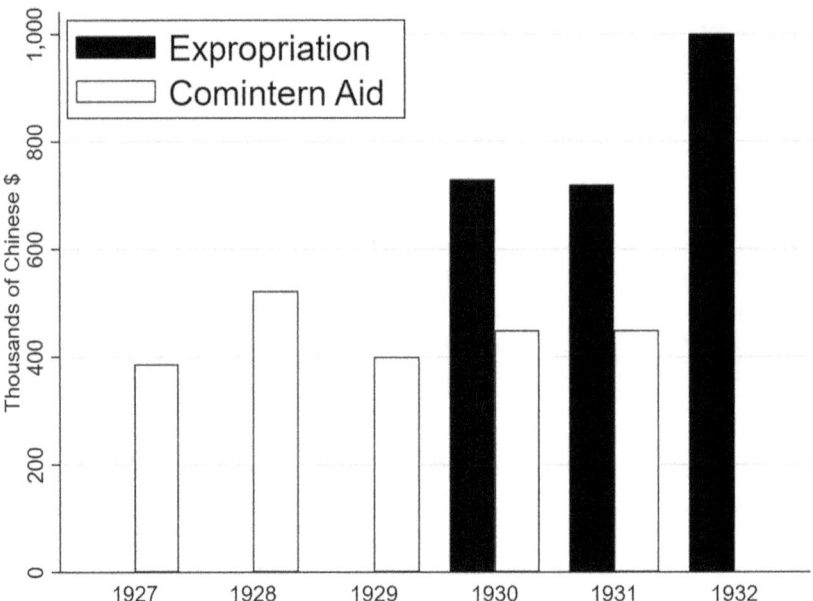

FIGURE 3.4 Comintern aid vis-à-vis expropriation (1927–1932)
Note: The Comintern aid data derive from the source noted in Figure 3.1. The data on expropriation come from Zhang and Xu (1999: 282–287).

The CCP internal party documents from the base areas consistently highlighted expropriation as the primary revenue source in the Soviet regions.[19] To put CCP's expropriation in perspective, Figure 3.4 illustrates the size of Comintern aid vis-à-vis expropriation by the Red Army in Jiangxi. As shown, expropriation raised around 730,000 Chinese yuan in preparation against the KMT's First Encirclement Campaign in 1930. A mere five months later, expropriation raised another 720,000 yuan in several counties during its preparation for the Second Encirclement Campaign in February 1931. Finally, the Red Army raised more than one million yuan after conquering Zhangzhou in April 1932. Altogether, the Red Army raised more than 2.45 million yuan through expropriation over the course of eighteen months, far exceeding the financial assistance offered by the Comintern. Notably, the size of expropriation in Figure 3.4 is likely to be understated because record keeping was poor, and it is based on only one Soviet area; the total expropriation by all the base areas would have, in fact, dwarfed the size of Comintern aid.

By contrast, CCP efforts in taxation were overshadowed by the success of expropriation. The CCP announced a series of progressive taxes – agricultural, business, and land – in late 1931 in both the Jiangxi and Fujian base areas.[20]

---

[19] See, for example, Zhang and Xu (1999) and Yu (1995).
[20] See Zhang and Xu (1999: 263–274). Note that tax collection did not start in most areas until 1932–1933. See also the discussion in Wang (2017) and Xu (1982 V2: 467).

3.2 The Triumph of Elite Resource Mobilization

However, the collection of 1932 taxes budgeted by the Soviet government still had not been completed by April 1933. In total, the Soviet governments collected only around 800,000 yuan in 1932 through land taxation, falling short of its one-million-yuan target. Tax collection worsened in 1933: Less than 10 percent of the budgeted tax revenue was collected by January 23, 1934 (Wang 2017: 66–67).

The Limits of Expropriation as an Instrument of Resource Mobilization. The short-term success of fiscal extraction through expropriation, however, comes at a heavy price. Documentation of the CCP's fiscal extraction in Jiangxi Ruijin Soviet base area between 1933 and 1934 shows that CCP strategies depleted local human and financial resources and led to severe repercussions (Huang 2011). For instance, the Red Army's manner of fiscal extraction was often coercive, targeting not only landlords and rich merchants but sometimes middle peasants and even poor peasants, who had been mislabeled as rich peasants. At some point the fiscal burden in the Ruijin base area even exceeded those in KMT-controlled areas (Huang 2011: 281–284). Beside fiscal extraction, the Red Army's conscription and labor mobilization exhausted local human resources; for example, between 40 and 80 percent of adult males aged 16–45 in the Ruijin base area were conscripted by the Red Army in its war mobilization from 1933 to 1934 (Huang 2011: 250–252). The excessive war mobilization of labor inevitably undermined economic production in the base areas, decreasing local residents' incentives to join the Red Army (Huang 2011: 254–255).

Most importantly, the reliance on expropriation as the primary instrument of resource mobilization undercut the expansion of party mobilization infrastructure. Compared to the Red Army, CCP party organizations were merely the "consumers," not the "producers" of resource mobilization. Hence the expansion of grassroots party organizations thrived only in areas where the Red Army had strong territorial control. For areas outside the CCP's territorial control, however, the development of CCP mobilization infrastructure remained a limited act. That the existence of most CCP grassroots organizations was ephemeral during this period is hardly a coincidence. Internal CCP communications attributed lack of funding as one of the main reasons for the challenges facing grassroots party organizations (Wang 2018). Ultimately, the CCP remained a party with very limited extractive capacity due to weak party mobilization infrastructure during this period.

3.2.2 The KMT: The Expansion of Extractive Capacity – An Unbalanced Act

After the successful Northern Expedition, the KMT became the ruling party in China by 1928, subsequently expanding its elite mobilization infrastructure and furthering its success in resource mobilization. The KMT's accomplishment benefited from two important factors. First, it relocated its capital from Guangzhou in Southern China to Nanjing in Eastern China, allowing it to continue the expansion of elite mobilization infrastructure in other affluent regions of China: Jiangsu and Zhejiang. Second, the CCP's radical insurgency tactics, including urban labor movements and rural expropriation, drove urban and rural elites into the arms of the KMT, who forged an alliance akin to "protection pacts." Therefore, the KMT succeeded in coopting many political and business elites into the party many of whom became members of the Nanjing Government or the National Legislature. The expansion of elite mobilization infrastructure meant that the KMT did not have to mobilize mass numbers of regular party members for resource mobilization; instead, it coopted existing political and business elites and achieved significant success in expanding KMT extractive capacity.

The KMT's success in resource mobilization is not without limits: Its elite mobilization infrastructure exhibited a pronounced urban bias in coastal China. This strategy served the KMT well during this period, as many scholars crediting the KMT for accomplishing state building in a hostile environment (Lin 2005; Strauss 1988; Remick 2002; Young 1971). The neglect of expanding KMT extractive capacity in rural China, nonetheless, planted the seeds for its demise during the Sino-Japanese War.

Strengthening the Elite Mobilization Infrastructure. The reliance on elite mobilization of economic resources was most evident when the KMT staffed the new Nanjing Government. At the national level, the KMT recruited numerous bureaucrats from the previous regime – Beiyang government – to assume important leadership roles in the new Nanjing Government instead of its own party members (Q. Wang 2010). The reasons for excluding KMT rank-and-file members in these leadership positions were twofold. Politically, Chiang Kai-shek's control over the KMT party organization was still limited at the time; therefore, Chiang was deeply concerned about the possibility of some KMT rival elites using their newfound access to the government bureaucracy to consolidate their own political power. From a practical standpoint, Chiang dismissed the majority of KMT members as lacking the necessary experience and maturity to effectively manage the complex bureaucracy essential for the functioning of his Nanjing Government.

At the local level, the KMT had no choice but seeking cooperation from local elites because the KMT completely abolished party apparatuses for mass mobilization after 1927.[21] Instead of devising a new strategy to strengthen KMT grassroots organizations, the KMT returned to the *baojia* system, which had been used by the central government in imperial China to outsource governance to local elites (Duara 1988). The head of the *baojia* had to meet a number of selection criteria, chief among them the endorsement of the county heads, who were local elites. Effectively, the return of the *baojia* system paved the way for the resurgence of traditional elites in local governance.

---

[21] See Chapter 7 for KMT party-building under Chiang during this period and the logic of party reorganization.

3.2 The Triumph of Elite Resource Mobilization

Consequently, local elites, not KMT grassroots party organizations, were the key players assisting the KMT to achieve policy compliance, for example, through tax collection.

The expansion of elite mobilization infrastructure for resource mobilization did not imply that the KMT always sought cooptation from the business community; at times, Chiang resorted to coercive tactics to compel business elites to meet his financial demands. By the same token, the business community did not embrace the KMT wholeheartedly, but the desire to maintain a stable business environment forced business elites to align themselves with the KMT. In fact, this is a common strategy for business elites in many societies – a protection pact between economic elites and the rulers.[22] In essence, business elites in urban China had to choose the lesser of two evils: the onerous fiscal burden from the KMT or the radical labor strikes and armed insurgencies from the CCP.

The KMT's relationship with business elites in Eastern China exemplifies its complexity.[23] The modernization of the Chinese economy since the early twentieth century has produced a plethora of industrialists and bankers, among them members of the highly influential Ningbo and Zhejiang financial guilds. Understanding economic elites' fear of instability in urban areas, Chiang Kai-shek suppressed the CCP-led labor movements and insurgencies. In return, Chiang extracted financial resources from the economic elites to finance his wars against his political rivals.

Chiang's relationship with these economic elites was initially cooperative, primarily because his government relied on their purchase of government bonds to help finance the Nanjing Government's expenditure. Finance Minister Soong Tse-ven skillfully created a liaison between Chiang and the economic elites, incentivizing the latter to provide financial resources while resisting Chiang's rising military expenses. As Chiang's demand for financial resources soared because of his expanding military campaign against the CCP, his relationship with economic elites turned sour. Chiang pursued various coercive tactics, including blackmail and abduction, to force economic elites to surrender greater financial resources. After Kung Hsiang-hsi replaced Soong Tse-ven as the new minister of finance in 1933, Chiang's fiscal demand for military expenses met with little resistance from the Ministry of Finance. Eventually, the Nanjing Government orchestrated a coup that took over the banking sector through the nationalization of the four largest banks in 1935. This move practically allowed the government to use the monetary supply to finance government expenses at will, most of which went to the military. To this end, Chiang obtained unlimited access to financial resources even though this strategy fueled the hyperinflation that eventually doomed the KMT in the 1940s.

---

[22] See Slater (2010) for the cooperation between authoritarian governments and business elites.

[23] Coble (1986) includes an excellent study detailing the complicated relationship between the KMT and business elites. Fewsmith (1985) also detailed attempts by business associations to influence the KMT.

The Transformation of KMT Extractive Capacity. During the transformation phase of state building, the KMT made a strategic decision to invest in fiscal institutions that prioritized taxing businesses and manufacturing in urban China as the primary means to establish stable revenue sources. The consideration was largely driven by the nature of the KMT elite mobilization infrastructure, which consisted primarily of emerging industrialists, merchants, and financiers but not traditional land elites. One should note that the strategic decision not to tax rural China was a matter of inability rather than unwillingness.

To begin, the historical infrastructure for the central government to collect land tax collapsed when the KMT assumed power in 1927. Land tax had historically been designated as a major source of revenue for the central government throughout China's history.[24] To ensure the enforcement of land tax collection, the imperial government allowed local officials to levy additional subtaxes on top of the land tax, serving as a fiscal compensation to local governments.[25] The collapse of the Qing dynasty and the ensuing power struggle among warlords forced the Beiyang government to enact the 1923 Constitution that designated land tax as local governments' revenue, a radical departure from previous fiscal arrangements between central and local governments.[26] Although the 1923 Constitution was later overturned, warlords retained land tax as de facto source of revenue for local government.

Recognizing the dominance of regional warlords and the limited involvement of land elites within the KMT's elite mobilization structure, the KMT sought a fiscal compromise that would ensure a stable source of revenue. Among the various sources of revenue, the KMT adopted a pragmatic strategy – prioritizing indirect taxation over direct taxation. The reason is that the KMT nationalist government struggled with limited bureaucratic capacity and insufficient control over local governments, making the effective implementation of direct taxation, such as the land tax, particularly challenging. This type of taxation requires a robust bureaucracy for accurate tax assessment and compliance enforcement.

During the KMT's North Expedition in 1927, Finance Minister Gu Yinfen put forth a temporary measure that allocated land tax as a revenue source for local governments while customs, the salt tax, and other business taxes were designated as the revenue source for the central government (Lin 2005: 121–124). When Soong Tse-ven became the new finance minister in 1928, he sought support from regional elites for indirect taxation by institutionalizing land tax as provincial government revenue. Effectively, the KMT gave up

---

[24] Wang (2022) constructed a dataset tracing the rise and decline of fiscal capacity of Chinese dynasties from the seventh to the early twentieth century. Focusing on the weak fiscal capacity in Qing dynasty, Zhang (2023) emphasizes the role of ideology in constraining the Qing government to raise revenues from land tax.
[25] See discussion in Ma and Rubin (2019), Wang (2022), and Zhang (2023).
[26] See Hou (2000) and Hao (2008) for a discussion of land tax reform during this period.

3.2 The Triumph of Elite Resource Mobilization

taxing agricultural production – the predominant economic activity in China at the time – in return for a stable indirect source.

Meanwhile, the KMT accomplished notable achievements in building institutions for indirect taxation (Strauss 1998). The KMT government successfully negotiated with foreign governments on customs arrangements, allowing it to regain a significant degree of tariff autonomy by 1928. In addition, the KMT established the Sino-Foreign Salt Inspectorate, an innovative arrangement in which authority was shared by Chinese and foreign tax inspectors to improve its credibility and insulate the organization from external pressures. Consequently, salt revenue swiftly emerged as a reliable and substantial source of income, ranking second among the KMT national government's revenue streams. The success of the KMT's retention of customs and salt revenues was rooted in the cooperation among the business elites and government bureaucrats who brokered the negotiation among the business community, foreign governments, and the KMT nationalist government. Soong Tse-ven made substantial contributions to the negotiations for the establishment of these institutions (Coble 1986).

The urban-centric resource mobilization paid off handsomely in expanding the KMT's extractive capacity. From 1929 to 1937, the total revenue collected by the KMT national government grew from 434 million to 1.251 billion, a three-fold increase (Figure 3.5). A closer look into the sources of revenue reveals that the KMT relied primarily on indirect taxation collected from business entities. For instance, the reliance on customs revenue ranged from 41 percent in 1929 to 30 percent in 1937. Revenue from salt, a type of indirect taxation, rose from 6.91 percent in 1929 to 15.75 percent in 1937. Most significantly, KMT tax reforms increased the share of consolidated tax

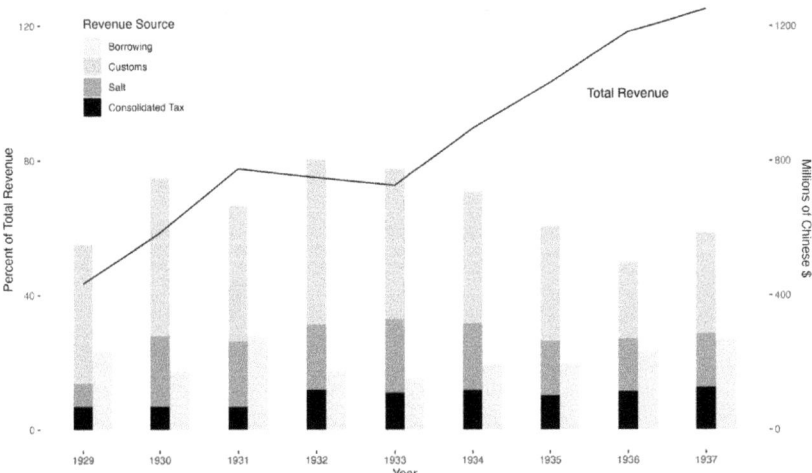

FIGURE 3.5 Sources of KMT fiscal revenue (1929–1937)
Note: Data are calculated based on Appendix 1 in Young (1971: 433–440).

revenues in total revenue from 6.91 percent in 1929 to 12.63 percent in 1937. Finally, although borrowing from domestic bonds and acquiring bank loans remained an important part of the fiscal revenue of the KMT, it was able to keep borrowing in check without a significant increase from 1929 to 1937. On average, borrowing accounted for 21.11 percent of KMT revenue during this period.

Some scholars attribute the refurbishment of the KMT fiscal foundation to an institutional explanation – the formation of the Nanjing national government legitimized the KMT's access to valuable state resources, such as revenue from customs duties and the salt monopoly, as well as monetary supply policies (Lin 2005; Strauss 1998). Nevertheless, the creation and functioning of these institutions hinged on the vital efforts of economic elites. The discussion above shows that the KMT employed cooptation and sometimes even the coercion of economic elites to mobilize financial resources (Coble 1986; Fewsmith 1985).

The Urban Bias in KMT Extractive Capacity in Coastal China. The KMT's extractive capacity exhibited two distinct characteristics on the eve of the Sino-Japanese War in 1937: an urban bias and a concentration in northern and coastal China. These characteristics were not accidental but instead the deliberate outcome of strategic calculations by the KMT nationalist government, which sought to navigate elite conflicts and leverage the comparative advantage of its elite mobilization infrastructure.

Specifically, customs, the salt tax, and consolidated tax accounted for nearly 75 percent of KMT government revenue by 1937, the sources of this revenue concentrated in urban centers in north China and coastal areas. For instance, Figure 3.6a shows the geographic location of major customs ports in China and the amount of customs revenue; four of the top five provinces were located on the east coast of China. Figure 3.6b illustrates the major salt production areas, which were concentrated in coastal cities in Tianjin, Shandong,

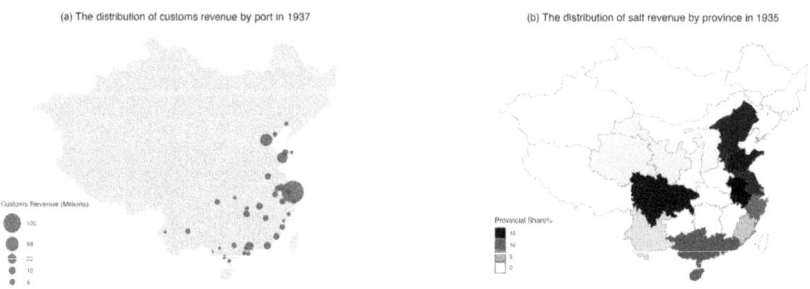

FIGURE 3.6 Prewar distribution of customs and salt production
Source: 1937 customs revenue data are from *Shi nian lai zhi hai guan* (*The Customs of the Past Decade*), 1943:9–12. Salt data derive from *Cai zheng nian jian* (*Finance Statistical Yearbook*) (1935, V2: 378–381).

3.3 Summary

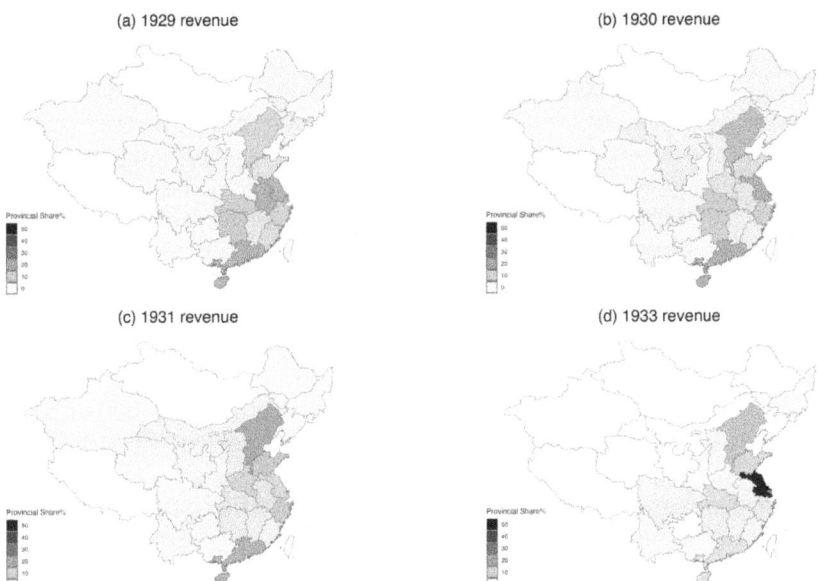

FIGURE 3.7 Prewar distribution of KMT national government revenue by province. Note: The visualization of the distribution of KMT national government revenue is based on *Cai zheng nian jian* (*Finance Statistical Yearbook*) (1935, VI: 151–158; 211–213; 421–423).

Zhejiang, Fujian, Jiangsu, Guangdong, and Anhui, primarily because of their proximity to abundant seawater sources. Consolidated and other business taxes targeted manufacturing, and these manufacturing hubs were again located in coastal China.

In addition, Figure 3.7 illustrates the shifting distribution of KMT national government revenue from various provinces in 1929, 1930, 1931, and 1933. First, the primary revenue contribution moved from southern China to eastern China over time. Second, persistent urban bias existed in coastal China for KMT's resource mobilization, the success of which unfortunately planted the seeds of its demise due to the Sino-Japanese War later: Jiangsu, Hebei, and Shandong accounted for more than two-thirds of KMT nationalist government's revenue on the eve of the war.

3.3 SUMMARY

On the eve of the Sino-Japanese War in 1937, the CCP and the KMT had developed two distinct types of mobilization infrastructure that led to different extractive capacities. The KMT relied on its elite mobilization infrastructure and significantly expanded its extractive capacity from 1928 to 1937.

By contrast, the CCP had a steep hill to climb in building a mass mobilization infrastructure. The weakness of its mobilization infrastructure failed to mobilize the necessary resources for the party's power struggle with its rivals.

With resource mobilization as the indicator of revolutionary party strength, Chapter 3 demonstrates why the CCP had a humble beginning and was on the brink of collapse twice (in 1927 and again in 1934) and why the KMT became a dominant party despite the intense power struggle among party elites. The KMT rapidly expanded its extractive capacity, leveraging its comparative advantage in elite mobilization infrastructure. Beneath the CCP's weakness lies in its fragile extractive capacity. The CCP's mass mobilization infrastructure failed to gain traction because of its inability to mobilize sufficient resources. The CCP's failure in resource mobilization is hardly a surprise. As highlighted in Chapter 2, building an effective mass mobilization infrastructure is highly costly, requiring substantial resource mobilization that mass mobilization parties do not have during the early stages of party formation. Elite mobilization infrastructure thus holds a comparative advantage in facilitating the rapid resource mobilization during the inception of the party, as exemplified by the remarkable success of the KMT.

4

Reversal of Fortune

Wartime Resource Mobilization (1937–1945)

The KMT solidified its position as the dominant ruling party in China by 1935, successfully expelling the CCP from the Jiangxi Soviet base area and amassing a formidable military force surrounding the remaining CCP troops in Shaanxi. The CCP, by contrast, barely survived the torturous Long March. On the eve of the Sino-Japanese War in 1937, the KMT boasted an impressive membership of 1.54 million, whereas CCP membership had dwindled to only 40,000. If not for the Xi'an incident, during which two KMT generals staged a coup and placed Chiang Kai-shek under house arrest on December 12, 1936, the CCP would have faced a fate akin to many revolutionary parties that succumbed to counterrevolutionary repression.[1]

Few could have predicted that the fortunes of these two parties would be radically reversed just eight years later. By the time the Sino-Japanese War ended in 1945, the CCP had amassed 1.2 million members, establishing a robust mass mobilization infrastructure in Northern China. Despite boasting a larger party membership of 6.9 million, the KMT further slipped into a fragile state, plagued by undisciplined members and dysfunctional party organizations. The rapid collapse of the KMT during the 1946–1949 Civil War caught everyone by surprise, including CCP leaders.

The shifting fortunes of the CCP and the KMT during the Sino-Japanese War have attracted enduring interests from both scholars and policymakers. I unveil a crucial factor contributing to the reversal of fortune of the two parties: The Sino-Japanese War altered the comparative advantages of party mobilization infrastructure for resource mobilization. In particular, the CCP successfully employed its mass mobilization infrastructure for resource mobilization in rural China. By contrast, the KMT's elite mobilization infrastructure

---

[1] See Fairbank and Feuerwerker (1986) and Zhang (2001) for the discussion of the Xi'an incident. For the role played by KMT General Zhang Xueliang, see Yang (2006).

became a liability because the Japanese invasion undermined the economic power of the very economic elites that the KMT sought to mobilize. The KMT's earlier decision in 1927 to forgo mass mobilization infrastructure proved fatal, depriving it of alternative means to effectively engage in wartime mass mobilization when it was most needed.

In the remainder of this chapter, I first document the impact of the initial fiscal shock stemming from the Sino-Japanese War on the CCP's and KMT's respective extractive capacity. I then trace the strategic responses by both parties to address the fiscal demand and supply shocks. I show that both parties were compelled to levy land-tax in kind (grains) as a response to their unsuccessful attempts to raise revenue from other sources. Furthermore, their distinct party mobilization infrastructures led to the divergent strategies and outcomes. I demonstrate that the mass mobilization infrastructure allowed the CCP to employ grassroots party organizations and adopt mobilized compliance as a tactic to facilitate successful fiscal extraction in a hostile environment. Conversely, the elite mobilization infrastructure forced the KMT to rely on economic elites for grain extraction, which in turn generated mass resentment due to inequity in the practice.

4.1 THE INITIAL WAR SHOCK (1937–1940)

The outbreak of the Sino-Japanese War began with the Marco Polo Bridge Incident of July 7, 1937, setting off a series of fiscal shocks to the KMT and the CCP. As the KMT faced an extreme fiscal demand shock to finance the war, the gradual loss of territorial control in northern and coastal China from 1937 to 1940 dealt a deadly blow to the KMT's extractive capacity because it was the region from which the KMT had drawn most of its revenue through its elite mobilization infrastructure. The CCP, on the other hand, initially experienced some fiscal relief at the outset of the War after forming the Second United Front with the KMT. As part of the agreement in the Second United Front, the KMT ceased its military campaign against the CCP and provided it with substantial financial support. The improvement in CCP fiscal revenue was ephemeral: The KMT abruptly withdrew all the financial support to the CCP after a skirmish erupted between the two parties in 1941. In addition, the Japanese military "mop-up" campaign and the economic blockade by the KMT further undercut the inflow of foreign assistance. By the end of 1940, both the KMT and CCP were confronted with a grim fiscal outlook.

4.1.1 The Crumbling Extractive Capacity of the KMT

As demonstrated in Chapter 3, the success of prewar KMT fiscal capacity building resulted in 75 percent of the Nationalist government's fiscal revenue originating from customs, salt monopoly revenue, and the consolidated tax in 1936. Most of the revenue was based on taxing business activities in northern and coastal China, a region where most of the Japanese occupation occurred later in the Sino-Japanese War.

4.1 The Initial War Shock (1937–1940)

Figure 4.1 visualizes the extent of fiscal demand and supply shocks to the KMT national government resulting from the Japanese invasion from 1937 to 1940. First, Figure 4.1a shows that in 1937 the Japanese immediately captured 213 counties across five provinces – Jiangsu, Hebei, Shandong, Zhejiang, and Hubei – the provinces where most of the KMT's fiscal revenue originated from. The Japanese occupation deepened in the next three years. By 1940, Jiangsu, Hebei, and Shandong had lost more than 75 percent of their counties to the Japanese invasion. Hubei lost 54 percent; Zhejiang, 30 percent.

Figure 4.1b depicts the amount of fiscal revenue collected from customs, salt monopoly revenue, and the consolidated tax, which was significantly outpaced by the uptick in defense spending during the same period from 1937 to 1940. The collapse of customs revenue fundamentally crippled the KMT's fiscal instruments (Boecking 2017). The divergence between the dwindling fiscal revenue from major sources and the soaring defense spending faced by the KMT became unmistakably clear.

Suffering the twin fiscal shocks of the War, the KMT had initially adopted two strategies in response – intensifying direct taxation and expanding monetary supply – but they quickly ran aground. For instance, the KMT initiated a tax reform on direct taxation in the urban sector, including excessive wartime profit tax and estate tax in 1938 and personal income tax in 1941 (Lin 2005). The KMT aimed to use direct taxation to compensate for the loss of revenue from indirect taxation resulting from the war. Nonetheless, the revenue from these new taxes could not offset the revenue losses incurred from Japanese occupation and catch up with the runaway fiscal demands required to finance the war.

To remedy the insufficient fiscal revenue, the KMT radically expanded the monetary supply in order to close the gap between government revenue and spending: Government borrowing drastically increased from an average of 21.11 percent of the budget before the war to 67.58 percent during the Sino-Japanese War.[2] The most devastating consequence of these responses was the rapid rise of hyperinflation, driven by insufficient tax revenue and the steep increase in the monetary supply. Prior to the Sino-Japanese War, China experienced relatively stable inflation from 1930 to 1937 despite the ongoing civil wars involving the KMT, the CCP, and the regional warlords. The year-to-year price index increased approximately 12 percent~18 percent during this period; however, inflation rocketed to 400 percent~665 percent in various regions of China from 1937 to 1940 and reached over 1,000 percent by 1941 (Chang 1958: 371).

4.1.2 Ephemeral Relief for CCP Extractive Capacity

The CCP's fiscal capacity initially benefited from the outset of the War after the formation of the Second United Front in 1937. The CCP agreed to accept KMT leadership and halted the radical land reforms in rural areas;

---

[2] Author's calculation. See Table C.8, Appendix C.

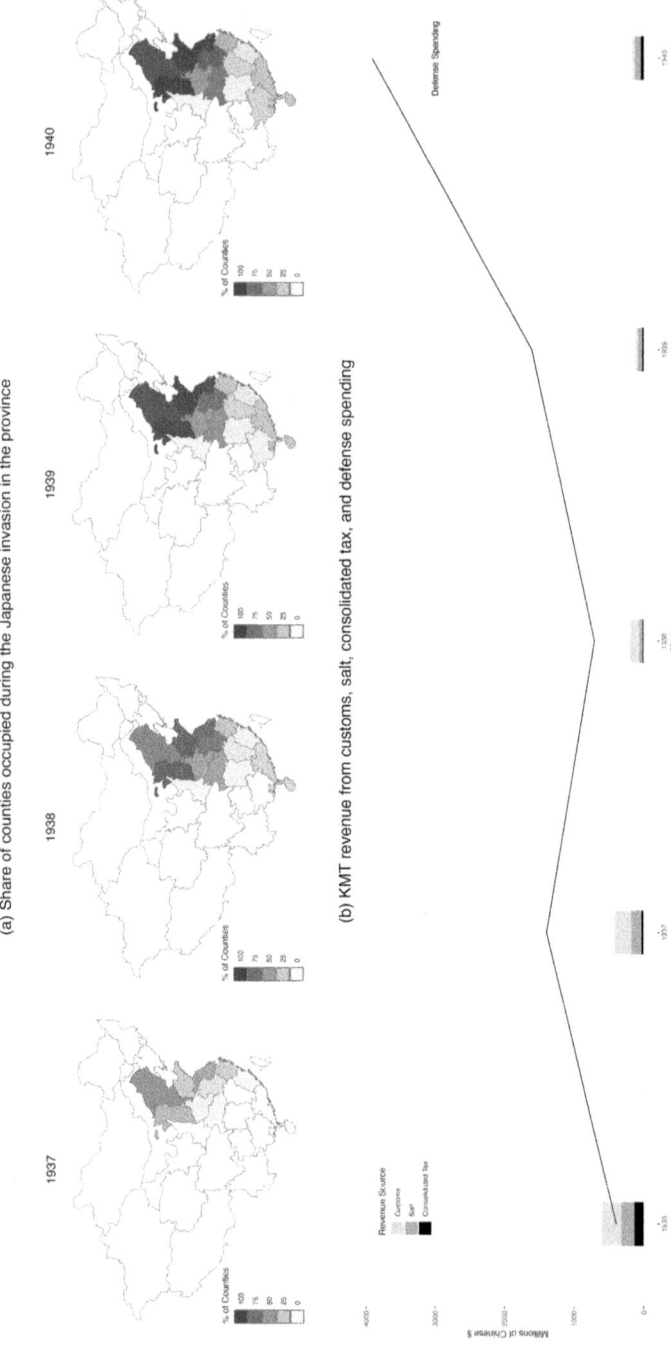

FIGURE 4.1 Wartime fiscal demand and supply shock to the KMT.
Note: The Japanese occupation data are based on Luo (2005: 26–58). The 1936 KMT revenue and defense spending data are from Young (1971: 433–440). The 1937–1940 KMT revenue and defense spending data are from Young (1965: 14). The 1939 customs revenue in the original source does not represent current customs collections in Free China in 1939, which were $33 million yuan (see note on Table 2 in Young 1971).

4.1 The Initial War Shock (1937–1940)

TABLE 4.1 *Outside assistance and CCP fiscal revenue*

	Total revenue	KMT financial assistance	Foreign assistance	Share of outside assistance (%)
1937	2,490,229.49	1,927,672.84	36,254.20	78.87
1938	7,361,971.44	4,480,157.16	1,973,870.97	87.67
1939	8,847,427.72	5,000,436.10	1,254,207.53	70.69
1940	14,329,696.10	4,997,074.11	5,505,901.69	73.30

Note: All the numbers are in *fabi* currency. The total revenue numbers, which differ from those reported in Shaan-Gan-Ning data, are from *Kang ri zhan zheng shi qi shaan gan ning bian qu cai zheng jing ji shi liao zhai bian (Shaan-Gan-Ning Border Region Finance and Economic Selective Historical Record During the Sino-Japanese War)* (1981, V6: 427), because I added the revenue from the KMT and foreign assistance as shown on pp. 428–429 in the same volume.

furthermore, the CCP reorganized the Red Army into the New Fourth Army and the Eighth Route Army that would be under the *de jure* command of the KMT National Revolutionary Army.[3] In return the KMT terminated its military campaign against the CCP and provided much-needed financial support to it.

During this phase of the Sino-Japanese War from 1937 to 1940, the CCP remained relying heavily on external financial assistance, which primarily originated from two key sources: the first, financial aid from the KMT, which was part of the agreement for the Second United Front[4]; the second, international assistance from the Comintern and other pro-Communist international organizations. Table 4.1 shows that outside financial assistance, especially KMT funding, accounted for up to 88 percent of its revenue in the Shaan-Gan-Ning area, where the Party Center of the CCP was located.

These external financial resources played a crucial role in enabling the CCP to recuperate and establish several anti-Japanese base areas without relying on expropriation for resource mobilization from the local population. Indeed, the CCP imposed a very light tax burden upon peasants from 1937 to 1940. In the Shaan-Gan-Ning base area, the share of grain levies in total agricultural output amounted only to 1.28 percent in 1937, 1.32 percent in 1938, and 2.92 percent in 1939.[5] In 1940, on the eve of the collapse of the Second United Front, grain

---

[3] The CCP still maintained de facto full control of its army, having learned from the failures of the first United Front, during which the party exerted little effort in establishing its own military forces because of the agreement. See Kataoka (1974) for the discussion of CCP operation during the Second United Front.

[4] See Li (2017) and Sun (2015) for more detail on KMT's military and financial assistance to the CCP.

[5] The Shaan-Gan-Ning data are from *Kang ri zhan zheng shi qi shaan gan ning bian qu cai zheng jing ji shi liao zhai bian (Shaan-Gan-Ning Border Region Finance and Economic Selective Historical Record During the Sino-Japanese War)*, (1981, V7: 59–60).

levies accounted for only 6.36 percent of local grain output and 18.54 percent of the CCP government's total fiscal revenues in Shaan-Gan-Ning.[6]

Unfortunately, the improvement in CCP fiscal capacity was short-lived: The KMT abruptly withdrew its financial support in January 1941, following the "South Anhui Incident" (皖南事变), which involved a military clash between the CCP's New Fourth Army and the KMT's nationalist army. The collapse of the Second United Front generated a severe fiscal supply shock to the CCP, which had heavily relied on KMT financial support in the previous four years.

The fiscal supply shock resulting from the withdrawal of KMT financial assistance in 1941 forced the CCP to explore several options at this critical juncture: 1941–1942. Specifically, the Party had explored four strategies to remedy the fiscal supply shock: (1) expansion of the monetary supply, (2) taxation of cross-border merchandise, (3) direct engagement in economic production, and (4) intensifying grain levies in kind. Despite its efforts the first three responses fell short of adequately responding to the fiscal supply shock.

For instance, the use of monetary expansion through the issuance of local currency sparked the rapid hyperinflation within the base areas. The monetary expansion increased 493.7 percent by June 1941 in the Shaan-Gan-Ning area, and inflation in Yan'an rocketed to 221.6 percent during the same period.[7] The inflationary trend continued throughout the second half of 1941, the annual inflation rate reaching 532.8 percent by December. Meanwhile, taxing cross-border merchandise was insufficient to close the gap in the budgetary shortfall because of a small tax base in CCP-controlled territories; furthermore, imposing greater indirect taxation on goods and business transactions fueled the rising inflation in the base areas.

Direct involvement in agricultural production provided some relief to the CCP's fiscal revenue in certain areas but not for the reasons the CCP often claimed. The self-production campaign to boost grain output was frequently highlighted as a key factor in the CCP's ability to endure in a challenging economic environment (Selden 1971). In reality, however, the full impact of grain cultivation was not realized until 1943–1944 because of the difficult agricultural conditions in the territories under CCP control, limiting significant increases in crop yields. Instead of grain cultivation, the cultivation and trading of opium, a highly valuable crop, brought critical short-term relief to the CCP.[8] Figure 4.2 illustrates that the profits from opium production immediately contributed 21.87 percent of Shaan-Gan-Ning's fiscal revenue in 1942. In the subsequent three years, profits from opium production remained an important source of Shaan-Gan-Ning government revenue, averaging 21.59

---

[6] See Appendix C for detailed data and their sources.
[7] The Shaan-Gan-Ning data are from *Kang ri zhan zheng shi qi shaan gan ning bian qu cai zheng jing ji shi liao zhai bian (Shaan-Gan-Ning Border Region Finance and Economic Selective Historical Record During the Sino-Japanese War)* (1981, V5: 125–129).
[8] Chen (1990) was one of the early scholars identifying the importance of opium production for CCP finance in the Shaan-Gan-Ning base area.

4.2 The Liability of KMT's Elite Mobilization

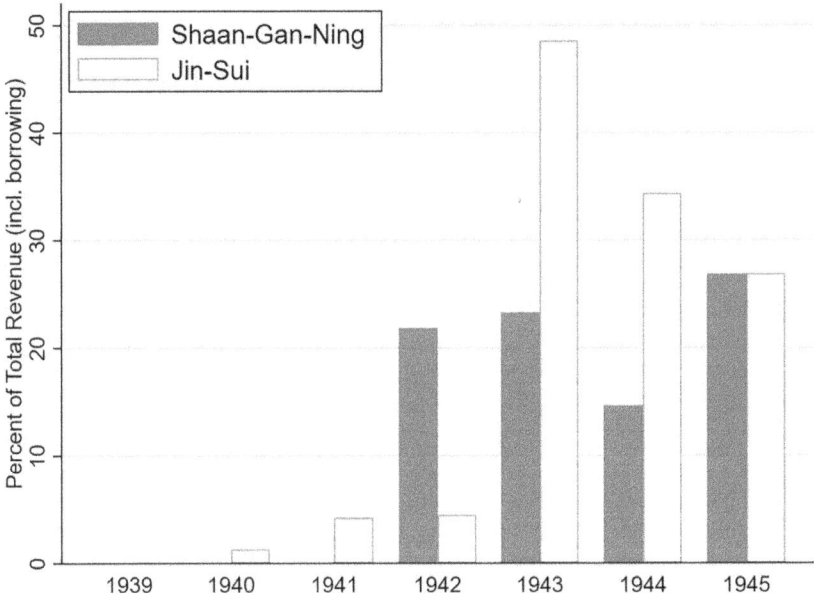

FIGURE 4.2 Share of opium revenue in Shaan-Gan-Ning and Jin-Sui
Note: The Shaan-Gan-Ning opium and total revenue data derive from *Kang Ri zhan zheng shi qi shaan gan ning bian qu cai zheng jing ji shi liao zhai bian* (Shaan-Gan-Ning Border Region Finance and Economic Selective Historical Record During the Sino-Japanese War) (1981, V6: 40–48, 57–62, 65–68, 77–83). The opium revenue was called "tecai [special product]" in the report of 1942 and 1943, and "maoyi shui [trade tax]" in 1944 and 1945. The Jin-Sui opium and total revenue data derive *Jin sui bian qu cai zheng shi zhi liao xuan bian* (Jin-Sui Border Region Finance and Economic Selective Historical Record) (1986, V2: 609–611). The opium revenue was called "yaoping bianjia [medicine price]."

percent from 1943 to 1945. Likewise, profits from opium production averaged around 36.61 percent of Jin-Sui government revenue from 1943 to 1945. Opium production was, however, limited only to these two revolutionary base areas; furthermore, the CCP leadership was very wary about the potential effect of the opium trade on its reputation.

4.2 THE LIABILITY OF KMT'S ELITE MOBILIZATION

As the war intensified and budgetary shortfalls grew, the KMT had no choice but to seek alternative revenue sources by tapping into rural economic resources. In this section, I first outline the KMT's strategic rationale for resorting to the grain levy by recentralizing the land tax. Nonetheless, the KMT's weak bureaucratic capacity and poor grassroots party organizations forced them to rely on local elites for grain levies. Although the KMT Central Government's overall grain levy burden was not considerably higher than the prewar level, the implementation of the grain levy provoked much resentment in rural China. Crucially, the KMT struggled to curb the ad hoc taxation and grain extraction imposed by local governments and military units, which frequently surpassed the official land tax revenue collected by the central government.

4.2.1 Centralization of Land Tax (Grain Levies in Kind) as a Fiscal Extraction Strategy

The KMT's centralization of land tax through grain levies was derived mainly from two considerations. First, the land tax, which had traditionally been the main source of central government revenue throughout China's history, was a source of untapped revenue, largely because the KMT government ceded it to provincial governments during the fiscal negotiations with regional strongmen in the 1920s, opting instead to prioritize indirect taxation from business activities. Even the U.S. advisor to the KMT urged Chiang to centralize the land tax as a strategy to address the budgetary shortfall (Young 1965).

Second, amid wartime challenges, particularly after the central government's relocation from Nanjing to Chongqing due to Japanese invasion, the KMT was confronted with the formidable responsibility of providing sustenance and compensation to military and government personnel. The challenges were further exacerbated by hyperinflation because the KMT had to procure grain to feed the military. For instance, the grain price index gradually increased 300 percent from 1937 to 1939, followed by a surge of nearly 100 percent in the first six months in 1940. By 1941 the grain price index had increased 2,716 percent from 1937 (Hao 2013). Consequently, the collection of taxes in monetary terms proved insufficient to keep pace with the escalating grain prices.

The KMT finally decided to centralize land tax in kind (田赋征实) in 1941, circumventing inflationary pressures by directly supplying food to the military and government personnel. In fact, several provinces had already experimented with collecting land taxes in kind prior to the KMT's centralization of the land tax. For example, Shanxi province, which was under the control of warlord Yan Xishan, first adopted a land tax through grain levies in kind as early as 1939. Provincial leaders in Fujian, Zhejiang, and Shaanxi provinces followed the initiative implemented in Shanxi in 1940. Although all four of these provinces adopted grain levies in kind for the land tax, the design of the policy varied.[9] Most importantly, Shanxi province's land tax policy reform mandated land tax payment completely through grain levies in kind, but the other three provinces' tax reform still allowed households to convert grain levies in kind into *fabi* as a form of tax payment.

The piloting land taxes through grain levies in kind in these four provinces offered the KMT a precedent to carry out the centralization of the land tax.

---

[9] For example, these provinces differed in effective tax rates, conversion rates between grain and tax obligations in monetary units, and revenue-sharing between provincial and county governments. See Hao (2008) for more discussion.

4.2 The Liability of KMT's Elite Mobilization

In the name of financing warfare and state building against Japanese invasion, Chiang Kai-shek formally proposed the centralization of land tax through grain levies in kind during the KMT Eighth Plenary Session of the Fifth Party Congress in April 1941 (Hao 2008: 53). With Chiang's endorsement, the KMT Executive Yuan passed a resolution to centralize the land tax and mandate grain levies in kind as a form of tax payment in June 1941. The KMT further established the Ministry of Food to take charge of collecting land taxes in kind and the Commission of Land Tax Management to conduct land tax assessment.

4.2.2 The Perils of Grain Extraction through Indirect Rule

The establishment of formal institutions does not automatically translate into effective policy implementation in societies where institutions are weak. The KMT faced the same challenge in the centralization of land taxes because of its limited bureaucratic capacity and mass mobilization infrastructure. First, the assessment of the land tax hinged on precise surveys of land ownership and grain output, which KMT governments lacked because the previous assessment system ceased to exist after the collapse of the Qing Dynasty in 1911. Second, although the KMT created new government agencies to facilitate grain levies in kind, it failed to invest enough economic and human resources because of budgetary constraints. Third, the initial institutional separation of land tax assessment and collection created a significant bureaucratic backlog even though the aim had been to avoid collusion between local bureaucrats and taxpayers. The KMT eventually merged these two bureaucracies at the local level in 1942.

The weak bureaucratic capacity left the KMT no choice but to delegate grain levies to provincial governments and local elites. At the outset, provincial governments were displeased with the fiscal centralization because the land tax was the most important source of revenue in many provinces during the prewar period.[10] In response to the KMT's centralization of land taxes, local elites leveraged policy implementation as a means of resistance because wartime needs prevented them from openly opposing the centralization of the land tax.

Importantly, the implementation of the KMT's grain levy policy was effectively shaped by the de facto power held by provincial governments and local traditional elites, which influenced various aspects of grain levies, including the allocation of overall grain quotas and the tax exemptions granted to local governments. For example, the provincial government in Sichuan province was initially reluctant to implement this policy even though the KMT central government relocated to the city of Chongqing in this province and Sichuan was a major grain-producing province. Despite pressure from the Ministry of Finance and even KMT leader Chiang Kai-shek, the Sichuan government did not establish a commission to study the policy implementation issue until March 1941, several months after the urging

---

[10] For example, land tax accounted for as much as 60 percent of provincial tax revenues on average in 1935 (Hao 2008).

by the Ministry of Finance (Hao 2008). The delay by Sichuan province set a precedent, albeit a poor one, for other provinces to delay their policy implementation. In 1941, despite the widespread hyperinflation in China, several provinces continued to collect land taxes in currency. Their rationale was that local government agencies were not adequately prepared to collect land taxes in kind. As a result, the provinces collecting land taxes in monetary terms experienced a comparatively lower tax burden than those collecting land tax in kind.

In addition, provinces with stronger relative bargaining power vis-à-vis the KMT central government were able to reduce their grain quota. Specifically, the KMT government had to assign grain quotas to each province to ensure it had sufficient grain to feed the military and government. The specific grain quotas were the result of negotiation between the MOF and provincial governments (Hao 2009). Provinces controlled by powerful regional strongmen, including Sichuan, Guangxi, Shanxi, and Yunnan, had a high degree of autonomy and were able to secure more favorable grain quotas.[11] The rise of relative power in Yunnan province exemplified strategic interaction between KMT central and local governments. Yunnan became a critical alternative pathway for China to receive external military aid as a result of the Japanese occupation and blockade of coastal China. Consequently, Yunnan's grain quota and tax rates were far lower than other provinces. Similar quota bargaining was replicated at the provincial – county level, distorting the quota distribution for local grain output.

Finally, local traditional elites exerted their influence in the process of grain collection at the grassroots level, leaving most of the grain burden to peasants instead of rich landlords. The KMT government emphasized the county head as the primary leader in local grain collection, but it did not have full control over the appointment of county officials. Hence, county heads had to seek cooperation from local traditional elites such as business leaders, members of the gentry, and landlords to assist with grain collection (Hao 2008; Yin 2017). The KMT even created local power-sharing organizations – county legislatures similar to what the CCP had done – in order to coopt local elites. Despite KMT efforts to promote a progressive grain tax burden, local elites sabotaged the implementation of this approach. The resistance resulted in poor grain levy collection in 1941. Thus, the KMT proposed a compromise, implicitly allowing an effective regressive tax rate.

Although the total grain tax burden on the local population was not significantly higher than the prewar level, the inequity in its distribution severely undermined the legitimacy of the KMT government (Eastman 1984; Hao 2008). The inequity in grain levy stemmed from various factors related to the execution of the grain levy policy (Eastman 1984; Young 1963). One significant issue was the perceived unfairness in the distribution of the grain quotas to individual households. Local elites had found ways to underreport grain output by concealing their land holdings, but not the peasantry. The challenge of accurately assessing land ownership significantly contributed to the KMT's failure in implementing

[11] See Eastman (1991) for KMT's lack of control of regional governments.

4.2 The Liability of KMT's Elite Mobilization

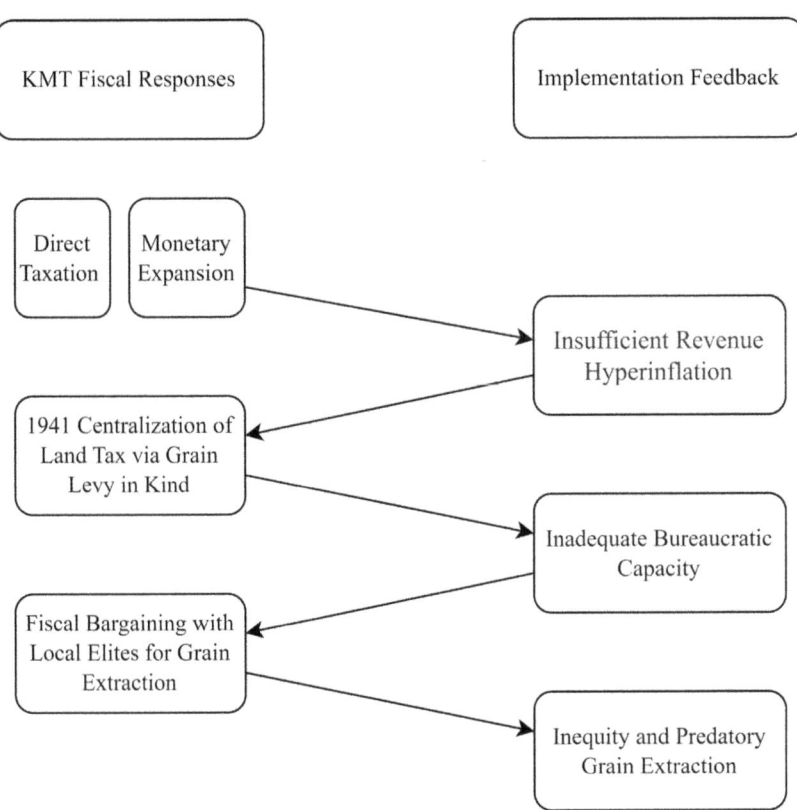

FIGURE 4.3 Evolution of KMT response to the wartime fiscal shock

progressive tax rates for land levies, resulting in a regressive distribution of the grain burden. Furthermore, the KMT's weak bureaucratic capacity and inadequate monitoring mechanisms exacerbated the problems associated with the grain levy. Corruption and embezzlement were prevalent because local officials used their positions to exploit or evade the levy. Such misconduct further eroded the trust and support of the rural population toward the KMT government.

Finally, the KMT failed to rein in the ad hoc taxation and grain extraction by local governments and military units, which imposed an additional grain levy that exceeded the land tax collected by the KMT central government. The reason for excessive local taxation was that the KMT centralized land tax without providing alternative revenue sources for local governments to compensate for the budgetary shortfall. Because the KMT relied on local elites to aid in grain extraction, it had to provide economic incentives through lack of oversight of these subtaxes, a tactic that had been a longstanding incentive mechanism in imperial China.

Figure 4.3 summarizes the KMT's responses to the increased fiscal demands caused by the Japanese invasion. It illustrates the KMT government's adaptive measures based on policy feedback on earlier failed strategies, leading to the eventual pursuit of centralized land tax collection through a grain levy in kind. Because of insufficient bureaucratic capacity, however, the KMT had to depend on local elites for collecting grain levies, resulting in significant inequities and exploitative practices in grain extraction.

4.3 THE RISE OF CCP'S MOBILIZED COMPLIANCE

Confronted with budgetary deficits and insufficient fiscal outcomes from other measures after 1941, the CCP focused on grain levies as a last ditch effort. Unlike the KMT, the CCP had bolstered its mass mobilization infrastructure between 1937 and 1940, as detailed later in Chapter 6, just in time before it had to intensify grain extraction. The CCP's grassroots party organizations emerged as the viable alternative to facilitate grain extraction. Specifically, the CCP employed a tactic that I call "mobilized compliance," leveraging grassroots party organizations to mobilize rural households. This involved encouraging accurate reporting of grain output and adherence to designated quotas, while redirecting the focal point of conflicts stemming from grain extraction. This approach did not necessarily aim to transform CCP members into bureaucrats; instead, it relied on their involvement in mobilizing ordinary peasants to act as party agents, ensuring mutual enforcement of grain assessment and compliance.

In the following section, I elucidate the strategic considerations of the CCP in pursuing the grain levy in-kind as a tactic to address budgetary shortfalls. I then trace the evolution of the CCP's grain levy strategies, which were devised in response to the myriad challenges encountered during the implementation of the policy.

4.3.1 Grain Levies in Kind as a Last Resort for Resource Mobilization

The ineffective responses to the fiscal shock in 1941, including monetary expansion and indirect taxation, sparked heated debates on grain levies among CCP leaders because the revenue shortfall became an impediment to political survival.[12] The debates centered primarily on two issues: (1) the trade-off between cutting fiscal spending and expansion of taxation, and (2) the distribution of the fiscal burden among classes of rural residents.

---

[12] For instance, CCP leaders overseeing finance and economic policies were deeply divided on monetary policies. The debates centered on key issues such as the extent of monetary expansion, regulation of currency exchange rates between *bianbi* (边币) issued by the CCP border government and *fabi* (法币) issued by the KMT government, inflation control, and the level of restriction on the circulation of *fabi*. See the discussion of the debate in *Jin sui bian qu cai zheng shi zhi liao xuan bian* (*Jin-Sui Border Region Finance and Economic Selective Historical Record*), (1986, V5: 205–365).

4.3 The Rise of CCP's Mobilized Compliance

Eventually, the CCP Senior Cadres Meeting (高干会议) in 1942 resolved the debate and reached a conclusion on the principle of resource mobilization through grain levies, as it was a practical strategy given that CCP-controlled territories were located mostly in rural areas, where agricultural production was the primary economic activity in local economies. Mao Zedong delivered an important speech justifying the CCP's new principle for fiscal policies[13] and criticized the prevailing principle of "benevolent governance (仁政)," characterized by hesitance to impose a tax burden on middle and poor peasants. Mao argued that the prevailing principle was outdated because the CCP's resource mobilization differed from feudal methods. Essentially, he adopted a perspective resembling the "ends justifying the means," asserting that the CCP's heightening tax burden would provide the necessary financing for a revolution that would ultimately liberate China. This meeting paved the way for the CCP to wholeheartedly expand fiscal extraction through grain levies in kind over austerity policies.

To meet the increasing demand of the growing military and government personnel, the CCP had no choice but to radically expand its tax base to over 90 percent of rural households, meaning that the fiscal burden fell on almost all classes of rural residents.[14] Gradually, the party had learned from its failed policies in the Jiangxi Ruijin Soviet base area in the early 1930s, which relied on a narrow tax base. The radical expropriation from rural affluent households was a short-sighted strategy tantamount to "killing the goose that lays golden eggs." The expropriation ultimately proved inadequate in generating a sustainable and reliable source of revenue in the long term, and most of the burden fell on landlords and rich peasants.[15]

4.3.2 Challenges of Grain Levy in Kind: Ineffective Bureaucratic Capacity

The drastic expansion of the grain levy, however, was met with two challenges. First, the CCP gradually recognized that coercive tactics, such as expropriation and apportionment of wealth by landlords and rich peasants in the past, were not a viable option for taxing middle and poor peasants, whom they needed to target as they expanded the tax base. If the CCP were to employ similar coercive tactics with middle and poor peasants in the grain levy, it risked eroding its popular support among the local population as had occurred in the Ruijin Soviet base area in the 1930s. Second, the bureaucratic capacity of the CCP was too weak for it to implement a broad-based taxation scheme by itself. Despite

---

[13] "抗日时期的经济问题和财政问题 [Economic and Financial Issues during the Anti-Japanese Period]," December 1942, in *Mao ze dong xuan ji (Mao's Selective Essays)* (1991, V3: 891–896).
[14] The CCP called for austerity policies by cutting spending through streamlining government bureaucracy in the base areas, but this approach was inadequate.
[15] See *Kang ri zhan zheng shi qi shaan gan ning bian qu cai zheng jing ji shi liao zhai bian (Shaan-Gan-Ning Border Region Finance and Economic Selective Historical Record During the Sino-Japanese War)* (1981, V7: 59–60).

the CCP's efforts to substantially intensify cadre training during wartime, the demands of cadres on government and military units outpaced the supply.[16]

Specifically, the CCP learned the harsh consequences of blunt coercive tactics during the early years of the Sino-Japanese War. CCP local cadres initially resorted to this type of coercion against landlords and wealthy peasants for grain extraction, mirroring their resource mobilization strategy in the Jiangxi Ruijin Soviet areas. Internal CCP reports spanning various base areas often included acknowledgement that local cadres employed violent tactics, sometimes excessively, to fulfill the grain quotas. In Shaan-Gan-Ning, for example, a CCP internal investigation revealed that local cadres forcibly demanded that peasants comply with arbitrary grain quotas and labor conscription from 1937 to 1940.[17] Meanwhile, CCP leaders in Jin-Sui launched the "Four Major Mobilization" (四大动员)" Campaign in 1940. During this campaign, local cadres placed most burden on landlords and rich peasants and intensified their use of violent tactics against them.[18] Similar findings had been reported in Jin-Cha-Ji from 1937 to 1941.[19]

These coercive tactics generated anxiety and resentment not only among well-to-do rural elites but also among middle and poor peasants. In the aftermath of the "Four Major Mobilization" Campaign, CCP internal reports revealed that over 900 households fled to KMT or Japanese-controlled territories. In addition, twenty-one cases of suicides were reported in Lan County and Ling County alone.[20] Similarly, in Shaan-Gan-Ning, the CCP's tactics led to the flight of over 800 households from Yan'an County and 500 households from An'sai County (Wang 2018: 35–36). The climax of resistance to CCP blunt-force tactics occurred in early 1940 when a coup erupted in Huan County (Li 2015; Zhang 2014). Initially labeled as a rebellion led by local bandits, the CCP's internal investigation later revealed that the uprising involved a diverse array of participants, including 235 party members, several local cadres, 900 members of village militias, and scores of peasants.[21] The CCP soon recognized that it was on its way to repeating the disastrous mistakes that led to the exhaustion of human and financial resources in the Jiangxi Ruijin Soviet areas.

---

[16] Huang (2024) documented the strategies and challenges in CCP cadre training during the Sino-Japanese War.

[17] "谢觉哉对庆环工作的意见 [Comments from Xie Jue Zai on Qing Huan Operation]" in *Zhong gong shaan gan ning bian qu dang wei wen jian hui ji (1940–1941) (Selection of CCP Party Documents in Shaan-Gan-Ning Border Area (1940–1941))* (1994: 434–447).

[18] "晋西北政权初建时期财政状况概述 [A Summary of Fiscal Condition during the Early Stage of Northwestern Jin Governing Body]" in *Jin sui bian qu cai zheng shi zhi liao xuan bian (Jin-Sui Border Region Finance and Economic Selective Historical Record)* (1986 V2: 3–7).

[19] For discussion of coercion in Jin-Cha-Ji, see Peng (1981 [1941]) and Zhou (2014).

[20] "晋绥边区历年公粮工作总结 [A Summary of Yearly Grain Work in *Jin sui bian qu cai zheng shi zhi liao xuan bian (Jin-Sui Border Region Finance and Economic Selective Historical Record)* (1986 V2: 494).

[21] "边区政府庆环工作团关于环县工作的报告 [Report on Huan County from Border Government Qing Huan Working Team]" in *Shaan gan ning bian qu zheng fu wen jian xuan bian (Selected Documents of Shaan-Gan-Ning Border Government)* (2013 V2: 333–338).

4.3 The Rise of CCP's Mobilized Compliance

Meanwhile, the CCP realized that the expansion of the tax base for grain levies beyond landlords and rich peasants requires a sophisticated bureaucratic capacity to ensure accurate assessment of grain output and secure compliance in grain payment from rural households. Unfortunately, such bureaucratic infrastructure was in short supply for the CCP because most of its cadres had neither substantial education nor work experience in government bureaucracies. The lack of experience was inevitable given the CCP's mass mobilization infrastructure. Despite the CCP's bolstering of its bureaucratic capacity by reintegrating intellectuals into the party following a shift in its party-building strategies after 1937, the majority of grassroots party members had neither the education nor the experience to run a government bureaucracy (Huang 2024). The CCP attempted to deploy cadres as a working team to various villages in order to monitor and organize grain levies, but doing so strained its limited human resources. The party had also attempted to use propaganda to rally peasants' tax morale to overcome its inadequate bureaucratic capacity, but it had limited impact: Most rural peasants in China at the time were uneducated and showed little interest in Communist ideology (Bianco 2001; Chen 1986).

4.3.3 The Compensation Effect of Party Mobilization Infrastructure

Given the insufficient bureaucratic capacity, the CCP turned to its party mobilization infrastructure for grain extraction. As detailed in Chapter 6, the CCP had evolved into a very different party by 1941, bearing little resemblance to its fragile state in the early 1930s.[22] The party had effectively transformed itself with a strong peasant mobilization infrastructure from 1937 to 1940. Membership sharply increased from 40,000 in 1937 to 800,000 in 1940 – a twenty-fold increase. The number of party cells during the same period surged from 617 to 4,794 while county party committees increased from 519 to 1,100. Most importantly, the CCP had resolved internal elite conflicts that generated self-defeating party-building strategies by 1940. The CCP mass mobilization infrastructure consisted primarily of peasants, accounting for more than 90 percent of party membership, and intellectuals were once again welcomed by the party.

The transformation of the CCP's party organization came at a critical moment when it needed to intensify resource mobilization through grain extraction to compensate its weak bureaucratic capacity. The party pursued a strategy that I call "mobilized compliance," in which grassroots party members mobilized ordinary peasants to become agents of the party for grain assessment and compliance enforcement. This tactic, while aiming for voluntary cooperation from peasants, also engendered a form of coercion stemming from pressures within the village communities themselves. It molds citizen behavior into "quasi-voluntary compliance [defined as] compliance motivated by a willingness to cooperate but backed by coercion" (Levi 2006: 7).

---

[22] Chapter 6 offered the detailed discussion concerning the expansion of CCP party organization during this period.

Mobilized compliance encompassed three tactics, refined through the trial and error experienced by CCP local cadres during the process of grain levies: (1) designation of the *village* instead of the *county* as the primary unit for grain levies, (2) the mobilization of peasants to participate in the assessment of the household grain burden resembling a prisoner's dilemma, and (3) the creation of a taxation scheme akin to a zero-sum game for the grain burden among rural households. Importantly, grassroots party organizations played a key role in facilitating the implementation of these tactics.

The emergence of mobilized compliance for the grain levy was hardly a preconceived plan. Instead, it evolved through a continuous process of adaptation between CCP grain levy policies and the challenges encountered during their implementation. The practice of mobilized compliance first evolved in the Jin-Cha-Ji base area around the borders of Shanxi, Chahar, and Hebei provinces in early 1940, quickly spreading to other base areas.

The Village as the Unit for Grain Levies. The CCP's first challenge of policy implementation was obstruction from existing rural elites. Historically, the county was the lowest level of Chinese bureaucracy. Policy implementation, such as tax collection, relied on traditional elites who served as the power brokers connecting the state and society;[23] nonetheless, traditional elites were reluctant to serve as brokers for the CCP. Although the CCP offered a power-sharing arrangement in local assemblies – the "three thirds" representation principle – in order to coopt these elites, many of them remained skeptical about the CCP and exerted little effort to assist it.[24] Consequently, the county-based designation often failed to meet the quotas of grain levies mandated by CCP border governments from 1937 to 1939, and local cadres had to fill the quotas by returning to coercive tactics aimed at landlords and rich peasants.[25]

Facing these challenges, the CCP made a strategic decision to shift the primary unit for grain levies from the county level to the village level, an approach that allowed it to circumvent the influence of traditional elites and directly mobilize the peasants. The CCP government in Jin-Cha-Ji was the first at a base area to experiment with designating the village as the primary unit for grain levy collection after 1938.

Designating the village as the unit for grain extraction quickly overtaxed the CCP's already limited bureaucratic capacity. To facilitate the grain levy, the CCP had to deploy working teams comprised of cadres to various villages to monitor and guide its implementation.[26] Nevertheless, this strategy placed a

---

[23] See the discussion of the important role of traditional elites in Duara (1988) and in Ma and Rubin (2019).
[24] Specifically, the CCP appointed these traditional elites to local government offices. In addition, the party even assimilated them into local legislatures through the three-thirds representation principle, allowing these traditional elites to occupy one-third of the seats in the local legislature. See Wei, Xing, and Fu (1984, V4: 679).
[25] See *Zhong guo nong min fu dan shi* (*The History of Peasant Burden in China*), (1994, V3: 281).
[26] See Wei, Xing, and Fu (1984, V4: 686–687).

4.3 The Rise of CCP's Mobilized Compliance

significant burden on the CCP's already strained bureaucratic capacity because the number of villages to manage far exceeded the number of cadres available. In response, the CCP established a village grain burden assessment committee, recruiting nonstate actors other than local elites to assist in collecting grain levies.[27] This committee initially comprised only representatives from peasant and business associations as well as the village heads, some of whom were CCP members. This committee was responsible for assessing the grain burden for each household. Unfortunately, the effectiveness of this committee varied significantly across villages, depending on the composition of the committee and the capability of the CCP members serving on it.

"Democratic Assessment" and Mobilization of Peasants. To address the varying quality of village committees for grain extraction, CCP leaders in Jin-Cha-Ji turned to mass "democratic assessment (民主评议)" meetings in 1940 to improve assessment and compliance. These assessment meetings were mass gatherings of all village households, during which each household revealed information not only about its own obligated grain burden but also about the accuracy of the grain burden reported by other households.

Effectively, the democratic assessment meetings created a prisoner's dilemma among peasants, forcing them to disclose truthful information about their grain outputs, as any underreporting would be exposed by other households within the village. Collusion among households was difficult because revealing truthful information about other households' grain output aligned with the peasants' best interest, particularly when it prevented others from exposing any falsehoods about their own grain output. Therefore, the democratic assessment meetings resolved the information deficiency faced by the CCP, as peasants had better information about the grain output of other households in the same village than the government.

CCP grassroots party cadres and members played the most critical role in mobilizing peasants to participate actively in democratic assessment meetings, thus ensuring accurate assessment and voluntary compliance with grain levies. CCP internal reports repeatedly reveal that the party encouraged and incentivized grassroots party members to become leaders in these meetings in order to manipulate the focal point of conflict and persuade peasants to participate.[28]

For instance, in a report by the local party branch in Pinbei County in the Jin-Cha-Ji base area, the local party committee specified detailed instructions for party members to lead these democratic assessment meetings.[29] The report

---

[27] Zhou (2014) has offered detailed studies of the effectiveness of assessment committees in the villages.
[28] See "晋西北行署关于公粮工作的指示信 [The Guidance Letter on Grain Collection Task by Jinxibei Bureau]" in *Jin sui bian qu cai zheng shi zhi liao xuan bian (Jin-Sui Border Region Finance and Economic Selective Historical Record)* (1986, V2: 194–197).
[29] See the discussion of party instructions on organizing these meetings in Wei, Xing, and Fu (1984, V4: 147–149).

recommended not only that local party members play an active role in these meetings but also encouraged them to recruit other local activists to help manipulate attitudes toward grain levies during these meetings. In addition, the report asked cadres to pay close attention to the use of various messages of political persuasion and the manipulation of sentiment in order to rouse peasants' emotions during these meetings. When tension over grain levies arose, the CCP cadres were urged to shift the focal point of taxation away from the government and emphasize instead the improvement of peasants' economic well-being if the CCP succeeded in the Sino-Japanese War. Finally, CCP cadres served as exemplars during this process, publicly overstating their own grain outputs in the hope that others would follow their lead.[30]

A Zero-Sum Game for the Allocation of Grain Burden among Households. Although the democratic assessment meetings mitigated challenges in grain assessment through a prisoner's dilemma, villages with strong social capital could still collude to underreport grain output, an equilibrium outcome typical of during a repeated prisoner's dilemma scenario (Hardin 1982). Indeed, internal CCP reports disclosed that grassroots party organizations encountered this issue in some villages (Zhou 2012, 2014). In response, the Jin-Chi-Ji government introduced a scheme resembling a zero-sum game in the allocation of household grain burdens.

The essence of this zero-sum grain burden distribution adhered the following principle, albeit with slight variations across regions. First, the CCP border government assigned a fixed grain quota to each village. Second, the nominal household grain burden for household i was determined using a point system which multiplied the household's grain output by the applicable progressive tax rates. Consequently, each household's nominal grain burden was converted into the number of points derived from this calculation. Third, the government aggregated the total nominal grain burden points from all households in the village and determined the grain burden per point by dividing the village grain quota by the total nominal points. Fourth, the actual grain burden facing each household was the nominal grain burden point multiplied the grain burden per point. The entire procedure of grain burden allocated to each household can be summarized in the following formula:

$$Grain\ Burden_i = \frac{Village\ Grain\ Quota}{\sum_i^n Nominal\ Grain\ Burden\ Point_i} \times Nominal\ Grain\ Burden\ Point_i$$

This zero-sum game in the allocation of grain burden implied that the actual burden of each household was intrinsically linked to the burdens placed on the other households within the village for the following reasons. The total

---

[30] See discussion in the practices of grain levies in various base areas in Zhou (2023).

4.3 The Rise of CCP's Mobilized Compliance

village grain quota was fixed, but not the value of each nominal grain burden point. If the total nominal points from the sum of all households were greater, the grain burden per point would be reduced accordingly. If one household reported a lower grain output, thereby reducing its nominal points, the sum of total points in the village would decrease. This, in turn, would lead to a higher grain burden per point, causing all households to bear a greater grain burden, even if their nominal points remained unchanged. Consequently, villagers had strong incentives to ensure other households truthfully reported their grain output; otherwise it would lead to an inflation of the grain burden per point for all households.

In preparation for grain levies in 1942, the Jin-Cha-Ji CCP Party Committee issued a memorandum laying out the zero-sum strategy above, drawing on the lessons learned from the previous year's grain collection efforts in 1941.[31] The memo revealed that the success in some villages in 1941 was largely the result of the role of grassroots party organizations in implementing the tactics of mobilized compliance. Although party members' own compliance established a good role model within the village, the memo also pointed out that low compliance occurred because assessment was controlled by village elites in some places with weak party organizations. A few months later, in another report by Liu Lantao, party secretary of Beiyue District in Jin-Cha-Ji, the CCP mandated each party cell to designate one party member to take responsibility for monitoring and implementing the mobilized compliance strategy in each village.[32]

From Blunt Coercion to Subtle Coercion. Did mobilized compliance lead to peasant voluntary cooperation? Although CCP propaganda garnered some support from the peasantry, numerous studies have highlighted the formidable challenges the CCP faced to maintain peasant support during the Sino-Japanese War. Hence, the tactic of mobilized compliance embodies quasi-voluntary compliance, which relies not only on cooperation from taxpayers but also on coercive mechanisms to sanction noncompliance (Levi 1989: 52–55).

On one hand, the system of mobilized compliance incorporated mechanisms such as the democratic assessment meetings and the zero-sum allocation of the grain burden, which created strong incentives for peasants to accurately report their grain output because of peer pressure. This dynamic made it difficult for individual households to cheat or collude without risking punishment, fostering a certain degree of voluntary compliance. On the other hand, despite these mechanisms, the compliance achieved through this strategy was not purely voluntary in the sense of being entirely self-motivated. The social pressure

---

[31] See "中共晋察冀北岳区党委关于1942年统一累进税工作的决定 [Decision on Consolidated Progressive Taxation in 1942 by the CCP Jin-Cha-Ji Beiyu District Party Committee]" in Wei, Xing, and Fu (1984, V4: 456–463).

[32] See "在区党委粮食会议上的结论 [Conclusion on the District CCP Party Commitment's Meeting on Grain Collection]" in Wei, Xing, and Fu (1984, V4: 200–206).

created played a critical role. Thus, while some peasants may have cooperated willingly to avoid the detrimental consequences of not doing so, others may have been coerced into compliance, particularly when the threat of collective punishment or the disruption of the social fabric loomed large.

Importantly, the enforcers of sanctioning shifted from state apparatuses to the peasants themselves. This strategic shift away from party-sponsored coercion was particularly crucial when the CCP had to intensify grain extraction to encompass over 90 percent of rural households. Alongside expanding the tax base and implementing progressive tax rates, these tactics effectively redirected discontent from state-society tensions to within-community conflicts. In other words, peasants' grievances originated from subtle coercion by their neighbors, relatives, and friends, not the brute-force tactics the CCP had previously employed against landlords and rich peasants. The genesis of this strategy stemmed from the CCP's bitter experience of relying primarily on coercion for resource mobilization. The previous coercive tactics carried a risk of alienating the very local population the CCP sought to win over.

The adaptation of the mobilized compliance strategy in response to local resistance is best exemplified in a CCP report on grain extraction from 1940 to 1947 in Jin-Sui.[33] In this report, the CCP acknowledged that the ineffectiveness of two initial grain mobilization campaigns in 1940, which employed violent tactics against landlords and wealthy peasants. These efforts failed to meet the CCP's own grain quotas and led to significant out-migration and suicides. In subsequent years, the Jin-Sui government abandoned the use of violent coercion and pursued mobilized compliance tactics. Consequently, the report reveals that peasants no longer held their resentment toward the CCP's grain demands. Even landlords and wealthy peasants informed CCP cadres that they were willing to contribute the required grain under the new system but emphasized that the previous violent tactics were an inappropriate strategy.

Diffusion of Mobilized Compliance in Grain Levies. The use of mobilized compliance tactics for grain levies in the Jin-Cha-Ji area diffused to other CCP-controlled territories after 1941, particularly the Jin-Sui and Shaan-Gan-Ning areas. The diffusion resulted from geographical proximity and organizational linkage. For instance, the Jin-Sui base area was geographically near Jin-Cha-Ji, southwest of it. Meanwhile, the Shaan-Gan-Ning base area was located west of the Jin-Sui base area. In addition, the party committees in both Jin-Cha-Ji and Jin-Sui fell under the CCP Northern Bureau prior to 1942; later, Jin-Sui and Shaan-Gan-Ning were part of the CCP Northwestern Bureau. These organizational linkages facilitated information exchanges between party committees and the government for policymaking.

---

[33] See "晋绥边区历年公粮工作总结 [A Summary of Yearly Grain Work in Jinsui Bianqu (1940.2–1947.10)]" in *Jin sui bian qu cai zheng shi zhi liao xuan bian (Jin-Sui Border Region Finance and Economic Selective Historical Record)* (1986, V2: 494–496).

4.3 The Rise of CCP's Mobilized Compliance

The Jin-Sui base area was among the first to adopt the mobilized compliance strategy. In late 1940 the Jin-Sui border government issued *Regulations on Anti-Japanese Grain Levies to Save the Country* (抗日救国公粮条例), in which a progressive tax rate was proposed and the use of political mobilization for grain levies was encouraged to expand the tax base.[34] The Jin-Sui border government further revised *Regulations*, which introduced the point system for the distribution of the household grain burden and promoted democratic assessment meetings as the main vehicle for mobilization in 1941 and 1943. A guidance letter issued in 1943 by the Jin-Sui border government encouraged local CCP cadres not to employ coercive tactics but to manipulate the relationships among villagers to achieve the zero-sum game at these democratic assessment meetings.[35] By 1944–1945, Jin-Sui fully implemented the mobilized compliance strategy and achieved significant success in the collection of grain levies (Zhou 2012).

In Shaan-Gan-Ning, the rollout of mobilized compliance followed the pattern established at Jin-Chi-Ji and Jin-Sui. Several counties first experimented with democratic assessment in Shaan-Gan-Ning in late 1941.[36] The success of grain levies in these counties later led to the formal adoption of these approaches across all counties in 1942, placing emphasis on manipulating public sentiment during the democratic assessment meetings about the household grain levy burden.[37] In addition, Shaan-Gan-Ning followed Jin-Cha-Ji in designing a progressive tax rate schedule with a built-in democratic assessment of the new grain levy regulations in 1943. Another internal CCP report attributed the success of the grain levies during 1944 and 1945 to the adoption of the mobilized compliance tactics in 1943.[38]

Figure 4.4 summarizes the evolution of CCP's mobilized compliance in grain extraction. A notable revelation is that the CCP did not possess an inherent blueprint for employing mobilized compliance in grain extraction. Instead, this approach emerged through a process of experimentation and trial and error, whereby the CCP learned to effectively leverage party organizations to mobilize the masses and ensure policy compliance, all while minimizing the risk of generating widespread resentment among the population.

---

[34] See *Jin sui bian qu cai zheng shi zhi liao xuan bian (Jin-Sui Border Region Finance and Economic Selective Historical Record)* (1986, V2: 94, 153).

[35] See "晋西北行署关于公粮工作的指示信 [Guidance Letter on Grain Levies Work by Jinxibei Xingsu Xingshu]" in *Jin sui bian qu cai zheng shi zhi liao xuan bian (Jin-Sui Border Region Finance and Economic Selective Historical Record)* (1986, V2: 194–197).

[36] Yan'an and Ansai counties were among the first group of counties to experiment with this approach.

[37] See *Kang ri zhan zheng shi qi shaan gan ning bian qu cai zheng jing ji shi liao zhai bian (Shaan-Gan-Ning Border Region Finance and Economic Selective Historical Record During the Sino-Japanese War)* (1981, V6: 402).

[38] See *Kang ri zhan zheng shi qi shaan gan ning bian qu cai zheng jing ji shi liao zhai bian (Shaan-Gan-Ning Border Region Finance and Economic Selective Historical Record During the Sino-Japanese War)* (1981, V8: 189).

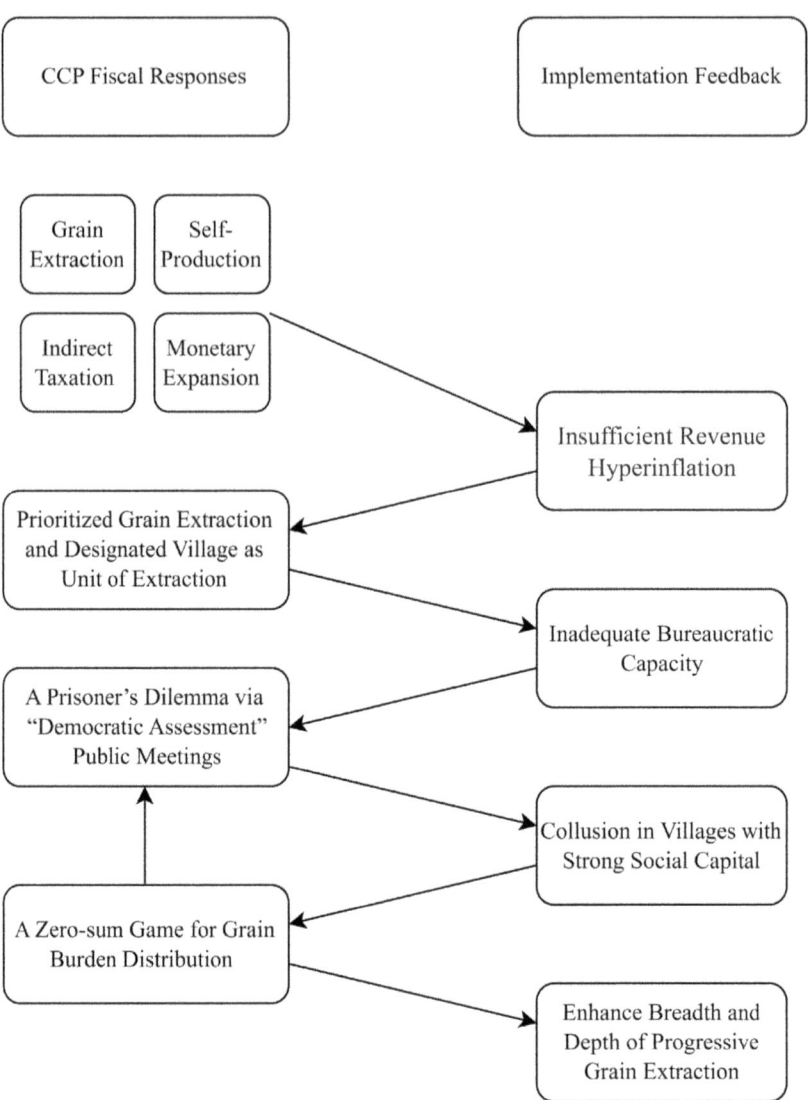

FIGURE 4.4 Evolution of CCP response to the wartime fiscal shock

4.4 THE DIVERGENCE OF GRAIN MOBILIZATION (1941–1945)

What had the CCP and the KMT accomplished in their resource mobilization through grain extraction? In this section I first investigate the degree of grain extraction and its contributions to the overall revenue for both parties from 1941 to 1945. I then illustrate that the CCP's grain extraction entails a

4.4 The Divergence of Grain Mobilization (1941–1945)

progressive distribution of the grain burden among rural households, which was in sharp contrast with KMT's regressive grain burden. Finally, I present quantitative evidence showing that party organization played a significant role in assisting with grain levies for the CCP but not for the KMT.

Historical records are notably sporadic for this period – particularly for the CCP – because the revolutionary base areas were decentralized and wartime record keeping was difficult. The quantitative and qualitative data in this section are based on various compendiums of CCP and KMT internal documents that detail party, government, economic, and financial activities. I also rely on county gazetteers to supplement the historical records of grain levies and grassroots party organizations.

4.4.1 Degree of Grain Extraction

First, I compare the degree of grain extraction in CCP and KMT territories. Given that the territories controlled by the KMT were much larger than those controlled by the CCP, I focus mainly on grain levies as a percentage of total grain output but not the total amount of grain being collected as the main measure for the degree of extraction. This measure parallels a conventional indicator of fiscal capacity – the share of taxation over GDP – employed by both economists and political scientists.[39] For the CCP, my primary focus is on three base areas: Shaan-Gan-Ning, Jin-Sui, and Jin-Cha-Ji, where reliable time series data on grain extraction are available. The KMT data cover twenty-one provinces (i.e., Free China) that were mostly behind battle lines.[40]

Figure 4.5 presents the degree of grain extraction by the CCP and the KMT between 1941 and 1945, and three important patterns emerge. First, the CCP had extracted a larger share of grain output than the KMT did. From 1941 to 1945, grain levies by the KMT central government amounted to an average of approximately 6.62 percent of local grain output; CCP grain levies averaged 10.35 percent (Shaan-Gan-Ning), 20.24 percent (Jin-Sui), and 11.85 percent (Jin-Cha-Ji).

Second, the degree of grain extraction varied significantly across CCP base areas. Jin-Cha-Ji, an early adopter of the mobilized compliance strategy, had a similar degree of grain levies compared to Shaan-Gan-Ning. By contrast, Jin-Sui had the highest level of grain levies of all three base areas, sometimes exceeding 20 percent of local grain output. Notably, the CCP obtained some revenues from the opium trade in both the Shaan-Gan-Ning and Jin-Sui base

---

[39] Scholars use the share of tax revenue in aggregate income (i.e., GDP) to reflect fiscal capacity in both economics and political science literature (Besley and Persson 2013).

[40] These provinces were Anhui, Fujian, Gansu, Guangdong, Guangxi, Guizhou, Henan, Hubei, Hunan, Jiangsu, Jiangxi, Jinyuan, Ningxia, Qinghai, Shandong, Shaanxi, Shanxi, Sichuan, Xikang, Yunnan, and Zhejiang.

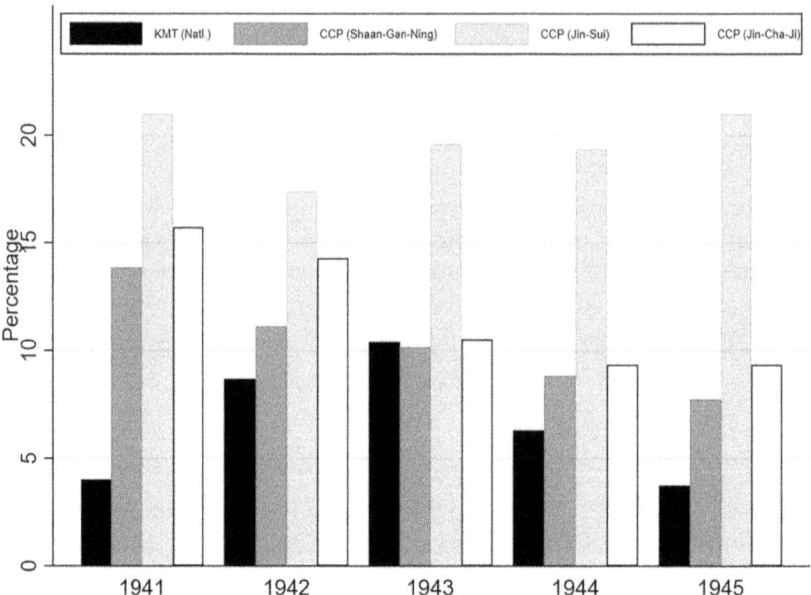

FIGURE 4.5 Degree of grain extraction by the CCP and KMT
Note: KMT grain data, which are from Chang (1958: 144) and Eastman (1984: 60), included levy (征实), borrowing (征借), and mandatory procurement (征购) of grain and rice by the KMT. KMT direct taxation data is calculated based on data from Young (1965). Shaan-Gan-Ning grain data is *from Kang ri zhan zheng shi qi shaan gan ning bian qu cai zheng jing ji shi liao zhai bian* (*Shaan-Gan-Ning Border Region Finance and Economic Selective Historical Record During the Sino-Japanese War*) (1981, V6). Jin-Sui grain data is from *Jin sui bian qu cai zheng shi zhi liao xuan bian* (*Jin-Sui Border Region Finance and Economic Selective Historical Record*) (1986, V2). Jin-Cha-Ji grain data are from Wei, Xing, and Fu (1984, V4). See Appendix C for detailed data and their sources.

areas after 1942, relieving some of its need to increase grain levies in territories without natural resources to significantly expand grain output.

Third, the trends of grain extraction over time are parallel in the CCP and the KMT as well as across CCP base areas, suggesting that they are affected by similar external shocks. The intensity of grain levies reached its peak around 1942 and 1943 and declined afterward. The trends in grain extraction were in part driven by the fluctuation of grain output and ongoing territorial control during the Sino-Japanese War.

4.4.2 The Contribution of Grain Levies to Overall Government Revenue

Given that both the CCP and KMT attempted to use grain levies to supplement their budgetary shortfalls, I evaluate the extent to which they accomplished

4.4 The Divergence of Grain Mobilization (1941–1945)

this goal. To this end, I compare the composition of government revenues by the CCP and KMT from 1939 to 1945.

I should note that comparing CCP and KMT government revenues from a variety of sources presents several challenges. First, grain levies in kind played a significant role as a direct form of fiscal extraction by the CCP; however, these levies were typically excluded from the overall fiscal revenue reporting found in the party archives. Instead, the archives separately documented grain levies in the base areas, distinct from the reporting of fiscal revenue. These levies were not considered part of the total government revenue in the archives, which encompassed direct and indirect taxes as well as revenue generated by government-sponsored businesses.

Second, another complicating factor is that monetary expansion is frequently omitted from the calculations of government revenues in these publications, making accurately assessing and comparing government revenues more difficult. Furthermore, several CCP base areas issued their local currencies after 1941, thus allowing them to essentially use monetary expansion to help finance government and military expenses. When comparing revenues across base areas, a significant challenge arises because of the varying currency units used in reporting.

Third, the CCP engaged in opium production and trade in two base areas (Shaan-Gan-Ning and Jin-Sui), aiming to compensate for the revenue shortfall after the KMT withdrew its financial assistance in late 1940 (Chen 1990); however, these financial records sometimes included codenames like "special production (特产)" or "medicine price (药品变价)" to disguise the nature of the revenue from opium trade.[41]

To address these problems, I first identified both CCP and KMT grain collection and the size of monetary expansion in these publications. I then converted fiscal revenue into grain units by using the grain prices for any given year in each base area. Finally, I added both grain collection and volume of monetary expansion to the overall revenue, all in grain units, to obtain a full picture of fiscal revenue obtained by the CCP and the KMT from several sources.

In Figure 4.6, I compare the sources of KMT revenue with those in the two most important CCP base areas: Shaan-Gan-Ning and Jin-Sui. The data illustrate distinct structures in the sources of government revenue that challenge conventional wisdom. First, one common narrative is that the KMT engaged in heavy taxation while the CCP used land reform and economic production to generate fiscal revenue. Using another indicator of fiscal capacity – share of direct tax in revenue in total revenue – reveals that direct taxation, which

---

[41] See *Jin sui bian qu cai zheng shi zhi liao xuan bian* (*Jin-Sui Border Region Finance and Economic Selective Historical Record*) (1986 V2: 13, 473, 543–544, 549–550) and *Kang ri zhan zheng shi qi shaan gan ning bian qu cai zheng jing ji shi liao zhai bian* (*Shaan-Gan-Ning Border Region Finance and Economic Selective Historical Record during the Sino-Japanese War*) (1981 V6: 426–427).

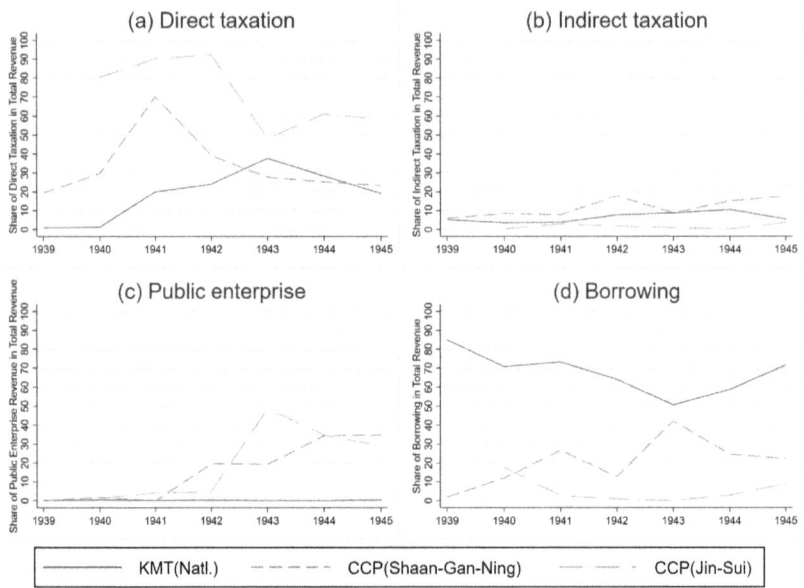

FIGURE 4.6 Sources of resource mobilization by the CCP and KMT (1939–1945). Note: KMT fiscal data derive from Young (1965); CCP (Shan-Gan-Ning) data, from *Kang ri zhan zheng shi qi shaan gan ning bian qu cai zheng jing ji shi liao zhai bian (Shaan-Gan-Ning Border Region Finance and Economic Selective Historical Record During the Sino-Japanese War)*, 1981, V4; and CCP (Jin-Sui) data, *Jin sui bian qu cai zheng shi zhi liao xuan bian (Jin-Sui Border Region Finance and Economic Selective Historical Record)*, 1981, V2. Direct fiscal extraction is measured by tax collection from personal and business income and grain collection in kind. Indirect fiscal extraction is measured by tax collection from business transactions and tariffs. Public enterprise revenue entails fiscal extraction from party- or state-sponsored businesses, including revenue from opium and salt. Bank borrowing entails both domestic bonds and monetary supply expansion by the government. See Appendix C.1 for detailed data and their sources.

includes grain levies, was a critical source of revenue for the CCP as much as for the KMT, especially during the height of the War from 1940 to 1942 (Figure 4.6a). Among the direct taxation collected by the CCP, most came from grain collection in kind. For instance, grain levies accounted for 87.46 percent of direct taxation in Shaan-Gan-Ning and 92.47 percent in Jin-Sui from 1939 through 1945. Hence, the contribution from direct fiscal extraction by the CCP was underestimated if grain levies are excluded. By contrast, the KMT achieved some success in raising revenues from direct taxation after 1940, following a series of tax reforms and grain levies; however, direct taxation remained insufficient, amounting to an average of 18.81 percent throughout this period.

Second, Figure 4.6b shows that indirect taxation on goods and services played a limited role in revenue collection for both the CCP and KMT. In

4.4 The Divergence of Grain Mobilization (1941–1945)

particular, the share of indirect taxation in the total revenue of the KMT government fell under 10 percent after 1939. By contrast, CCP tax reforms, mostly through tariffs and merchandise taxes, increased the share of indirect taxation in CCP revenue to some extent, particularly in the Shaan-Gan-Ning base area.

Third, Figure 4.6c reveals that public enterprise revenues became an important source of CCP revenue in these two base areas after 1942. Notably, the public enterprise revenue of the CCP consisted primarily of the production and sale of opium instead of the goods and services it produced. This pattern of opium profits is consistent with earlier findings that detailed the opium trade in Yan'an, the heart of the Shaan-Gan-Ning base area (Chen 1990).

Finally, Figure 4.6d suggests that the primary source of KMT revenue still derived from bank borrowing, ranging from 50.64 percent to 76.27 percent during the period from 1939 to 1945. Meanwhile, the CCP also relied on the expansion of monetary supply but to a lesser degree than the KMT. At some point, bank borrowing accounted for as much as 30 percent in 1943 in the Shaan-Gan-Ning base area.

4.4.3 Distribution of Grain Burden across Rural Residents

The preceding analysis unveils a strikingly higher level of grain extraction by the CCP in comparison to the KMT during the Sino-Japanese War, which challenges the prevailing notion that the KMT was notorious for its burdensome taxation. Despite the significant grain extraction by the CCP, however, it incited less resentment than that experienced under KMT rule. Illustrated in Section 4.3, the CCP employed a strategy of mobilized compliance in grain extraction, effectively shifting the focal point of tension from "state–society" to "within-community." Another crucial factor contributing to the divergence of public sentiment lies in the differing distribution of the grain burden among rural residents. This section highlights how the CCP implemented a progressive distribution of the grain burden to alleviate tension, while the KMT maintained a regressive distribution because of its dependence on local elites as intermediaries in the process of grain extraction.

Regressive KMT Grain Burden Distribution. To be fair, the KMT had attempted to implement a progressive tax rate on grain extraction, considering the grain income of individual rural households (Hao 2008: 229, 231). The implementation of a progressive taxation relied heavily on the KMT's bureaucratic capacity to accurately assess grain output and ensure compliance from rural residents, which was inadequate during wartime. Furthermore, the KMT encountered strong opposition from local elites who would have shouldered a heavier burden under the progressive grain extraction scheme. Because of both a lack of bureaucratic capacity and political will, the KMT's grain extraction adhered to the regressive land tax scheme that imposed a fixed tax rate based on landownership rather than on the actual grain output.

The regressive land tax implemented by the KMT resulted in a notable issue of inequity (Hao 2008: 225–227, 2011; Xiao 2010). Although the tax was intended to be levied solely on rural households that owned land, in practice, landlords frequently shifted their grain burden onto tenants who rented land from them. A survey conducted in two counties in Hubei shows that around 20 percent of landlords managed to evade paying any land tax in kind, and that nearly 15 percent of peasants were burdened with paying land tax despite not owning any land (Zhu 1963). Landlords often passed the grain burden to their tenants by increasing land rents, and because of pervasive corruption in rural China, rural elites resorted to fraudulent practices to underreport the size of their land ownership, thus evading the land tax imposed on them.

Because the KMT failed to execute progressive grain extraction, the government did not bother to maintain systematic data on the distribution of grain burden across rural households by income and wealth. Some news reporting at the time suggested that the effective rates of land tax in kind for landlords were approximately between 3 and 8 percent in KMT controlled territories;[42] by contrast, the effective land tax in kind for peasants ranged from 13 to 30 percent during the same period.

The inequity of KMT's grain burden distribution has been noted by scholars in earlier studies. Eastman (1984) attributed the inequity in grain extraction, conscription, and corruption as the primary causes that eroded peasants' support of the KMT. Young (1965) made a parallel observation, highlighting the KMT's wartime fiscal extraction, not inflation, as the leading factor of the disillusionment of peasants. Because rural residents relied primarily on agricultural production rather than monetary income, their grievances stemmed from the KMT's actions during the war.

Progressive CCP Grain Burden Distribution. Based on data from the CCP's own surveys in several base areas, Figure 4.7 illustrates the distribution of the grain burden across classes of rural residents across base areas from 1940 to 1945, and it is in stark contrast with the distribution of the grain burden by the KMT government. The average effective grain levy rates imposed by the CCP were 30.65 percent for landlords and 25.32 percent for rich peasants across all the base areas during this period. In contrast, middle peasants and poor peasants faced lower rates, with averages of 14.32 percent and 7.19 percent, respectively.

Among the base areas, Jin-Sui imposed the greatest grain burden across all classes of rural residents, which is consistent with an earlier finding indicating that the degree of grain extraction by the CCP was the highest in this base area, amounting to over 20 percent throughout the war. For instance, the average grain levy rate on landlords was 39.1 percent; even poor peasants had to pay 10.19 percent of their grain output. By contrast, Shandong and Jin-Cha-Ji imposed relatively lighter grain burden in part because these two base areas were located behind the Japanese occupation, and the CCP did not have a firm territorial control.

---

[42] Fei (1944) suggested 3–5 percent; Hao (2008) estimated between 5 and 8 percent.

4.4 The Divergence of Grain Mobilization (1941–1945)

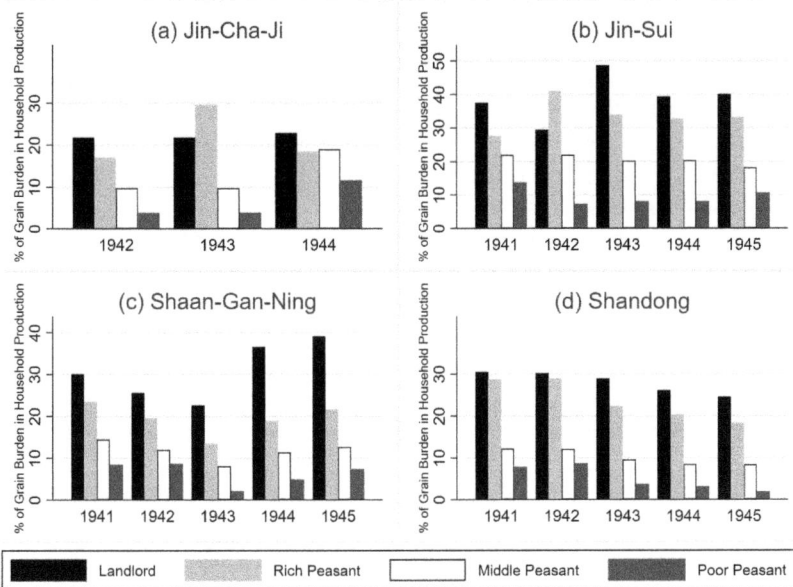

FIGURE 4.7 Distribution of grain burden across classes of rural residents (1941–1945).
Note: Author's data. See Appendix C for data source.

4.4.4 Grassroots Party Strength and Grain Extraction

How much can we attribute the CCP's success and the KMT's failure in grain extraction to their party mobilization infrastructure? In this section I offer a quantitative analysis to shed light on the correlation between party mobilization capacity and fiscal extraction.[43] The main dependent variable is the respective amount of grain collected by the CCP and KMT governments. To measure party grassroots mobilization infrastructure – the independent variable – the optimal metric would be the elite-mass composition of party membership. Unfortunately, systematic data on party membership for both parties at the subnational level are spotty and limited. Consequently, I have resorted to party membership as a proxy.

Collecting systematic data on grain levies and the grassroots party organizations at the subnational level during the Sino-Japanese War is a challenging task because of poor records. Hence, I constructed a my dataset from various sources. First, I constructed a base-level panel dataset for the CCP and a province-level panel dataset for the KMT from 1941 to 1945. Although this level of analysis renders a small number of observations, it offers better

---

[43] For a more extensive quantitative analysis of party strength and grain extraction by the CCP and KMT, see Lü (2025).

systematic data on grain levies and party size. The KMT data cover twenty-one provinces that were under its control during wartime. The data on party membership derive from KMT party organization archives,[44] and the data on grain levies come from KMT internal government documents.[45] Meanwhile, the CCP data cover three base areas (Jin-Sui, Shaan-Gan-Ning, Shandong), and I collected the CCP grain and other fiscal data from various compendiums of party archives across base areas (see Appendix C).

Second, I constructed a county-level panel dataset for all counties in six provinces (Hebei, Gansu, Ningxia, Shanxi, Shaanxi, and Shandong) from county gazetteers for the same period. Some of the counties in these six provinces were part of CCP base areas (Jin-Sui, Jin-Cha-Ji, Shaan-Gan-Ning, and Shandong), where territorial integrity was best maintained during wartime; others were controlled by the KMT government. The advantage of a county-level dataset is the sample size, which renders better statistical power. The drawback of county-level panel analysis is that the missing data issue is more prevalent, especially for grain collection data and KMT membership.

To address the missing data issue, I use *MissForest*, a nonparametric missing value imputation based on a random forest (Stekhoven and Bühlmann 2012). I chose a method based on the following considerations. First, during this period the party membership and grain levies data underwent radical changes due to the war, hence imputation based on parametric models, such as the Amelia package (Honaker, King, and Blackwell 2011), generate poor imputation results. Second, *MissForest*, a random forest imputation, is an ensemble machine-learning method that does not rely on a linear, additive model with the potential to accommodate flexible dependencies between variables (Marbach 2021).

The baseline results mainly follow two model specifications with or without the location (i) and year (t) fixed effects. In addition, I include a time trend to capture potential series correlation over time.

$$Log(Grain)_{i,t} = \beta_1 * Log(Party\ Members)_{i,t} + \beta_j \sum_1^j X_{i,t} + year_t + \epsilon_{i,t} \quad (4.1)$$

$$Log(Grain)_{i,t} = \beta_1 * Log(Party\ Members)_{i,t} + \beta_j \sum_1^j X_{i,t} + \alpha_i + \gamma_t + year_t + \epsilon_{i,t} \quad (4.2)$$

---

[44] Provincial party membership data are from Li (1993).
[45] Hao (2008) compiled the data from primary sources at the Second Historical Archives of China in Nanjing; these records are inaccessible to scholars outside China.

4.4 The Divergence of Grain Mobilization (1941–1945)

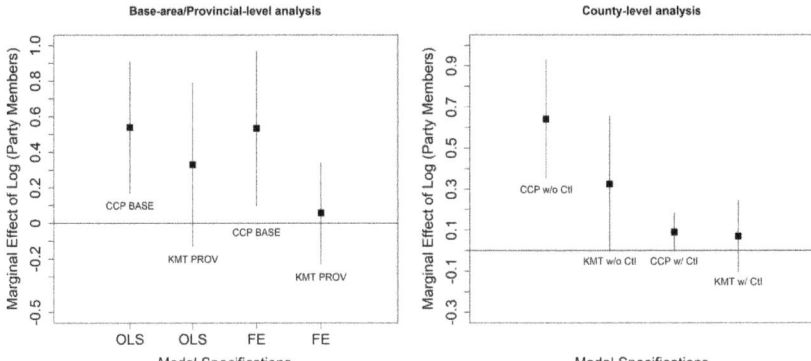

FIGURE 4.8 Statistical analyses of grain levy and party size.
Note: The dependent variable is *log(grain)* for all analysis. Panels (a) and (b) show the point estimates of *log(party member)* and 95% confidence interval in model specifications for the analysis of grain levy by the CCP and KMT. See Tables D.1 and D.2 in Appendix D for detail regression results reported in Panel (a) and Panel (b), respectively.

When the unit of analysis is at the base or provincial level, I controlled for other sources of revenue that indicate fiscal pressure faced by the governments. In county regression analysis, I controlled for the integrity of territorial control by including the percentage of counties that had established a functioning CCP, KMT, and Japanese puppet government on a yearly basis. Notably, two or more governments ruled by different parties coexisted at the same time.

Figure 4.8 reports the point estimates of *Log(Party Members)* in different model specifications for the analysis of grain levy by the CCP and KMT. For the analysis at the baselevel, I found a strong correlation between CCP membership and grain extraction in models with or without fixed effects (Figure 4.8a), controlling for other resources of revenue. The baseline models suggest a 10 percent increase in party membership associated with an approximately 5.4 percent increase in grain extraction. The coefficient estimates are robust even after I included year and base fixed effects and the time trend in the model specification. Turning to the KMT, Figure 4.8a shows mixed results for the correlation between KMT membership and grain extraction. At the provincial level, I initially found a positive correlation between KMT membership and grain extraction, but the estimate is not statistically significant at the 0.1 level. The estimate becomes close to zero and is no longer statistically significant in the analysis of a two-way fixed effect model with the time trend.

I then conducted the county-level analysis by using the two-way fixed effect models with a time trend and found the correlation between CCP membership and grain extraction remains positive and statistically significant (Figure 4.8b). For the KMT, I initially found a positive correlation when I excluded any control variable; however, once I controlled for the existence of governments controlled by several entities (i.e., CCP, KMT, and Japanese), the coefficient estimate again becomes close to zero and is no longer statistically significant.

I examined various alternative arguments that may account for the grain extraction patterns of the CCP and KMT. Although some of these arguments have merits, I established that the principal findings persisted despite these factors.

Scale of Government. A possible argument is that the KMT – as the ruling party – had to bear a greater fiscal burden to finance the warfare compared to the CCP, which relied on guerrilla tactics and faced a less severe fiscal demand shock. If comparing the total amount of grain extracted, the KMT government would be found to have extracted more than the CCP; however, keeping in mind that the KMT had control over a larger territory than the CCP is essential. Importantly, the CCP had also significantly expanded its military and bureaucracy during the war,[46] thus facing a fiscal uptick similar to the KMT. To obtain a more accurate measure of the intensity of fiscal extraction, examining the extent to which the government can extract economic resources from the total economic activities is necessary. Figure 4.5 shows that the CCP base areas consistently extracted a greater share of grain in total grain output than the KMT, which provides evidence that the CCP's grain extraction strategy was more intensive.

Other Sources of Revenue. The KMT had better access to state resources than the CCP did, perhaps relieving some pressure in grain extraction. I should note that the statistical analysis had already controlled for other sources of revenue; furthermore, the patterns of other sources of revenue contradicted the notion that the KMT faced a less severe fiscal supply shock. For instance, Figure 4.6 shows that the CCP and KMT had collected similar shares of indirect taxation in total revenue. Meanwhile, the CCP Shaan-Gan-Ning and Jin-Sui base areas benefited from opium production, which would have reduced the intensity of grain extraction by the CCP in those areas (Figure 4.5). Finally, both the CCP and KMT had the option of financing the war through monetary expansion because the CCP Border Region governments also issued their own currency; however, the CCP decided not to overly rely on borrowing to finance the war (Figure 4.6).

Informal Institutions. Recent scholarship has attributed the CCP's success in insurgency mobilization from 1928 to informal institutions and lineage networks; however, this argument does not mean that CCP grassroots organizations and informal village institutions are substitutional – they are complementary. To proxy for the CCP's penetration in local informal institutions,

---

[46] For instance, the size of CCP military rose from approximately 74,000 to 780,000, a tenfold increase (see *Zhong guo ren min jie fang jun quan shi* (*The Complete History of Chinese People's Liberation Army*), 2000 V3: 378 and V4: 440).

I included two variables indicating whether the CCP county head and county party secretary governed in their birthplaces (籍贯). Table D.3 in Appendix D shows that the effects of party membership size still had a strong correlation with grain extraction despite the positive correlations between the CCP's penetration of informal institutions and grain extraction.

Reversed Causality. Access to various types of economic resources could have a profound impact on party building and rebel organizations. I contend that reverse causality is not a major concern in this case. As demonstrated in Chapters 6 and 7, both parties experienced a transformation of mobilization infrastructure from 1937 to 1940, prior to their intensifying grain extraction in 1941.

4.5 SUMMARY

Focusing on the efforts by the CCP and KMT to extract grain from rural households, a form of direct taxation during the Sino-Japanese War, I show the success of the CCP stemmed from its mass mobilization infrastructure prior to the onset of grain levies. Employing the tactics through mobilized compliance, the CCP was able to extract substantial grain from local production without losing the popular support of peasants. In contrast, the KMT had neglected building its mass mobilization capacity before the war, opting instead to rely on local elites for grain extraction. Despite effectively extracting a substantial amount of grain, which constituted a smaller share of total local grain output compared to the CCP, the KMT's strategies led to an inequitable distribution of grain burden. This sparked widespread resentment and ultimately contributed to the downfall of the KMT during the Civil War from 1946 to 1949.

Recent research has emphasized the significance of bureaucratic capacity for modern fiscal states; nonetheless, building bureaucratic capacity is an incremental process, but war finance requires immediate fiscal intake. I demonstrate that political parties can effectively compensate weak bureaucratic capacity for wartime resource mobilization only if they have developed strong mass mobilization capacity prior to the onset of the war. Unfortunately, parties that rely on mobilizing existing economic elites may fail to address the fiscal demand shock caused by war, especially if the wealth of these economic elites is severely diminished by the conflict.

The reversal of fortunes of the CCP and KMT, however, was not completely inevitable. Had the CCP failed to significantly expand its mass mobilization infrastructure in rural China prior to 1941, the Sino-Japanese War may not have helped it to lay the foundation for its rise after the war. One should note that the CCP had followed Leninist doctrine by emphasizing the recruitment of workers as the "vanguard" of the Communist Revolution during the early phase of party formation. Hence the expansion of rural mobilization infrastructure was hardly a natural step. By the same token, the KMT might have survived the war and maintained its domination over the CCP had it not abandoned the expansion of mass mobilization infrastructure in 1927.

Indeed, the KMT had undergone a radical party reform, aiming to transform itself into a "Leninist Party" after the formation of the First United Front in 1924. Hence, the KMT had the potential to become a truly mass party, yet the anti-Communist purge in 1927 all but eliminated the KMT's opportunity to build its mass mobilization infrastructure.

In Chapters 5, 6, and 7, I delve into the fateful choices made by CCP and KMT leaders to develop their respective mobilization infrastructure prior to the Sino-Japanese War. Combining qualitative and quantitative evidence, I substantiate the theoretical framework presented in Chapter 2, illuminating how internal power struggles influence the strategies employed in building their respective mobilization infrastructures.

5

The CCP

Elite Conflict & Party Struggle (1921–1934)

To this point I have demonstrated that the reversal of fortune of the CCP and KMT was closely tied to their capacity for resource mobilization rather than the size of party membership or internal organizational structure. The natural question then becomes why the CCP and KMT pursued different party-building strategies in developing their mobilization infrastructure, and why their mobilization infrastructure achieved uneven outcomes over time. Specifically, why did the CCP struggle to build a resilient mobilization infrastructure before the Sino-Japanese War despite its persistent efforts? The transformation of the CCP from a fragile organization into a party with formidable peasant mobilization capacity – a feat it had repeatedly failed to achieve in its early years – is puzzling. Meanwhile, why did the KMT repeatedly fail to resolve internal elite conflicts, which resulted in an ineffective party organization fully exposed during the Sino-Japanese War? Despite its seemingly large membership and early efforts by its founding father to build a Leninist party, why did the KMT struggle to transform into a mass party and effectively penetrate society? These perplexing yet crucial questions shift the focus onto the origins of party mobilization infrastructure itself.

I contend that the answers to these questions lie in the power struggle among party elites that shapes their choices in party-building tactics. This, in turn, exerts a profound impact on the effectiveness of party mobilization infrastructure. Specifically, contested party leadership often leads to conflicting party-building strategies, weakening the effectiveness of party mobilization infrastructure. Conversely, the presence of a dominant party leader plays a crucial role in fostering the coherence of party-building strategies, thereby fortifying the party's mobilization infrastructure. Importantly, the intraparty power dynamics under contested and dominant leadership is self-reinforcing. Therefore, contingent events, rather than the strategic maneuvers of party elites, play a pivotal role in disrupting the balance of power among party elites. These shifts, in turn, engender a radical departure from previous party-building strategies.

I employ process tracing as the principle analytical tool to uncover the cascading effects of intraparty elite power struggles on party-building strategies and the resulting attributes and strength of party mobilization infrastructure. I distinguish party-building *intentions* from party-building *outcomes* and use specific indicators to guide the analysis, particularly in relation to mobilization infrastructure. To discern party-building intentions, I closely scrutinize the statements of party elites, identifying shifts in their endorsed strategies pertaining to recruitment and training that arise from the evolving balance of power among party elites. To measure the outcome of party-building strategies, I draw on two sets of variables that reflect the attributes and strength of elite-centric and mass-centric mobilization infrastructures, respectively. The first set encompasses both the quality and socioeconomic backgrounds of party members, unveiling the breadth and efficacy of the mobilization infrastructure in engaging diverse segments of society. The second set centers on operational effectiveness of grassroots party organizations, serving as a gauge of the party's capacity to permeate society.

In the remainder of this chapter, I delve into the underlying causes of the CCP's fragility prior to 1935, illuminating the intraparty elite conflict as a main culprit in its failure to build a robust mass mobilization infrastructure. I begin by examining the initial power dynamics and party-building approach during its inception from 1921 to 1927. With Chen Duxiu as a relatively weak leader and a lack of mass appeal, the CCP operated under the shadow of the Comintern, whose opinions significantly influenced party leadership turnovers and party-building strategies. An intense power struggle emerged among CCP elites after Chen Duxiu was forced to resign in 1927. Internal CCP party archives shed light on how elite conflicts within the party led to debates and difficulty in defining the true representatives of the "vanguard" of the proletariat revolution in China. These debates resulted in conflicting strategies regarding which class of the masses the CCP should prioritize in terms of recruitment and promotion. Compounded by suppression from the KMT and regional warlords, incoherent party-building strategies resulted in a weak mass mobilization infrastructure. Unsurprisingly, the CCP found itself on the brink of collapse twice during this period, when its membership suffered sharp declines and many grassroots party organizations were wiped out.

Chapter 6 will shift its focus to the period between 1935 and 1945, with particular emphasis on the critical years from 1935 to 1938, which marked the pivotal phase in Mao Zedong's rise to power within the CCP. Mao's rise enabled the CCP to embark on a cohesive journey toward building a resilient mass mobilization infrastructure in rural China. Finally, Chapter 7 analyzes elite power struggles and party building within the KMT, exposing the persistent conflicts among KMT elites and highlighting Chiang Kai-shek's inability to consolidate his power and became a dominant leader, which ultimately led to conflictual party-building strategies and party mobilization infrastructure of mixed quality, particularly in rural China.

5.1 A TEPID COMMUNIST MOVEMENT (1921–1927)

The inception of the Communist revolution in China did not spark a fervent movement. Like numerous other revolutionary parties, the CCP was born weak. Chen Duxiu, the first CCP leader, lacked strong leadership qualities despite facing minimal challenges from other party elites. During the early phase of party formation, the CCP sought to emulate the Communist revolution in the Soviet Union and found itself heavily influenced by the Comintern, which exerted their influence through crucial financial and strategic support. Meanwhile, the mobilization infrastructure of the CCP was still in its infancy, rendering it susceptible to external repression.

5.1.1 Chen Duxiu, a Weak Party Leader (1921–1927)

Chen Duxiu was elected secretary of the Provisional Central Executive Bureau when the CCP was founded in 1921, and his source of power stemmed primarily from his esteemed reputation as a prominent intellectual and his early advocacy for the Communist revolution dating back to 1915.[1] Together with Li Dazhao, Chen played a vital role in disseminating Communist ideas, inspiring Chinese youth, and captivating the intellectual circles (Meisner 1967). Chen was an intellectual first but not a grassroots organizer; therefore, the assistance and guidance of Henk Sneevliet (also known as Maring), a representative of the Comintern, were instrumental in shaping the CCP's party-building strategies and tactics under Chen's leadership (Saich 1991).

The formation of the First United Front with the KMT became a turning point in the CCP elite conflict and the downfall of Chen Duxiu. Seeking to counter the influence of regional warlords, Maring advocated for a political alliance between the CCP and the KMT.[2] The extent and nature of collaboration between these two parties became contentious matters among CCP party leaders during the Third Party Congress in 1923. In particular, Zhang Guotao, a prominent figure in the labor movement and a member of the Central Executive Bureau, opposed placing the CCP under the leadership of the KMT even with the condition that CCP members could have joined the KMT simultaneously without relinquishing their party affiliation. Ultimately, Chen sided with Maring in endorsing the First United Front with the KMT despite his early hesitation,[3] and Zhang was marginalized within the Central Committee after the CCP Third Party Congress.

---

[1] Chen founded the journal *Youth*, renamed *New Youth* (新青年) in 1915; it was one of the most influential publications attracting eager Chinese youth to the CCP.
[2] The First United Front was codified in 1924 after Sun Yat-sen, founder of the KMT, decided to adopt the party reform known as "Uniting with the Soviet and Accommodating the CCP" in 1923. For more details about the rise and fall of the First United Front, see Saich (1991) and Yang (2012).
[3] "陈独秀致吴廷康的信 – 反对共产党及青年团加入国民党 [Letter from Chen Duxiu to Wu Tingkang–Opposing the CCP and its Youth League Joining the KMT]," April 4, 1922, in *Zhong gong zhong yang wen jian xuan ji* (*CCP Party Center Selected Documents*) (1989 VI: 31–32).

The First United Front proved a short-lived marriage between the CCP and the KMT. The rising influence of the CCP within the KMT organization generated friction, leading to the rise of an anti-Communist movement within the KMT in 1926. The CCP under Chen initially succumbed to pressure from the KMT and adopted several compromises.[4] These retreats further emboldened Chiang Kai-shek, who orchestrated a bloody purge of CCP members on April 12, 1927.[5]

The collapse of the First United Front effectively discredited the leadership of Chen Duxiu, who was scapegoated for the failure of CCP strategies dealing with the KMT. The Comintern accused Chen of ignoring its advice to resist KMT aggression after 1926.[6] For example, it accused the CCP under Chen of resisting the Comintern's call to cut ties with the KMT; instead, Chen issued a resolution to advocate strengthening the coalition with the KMT-Left faction. In fact, Chen intended to use this coalition-building strategy to outmaneuver Chiang and the KMT-Right faction.[7] Chen even issued an ill-timed joint statement with Wang Ching-wei, a KMT-Left leader, to promote cooperation between the CCP and the KMT-Left faction on the eve of the April 12 anti-communist purge in 1927.[8]

In reality, Chen's apparent defiance of Comintern stemmed from the ambivalent Soviet attitudes towards the KMT's increasing aggression. If anything, Chen's strategy of collaborating with the KMT-Left faction was officially approved by the Comintern in May 1927, a month after Chiang's bloody purge, but Comintern's stance shifted two months later.[9] The Comintern's

---

[4] For instance, CCP leaders under Chen agreed to resign from KMT party leadership positions after the Second Party Congress of the KMT in 1926.
[5] The April 12 incident refers to an event during which Chiang Kai-shek, with the help of underground mafia and gangster organizations, arrested and murdered thousands of CCP members in Shanghai.
[6] See Yang (2012) for more discussion of the Zhongshanjian Incident. For example, Borodin, the Comintern representative, urged the CCP cut ties with the KMT after this incident.
[7] "中央致粤区信 – 关于国民政府迁汉后应付粤局的策略 [Letter from the Party Center to the Guangdong Bureau: Concerning Strategies in Guangdong after the National Government Relocated to Wuhan]," December 4, 1926, in *Zhong gong zhong yang wen jian xuan ji* [*CCP Party Center Selected Documents*] (1989, V2: 471-475); "政治报告 – 一九二六年十二月十三日中央特别会议 [Political Report of the Party Center Special Meeting on December 13, 1926]," December 13, 1926, in *Zhong gong zhong yang wen jian xuan ji* (*CCP Party Center Selected Documents*) (1989, V2: 559-569).
[8] "汪精卫、陈独秀联合宣言 [A Joint Announcement by Wang Ching-wei and Chen Duxiu]," April 5, 1927, in *Zhong gong zhong yang wen jian xuan ji* (*CCP Party Center Selected Documents*) (1989, V3: 593-594).
[9] According to "共产国际执行委员会第八次全体会议关于中国问题决议案 [The Resolution on China Issues at the No. 8 Full Meeting of the Communist International Executive Committee]," May 1927, in *Zhong gong zhong yang wen jian xuan ji* (*CCP Party Center Selected Documents*) (1989, V3: 595-612), the Comintern's endorsement came in May, but it reversed its course in July as shown in "共产国际执行委员会关于中国革命目前形势的决定 [The Decision on Current

5.1 A Tepid Communist Movement (1921–1927)

initial support of CCP cooperation with the KMT-Left faction resulted from Stalin's intention to use the KMT Wuhan government to strengthen the Communist movement in China (North 1963). Nonetheless, the degradation of the First United Front presented an opportunity for some Soviet elites to criticize Stalin, leading to the withdrawal of support from the Comintern (Yang 2012). Under pressure from the Comintern, Chen was forced to resign from his position, removed from the CCP Politburo altogether a few months later on August 7, 1927.

5.1.2 Building a Party by Mimicking the Soviets

Aiming to imitate Soviet success, the CCP followed Soviet doctrine closely in its early party-building strategies, reflected in its first Party Manifesto.[10] In this Manifesto, the CCP emphasized constructing a Leninist party organization characterized by a hierarchical organizational structure and mass grassroots party organizations. Second, the CCP regarded itself as the vanguard of the proletariat, exclusively encompassing workers.[11] Third, the Manifesto established the boundary of its mobilization infrastructure that targeted the masses, prohibiting CCP members from holding any position in existing governments or legislatures. In essence, the exclusion of individuals from existing political institutions signaled the constraining effect of CCP ideology by exclusively developing a mass mobilization infrastructure, a stance reaffirmed at the Third Party Congress thereafter.[12]

Like Karl Marx, the peasantry was an afterthought by the CCP as a potential force of Communist revolution. CCP leaders viewed peasants as "loose sand" with diffuse interests, presenting a significant obstacle for mass mobilization.[13] In addition, the CCP viewed peasants as a backward population with little understanding of Communist ideology. Hence, the goal of the

---

Chinese Revolution Movement by the Communist International Executive Committee]," July 1927, in *Zhong gong zhong yang wen jian xuan ji* (*CCP Party Center Selected Documents*) (1989, V3: 622–628).

[10] "中国共产党第一个纲领 [The First Manifesto of the Chinese Communist Party]," July 1921, in *Zhong gong zhong yang wen jian xuan ji* (*CCP Party Center Selected Documents*) (1989, V1: 3–5).

[11] For example, the CCP emphasized worker recruitment as a key justification for joining the Comintern. "中国共产党加入第三国际决议案 [Resolution on the CCP Joining the Communist International]," July 1922, in *Zhong gong zhong yang wen jian xuan ji* (*CCP Party Center Selected Documents*) (1989, V1: 67–72).

[12] "关于党员入政界的决议案 [Resolution on Party Membership Joining the Existing Government]," July 1923, in *Zhong gong zhong yang wen jian xuan ji* (*CCP Party Center Selected Documents*) (1989, V1: 152).

[13] "第三次全国劳动大会关于职工运动总策略决议案 [Resolution on Labor Mobilization Strategy at the Third Annual National Labor Conference]," May 1926, in *Zhong gong zhong yang wen jian xuan ji* (*CCP Party Center Selected Documents*) (1989, V2: 96–100).

CCP propaganda campaign in rural areas prioritized class struggle and tax revolt, not Communist ideology, to mobilize peasants.[14]

The subsequent resolutions and bylaws outlining its strategies for party building from 1921 to 1926 continued to reveal the CCP elites' intention to build a Communist party resembling that in the Soviet Union (Table 5.1). For example, early party documents consistently targeted workers in CCP recruitment strategies with little attention paid to peasant mobilization. The Party Center repeatedly emphasized establishing unions and grassroots party cells in urban areas, even maintaining that worker well-being was the ultimate priority guiding party operations. Meanwhile, party documents barely mentioned peasant mobilization in rural areas during this period, a jarring omission given that China was a predominantly agrarian society at the time.

In 1925, CCP leaders finally turn their attention to peasant mobilization because of escalating hostility from Chiang and the KMT-Right faction. CCP leaders revised their strategies by broadening their alliance with the KMT-Left faction and the peasantry, aiming to forge a cohesive partnership. For instance, the CCP initiated peasant mobilization in Guangdong, where the KMT-Left faction was based.[15] Chen Duxiu issued a letter to all CCP grassroots party branches, calling on their members to strengthen the mobilization and recruitment of peasants in 1926.[16] In a report on dealings with the KMT, Chen urged the party to issue a manifesto targeting peasants, allowing the CCP to strengthen the KMT-Left faction to compete with Chiang and the KMT-Right faction.[17] The Party Center later issued a draft of its manifesto for peasants, promoting a coalition with both peasants and tenants.[18]

The CCP recognized the importance of appealing to peasants' interests, but its party-building strategies still treated peasants as a class inferior to workers.

---

[14] "关于农民运动之议决案 [Resolution on the Peasant Movement]," February 1925, in *Zhong gong zhong yang wen jian xuan ji (CCP Party Center Selected Documents)* (1989, V1: 358–364).

[15] See, for example, "对于广东农民运动议决案 [Resolution on the Peasant Movement in Guangdong]," February 1925, in *Zhong gong zhong yang wen jian xuan ji (CCP Party Center Selected Documents)* (1989, V1: 238–258); "中央通告第四号（龙字第一号 – 成立农委发展农民运动并定期报告农运工作 [No. 4 Announcement by the Party Center–Establishing a Peasant Commission to Develop a Peasant Movement with Regular Report]," August 4, 1926, in *Zhong gong zhong yang wen jian xuan ji (CCP Party Center Selected Documents)* (1989, V2: 284–285).

[16] "陈独秀给各级党部的信 – 对于扩大党的组织的提议 [Letter from Chen Duxiu to the Grassroots Party Organization – A Suggestion on Expanding Party Organization]," October 17, 1926, in *Zhong gong zhong yang wen jian xuan ji (CCP Party Center Selected Documents)* (1989, V2: 635–636).

[17] "陈独秀关于国民党问题报告 [Report on the KMT Issued by Chen Duxiu]," November 4, 1926, in *Zhong gong zhong yang wen jian xuan ji (CCP Party Center Selected Documents)* (1989, V2: 422–430).

[18] "中国共产党关于农民纲领的草案 [Draft of CCP's Peasant Program]," November 4, 1926, in *Zhong gong zhong yang wen jian xuan ji (CCP Party Center Selected Documents)* (1989, V2: 434–437).

5.1 A Tepid Communist Movement (1921–1927)

TABLE 5.1 *CCP resolutions and internal reports on party building (1921–1926)*

Year	CCP documents	Targeted population	
		Workers	Peasants
July 1921	"中国共产党第一个决议 [The First Resolution of the Chinese Communist Party]"[19]	Organized worker unions and schools	Not mentioned
November 1921	"中国共产党中央局通告 – 关于建立与发展党团工会组织及宣传工作等 [CCP Party Center Announcement – Issues concerning the Development of Party and Labor Union Organization and Propaganda Work]"[20]	Mandated the strategy for organizing unions in cities across China	Not mentioned
June 1922	"中共中央执行委员会书记陈独秀给共产国际的报告 [Report to the Comintern by the CCP Central Executive Committee Secretary Chen Duxiu]"[21]	Reported CCP activities in mobilizing workers	Not mentioned
July 1922	"关于'国际帝国主义与中国和中国共产党'的决议案 [Resolution on 'International Imperialism and China as well as the CCP']"[22]	Adopted well-being of the worker class as the top priority for the party	Not mentioned
July 1922	"中国共产党章程 [CCP Bylaws]"[23]	Prioritized mobilizing workers, intellectuals, youth, and women	Not mentioned
January 1925	"对于农民运动之议决案 [Resolution on Peasant Movement]"[24]		Peasant mobilization without party recruitment
January 1925	"对于组织问题之议决案 [Resolution on Party Organization]"[25]	Focused on areas with most workers for party expansion	Not mentioned

[19] Full documents in *Zhong gong zhong yang wen jian xuan ji* (*CCP Party Center Selected Documents*) (1989, V1: 6–9).
[20] Ibid., (1989, V1: 26–27).
[21] Ibid., (1989, V1: 47–55).
[22] Ibid., (1989, V1: 61–63).
[23] Ibid., (1989, V1: 93–98).
[24] Ibid., (1989, V1: 358–364).
[25] Ibid., (1989, V1: 379–382).

For instance, the CCP insisted upon worker leadership over peasants in rural party organizations. The CCP even declared that workers and peasants did not belong to the same alliance; Workers were the leaders of peasants in the Chinese Communist revolution and the vanguard of the movement.[26]

5.1.3 A Worker-Centric Mobilization Infrastructure in Infancy

In its early days, the CCP was far from being a disciplined and resilient Leninist party. The CCP focused on recruiting urban workers and building a mobilization infrastructure centered around the working class guided by the Party Center's strategies. The expansion of this infrastructure, however, experienced a sluggish start, gaining momentum only after the formation of the First United Front in 1924 and the May 30 labor movement in 1925.

Despite the mandate in the CCP Manifesto, the worker-oriented party-building strategies did not register immediate success prior to the formation of the First United Front. CCP membership grew slowly from twenty-seven members in 1921 to 420 in 1923 (Figure 5.1). Repeatedly, local party branches reported challenges in recruiting workers into the party. For instance, a report from the Shanghai branch[27] indicated that only eight of forty-seven party members (17 percent) were workers, a dismal outcome given that Shanghai was a major industrial hub. The Shanghai report even conceded that the CCP-led labor mobilization had all but failed to penetrate worker organizations. Similar patterns were also found in reports from party branches in Beijing,[28] Hankou,[29] Hunan,[30] and Shandong.[31]

The expansion of the party was finally sparked by the formation of the First United Front with the KMT in 1924 and the May 30 Labor Movement in 1925.[32] CCP membership jumped to 3,000 in 1925, more than ten times the number in 1924. During the next two years, from 1926 to 1927, the CCP more

---

[26] "中国共产党中央执行委员会致广东省第二次农民代表大会祝词 [Message to the Second Peasant Representation Conference in Guangdong from the CCP Party Central Executive Committee]," May 1926, in *Zhong gong zhong yang wen jian xuan ji (CCP Party Center Selected Documents)* (1989, V2: 116–117).

[27] "上海地方报告 [Report of Shanghai]," June 1, 1924, in *Zhong gong zhong yang wen jian xuan ji (CCP Party Center Selected Documents)* (1989, V1: 256–261).

[28] "京区报告 [Report of Beijing]," June 1, 1924, in *Zhong gong zhong yang wen jian xuan ji (CCP Party Center Selected Documents)* (1989, V1: 274–276).

[29] "汉口报告 [Report of Hankou]," June 1, 1924, in *Zhong gong zhong yang wen jian xuan ji (CCP Party Center Selected Documents)* (1989, V1: 262–264).

[30] "湘区报告 [Report of Hunan]," June 1, 1924, in *Zhong gong zhong yang wen jian xuan ji (CCP Party Center Selected Documents)* (1989, V1: 265–273).

[31] "山东报告 [Report of Shandong]," June 1, 1924, in *Zhong gong zhong yang wen jian xuan ji (CCP Party Center Selected Documents)* (1989, V1: 277–281).

[32] It was a major labor and anti-imperialist movement in response to the massacre of Chinese protesters by Shanghai municipal police.

5.1 A Tepid Communist Movement (1921–1927)

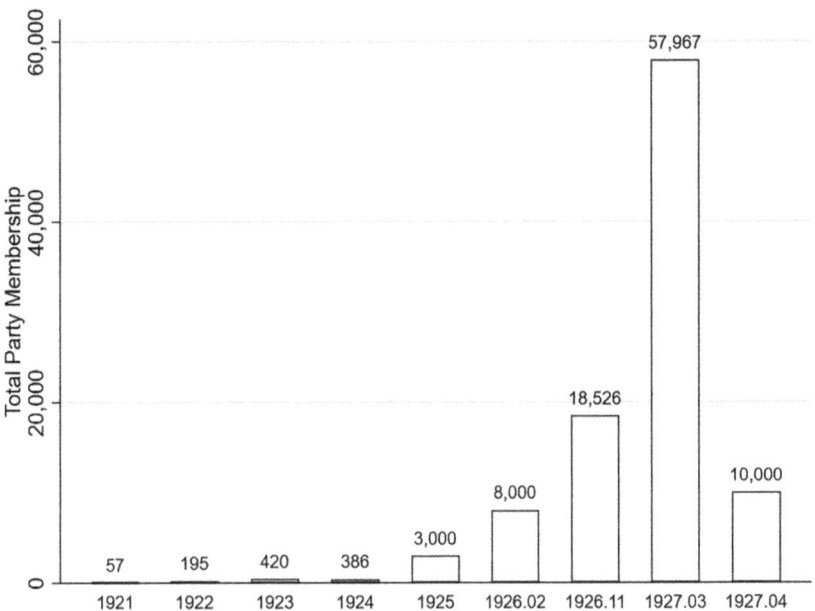

FIGURE 5.1 CCP membership (1921–1927)
Note: See Appendix A for data source.

than doubled its membership over the previous year, reaching 57,967 members in March 1927 on the eve of KMT's anti-Communist purge.

During this phase of party expansion, a worker-centric mobilization infrastructure started to emerge. Although the party was initially dominated by intellectuals, a deliberate effort to increase the representation of workers became effective over time. The overall worker representation in the party accounted for 11 percent of party membership in 1922 but soared to 60 percent in November 1926.[33] Although the CCP only mobilized peasants in late 1926, workers still accounted for 51 percent of party membership by early 1927 (Figure 5.2a). Not surprisingly, worker representation was higher in industrial hubs, registering 84.32 percent in Shanghai and 63.7 percent in the Northern region. Even in less industrial regions, worker representation accounted for more than 40 percent of the party membership (Figure 5.2b).

The expansion of CCP grassroots party cells (支部) mirrored the growth of party membership – a slow start from 1921 to 1923 but a rapid expansion after 1925. The total number of party cells increased from 69 in 1924 to 461 in 1925, skyrocketing to 3,232 in 1927 (Figure 5.3a). Similarly, county party committees reached 295 by 1927, amounting to more than 10 percent of the counties in China at the time (Figure 5.3b).

---

[33] See Table A.2 in Appendix A for data source.

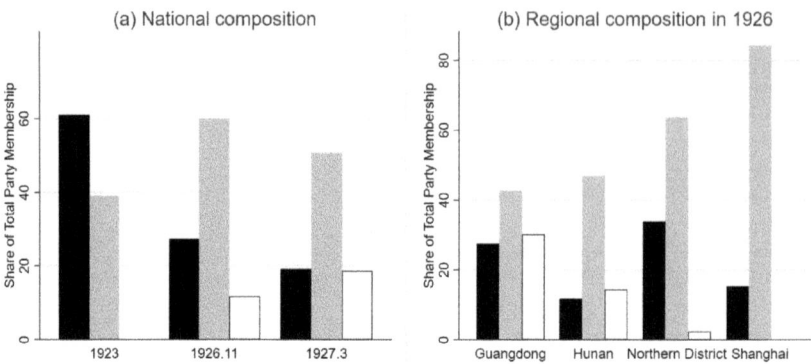

FIGURE 5.2 Class backgrounds of party membership.
Note: See Table A.2 in Appendix A for data source of national party membership composition. Regional party membership composition is from "中央局报告 (十, 十一月份) [Report of the Party Central Bureau (October and November)]," December 5, 1924, in *Zhong gong zhong yang wen jian xuan ji* (*CCP Party Center Selected Documents*) (1989, V3: 476–504).

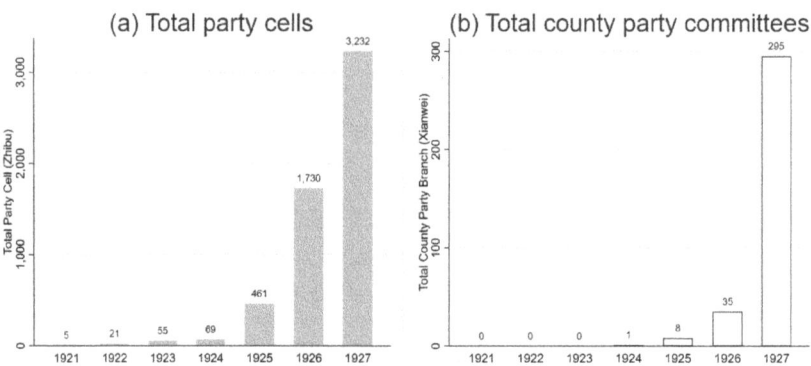

FIGURE 5.3 CCP grassroots party cells and county committees (1921–1927).
Note: Author's dataset. See Table A.1 in Appendix A, for data source.

The significant expansion of CCP party membership and grassroots organizations after 1925 largely concentrated in Guangdong, followed by Hunan and Hubei (Figure 5.4). The success of the CCP in Guangdong can be attributed to its strategic alliance with the KMT, whose headquarters located in Guangdong. Thus, the establishment of the First United Front provided a safe harbor for the CCP's party expansion, protecting it from the repression imposed by regional warlords in other provinces. The CCP organized both labor and peasant movements in Guangdong, capitalizing on the revolutionary fervor in both urban and rural populations. One key figure in this effort was Peng Pai, who

5.2 Elite Conflict & Party Fragility (1927–1935)

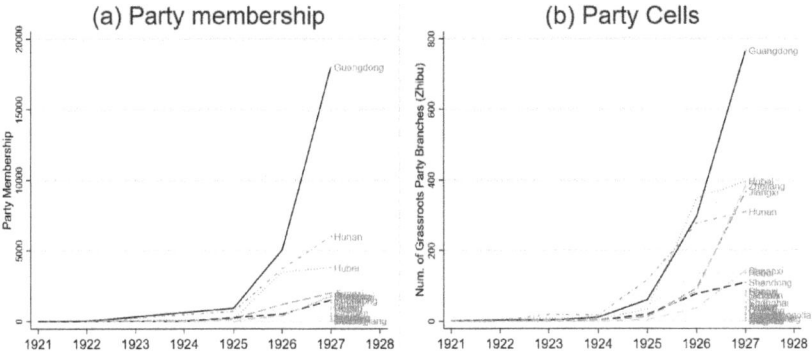

FIGURE 5.4 CCP membership and party cells by province (1921–1927).
Note: The data was constructed by the author based on provincial party organization history (组织史资料) in the following twenty-eight provinces: Anhui, Beijing, Chongqing, Fujian, Gansu, Guangdong, Guangxi, Guizhou, Hainan, Hebei, Heilongjiang, Henan, Hubei, Hunan, Jiangsu, Jiangxi, Jilin, Liaoning, Neimenggu, Ningxia, Shaanxi, Shandong, Shanghai, Shanxi, Sichuan, Tianjin, Yunnan, and Zhejiang.

played a pivotal role in initiating peasant mobilization in Haifeng and later contributed to the establishment of the Peasant Movement Training Institute in Guangzhou.[34]

The rapid party expansion after 1925 does not necessarily imply that the CCP had developed a resilient mass mobilization infrastructure. Demonstrated in Chapter 3, the CCP had little extractive capacity to mobilize crucial financial resources because the worker-centric mobilization infrastructure was in its infancy. Importantly, the central leadership of the CCP did not wield the level of authority over its members that is often assumed (Van de Ven 1991). A continuous conflict simmered between the party center and the local party branches, initially with the Shanghai branch and later with the Guangdong branch. The vulnerability of the CCP was exposed in the aftermath of the April 12 Shanghai purge in 1927. This event ignited a fierce power struggle among party elites and significantly weakened the effectiveness of its mass mobilization infrastructure for the subsequent eight years.

5.2 CCP ELITE CONFLICT AND PARTY FRAGILITY (1927–1935)

The prevailing understanding is that the CCP elite conflict between 1927 and 1935 primarily revolved around tactical differences, commonly known as the "two-line struggle" – left-leaning versus right-leaning strategies, worker

---

[34] For Peng Pai's early peasant mobilization, see Ye (2011).

mobilization versus peasant mobilization, and radical insurgency versus guerrilla warfare.[35] Beneath the surface lay a fierce power struggle among the CCP party elites, who pursued strategies to bolster their own power at the expense of their rivals. The self-inflicting party-building strategies inevitably undermined the CCP's efforts to build a resilient mass mobilization infrastructure.

The ongoing power struggle among party elites prevented the CCP from adapting to the evolving political landscape in China. In particular, the radical turn of CCP policies on strikes, armed uprising, and expropriation in both urban and rural areas alienated business communities from large to small, driving them into the arms of the KMT that promised to offer a stable environment for business operations.[36] At the very moment the political environment became hostile to the CCP operation in urban China, the CCP Center doubled down on the worker-centric party-building strategies and prioritization in urban insurgency by those elites aiming to please the Comintern. Hence, the CCP's expansion efforts became futile, and the party organization succumbed to external repression.

5.2.1 CCP Leadership in Turmoil

The departure of Chen Duxiu marked the beginning of intense conflict among CCP elites, primarily between two groups of CCP leaders: those aligned with the Comintern[37] and those associated with leading the Soviet base areas. Because the CCP relied on the Comintern for financial support and strategic guidance, the Comintern influence loomed large in CCP leadership turnovers. Hence, some CCP elites pursued radical strategies in order to gain favor with the Comintern. Meanwhile, the establishment of Soviet bases enhanced the de facto power of other CCP leaders, solidifying their resistance to the party center that was dominated by Comintern-backed elites.

Turbulent CCP Central Leadership Turnovers. From 1927 to 1931, CCP leadership had experienced radical reshuffling several times. Both the CCP and the Comintern justified changes in leadership by attributing the failures of CCP insurgency tactics to mistakes made by party leaders.[38] For instance, the Comintern accused CCP leaders of adopting erratic tactics without recognizing

---

[35] See, for example, Chen (1998), Gao (2000), Saich (2021), Saich and Yang (1996), and Teiwes (1994).
[36] Coble (1986) offers an insightful account of the unwilling alliance between the banking industry and the KMT in China at the time.
[37] Some called this group the "Returned Student Faction" because many of its members had studied in the Soviet Union (Teiwes 1994); however, in reality they were hardly an organized faction because each individual elite was trying to win favor from the Comintern and the Soviet leaders.
[38] Qu Qiubai and Li Lisan were two main CCP leaders shouldering the blame for the CCP's failed insurgencies during this period.

5.2 Elite Conflict & Party Fragility (1927–1935)

that the Chinese revolution was still too immature for radical insurgencies. In addition, the Comintern also blamed CCP leaders for failing to adhere closely to its guidance.

The reality was that the CCP elites in leadership positions were "overachievers," who frequently adopted radical tactics to demonstrate their loyalty and commitment to the Comintern. These elites recognized that their source of power derived from the support of the Comintern; therefore, a vicious cycle of CCP leadership changes and the adoption of radical party policies ensued. When the radical insurgencies failed, Comintern-supported CCP leaders became the scapegoats,[39] prompting the next CCP leader to pledge greater adherence to the Comintern's directives and to double down on radical party-building strategies.

The vicious cycle can be illustrated in CCP leader behaviors after the KMT's anti-Communist purge in 1927. Following the purge, the CCP held the August 7 Emergency Conference in 1927 under the guidance of Besso Lominadze, a Comintern representative sent by Stalin.[40] The CCP elected a three-person Standing Committee comprising Qu Qiubai, Li Weihan, and Su Zhaozheng, with Qu acting as Chairman of the CCP Politburo and the de facto leader of the party. Qu immediately instructed the CCP to pursue radical insurgencies in both urban and rural areas, demonstrating to the Comintern his firm stance against the KMT's betrayal and marking a clear departure from the previous "compromising position" that had led to Chen Duxiu's downfall. Unfortunately, most of the insurgencies were doomed from the outset because the CCP was unprepared to carry out large-scale armed uprisings.

Qu's failure led to another CCP leadership change only a year later during the Sixth Party Congress of the CCP in 1928. This Party Congress was held in Moscow, implying an inevitable Soviet influence on this party congress. Qu was marginalized at this meeting, and the Sixth Party Congress issued a resolution endorsing the Comintern to bypass the CCP Central Committee and directly mobilize CCP party members to jump-start the revolutionary strategy.[41] By the end of the Sixth Party Congress, the Comintern appointed Xiang Zhongfa, a leader of the labor movement, as the CCP leader despite his scant experience in party affairs.

Because of Xiang's lack of experience in managing party affairs, the responsibility for party and military operations fell to two CCP party elites: Li Lisan

---

[39] For example, North (1963) suggests that Kremlin leadership played an important role in shaping Li Lisan's radical strategies for uprisings, and the leaders in Moscow contrived directives in a manner that could be interpreted to their advantage no matter the outcome of these directives.

[40] Stalin sent two Comintern agents to China after the collapse of the First United Front. Besso Lominadze was responsible for carrying instructions for an uprising soon to take place in Nanchang, and Heinz Neumann, who called a special meeting of Chinese party elites, organized the Canton Uprising (North 1963).

[41] "政治议决案 [A Political Resolution of the Sixth Party Congress]," July 9, 1928, in *Zhong gong zhong yang wen jian xuan ji* (*CCP Party Center Selected Documents*) (1989, V4: 295–328).

and Zhou Enlai. Zhou was an experienced bureaucrat placed in charge of military affairs after the August 7 Emergency Conference, and he became a member of the Standing Committee after the Sixth Party Congress. By contrast, Li Lisan, a leader of the labor movement, was elected an alternate member of the Standing Committee. Li Lisan later replaced Cai Hesen in the Politburo in November 1928, challenging the more cautious Zhou Enlai (Saich and Yang 1996). Neither Zhou nor Li could dominate each other, but Li continued to pursue radical policies, hoping to impress the Comintern. The radical insurgence led to severe casualties among CCP personnel and military forces. As with Chen Duxiu and Qu Quibai, the failures of CCP's revolutionary tactics led to Li's downfall in 1931.

The ascent of Wang Ming following Li Lisan's downfall served as another clear demonstration of the pivotal role played by Comintern influence in shaping the balance of power during the CCP elites' power struggle. Compared to other CCP elites, Wang was only a junior CCP figure when he gained prominence in the party as a student at Moscow Sun Yat-sen University, not a leader of the early Communist movement. Specifically, Wang was trusted by Comintern leaders in part because he actively participated in the factional fight within the university, a spillover from the Soviet elite factional struggle.[42]

With support from Pavel Mif, a new Comintern leader at the Far East Bureau, Wang returned to China from Moscow and orchestrated a "coup" that resulted in sweeping change to CCP leadership during the Fourth Plenum in 1931. Although Wang Ming was not even a member of the CCP Central Committee prior to the 1931, he became a full member of the Politburo after the meeting. Qu Qiubai, Li Weihan, and Li Lisan were dismissed from their Politburo positions; and Wang Ming, Ren Bishi, Liu Shaoqi, and Wang Kequan, many of whom were students returned from the Soviet Union, were elected to the Politburo. Although Xiang Zhongfa remained the general party secretary, Wang Ming and other CCP elites closely connected to the Comintern became the de facto leaders.

The 1931 Fourth Plenum "coup" sparked the first major party split, leading to an attempt to establish an alternative party center. Luo Zhanglong, an alternate Central Committee member, spearheaded the opposition against the leadership change orchestrated by the Comintern. He sought to establish alternative CCP Politburo and Provincial Party Committees in Jiangsu and Shanghai (Luo 2005; Zhao 1987); however, this party-splitting strategy failed to gain support from key party elites, including Zhou Enlai and Qu Qiubai. Within a few months Luo's effort collapsed, and his CCP membership was revoked.

The Rise and Fall of CCP Elites from Soviet Base Areas. The turbulent leadership turnover at the Party Center from 1927 to 1931 concealed the rise of a new class of CCP elites, who were able to expand their power by cultivating

---

[42] Wang often served as a translator during meetings between Soviet and Comintern leaders and CCP representatives, allowing him to obtain access to Soviet elites (Guo 2014).

5.2 Elite Conflict & Party Fragility (1927–1935)

personal networks, doing so by establishing the Soviet base areas in Jiangxi and Hubei provinces after the KMT purge.[43] This new class of base area leaders later rapidly ascended into the CCP leadership circle after the Comintern influence faded.

Mao Zedong was among these prominent emerging CCP elites, who led the Autumn Uprising and established the Jinggangshan base area, one of three major Soviet base areas formed in 1927.[44] Along with Zhu De, Mao led the Fourth Red Army, significantly expanding the CCP military force and party organization. In fact, 26 percent of the Fourth Red Army controlled by Mao and Zhu were party members in 1929.[45] Success in building a rural base propelled Mao's rise to CCP leadership: He was elected to the Central Committee after the Sixth Party Congress in 1928 even when he was unable to travel to Moscow for it. Although Mao was not in contention for CCP leadership from 1927 to 1931, his success in building a power base in the Jiangxi Soviet base area allowed him to develop important bonds with CCP and military leaders (Gao 2000).

Unfortunately, CCP leaders in the base areas faced severe challenges to their power after the CCP Party Center was forced to move its headquarters from Shanghai to the Jiangxi Soviet base area in 1931. The relocation of the Party Center inevitably generated a clash between the central and local CCP leaders, which emerged as the focal point of the CCP elite power struggle. The fundamental source of conflict stemmed from contention among CCP Central elites to gain control of military and financial resources in the Soviet base areas.[46]

The onset of the CCP elite power struggle during this phase began when the KMT intensified suppression of CCP urban operations in Shanghai in 1931. Several CCP leaders at the Party Center were soon arrested, including the CCP General Party Secretary Xiang Zhongfa.[47] These arrests made Shanghai an untenable location for Party Center headquarters, forcing relocation to the Jiangxi Soviet base area. The Central Soviet Bureau was established after the

---

[43] See Esherick (2022) and Fewsmith (2022) for an excellent study of the bottom-up origins of these base areas.

[44] The other two important Soviet bases were the Xiang-Exi (湘鄂西) Soviet base area in west Hunan-Hubei led by He Long and the E-Yu-Wan (鄂豫皖) Soviet base area in Hubei-Henan-Anhui led by Xu Xiangqian (Saich and Yang 1996).

[45] "红军第四军前委书记毛泽东给中央的报告 [The Report to CCP Party Central by the Fourth Red Army Party Secretary Mao Zedong]," June 1, 1929, in *Zhong gong zhong yang wen jian xuan ji (CCP Party Center Selected Documents)* (1989, V5: 681–687) and "陈毅关于朱毛红军的党务概况报告(二) [The Report of Party Affairs in the Zhu Mao Red Army by Chen Yi, II]," September 1, 1929, in *Zhong gong zhong yang wen jian xuan ji (CCP Party Center Selected Documents)* (1989, V5: 772–790).

[46] Esherick (2022) and Fewsmith (2022) systematically documented these clashes in Shanxi and Jiangxi, respectively.

[47] For instance, Xiang Zhongfa, the CCP general party secretary, betrayed the underground CCP operation in Shanghai after his arrest.

Fourth Plenum in January 1931, and a delegation was sent to the Jiangxi Soviet base area three months later.[48] The arrival of Party Center delegation spelled the end of Mao's dominant power in the base area. Mao lost direct control over the Red Army and was named only to the newly created post of chairman of the Soviet Government in the Jiangxi base area. Mao was further marginalized after the Ningdu Conference in October 1932, during which he was removed from the front line of the Red Army (Saich and Yang 1996). Zhou Enlai and Zhu De then formed the collective leadership in control of the First Red Army.

5.2.2 The Onset of Discriminatory Party-Building Strategies

Leadership turmoil and elite conflicts within the CCP led to a series of radical swings in party-building strategies, often detrimental to the very party mobilization infrastructure that the CCP aimed to strengthen. In this section, I highlight three pivotal moments in which changes in power dynamics among party elites were closely associated with radical shifts in party-building strategies.

Pivotal Moment 1: The Exclusion of the Intelligentsia after Chen Duxiu's Fall. Discriminatory measures for party building started to emerge after Chen Duxiu was removed from CCP leadership. Prior to his fall in August 1927, the CCP rarely discriminated against any nonelites because of their family and occupational backgrounds despite the party's emphasis on recruiting workers.[49] In fact, the CCP party-building strategy showed little departure during the Fifth Party Congress held from April 27 to May 9, 1927, following the KMT's anti-Communist purge. The only differential treatment among nonelites was a revision of recruitment policy in the Party Bylaws approved by the Politburo, in which laborers (e.g., workers, peasants, clerks, and soldiers) were subject to no probation but nonlaborers (e.g., intellectuals and freelancers) were subject to a probationary period of three months.[50] The Party Congress even issued an announcement to accelerate the building of party organizations among poor peasants.[51]

Chen's resignation in July, three months after the Party Congress, changed everything. The new leadership under Qu Qiubai, who was endorsed by the

---

[48] The delegation comprised Ren Bishi, Gu Zuolin, and Wang Jiaxiang.
[49] For instance, one resolution emphasized the recruitment of workers, progressive peasants, and revolutionary intelligentsia into the party. See "组织问题议决案 [Resolution on Party Organization]," April 27, 1927, in *Zhong gong zhong yang wen jian xuan ji* (*CCP Party Center Selected Documents*) (1989, V3: 87–89).
[50] "中国共产党第三次修正章程决案 [Resolution on the CCP's Third Revision of the Party Manifesto]," June 1, 1927, in *Zhong gong zhong yang wen jian xuan ji* (*CCP Party Center Selected Documents*) (1989, V3: 142–155).
[51] "中央通告农字第八号 – 农运策略的说明 [No. 8 Nong Announcement of the Party Center: Explanation of Peasant Movement Tactics)]," June 14, 1927, in *Zhong gong zhong yang wen jian xuan ji* (*CCP Party Center Selected Documents*) (1989, V3: 178–194).

5.2 Elite Conflict & Party Fragility (1927–1935)

Comintern, initiated a radical shift in CCP recruitment strategies during the Provisional Politburo Enlarged Conference on November 9, 1927. At this meeting the CCP announced a set of discriminatory criteria based on family and occupational background for membership recruitment and cadre promotion. The intelligentsia was the target of this first onslaught of discrimination largely because Chen Duxiu was an intellectual. The Politburo justified this radical shift by attributing past setbacks to CCP cadres who were intellectuals and failed to carry out directives issued by the Party Center wholeheartedly.[52] The resolution proposed remedying the situation by demoting CCP cadres from intellectual backgrounds and promoting those with origins among workers or poor peasants. This policy shift aligned with the spirit of putting the proletariat revolution in the hands of the proletariat once the CCP equated the intelligentsia with the bourgeoisie.

Although the CCP did not initially purge intellectuals from the party outright, the Party Center later issued several resolutions establishing quotas for workers and poor peasants in both membership recruitment and cadre appointments, effectively marginalizing the intelligentsia. For instance, on January 3, 1928, the Politburo issued a resolution that set quotas for new recruits in a membership drive: 60 percent for workers and 30 percent for peasants.[53] In another announcement to local party organizations in the same month, the Party Center mandated that cadres organizing labor and mobilizing peasants should comprise primarily workers and peasants, respectively.[54]

Pivotal Moment 2: Following in the Soviet Union' Footsteps amidst Leadership Turmoil. From 1928 to 1931, CCP leadership underwent reshuffling several times. Consequently, party building was in disarray for the CCP because elite conflicts resulted in radical changes in party-building strategies. During this critical period of leadership transition, newly appointed CCP leaders closely monitored the winds of Soviet politics, aiming to closely follow the preferences of Soviet leaders. To illuminate the cascading effect of the intraparty elite power struggle on party-building strategies, I trace the sequences of two radical policy shifts originating in Soviet politics concerning the treatment

---

[52] "最近组织问题的重要任务议决案 [Resolution on Recent Party Organizations' Important Tasks]," November 14, 1927, in *Zhong gong zhong yang wen jian xuan ji (CCP Party Center Selected Documents)* (1989, V3: 468–477).

[53] "广州暴动之意义与教训 [The Significance and Lessons from the Guangzhou Insurgency]," January 3, 1928, in *Zhong gong zhong yang wen jian xuan ji (CCP Party Center Selected Documents)* (1989, V4: 1–44).

[54] See, for example, "中央关于中国政治现状与最近各省工作方针议决案 [Resolution on the Current Political Condition and Recent Provincial Guidance]," January 22, 1928, in *Zhong gong zhong yang wen jian xuan ji (CCP Party Center Selected Documents)* (1989, V4: 85–111); "中央通告第三十二号 – 关于组织工作 [No. 32 Announcement of the Party Center–Concerning Organizational Tasks)]," January 30, 1928, in *Zhong gong zhong yang wen jian xuan ji (CCP Party Center Selected Documents)* (1989, V4: 76–85); "中央致朱德、毛泽东并前委信 [Letter from the Party Center to Zhu De and Mao Zedong]," June 4, 1928, in *Zhong gong zhong yang wen jian xuan ji (CCP Party Center Selected Documents)* (1989, V4: 239–257).

of workers and rich peasants. The policy cascade exemplifies how certain CCP elites embraced party-building strategies catering to the Comintern and Soviet leaders as they conferred power upon these elites.

Prioritizing Workers at All Costs. From 1927 to 1930, the Soviet Union initiated a proletarianization drive for party recruitment, calling for a proportional increase in the number of Communist workers in order to facilitate its acceleration of industrialization in 1927 (Rigby 1968). The left-leaning policy shift in the Soviet Union led to a policy shift at the Sixth World Congress of the Comintern. Bukharin delivered a speech on behalf of the Comintern at the Sixth Party Congress of the CCP in 1928, emphasizing worker leadership over peasants as a strategy for China's Communist revolution.[55]

Sensing the shift in policy orientation, the CCP issued a resolution on party organization that signaled worker-centric proletarianization while marginalizing peasants during the Sixth Party Congress in 1928.[56] The CCP Central Committee further emphasized the importance of mobilizing workers, insisting that they should serve as the leaders in rural mobilization.[57] Upon the Comintern's recommendation to evaluate local party organizations based on the size and composition of their new membership, the CCP responded by intensifying its directives to local party branches.[58] These directives stressed the importance of meeting recruitment quotas for individuals with worker backgrounds, particularly those employed in modern industries across a range of provinces. By contrast, the CCP set no specific quotas for peasant recruitment in rural areas.[59] The emphasis on worker cadres in leadership positions stirred up conflicts among party elites at local party organizations during the

---

[55] "中国革命与中共的任务 – 国际代表在中国共产党第六次大会上的政治报告（节录）[The Chinese Revolution and the CCP's Tasks – Report by the Comintern Representative at the Sixth Party Congress of the CCP (Selected)]," 1928, in *Zhong gong zhong yang wen jian xuan ji* (*CCP Party Center Selected Documents*) (1989 (V11: 133–146).

[56] This resolution criticized an trend in which peasants instead of workers filled the void in local leadership after the purge of intellectuals. "关于组织问题草案之决议 [Resolution on the Draft of Organizational Issues]," July 10, 1928, in *Zhong gong zhong yang wen jian xuan ji* (*CCP Party Center Selected Documents*) (1989, V4: 441–466).

[57] "中国共产党中央委员会告全体同志书 [CCP Central Committee Announcement to All Party Members]," November 11, 1928, in *Zhong gong zhong yang wen jian xuan ji* (*CCP Party Center Selected Documents*) (1989, V4: 695–710); "组织问题决议案 [Resolution on Organization Issues]," June, 1929, in *Zhong gong zhong yang wen jian xuan ji* (*CCP Party Center Selected Documents*) (1989, V5: 213–248).

[58] "中国共产党的最近组织任务 – 共产国际东方部议决案 [Recent Organizational Tasks of the CCP – Resolution by the Comintern Eastern Bureau]," August, 1930, in *Zhong gong zhong yang wen jian xuan ji* (*CCP Party Center Selected Documents*) (1989, V6: 596–607).

[59] For instance, see "中央通告第七十三号 – 发展产业工人党员加强党的无产阶级基础 [No. 73 Announcement of Party Center–Further Recruitment of Workers to Strengthen the Proletariat Foundation of the Party]," March 22, 1930, in *Zhong gong zhong yang wen jian xuan ji* (*CCP Party Center Selected Documents*) (1989, V6: 49–54); see "全国组织报告的决议案 [Resolution on the National Report of Organization]," May 1, 1931, in *Zhong gong zhong yang wen jian xuan ji* (*CCP Party Center Selected Documents*) (1989, V7: 228–235).

5.2 Elite Conflict & Party Fragility (1927–1935)

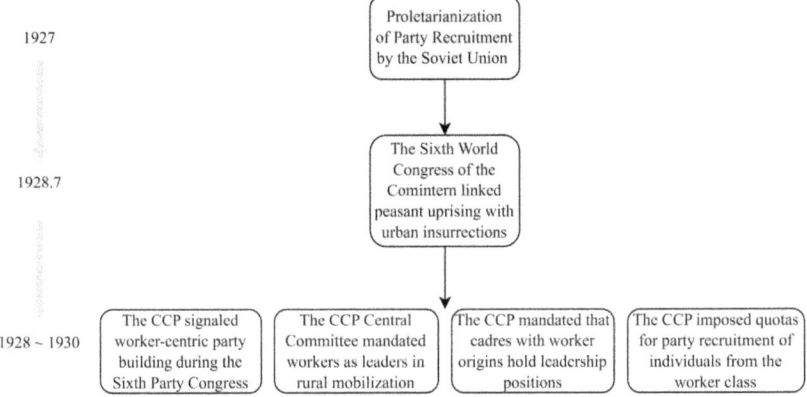

FIGURE 5.5 The policy cascade on the rise of worker

process of cadre (re)appointment, forcing the Party Center to issue a resolution to resolve factional conflicts within the party.[60]

Notably, CCP central leaders radicalized their policy shift even though neither the Soviet Union nor the Comintern explicitly advocated discriminatory policies against other social classes. When Li Lisan took over the operation of the Party Center in 1929, he initiated a series of leftist policies (左倾主义) in the hope of preempting accusations of being rightist (右倾主义) by the Comintern.[61] Under Li's leadership, the CCP not only escalated radical insurgencies in both urban and rural areas but also placed exclusive emphasis on an individual's socioeconomic background as the sole criterion for party recruitment and cadre promotion, giving priority to workers over all other proletariat classes. The policy cascade is illustrated in Figure 5.5.

Turning against Rich Peasants. The 180-degree turn in CCP policies toward rich peasants (富农) exemplifies another radical shift in CCP party-building strategies resulting from the policy cascade from Soviet politics and the Comintern. Prior to policy shifts in the Soviet Union, the CCP expanded peasant recruitment without rejecting rich peasants. In "A Political Resolution," issued by the Sixth Party Congress of the CCP held in Moscow in 1928, the Politburo even explicitly stated its error in struggling against rich peasants while recognizing that poor peasants constituted the core of the proletariat and middle peasants were part of the broader coalition.[62] In another resolution concerning rural

---

[60] See discussion of this resolution on party-building outcomes during this period. "中央关于党内宣传派别问题决议案 [Resolution on Party Propaganda on Social Origins Issue]," January 18, 1929, in *Zhong gong zhong yang wen jian xuan ji* (*CCP Party Center Selected Documents*) (1989, V5: 13–16).
[61] See Yang (1991).
[62] "政治议决案 [Political Resolution]," July 9, 1928, in *Zhong gong zhong yang wen jian xuan ji* (*CCP Party Center Selected Documents*) (1989, V4: 295–328).

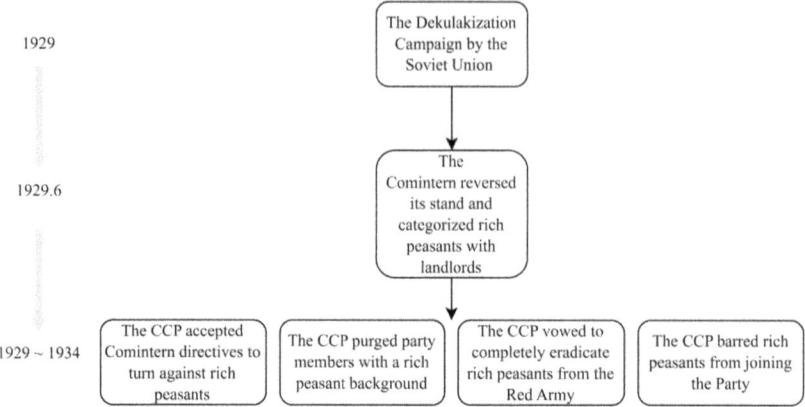

FIGURE 5.6 The policy cascade on the demise of rich peasants

mobilization in early 1929, the Politburo maintained that rich peasants could still have been revolutionaries, hence the party should try to coopt them into their campaigns against warlords, landlords, and rural tycoons.[63]

Just when the CCP leaders had begun to embrace rich peasants, it was forced to swiftly change direction shortly after Stalin initiated a campaign to liquidate kulaks as a class as part of rural collectivization in the Soviet Union in 1929.[64] In June 1929 the Comintern immediately changed its position toward rich peasants, categorizing them along with landlords and criticizing the CCP's lenient policy toward them.[65] The directive explicitly rejected the cooptation of rich peasants, citing Lenin's thoughts on the alliance between the proletariat and peasants (Figure 5.6).

In August 1929 the CCP promptly issued a resolution, aligning with the Comintern's directive from the previous month, which explicitly barred rich peasants from joining the peasants' association.[66] The CCP further accepted the new directives from the Comintern, categorically rejecting the admission of rich peasants into the party.[67] The CCP vowed to eradicate rich peasants from

---

[63] "中央通告第二十八号 – 农民运动的策略 (一) [No. 28 Announcement of Party Center – The Tactics of Peasant Movement]," February 3, 1929, in *Zhong gong zhong yang wen jian xuan ji* (*CCP Party Center Selected Documents*) (1989, V5: 17–22).

[64] See discussion in Rigby (1968).

[65] For directive from the Comintern, see "共产国际执行委员与中国共产党书 [Letter from Comintern Executive Committee to the CCP]," June 7, 1929, in *Zhong gong zhong yang wen jian xuan ji* (*CCP Party Center Selected Documents*) (1989, V5: 688–699).

[66] "中央关于接受共产国际对于农民问题之指示的决议 [Resolution on Accepting Comintern's Directives on the Peasant Issue]," August, 1929, in *Zhong gong zhong yang wen jian xuan ji* (*CCP Party Center Selected Documents*) (1989, V5: 446–460).

[67] "中国共产党的最近任务 – 共产国际东方部议决案 [Recent Tasks of the CCP – Resolution from the Comintern Eastern Bureau]," August, 1930, in *Zhong gong zhong yang wen jian xuan ji* (*CCP Party Center Selected Documents*) (1989, V6: 596–609).

5.2 Elite Conflict & Party Fragility (1927–1935)

the party through a series of resolutions in ensuing months.[68] These purges even preceded the great purges by Stalin in the 1930s. Ironically, the CCP initiated the purge of rich peasants even though the concept of *kulaks* in the Soviet Union was very different from that of rich peasants in China because the means of production in rural areas differed widely in these two societies (Yang 2009). Consequently, the CCP struggled to define "rich peasant" during the implementation of party policies in rural areas, sometimes using the concept subjectively in order to categorize those middle peasants who did not support CCP policies.[69]

Pivotal Moment 3: The Fall of Li Lisan and the Center – Local Conflict. The fall of Li Lisan and the 1931 "coup" elevated proletarianization among the CCP's party-building strategies to a new level. Aiming to gain the blessing of the Comintern and Soviet leaders, the new CCP leaders reinforced worker-centric party-building strategies while purging party members with rich peasant background from the membership roll. The radical left turn of CCP party-building strategies encountered pushback by CCP leaders in Soviet base areas, where political survival rested on a peasant-centric mobilization infrastructure.

The clash between CCP central and local leaders manifested in their conflicting party-building strategies. On one hand, through a series of resolutions and correspondence, the Politburo urged local party branches to initiate a leadership transformation in grassroots party organizations and emphasize the recruitment of workers even in remote rural areas within the Soviet territories.[70] These directives went as far as mandating the purge of CCP

---

[68] "中央通告第八十四号 [Party Central No. 84 Announcement]," July 21, 1930, in *Zhong gong zhong yang wen jian xuan ji (CCP Party Center Selected Documents)* (1989, V6: 173–177).

[69] For instance, the Party Center issued a letter to the Central Bureau for the Soviet areas to reject their definition of rich peasants on November 10, 1931, contending that household grain yields should not be used as the criterion to define rich peasants but whether a household hired any tenants in the production process. See more details in "中央为土地问题致中央苏区中央局信 [Party Center's Letter on Land Issue to Central Bureau of the Soviet Base Areas]," November 10, 1931, in *Zhong gong zhong yang wen jian xuan ji (CCP Party Center Selected Documents)* (1989, V7: 500–511). Yang (2009), however, points out that hiring tenants, leasing land, issuing small loans, and operating small businesses were typical in the traditional Chinese economy regardless of wealth status but not necessarily a form of expropriation.

[70] "全国组织报告的决议案 [Resolution on the National Report of Party Organization]," May 1, 1931, in *Zhong gong zhong yang wen jian xuan ji (CCP Party Center Selected Documents)* (1989, V7: 228–235); "中央关于鄂豫皖省委的决议 [Resolution on the E-Yu-Wan Provincial Committee by the Party Center]," May 6, 1931, in *Zhong gong zhong yang wen jian xuan ji (CCP Party Center Selected Documents)* (1989, V7: 250–257); "中央给赣东北省委的信 [Letter to the North Jiangxi Provincial Committee by the Party Center]," May 6, 1931, in *Zhong gong zhong yang wen jian xuan ji (CCP Party Center Selected Documents)* (1989, V7: 236–249); "中央致闽粤赣苏区省委的信 [Letter to Fujian, Guangdong, Jiangxi, and Jiangsu Provincial Committees by the Party Center]," August 29, 1931, in *Zhong gong zhong yang wen jian xuan ji (CCP Party Center Selected Documents)* (1989, V7: 347–354); "中央关于苏维埃区域党的组织决议案 [Resolution on Soviet Area Party Organization by the Party Center]," May 1931,

members with rich peasant backgrounds and imposing a prohibition on their admission into the party. In particular, the Party Center was critical of Mao's leadership because of the predominance of cadres with peasant backgrounds within the Red Army.[71]

On the other hand, CCP leaders in Soviet base areas resisted the call from the Party Center to implement strictly discriminatory measures in party building. The leadership of the Soviet areas insisted upon treating workers, poor peasants, and tenants as equals.[72] Some local CCP leaders actually criticized the discriminatory approach as a narrow-minded and rigid application of a principle that disregarded reality.[73] In particular, the Soviet Central Bureau issued a resolution[74] in 1933 explicitly criticizing leftist party-building strategies that prohibited the recruitment of members of the intelligentsia sympathetic to the worker class and purged party members simply because of their social status as rich peasants or intellectuals.

5.2.3 An Out of Sync Mass Mobilization Infrastructure

The development of CCP party mobilization infrastructure during the period from 1927 to 1935 was marked by a paradox. On the one hand, the party demonstrated resilience, swiftly recovering from the KMT purge in 1927 and registering significant expansion in membership over the next eight years. On the other hand, most grassroots party organizations lasted for only a few years,

---

in *Zhong gong zhong yang wen jian xuan ji* (*CCP Party Center Selected Documents*) (1989, V7: 268–272); "中央关于目前农民斗争的形势与我们的任务的决议 [Resolution on Current Situation of the Peasant Struggle by the Party Center]," September 15, 1932, in *Zhong gong zhong yang wen jian xuan ji* (*CCP Party Center Selected Documents*) (1989, V8: 468–482).

[71] "关于目前政治形势及中共党的紧急任务决议案 [Emergent Resolution of the CCP Concerning Current Political Affairs]," May 9, 1931, in *Zhong gong zhong yang wen jian xuan ji* (*CCP Party Center Selected Documents*) (1989, V7: 258–267); "中央给苏区各级党部及红军的训令 [Instruction to All Levels of Party Branches and the Red Army in Soviet Areas by the Party Center]," June 16, 1931, in *Zhong gong zhong yang wen jian xuan ji* (*CCP Party Center Selected Documents*) (1989, V7: 309–329); "中央给苏区中央局并红军总前委的指示信 [Instruction Letter to Soviet Central Bureau and Frontline Commanding Center of the Red Army by the Party Center]," August 30, 1931, in *Zhong gong zhong yang wen jian xuan ji* (*CCP Party Center Selected Documents*) (1989, V7: 355–375).

[72] "党的建设问题决议案 [Resolution on Party Building Issues]," November 1–5, 1931, in *Zhong gong zhong yang wen jian xuan ji* (*CCP Party Center Selected Documents*) (1989, V7: 464–484); "苏区中央局关于争取和完成江西及其邻近省区革命首先胜利的决议 [Resolution on Soviet Central Bureau's Goal to Achieve First Revolution Success in Jiangxi and Nearby Provinces]," June 17, 1932, in *Zhong gong zhong yang wen jian xuan ji* (*CCP Party Center Selected Documents*) (1989, V8: 240–261).

[73] "红军问题决议案 [Resolution on the Red Army Issue]," November 1–5, 1931, in *Zhong gong zhong yang wen jian xuan ji* (*CCP Party Center Selected Documents*) (1989, V7: 485–491).

[74] "苏区中央局关于纠正发展和巩固党的组织中错误倾向的决议 [Soviet Central Bureau Resolution on Correcting, Developing, and Consolidating the Mistaken Trend in Party Organization]," May 29, 1933, in *Zhong gong zhong yang wen jian xuan ji* (*CCP Party Center Selected Documents*) (1989, V9: 201–205).

5.2 Elite Conflict & Party Fragility (1927–1935)

and party membership shrank by 90 percent after the loss of the Jiangxi Soviet area in 1934. Although brutal repression by the KMT contributed to the CCP's misfortunes, the fundamental source of its fragility lay in its weak mobilization infrastructure, which was the product of the conflictual and sometimes self-defeating party-building strategies revealed earlier. The fluctuating and occasionally radical shifts in party-building strategies engendered a sense of uncertainty among grassroots party organizations, leaving their members unsure about the path to take in developing mass mobilization infrastructure.

The weakness of the CCP's mobilization infrastructure is best captured by two contradictions. First, despite a rapid increase in party membership, the number of grassroots party organizations steadily declined, indicating a lack of effective organization at the grassroots level. Second, while the central and local party leadership shifted toward a worker-centric background, the majority of party expansion came from recruiting peasants, resulting in a disconnect between the leadership and the members in terms of mindset and background. These contradictions highlight the lack of effective communication channels and organizational structures within the CCP, impeding the implementation of party policies.

A Plate of Loose Sand: Mass Party Membership without Mass Grassroots Organizations. At first glance, CCP membership seemed to rebound quickly after the 1927 anti-Communist purge by the KMT. Although membership fell sharply to 10,000 after the purge, the establishment of rural base areas provided much-needed territorial protection to the CCP in party expansion. By 1929 the overall party membership surpassed its height on the eve of the 1927 purge in a mere two-year span. Nevertheless, the elite power struggle and conflictual party-building strategies generated several setbacks in the CCP's efforts to expand its mobilization infrastructure, as demonstrated in Figure 5.7.

For instance, the abrupt shift toward worker-centric recruitment and the purging of the intelligentsia led to a decline of party membership from 1929 to 1930. Although party membership doubled in six months in early 1930, the sudden shift against rich peasants and the 1931 Fourth Plenum "coup" again slowed down the party membership expansion. After 1931 the Party Center was occupied by fighting against KMT repression in urban China, which gave local leaders in Soviet base areas some autonomy in building the party as well as the Red Army. Party membership dramatically increased threefold from 1931 to 1934; nevertheless, the CCP suffered another deadly blow when the Jiangxi Soviet base fell during the KMT Fifth Encirclement campaign in 1934. This resulted in a steep decline in CCP membership, plummeting from 411,000 to approximately 40,000 on the eve of the Sino-Japanese War in 1937.

The substantial growth in party membership served as a veil, concealing the inherent weaknesses in the CCP's mobilization infrastructure. Notwithstanding the overall increase in membership, the grassroots organizations, including party cells and branches, were unable to keep pace with this expansion and in

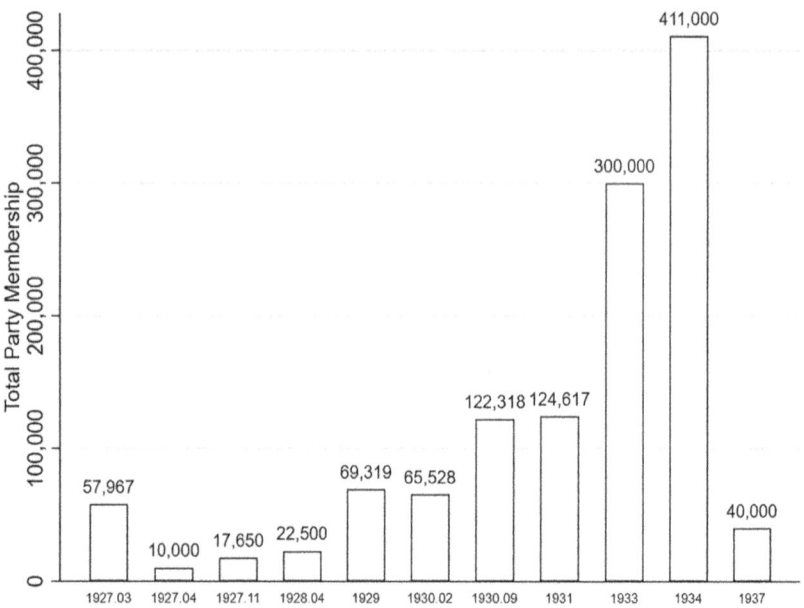

FIGURE 5.7 CCP membership (1927–1937).
Note: Author's database. See Appendix A for data source.

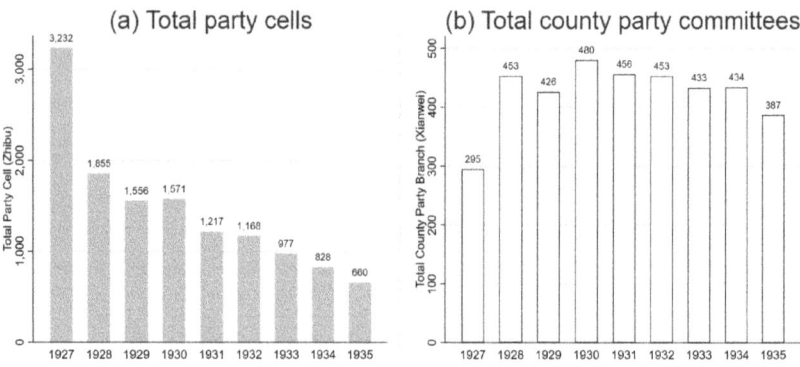

FIGURE 5.8 CCP grassroots party cells and county party committees (1927–1935).
Note: Author's database. See Appendix A for data sources.

fact experienced a decline during the same period. Figure 5.8 shows a steady decline in the number of grassroots party cells (支部) from 1927 to 1935. In its peak year of 1927, the CCP boasted a total of 3,232 party cells spread across the country; however, the number of party cells declined by nearly half in 1928 because of the anti-Communist purge and ill-fated radical uprisings.

5.2 Elite Conflict & Party Fragility (1927–1935)

Over subsequent years this contraction continued, resulting in only 660 party cells remaining by 1935. The number of CCP county committees followed a similar trend, but the decline was not as steep as that of party cells. This pattern stands in stark contrast to the period from 1921 to 1927, when the number of CCP grassroots party cells consistently grew over time. The contrasting patterns of party membership and party cells suggest that during this period, most party members were loosely organized, lacking a cohesive organization gluing them together at the grassroots level.

Internal party communications offer a vivid illustration of the chaotic and ineffective nature of grassroots party operations as exemplified by the provincial party committee in Hebei.[75] Over the span of ten years from 1927 to 1937, two provincial CCP committees (顺直省委[Shunzhi shengwei] and 河北省委[Hebei shengwei]) were established in the province. From 1927 to 1930, the Shunzhi committee embarked on a tumultuous journey marked by an extraordinary ten reorganizations and nine changes in the position of provincial party secretary. The provincial committee was completely dismantled twice, triggered by defections of provincial party leaders. This dysfunction persisted from 1930 to 1937 after it was reorganized as the Hebei provincial committee: It experienced another turbulent period characterized by five cycles of destruction, eleven reconstructions as a temporary provincial committee, six reestablishments, and twelve changes in provincial party secretary.

Although the instability of the Hebei provincial committee may be attributed to KMT suppression, the situation in the Jiangxi Soviet base area, once home to the Party Center, fared no better. From 1930 to 1934, the base area witnessed a turbulent period marked by a violent purge targeting the so-called "AB League" within the local party, government, and military organizations.[76] The purge resulted in frequent leadership changes within these organizations and the tragic deaths of thousands of CCP members, Red Army soldiers, and cadres. The tumultuous events significantly weakened the mobilization infrastructure and party cohesion, contributing to the eventual fall of Jiangxi base area to the KMT.[77]

Tension in the Transformation of Party Membership Composition. The contrasting composition of party membership between the leadership and rank-and-file members is another important indicator of the CCP's weak mobilization infrastructure. The tension manifested mainly between dogmatic worker-oriented party-building strategies and pragmatic approaches in the Soviet base areas. This incongruity highlights the lack of an effective mobilization infrastructure as party leaders and rank-and-file members shared little common ground.

---

[75] See *Zhong guo gong chan dang he bei sheng zu zhi shi zi liao: 1922–1987* (*The CCP Hebei Province Party Organization History Documents: 1922–1987*) (1990: 90).
[76] For the discussion of the AB League purge, see Gao (1999) and Dai and Luo (1994).
[77] See Fewsmith (2022) for a study of party struggle in Jiangxi during this period.

To begin, the peasantry primarily contributed to the rapid expansion of rank-and-file party membership despite the Party Center's repeated calls for increased recruitment of workers and for the establishment of party cells in urban areas. Although total party membership rebounded in 1928 to around 40,000, workers amounted to no more than 4,000 because they did not respond enthusiastically to urban mobilization by the CCP.[78] Another 1928 report suggests that party members with worker origins accounted for only 10.9 percent, and those with peasant origins accounted for 76.6 percent of total party membership.[79] This pattern sharply contrasts with the situation prior to the anti-Communist purge in 1927 when workers accounted for 50.8 percent of CCP membership. Although the CCP had expanded its membership to 120,000 by 1930, the number of workers from modern industries comprised only around 2,000 members, representing a mere 1.6 percent of the total membership.[80]

The decline in the share of workers in rank-and-file party membership prompted the Party Center to issue multiple memorandums to local party organizations, cautioning them about this "concerning" trend. In a 1928 memorandum,[81] for example, the Party Center warned that party organizations had basically ceased to function in major urban centers across the country because of a lack of worker mobilization. In yet another resolution in 1928, the CCP expressed its dismay over the growing disparity between the number of party members with peasant origins, which was seven times higher than that of those with worker origins. Party Center leaders of the CCP were deeply concerned that this alarming trend could lead to workers blaming the CCP for neglecting their interests and prioritizing peasants instead.[82]

Meanwhile, CCP leaders in Soviet base areas continued to sidestep the call from the Party Center and pursued a pragmatic approach by recruiting peasants into the party. A 1933 party organization report on regional party building in Jiangxi exemplified the patterns of party membership expansion in

---

[78] "中共中央政治局向国际的报告 [CCP Politburo Report to the Comintern]," November 28, 1928, in *Zhong gong zhong yang wen jian xuan ji (CCP Party Center Selected Documents)*, (1989, V4: 714–722).

[79] "关于组织问题草案之决议 [Resolution on the Draft of an Organizational Issue]," July 10, 1928, in *Zhong gong zhong yang wen jian xuan ji (CCP Party Center Selected Documents)*, (1989, V4: 452).

[80] "关于传达国际决议的报告 [Report on Conveying the Resolution from the Comintern]," September 24, 1930, in *Zhong gong zhong yang wen jian xuan ji (CCP Party Center Selected Documents)*, (1989, V6: 359–388).

[81] "中央通告第三十二号－关于组织工作 [No. 32 Announcement by the Party Center–Concerning Organizational Work]," January 30, 1928, in *Zhong gong zhong yang wen jian xuan ji (CCP Party Center Selected Documents)*, (1989, V4: 76–84).

[82] "关于组织问题草案之决议 [Resolution on the Draft of an Organizational Issue]," July 10, 1928, in *Zhong gong zhong yang wen jian xuan ji (CCP Party Center Selected Documents)* (1989, V4: 441–466).

Soviet base areas.[83] Party expansion increased threefold during the "Red May Recruitment Campaign" – from around 30,000 members in early 1932 to 97,451 by September 1933. Nonetheless, only 13.43 percent of the new recruits were workers, falling short of the intended target of recruiting at least 30 percent workers. Of the 17,507 new members added, 56 percent were poor peasants.

The Party Center's urge to build a worker-centric mobilization infrastructure only succeeded in transforming both central and local leaderships. In a report to the Comintern,[84] the CCP proudly highlighted the transformation of the Politburo following the Fourth Plenum in 1931 as one of its notable achievements, with 10 of 16 (62.5 percent) Politburo members coming from worker origins. The composition of the Politburo stood in stark contrast with the CCP rank-and-file membership at the time – less than 5 percent of the party members had worker origins in 1930.[85]

Similarly, the quota for worker representation led to a transformation in grassroots party leadership positions. Most of these new cadres, nevertheless, were inexperienced and uneducated, spelling problematic leadership for grassroots party organizations. In a cadre survey in Jiangxi, the CCP reported that among 419 cadres in 16 counties, 192 of them (46 percent) had worker origins and 184 of them (44 percent) had poor peasant origins. Among these local cadres, only thirteen of them joined the party before 1927 (3.1 percent), and 55 percent of them had joined the party fewer than two years later. Meanwhile, 20 percent of the cadres were found to be completely illiterate, and 43 percent could read but not write. As a result, nearly two-thirds of the cadres in Jiangxi were unable to provide written reports to higher-level party organizations, hindering the effective communication and functioning of the party. In addition, forty-one cadres were purged from the party during this period, more than 50 percent of whom had a background as landlords or rich peasants.

5.3 SUMMARY

Drawing upon internal party documents and communications, I illuminate the link between the power struggle among CCP elites and the detrimental party-building strategies that led to a feeble mass mobilization infrastructure spanning 1921–1937. One may argue that the disagreement in CCP

---

[83] The statistics were reported in "党的组织状况 [Current Stage of the Party Organization]" in *Zhong yang ge ming gen ju di shi liao xuan bian (The selection of central party revolutionary base historical documents)* (1982 V1: 674–675).

[84] "中共中央总书记向忠发给共产国际的报告 [Report to the Comintern by CCP General Party Secretary Xiang Zhonfa]," February 22, 1931, in *Zhong gong zhong yang wen jian xuan ji (CCP Party Center Selected Documents)* (1989, V7: 115–138).

[85] For the composition of workers in total CCP membership, see "目前政治形势与党的组织任务 [Current Political Situation and the Tasks of Party Organization]," July 22, 1930, in *Zhong gong zhong yang wen jian xuan ji (CCP Party Center Selected Documents)* (1989, V6:185).

revolutionary strategies fueled intense conflicts among party elites; in reality, the disagreement over party policies was not the root cause but instead a consequence of the ongoing power struggle among CCP elites. Party elites' animosity was fundamentally motivated by disputes over personal power, manifested in control over financial and military resources.

The CCP elite power struggle began after Chen Duxiu's loss of leadership in 1927. Within this intense period of power struggle among CCP elites, the party implemented discriminatory practices in recruitment and promotion that were detached from the realities. These practices were primarily motivated by some party elites' aspirations to follow closely the preferred strategies promoted by the Comintern and the Soviet leaders, which wielded significant influence over the selection of CCP leaders. Consequently, the CCP party organization became fragile and susceptible to external repression, an unexpected outcome.

By 1935 the CCP appeared to be on the verge of collapse. Party membership declined by 90 percent, and the party lost control of all its Soviet base areas. This loss of territorial control, coupled with a significant decrease in human and financial resources, left the CCP ill-equipped to withstand the KMT's military onslaught. When the Party Center of the CCP and its remaining forces finally settled in Shaan-Gan-Ning in 1935, they found themselves once again surrounded by KMT troops.

Well-known by now, this was not the last chapter for the CCP. The party underwent a remarkable transformation, successfully building a strong mass mobilization infrastructure in rural areas. In the next chapter, I delve into its internal dynamics and the impact of external contingent events that contributed to the significant transformation achieved by the CCP after 1935.

6

Mao's Rise and the Birth of a Strong Party (1935–1945)

Upon their arrival in northern Shaanxi in October 1935, the CCP and its First Red Army were a group of exhausted and demoralized men and women who exhibited few if any signs of a resilient revolutionary party in the making. Party membership had shrunk to 40,000, and most grassroots party organizations had ceased to function. Any observers would have anticipated the CCP's imminent collapse at that time, and few would have predicted the remarkable turnaround by the end of Sino-Japanese War in 1945 marked by a mass membership exceeding 1.2 million and a dynamic mobilization infrastructure in rural areas. Importantly, the CCP's resilient rural mobilization infrastructure was able to facilitate the mobilization of crucial financial resources from rural China without provoking widespread resentment.

How did the CCP manage to undergo such a remarkable organizational transformation? Johnson (1962) pinpoints the Sino-Japanese War as a crucial factor because it engendered a political opportunity for the CCP's revival through nationalism. Similarly, Koss (2018) highlights the political vacuum behind enemy lines, created by the Japanese invasion, enabling the CCP to expand its operations and influence. Meanwhile, Selden (1971) attributes the CCP's success to the land distribution and economic program that won the hearts and minds of peasants. Although these arguments hold some truth, one must not overlook the mounting evidence that the CCP continuously struggled in garnering popular support – even within CCP base areas – during the Sino-Japanese War.[1] These struggles reveal that the CCP had no inherent appeal for peasants, and the Sino-Japanese War did not naturally make the peasantry embrace the Party. In fact, Johnson (1977) and Selden (1995) later acknowledged the limitations of their arguments. The difficulty of relying

---

[1] See Saich and Yang (1996) and Saich (2021) for excellent summaries of the key findings in the studies of base areas.

solely on ideology and nationalism to garner peasant support is unsurprising because the communist movements in the Southeast Asia encountered similar challenges.[2]

The catalyst for the CCP's transformation during the Sino-Japanese War, I contend, emerged between 1935 and 1938. Specifically, the shifting tides in elite politics from 1935 to 1938 laid the foundation for Mao's later dominant leadership, enabling him to successfully fend off challenges posed by his main intraparty rivals: Zhang Guotao and Wang Ming. This power consolidation by Mao was instrumental in shaping the subsequent party-building strategies: It brought about favorable circumstances for the CCP to abandon discriminatory party-building tactics and instead embark on a significant expansion of its rural mobilization infrastructure. Not only did the CCP prioritize building a peasant-centered mobilization infrastructure and strengthen its presence in rural areas, but the assimilation of intellectuals also bolstered the party's bureaucratic capacity.[3] This expansion prepared the party for the subsequent grain extraction after the fiscal shock of 1941 (see Chapter 4).

Tracing the cascading effect of elite politics on party building reveals another important observation: The significance of contingent events in reshaping the power dynamics among CCP elites. Scholars commonly consider the Yan'an Thought Rectification campaign as a pivotal moment that elevated Mao to a dominant leadership position.[4] Nevertheless, Mao would not have been able to launch that campaign without his earlier triumphs in overcoming challenges from Zhang Guotao and Wang Ming. Although Mao strategically plotted the campaign to consolidate his power, the tipping point in shifting the balance of power had as much to do with the misfortunes of his rivals as it did with his own maneuvers: The military failure of the Fourth Red Army led by Zhang and the erosion of the support of Wang by the Comintern and Stalin. In essence, these unexpected events seriously weakened the sources of power of his rivals, clearing the obstacles to Mao's power consolidation.

6.1 FROM CONTESTED LEADERSHIP TO DOMINANT LEADERSHIP

From 1935 to 1945, Mao slowly but steadily consolidated his power, becoming the CCP's paramount leader. Undoubtedly, Mao's adeptness in

---

[2] Staniland (2014) offers compelling evidence by comparing communist movements in the Philippines, French Indochina, and Malaya.
[3] Huang (2024) provides a detailed account of the training of CCP cadres and the assimilation of intellectuals by the CCP during the Sino-Japanese War.
[4] See Gao (2000) and Teiwes (1994). *The Vladimirov Diaries* also depicts Mao's strategic behaviors in manipulating tensions among CCP elites and marginalizing Wang Ming and Zhang Guotao in Yan'an (Vladimirov 1975).

6.1 From Contested Leadership to Dominant Leadership

outmaneuvering rival CCP elites can be attributed to his strategic manipulation of elite relations and the patronage network he cultivated during his leadership in the Jiangxi era, particularly in spearheading the peasant revolution. The establishment of Soviet base areas and the leadership of the Red Army in rural China provided Mao with the crucial political capital and prestige that set him apart from other CCP elites. Nevertheless, a careful study of the sequence of events leading to Mao's ascent highlights the significance of external factors and contingent events.

Compared to the earlier period, the diminishing influence of the Comintern during the Long March emboldened Mao in this quest for power. The CCP leadership often had to make critical decisions regarding military and party tactics without the guidance or consultation of the Comintern because of the loss of its communication channel. The dissipating Comintern influence benefitted CCP elites whose source of power stemmed from the domestic patronage network.

6.1.1 The Zunyi Meeting: The Launchpad for Mao's Return to the CCP Leadership Circle

The first monumental event for Mao's power ascent occurred during the Long March. The KMT's Fifth Encirclement Campaign finally broke the CCP's defense in 1934, forcing it to abandon the Jiangxi Soviet base area and launched the Long March. The military campaign was a success for the KMT, but it inadvertently facilitated Mao's return to the CCP leadership circle by undermining the source of power possessed by Mao's rivals.

Mao's return to CCP's leadership circle began at the outset of the Long March. The CCP held the expanded Politburo Conference in Zunyi in January 1935, a meeting that was one of the most critical turning points in the resurrection of Mao's leadership.[5] On the main agenda of the Zunyi Conference was the reevaluation of CCP military tactics in response to the military debacle at Jiangxi Soviet base area. With support from Zhang Wentian and other party leaders, Mao became the leading voice of opposition to the previous party line and military tactics upheld by Bo Gu and Otto Braun in this conference. Desperate for alternative strategies to revive the CCP, many party and military leaders sided with Mao. At its conclusion, Mao joined the Standing Committee of the Politburo, becoming one of five CCP leaders in charge of Party and military decisions. Although Mao's status initially rose in the military command, not in the party ranks, the Zunyi Conference marked the first crucial step in his ascent to the pinnacle of CCP leadership.

Notably, the Zunyi Conference did not immediately elevate Mao to the highest leadership position within the party or the military command. Instead,

---

[5] See Braun (1982), Cheng (2006), Teiwes (1994), Wu (2013b), and Yang and Yang (1986) for detailed discussion of elite struggle during the Zunyi meeting.

Zhang Wentian, who had ranked No. 2 in the Party after 1931, replaced Bo Gu to become the General Secretary of the CCP.[6] The military command leadership was shared by Zhou Enlai and Zhu De, who helped lead the First Red Army and the Fourth Red Army, respectively. In the division of labor among members of the Standing Committee of the Politburo, Mao was tasked with assisting Zhou Enlai as military commander.[7]

Nonetheless, Mao seized the moment and gained considerable power from 1935 to 1938, benefiting from Zhang Wentian's collective leadership style and Zhou Enlai's untimely illness. Zhang Wentian was an intellectual who had been responsible for the CCP Propaganda department since 1931 (Cheng 2006). He was one of the key CCP elites who aligned with Mao during the Zunyi Conference. The alignment largely stemmed from their repeated interactions in the same military unit during the Long March, which provided Zhang with numerous opportunities to engage in extensive discussions with Mao (Cheng 2006: 130–134). Because military strategy was crucial for CCP survival during this period – an area outside Zhang's expertise – he adopted a collective leadership by delegating key military decisions to other CCP leaders with greater military expertise (Wu 2013b). Meanwhile, although Zhou Enlai was responsible for the CCP military command after January 1935, he contracted amoebic dysentery in August 1935. Consequently, Mao became the de facto military commander of the First Red Army, with Zhou assuming the role of his assistant. Mao's increasing influence within the party can be witnessed in the telegrams sent out by the CCP Politburo from October 1935 until October 1938: Among 451 with Zhang Wentian's signature, 64 percent of them were cosigned by Mao (Zhang and Zhou 2012, Zhang 2013). By the time three major Red Army forces met in October 1936, Mao had obtained the highest military commander position within the CCP (Wu 2013b: 55–57).

6.1.2 The Strategic Mistake by Zhang Guotao as a Helping Hand to Mao

After the Zunyi Conference, Mao faced perhaps the most critical challenge from Zhang Guotao, who attempted to wrest power from Mao and other CCP leaders.[8] This confrontation led to a split in both the party and the military

---

[6] See Wu (2013b: 46–48) for reasons Zhang Wentian became the CCP General Party Secretary after Bo Gu resigned.
[7] The meeting record of the Zunyi Conference remained elusive among party historians. The most crucial revelation came from detailed notes recorded by Chen Yun, later published as "(乙) 遵义政治局扩大会议[(Second) Zunyi Enlarged Politburo Conference]" in *Zhong gong dang shi zi liao (Historical Documents of Chinese Communist Party Center)* (1982, V6: 1–12). See Chen (1982 [1935]).
[8] In an interview with Edgar Snow in 1960, Mao reflected that the struggle with Zhang Guotao during the Long March in 1935 was the darkest period of his life because the party faced a critical risk of fragmentation that could have led to its doom Wu (2013b: 45).

a few months later in 1935. Unfortunately for Zhang, his miscalculation in military strategy resulted in a disastrous defeat for his troops, effectively discrediting his bid for CCP leadership.

Like Mao, Zhang Guotao accumulated his power through years of experience in managing CCP party and military affairs. Zhang was one of the delegates attending the First Party Congress in 1921 and a leader in the labor movement. After appointed as the leader of the E-Yu-Wan Soviet base area in April 1931, Zhang gained considerable influence and power. This base area housed the Fourth Red Army, one of the strongest CCP military units at that time. To expand his patronage network, Zhang initiated several purges and reshuffled local leaders in both party organizations and in the Fourth Red Army shortly after his arrival (Sheng 1985: 41–45). The Fourth Red Army continued to expand, fueling Zhang's ascent within the CCP.

The clash between Mao and Zhang Guotao intensified during the Long March when they held divergent opinions on CCP military tactics. Although Mao had returned to the highest leadership circle of the CCP after the Zunyi Conference in January 1935, the First Red Army led by Mao was less equipped (under 20,000 military personnel) compared to the Fourth Red Army led by Zhang (80,000 men strong).[9] When Mao's First Red Army and Zhang's Fourth Red Army met in June 1935 during the Long March, the CCP held an expanded Politburo meeting in Liangherkou,[10] trying to reach a consensus on the military strategies and leadership conflict between Mao and Zhang. During this meeting, a fierce disagreement erupted between Zhang and Mao regarding the next military move. Mao advocated for marching north to occupy the Shaanxi and Gansu areas, where the KMT control was weak; but Zhang insisted on moving south to establish a base area in Sichuan, citing its abundance of economic resources.[11] Eventually a compromise seemed within reach at the meeting: Mao's suggestion to march north was adopted by the Politburo during this meeting, and Zhang was named the political commissar of the Red Army, replacing Zhou Enlai (Wu 2013a: 31).

The compromise quickly fell apart after the Red Army was divided into two groups during the next phase of the Long March. The Party Center and the First Red Army, led by Mao's group consisting of eight Central Committee members and seven alternate members, marched north. Against the agreement reached at the June Liangherkou meeting, Zhang's group, which consisted of seven Central Committee members and three alternate members as well as the Fourth Red Army, turned south (Sheng 1985: 77). During the next few months, Zhang Guotao repeatedly defied orders from the Party Center to march north,

---

[9] See Saich and Yang (1996) for the size of the military forces of these two parties.
[10] See Wu (2013a) for the discussion on the split between the First Red Army and the Fourth Red Army.
[11] See Chen (1998), Gao (2000), and Wu (2013a) on the conflicts between Mao and Zhang during the Long March.

and he even established an alternative Party Center in October 1935. In the name of the new "Party Center," Zhang Guotao issued a "resolution" that would remove Mao Zedong and Zhou Enlai along with other key CCP elites from the CCP Central Committee and even revoke their CCP membership (Sheng 1985: 67).

Zhang Guotao's contention for party power took an unfortunate turn when his southern expedition ended in military disaster. The Fourth Red Army suffered severe casualties at the hands of KMT troops stationed in Sichuan. By February 1936, just a few months after splitting from Mao's troops, Zhang's Fourth Red Army was reduced by half to 40,000 (Sheng 1985: 72). Forced to abandon his southern expedition, Zhang moved his troops northward. Nevertheless, he remained defiant by attempting to establish another base area in northwest China near the Tibet–Xinjiang border, yet these military maneuvers all ended in defeat. Unwillingly, Zhang's Fourth Army finally arrived in Yan'an in December 1936.

Ultimately Zhang Guotao's power base was depleted because of his disastrous military tactics: Close to 80 percent of his troops were lost on the battlefield. After Zhang arrived in Shan-Gan-Ning, he was deprived of his leadership of the Fourth Red Army, and his troops were disbanded and merged into other military units. Forced to admit his mistakes at several party meetings in 1937, Zhang was subsequently relegated to the margins of CCP leadership.[12] Unhappy with his political misfortunes within the CCP, Zhang Guotao defected to the KMT in 1938 and was stripped of his CCP membership, marking the end of his power contestation with Mao.[13]

6.1.3 Wang Ming's Loss of Support from the Soviet

Just when Mao Zedong eliminated Zhang Guotao as a threat to his leadership, the return of Wang Ming from Moscow in November 1937 marked a new challenge. Believing that he had Stalin's blessing and support, Wang immediately inserted himself into the CCP leadership circle upon his return and attempted to reshuffle CCP leadership during the Politburo meeting in December 1937 (Gao 2000). Or so he thought.

Unlike Zhang Guotao, who was able to build a formidable power base by expanding the Fourth Red Army and leading the E-Yu-Wan Soviet base area, Wang's de facto power derived mainly from his connection with the Comintern. Wang was acutely aware of the absence of a domestic patronage

---

[12] "中央政治局关于张国焘同志错误的决议 [The Politburo Resolution on Comrade Zhang Guotao's Mistakes]," March 31, 1937, in *Zhong gong zhong yang wen jian xuan ji* (*CCP Party Center Selected Documents*) (1989, VII: 164–168).

[13] "中共中央关于开除张国焘党籍的决定 [The CCP Party Center Decision to Revoke Zhang Guotao's Party Membership]," April 18, 1938, in *Zhong gong zhong yang wen jian xuan ji* (*CCP Party Center Selected Documents*) (1989, VII: 492–493).

6.1 From Contested Leadership to Dominant Leadership 143

network within both the party and the Red Army. To overcome this limitation, he sought to establish his own personal network, only to see his efforts thwarted by external forces. For instance, Wang promoted several CCP cadres with Comintern connections in both party and military organizations before his departure to Moscow in 1931; however, the CCP elites with worker backgrounds suffered from severe casualties due to KMT repression in the following years. The proportion of CCP Central Committee members with worker backgrounds consistently declined from 45 percent in 1931 to 21 percent in 1935. In contrast, the number of Central Committee members with peasant backgrounds increased from approximately 17 percent to 34 percent during the same period (Figure 1.2).

Upon his return to Yan'an from Moscow in late 1937, Wang again asserted his views forcefully during the December Politburo meeting, advocating for the establishment of a CCP Yangtze Bureau to prepare for the formation of the Second United Front with the KMT. After the establishment of this bureau, Wang became the secretary of the Yangtze Bureau and moved to Wuhan on December 23, 1937. To strengthen his influence and challenge Mao's stronghold in Yan'an, Wang saw the Yangtze Bureau as an opportunity to cultivate his own patronage network. He persistently urged Yan'an to dispatch more cadres to Wuhan to revive the labor movement, envisioning it as a means to expanding his political influence. In addition, Wang saw the successful formation of the Second United Front with the KMT as a potential avenue to enhance his political capital beyond the confines of the CCP.

The assertion of power by Wang Ming was short-lived after a series of events quickly diminished his hope to cultivate his personal power base. First, Wuhan fell to the Japanese invasion in October 1938, effectively ending Wang's attempts to build his own domestic patronage network. Second, the friction between the CCP and the KMT remained intense, suggesting the Second United Front was not a viable option for Wang to expand his influence. Third, and more importantly, Wang lost the endorsement of Stalin and the Comintern, depleting his primary source of power. During the Sixth Plenum in November 1938, Ren Bishi returned from Moscow and made an announcement on behalf of the Comintern,[14] stating that CCP leadership should center around Mao Zedong and criticizing Wang's effort to challenge Mao's leadership (Teiwes 1994). By the time the Sixth Plenum concluded, Mao had formally achieved the highest rank in the Politburo, and Wang found himself left out of the CCP elite inner circle, retaining only responsibility for nonessential party affairs.

---

[14] Instead of sending Comintern agents to China to guide the CCP revolutionary strategy, the Comintern decided that the CCP should keep a delegation in Moscow after the Sixth Party Congress in 1928. The CCP delegation would serve as the communication bridge between the Comintern and the CCP (Yang and Yang 1986).

Notably, Wang's loss of Comintern support was not only a result of his strategic miscalculation but in part originated from factional struggles in the Soviet Union. The Great Purge in the Soviet Union led to the removal of Pavel Mif, the key Comintern leader aiding Wang's rise to power. The fall of Mif led to the Soviet leadership's distrust of his close associates, among whom Wang was a key member. Furthermore, Stalin decided to support Mao to resolve CCP elite power struggle because he realized that the Sino-Japanese War was a prolonged warfare and that a unified CCP would be more effective in engaging with the Japanese, relieving military pressure on the Soviet Union (Chen 1998). The loss of support from the Comintern effectively obliterated the edifice of Wang's de facto power within the CCP.

After eliminating Wang Ming in CCP leadership contestation during the Sixth Plenum by the end of 1938, Mao remained dissatisfied with his power consolidation, viewing the Comintern as the fundamental obstacle that could still challenge his power in the future (Gao 2000). To remove the lingering influence of the Comintern, Mao plotted a strategy to shift the mindset of CCP elites away from the absolute dominance of Marxist and Soviet revolutionary doctrine. He introduced his concept of the "Sinification of Marxism," aiming to reshape the guiding principles of the CCP's revolutionary strategy. Mao launched the Yan'an Rectification Movement in 1942 after careful preparation.[15] The success of this campaign, combined with the dissolution of the Comintern in 1943, became the final nail in the coffin for Wang Ming and other CCP elites whose power relied on their connection with the Comintern. By the time the CCP held the Seventh Party Congress in 1945, Mao was able to handpick members of the Politburo and the Central Committee. Wang Ming and Bo Gu, the key leaders whose source of power stemmed from the Comintern, failed to gain even a seat in the new CCP Politburo.

6.2 UNIFYING PARTY-BUILDING STRATEGIES

The pivotal shifts in balance of power among CCP elites during the crucial period of 1935–1938 were indeed consequential for CCP party-building strategies. The party moved away from contentious worker-oriented party-building strategies as Mao consolidated his power. Instead, grassroots party organizations were encouraged to welcome intellectuals and even rich peasants into their ranks. In some localities, the CCP went as far as recruiting leaders of secret societies and coopting local elites to enhance its mass mobilization capacity. The shifts in party-building tactics paved the way for the CCP to build a robust mobilization infrastructure in rural China.

---

[15] Gao (2000) provided the most detailed account of the origin and process of the Yan'an Rectification Movement, tracing Mao's strategies in preparing and conducting it.

6.2 Unifying Party-Building Strategies

6.2.1 The Shift in 1935 during Mao's Rise and Zhang's Fall

The departure from acrimonious party-building tactics immediately took effect following the Zunyi Conference in January 1935 with Mao's return to the CCP leadership circle. Importantly, some of these policy changes occurred prior to the establishment of the Second United Front with the KMT, indicating that they were driven mainly by intraparty dynamics rather than external influences.

The treatment of rich peasants amounted to one of the most important departures in the CCP's party-building strategies. Days after Mao returned to the CCP leadership circle during the Zunyi Conference in January 1935, the Political Commissar Department of the Red Army first signaled a change of heart toward previous discriminatory party-building policies, advising grassroots party organizations to adopt more flexible criteria when engaging with rich peasants, businesspersons, and intellectuals.[16] The guidance rescinded the radical expropriation policies toward rich peasants and merchants and called upon grassroots organizations to approach members of both the intelligentsia and secret societies (e.g., 哥老会). In another secret letter to local party leaders, the Party Center moderated its stance on the bourgeoisie to unify all forces necessary to counter the KMT and the Japanese.[17] In the "Party Center's Resolution on Shifting Tactics toward Rich Peasants" on December 6, 1935,[18] the Party Center justified the policy shift by suggesting that the external political environment had changed and the CCP had to expand its coalition building to other classes of citizens for the Chinese revolution, including the rich peasants.

The CCP's departure from previous discriminatory party-building strategies was further emboldened by the return of Zhang Hao in October 1935, who was the CCP representative at the Comintern. Zhang brought news that the Comintern had embarked on a strategic shift toward building a United Front Against Fascism as outlined during the Seventh Comintern Congress a few months earlier.[19] Seizing this opportunity, the CCP immediately held an expanded Politburo meeting in Wayaobu, December 17–25, 1935, to further revise the party line and military strategy (Zhao 1987: 122–123). The CCP Politburo concluded the meeting by issuing a resolution calling for the

---

[16] "总政治部关于地方工作的指示信 [Guidance Letter on Local Party Work by Political Bureau]," January 14, 1935, in *Zhong gong zhong yang wen jian xuan ji*, (CCP Party Center Selected Documents) (1989, V10: 448–451).
[17] "中央为目前反日讨蒋的秘密指示信 [Secret Guidance Letter on Current Anti-Japanese and Campaign against Chiang by the Party Center]," October, 1935, in *Zhong gong zhong yang wen jian xuan ji*, (CCP Party Center Selected Documents) (1989, V10: 561–571).
[18] In *Zhong gong zhong yang wen jian xuan ji* (CCP Party Center Selected Documents) (1989, V10: 583–597).
[19] "The Fascist Offensive and the Tasks of the Communist International in the Struggle of the Working Class against Fascism" in Dimitrov (1972 V2: 7–88).

termination of using social class as the primary criterion for the recruitment and promotion of party members.[20]

On December 27, two days after Wayaobu meeting, Mao delivered an important speech, urging the Party to swiftly revise its party-building tactics for a broader unified front across social classes.[21] He criticized the previous practice as a closed-door doctrine, arguing that reliance solely on the working class was insufficient for the CCP to achieve political power. The Wayaobu meeting and Mao's speech set the tone for a radical shift in CCP party-building strategies. A year later, the Politburo issued a resolution on the anti-Japanese movement and toned down the mobilization strategy centered on "class struggle,"[22] a significant departure from Marxist and Leninist doctrines that the CCP had followed earlier when it was dominated by Comintern-backed CCP elites.

As Mao continued to consolidate his power within the party, the CCP formally promoted the recruitment of workers, peasants, and intellectuals into the party without privileging one over the other in 1937. The Party Center issued two important policy documents, attributing the failures of the previous closed-door party-building policies to the exclusion of individuals from the nonworker classes.[23] One document responded to an earlier call that the CCP should consider recruiting traditional local elites, including *baojia* and KMT grassroots officials, because of their possession of social capital that could effectively mobilize the masses. The Party Center repeatedly mandated party organizations to penetrate local peasant associations and recruited their key leaders, who had strong mobilization capacity in these associations. Although one cannot ignore the external political environment – the formation of the Second United Front in December 1936 – that played an important role in these changes of CCP policies, the CCP had deviated from previous discriminatory party-building strategies as early as 1935.

---

[20] "中央关于目前政治形势与党的任务决议 [Resolution on the Party's Primary Tasks Given the Current Political Climate]," December 25, 1935, in *Zhong gong zhong yang wen jian xuan ji* (*CCP Party Center Selected Documents*) (1989, V10: 598).

[21] "论反对日本帝国主义的策略 [On the Strategy to Fight with Japanese Imperialism]," December 27, 1935, in *Mao ze dong xuan ji* (*Mao's Selective Essays*) (1991, V1: 142–169).

[22] "中央关于抗日救亡运动的新形势与民主共和国的决议 [Resolution on the Anti-Japanese and Nation-Saving Campaign as well as the Democratic Republic by the Party Center]," September 17, 1936, in *Zhong gong zhong yang wen jian xuan ji* (*CCP Party Center Selected Documents*) (1989, V10: 92–99).

[23] "苏区党代表会议组织问题报告提要 [Report on the Party Organization in Soviet Areas at the Soviet Party Representative Conference]," May 10, 1937, in *Zhong gong zhong yang wen jian xuan ji* (*CCP Party Center Selected Documents*) (1989, V11: 213–223) and "白区党目前的中心任务 [Primary Tasks of the Party Organization in the White Area]," June 6, 1937, in *Zhong gong zhong yang wen jian xuan ji* (*CCP Party Center Selected Documents*) (1989, V11: 224–264).

6.2 Unifying Party-Building Strategies

6.2.2 CCP Party-Building Strategies during the Mao–Wang Power Struggle

Wang Ming's return to Yan'an in late 1937 resulted in a brief deviation from Mao's vision in a united front party-building strategy, but Wang's efforts ultimately proved unsuccessful. Wang again attempted to steer the CCP toward a worker-centric party-building strategy during the March 1938 Politburo Meeting[24] but was met with a different outcome. The shift in the balance of power between Mao and Wang began with the fall of Wuhan and the withdrawal of Comintern support to Wang in 1938. As Mao's influence prevailed, the CCP continued to adopt consistent party-building strategies that no longer relied on social class as the sole criterion to screen and evaluate party members.

For instance, the CCP issued an important resolution after the March 1938 Politburo Meeting to expand party membership regardless of social class, indicating that Mao retained strong control over party decision-making.[25] This policy eliminated social class as the sole criterion for recruitment and promotion and removed or reduced probation for new party members. Once Mao completely marginalized Wang after the 1938 Sixth Plenum, the CCP issued another resolution[26] to recommend the assimilation of the intelligentsia into the party and the Red Army, which Mao endorsed.[27]

Even during the Yan'an Thought Rectification Campaign, an internal CCP document emphasized the importance of self-criticism to demonstrate loyalty to the party rather than relying solely on one's social class as was done in previous purges of peasants and intellectuals. Effectively, the screening device for party member loyalty rested on the actions of party members instead of a dogmatic measure based on social class. By the time the CCP held its Seventh Party Congress in 1945, the revised Party Constitution had become a codified set of criteria for party membership recruitment based on social origin.[28]

---

[24] "三月政治局会议的总结 [Summary of the March Politburo Meeting]," March 11, 1938, in *Zhong gong zhong yang wen jian xuan ji* (*CCP Party Center Selected Documents*) (1989, V11: 430–465).

[25] "中央关于大量发展党员的决议 [Resolution on Significantly Expanding Party Member Recruitment]," March 15, 1938, in *Zhong gong zhong yang wen jian xuan ji* (*CCP Party Center Selected Documents*) (1989, V11: 466–468).

[26] "总政治部关于大量吸收知识分子和培养新干部问题的训令 [Instruction on Intensifying the Recruitment of Intellectuals and the Training of New Cadres by Political Bureau]," June 25, 1939, in *Zhong gong zhong yang wen jian xuan ji* (*CCP Party Center Selected Documents*) (1989, V12: 134–135).

[27] "毛泽东: 大量吸收知识分子 [Mao Zedong: Intensifying the Recruitment of Intellectuals]," December 1, 1939, in *Zhong gong zhong yang wen jian xuan ji* (*CCP Party Center Selected Documents*) (1989, V12: 204–206).

[28] "中共产党党章 [Bylaws of the Chinese Communist Party]," June 11, 1945, in *Zhong gong zhong yang wen jian xuan ji* (*CCP Party Center Selected Documents*) (1989, V15: 115–136).

For most nonelites, the only difference was the probation period, ranging from six months to one year. Importantly, the CCP did not establish quotas for recruiting party members from specific backgrounds.

6.3 THE EMERGENCE OF RURAL MOBILIZATION INFRASTRUCTURE

The preceding discussion has revealed that external factors created favorable conditions for the expansion of the CCP, but the internal dynamics of the elite power struggle led to the crucial departure of previous discriminatory party-building strategies. Consistent with the changing winds of elite politics, this section demonstrates that the crucial turning point for the CCP's expansion occurred prior to the land reform and economic production initiatives in 1942 and was not driven by changes in Japanese aggression.

Indeed, the pattern of CCP expansion during this period is more closely tied to fluctuations in the CCP elite power struggle and evolution of party-building strategies rather than primary influence by external factors (Figure 6.1). For instance, if nationalism had been a major driver for the rise of Communism in China, the Nanjing Massacre from December 1937 to January 1938 would have prompted an extreme surge in party membership. Nonetheless, CCP party membership only doubled its size to 90,000 members by the end of 1938.

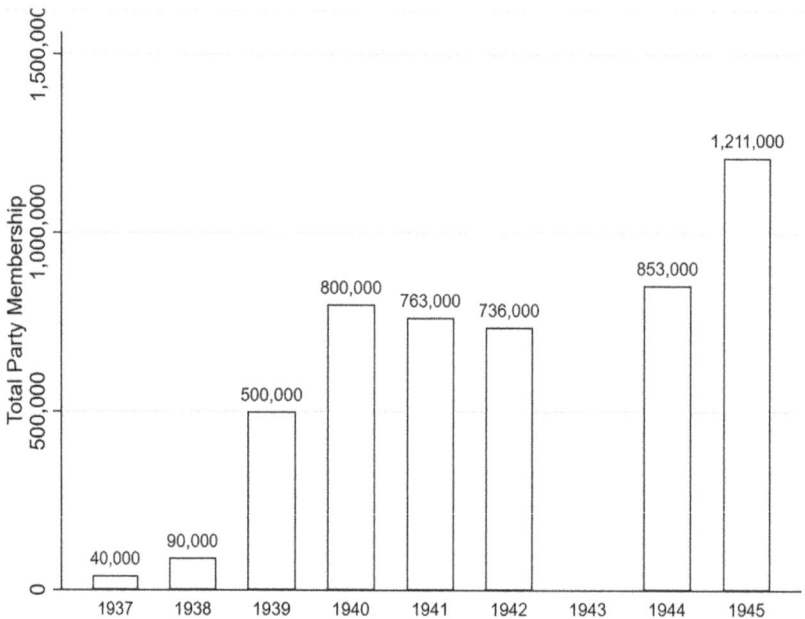

FIGURE 6.1 CCP membership (1937–1945)
Note: Author's database. See Appendix A for data source. The party membership data for 1943 was missing.

6.3 The Emergence of Rural Mobilization Infrastructure

By contrast, CCP membership witnessed a substantial expansion following a party resolution in October 1938, calling for a significant increase in party membership,[29] which surged to 500,000 in 1939 and 800,000 in 1940. Importantly, the resolution emphasized not nationalism as a recruitment device but quantity over quality in party expansion in base areas.[30] The significant surge in party membership over the course of two years compelled the CCP to pause the rapid expansion and consolidate the party organization in order to ensure the quality of its new recruits.[31]

The party expansion briefly slowed down after 1940 because of a series of events: The Japanese aggression in northern China in 1941–1942, the internal party membership reevaluation and consolidation in 1940, and the Yan'an Thought Rectification Campaign in 1942. Thus, CCP membership remained stagnant and even experienced a slight decline in 1942. Only after Mao concluded the Yan'an Thought Rectification Campaign in 1943 did CCP membership expansion resume, eventually reaching 1.2 million by 1945.

Crucially, the CCP enhanced its mobilization infrastructure not only by expanding party membership but also by transitioning from a worker-centric recruitment strategy to a more inclusive approach as Mao started to consolidate his power after 1935. The transformation did not necessarily occur because the CCP exclusively recruited peasants and discriminated against workers and intellectuals but because the base areas were located only in rural China, where its population was the base for CCP party expansion. The inclusive recruitment strategies, therefore, primarily benefited the recruitment of peasants, and the reconciliation with intellectuals facilitated the CCP's efforts to strengthen its bureaucratic capacity. For instance, party members in the peasant class rose from below 50 percent in 1927 to 95 percent in the Shaan-Gan-Ning base area and close to 80 percent in Shandong by 1941 (Figure 6.2). Meanwhile, intellectuals played a crucial role in the CCP's early efforts to establish grassroots party organizations in rural China. According to a survey taken in 1942 by the Northwest Bureau, 85 percent of rural party cells were initially established by party members with intellectual backgrounds (Huang 2024: 221).

The CCP's experience in the early 1930s reveals that a growing membership is insufficient for a robust mobilization infrastructure; it requires the

---

[29] "关于抗日民族统一战线与党的组织问题 [Issue Concerning the Anti-Japanese and National United Front and the Party Organization]," October 15, 1938, in *Zhong gong zhong yang wen jian xuan ji* (*CCP Party Center Selected Documents*) (1989, V11: 663–721).

[30] Huang (2024: 32) suggested that the guiding principle for 1938 CCP party expansion was "expansion first, training and exclusion later."

[31] "中央政治局关于巩固党的决定 [Decision to Consolidate the Party by the CCP Politburo]," August 25, 1939, in *Zhong gong zhong yang wen jian xuan ji* (*CCP Party Center Selected Documents*) (1989, V12: 155–158); "中央关于审查干部问题的指示 [Instruction on the Issue Concerning Cadre Evaluation by the Party Center]," August 1, 1940, in *Zhong gong zhong yang wen jian xuan ji* (*CCP Party Center Selected Documents*) (1989, V12: 444–447). See Huang (2024) for a detailed account of CCP cadres training during this period.

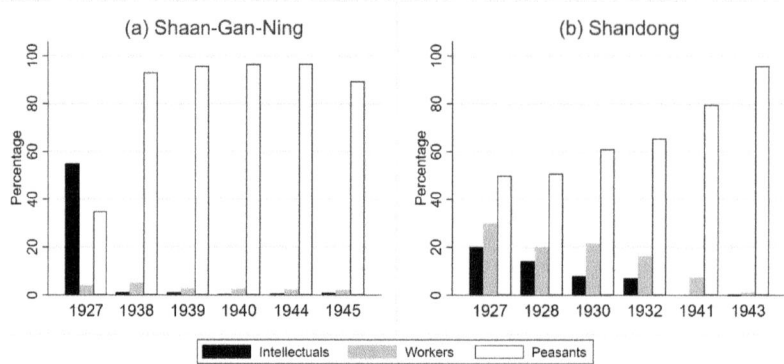

FIGURE 6.2 CCP membership class backgrounds in Shaan-Gan-Ning and Shandong base areas (1927–1945).
Note: The Shaan-Gan-Ning data on CCP membership class background derive from *Zhong guo gong chan dang shan xi sheng zu zhi shi zi liao* (*CCP Shaanxi Provincial Party History Documents*) (1994); the Shandong data derive from *Shandong dang shi zi liao wen ku* (*Shandong Party History Selective Documents*) (2015, V1, V2, V4, V5).

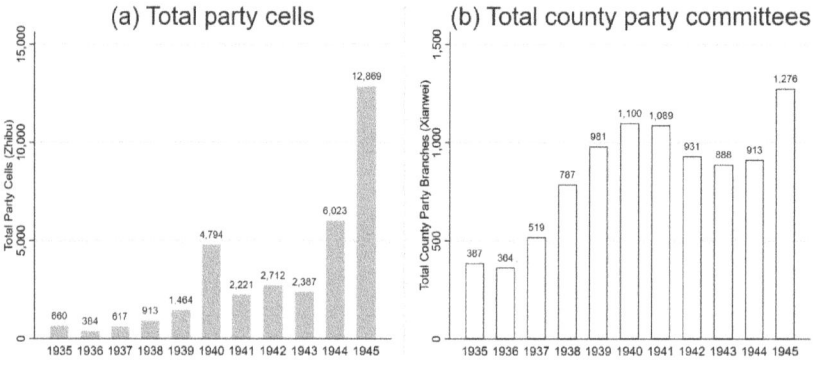

FIGURE 6.3 CCP grassroots party cells and county party committees (1935–1945).
Note: Author's dataset. See Appendix A for data source.

organization of party members through grassroots party apparatuses. The CCP's earlier expansion was not accompanied by the extreme expansion of grassroots party organizations, resulting in a weak mobilization infrastructure that failed to penetrate the society. Learning from this lesson, the CCP witnessed a rapid expansion of grassroots party cells during the period of 1937–1940 (Figure 6.3a). Although this expansion faced resistance following the collapse of the Second United Front and Japan's military strategies in northern China in 1941 and 1942, the CCP's party cells regained momentum for exponential growth in 1944 and 1945. By the end of the Sino-Japanese War in 1945, the CCP had successfully established a remarkable 12,869 party branches across China.

Notably, the establishment of CCP grassroots party branches was not limited to the base areas under CCP control. The CCP had established county party committees across China, showing the breadth and depth of its grassroots penetration (Figure 6.3b). By 1945, the CCP had created 1,276 county party committees across China, covering more than 50 percent of its counties.

6.4 SUMMARY

Tracing the intraparty power struggle to party-building strategies, this chapter reveals two important observations. First, the transformation of the CCP's mobilization infrastructure closely followed Mao's power consolidation within the party starting in 1935, setting off a remarkable turn in CCP party-building strategies: Transitioning from contentious and discriminatory approaches to a more unified and coherent vision. Mao's power consolidation dismantled the party's self-defeating policies, and the CCP developed a resilient rural mobilization infrastructure during the crucial period of 1935–1941 before it was forced to expand grain extraction in rural China (see Chapter 4). In stark contrast, the intense power struggle among CCP elites between 1931 and 1935 gave rise to discriminatory practices in recruiting and promoting members, which proved detached from the realities on the ground. The CCP's party organization grew fragile and susceptible to external repression.

Second, the realignment of power dynamics among CCP party elites during this period, including Mao Zedong himself, was partly driven by external contingencies, such as the disastrous military and insurgency strategies pursued by their rivals as well as waning support from the Comintern due to internal politics within the Soviet Union. These exogenous influences played a crucial role in shaping the landscape of CCP leadership struggle and decision-making. The realignment challenges conventional wisdom that suggests the 1942 Yan'an Thought Rectification Campaign as a pivotal moment in Mao's ascent to power. This chapter demonstrates that although strategic calculation by Mao played a key role in his ascendancy, external circumstances and unexpected events from 1935 to 1938 had a profound impact on tilting the balance of power among party elites in his favor. Had Mao's main rivals not employed disastrous military tactics or lost the support of the Comintern, Mao may not have been able to consolidate his power within the CCP.

7

The KMT

Revolutionary Party Aborted

The pre-1949 KMT is often portrayed as a party marred by factional disputes and a loose organizational structure, but closer examination reveals some paradoxical developments. Despite its revolutionary origin,[1] external threats and violent conflicts had failed to foster elite cohesion and party discipline. In addition, the KMT's organizational weakness did not result from a lack of effort on the part of its leaders: The party twice attempted but failed to transform itself into a mass party, initially during the First United Front (1923–1927) and later during the Sino-Japanese War. Finally, elite conflicts had not prevented the KMT from becoming a ruling party in 1928; in fact, it had benefited early from its elite mobilization infrastructure and consistently surpassed the CCP both in terms of military might and party size. The domination, however, evaporated over the course of the Sino-Japanese War as the comparative advantage of the KMT's mobilization infrastructure diminished, and the party struggled to effectively mobilize financial resources from rural China.

How should the rise and fall of the KMT be understood? To answer this question, I trace the evolution of the KMT elite power struggle, party-building strategies, and mobilization infrastructure from 1921 to 1945. The analyses offer three important insights. First, the practice of KMT party ideology, originating in Sun Yat-sen's Three Principles of the People, fostered an elite mobilization infrastructure, which in turn offered a comparative advantage in resource mobilization (see Chapter 3).

---

[1] Levitsky and Way (2022) do not consider the KMT a revolutionary organization because it did not rely heavily on mass mobilization in its revolutionary efforts; however, this chapter reveals that the KMT exhibited numerous traits of revolutionary parties and initially sought to engage in mass mobilization. Only because of internal elite conflicts and party ideology did the KMT eventually revert to an elite mobilization structure.

7.1 The KMT under a Dominant Leader (1921–1925)

Second, the KMT's elite mobilization infrastructure, designed to attract ambitious political actors, created a breeding ground for internal power struggles. Under the dominant leadership of Sun Yat-sen, the party experienced relative unity as he used his prestige to maintain party cohesion. In fact, Sun was able to force the formation of the First United Front with the CCP in an effort to reform the party over the objections of many party elites. Unfortunately, the ensuing succession battle after Sun's untimely death ignited an intense elite power struggle. In their attempts to outmaneuver their intraparty rivals, KMT party elites, characterized by their ambition, strong patronage networks, and ample resources, constantly pursued opportunities to wield their power and outmaneuver their rivals, even to the detriment of the party's unity and cohesion. The prevalence of elite conflict within the party undermined KMT party organizational strength.

Third, the balance of power among KMT elites was frequently shaped and shifted by external factors and unforeseen events. The influence of the Comintern and the Japanese invasion as well as assassinations and personal health circumstances played pivotal roles in breaking stalemates and shifting the balance of power among KMT elites.

Unlike the CCP, which transitioned from contested leadership to dominant leadership during from 1928 to 1945, the KMT witnessed a fluctuating balance of power among its party elites. In the remainder of this chapter, I analyze the elite power struggle within the KMT and its party-building process through three distinct phases based on the balance of power among KMT elites:

1) Dominant Leadership under Sun Yat-sen (1921–1925)
2) The Era of Violent Elite Contestation (1925–1937)
3) The Rise of Chiang Kai-shek as the Quasi-Dominant Party Leader (1938–1945)

7.1 THE KMT UNDER A DOMINANT LEADER (1921–1925)

The KMT was a successor to several revolutionary organizations and secret societies that overthrew the Qing Dynasty during the 1911 Chinese Revolution. As the leader of this organization, Sun Yat-sen was widely considered the "Father of the Nation" by both the CCP and the KMT. Not only did he craft a visionary ideology with which he sought to bring independence, equality, and prosperity to China, but he also spearheaded various revolutionary organizations to translate his ideology into action. Sun wielded absolute authority within the KMT, driving a series of sweeping changes in party-building strategies. Among these transformative initiatives, the formation of the First United Front with the CCP and collaboration with the Comintern stood out as the most momentous endeavors. The formation of the First United Front with the CCP – and more importantly, the financial and military aid from the Soviet Union – propelled the KMT in a promising direction.

7.1.1 Sun Yat-sen as a Dominant Leader

By many measures, the KMT began as a genuine revolutionary party, with its origins tracing back to numerous clandestine revolutionary groups that played a pivotal role in toppling the Qing Dynasty during the 1911 Chinese Revolution.[2] Despite suffering a temporary dissolution due to the treacherous actions of warlord Yuan Shikai in 1913, the KMT reemerged in the wake of the May 4 Student Movement in 1919.

The unwavering leadership of Sun Yat-sen in these revolutionary organizations was pivotal in steering the Chinese Revolution through numerous obstacles encountered since 1894; therefore, Sun had enjoyed unparalleled prestige and respect within the KMT. His domination stemmed from two sources of power (Cui 2013). First, Sun authored the Three Principles of the People, a political manifesto that served as the beacon of light generating widespread appeal to political activists across China. Second, Sun's exceptional ability to mobilize financial and human resources set him apart as one of the most effective revolutionary elites of his time. His adeptness in harnessing these resources formed the bedrock of the insurgency against the Qing Dynasty and proved instrumental in countering the suppression orchestrated by regional warlords.

Sun's domination was on full display when he exerted his personal influence to impose the strategy known as "Alliance with Russia and Accommodating the CCP" (联俄容共) against strong opposition within the party. The motivation behind this radical shift was twofold. First, Sun found himself in dire need of external assistance to rejuvenate the Chinese revolution in the face of significant setbacks caused by the betrayal of regional military strongmen. Maring, a Comintern agent, convinced Sun to form an alliance with the CCP through the First United Front.[3] In return, the KMT received much-needed military and financial support from the Soviet Union. Second, Sun's aspiration was to forge a strong and united KMT capable of fulfilling its revolutionary objectives.[4] Recognizing the need for a revitalized KMT organization, he embraced Leninist party principles in his quest to reshape the party into a disciplined and formidable force, marked by the establishment of vibrant grassroots party organizations.

The accommodation of the CCP was highly divisive, splitting KMT elites into two factions: the KMT-Left faction, which endorsed Sun's strategic

---

[2] The KMT was a successor party to several revolutionary organizations – the Xinzhonghui (1894~1905), Tongmenghui (1905~1912), Guomindang (1912~1914), and Zhonghua Gengmingdang (1914~1919) – until it was named Zhongguo Guomindang (Kuomintang) in 1919. For studies of these revolutionary organizations, see, for example, Cui (2013) and Fairbank and Feuerwerker (1986).

[3] For a detailed discussion of Sun's acceptance of Soviet aid and background on the formation of the First United Front, see Li (1987), Saich (1991), Q. Wang (2010), and Yang (2012).

[4] For instance, Sun gave an important speech after the First Party Congress of the KMT in 1924, emphasizing party building at the grassroots level (Q. Wang 2010).

7.1 The KMT under a Dominant Leader (1921–1925)

alliance with the CCP; the KMT-Right faction, which opposed it. The primary source of opposition arose from the perceived ideological incongruence of the inclusive vision outlined in the Three Principles of the People because the CCP's communist ideology embodies an exclusive emphasis on class struggle. Furthermore, the KMT-Right faction expressed doubts about the CCP's reliability as a partner, fearing that the inclusion of CCP members could lead to the expansion of the CCP at the expense of the KMT.[5]

Despite the strong opposition from the KMT-Right faction, Sun used his personal power to force the formation of the First United Front. Specifically, he muted leading voices of the KMT-Right faction by revoking the party memberships of several key opponents.[6] Furthermore, Sun facilitated the appointments of CCP members in several important leadership positions within the newly reformed party organization. When the First Party Congress of the KMT concluded in January 1924, for instance, CCP members occupied three of twenty-four formal seats and seven of seventeen alternate seats on the KMT Central Committee.[7] In addition, several CCP members were appointed department heads in the KMT organization.[8] Meanwhile, several members of the KMT-Left faction, including Liao Zhongkai and Zeng Xing, also held important leadership positions in the KMT.

7.1.2 An Elite-Centric Mobilization Infrastructure Flirting with the Leninist Principle

Given the preeminent status of Sun Yat-sen, KMT party-building strategies closely aligned with his preferences in two distinct phases during his tenure. In the first phase, Sun pursued an elite-centric mobilization infrastructure by relying on his personal charisma rather than strict adherence to organizational principles to appeal to political and economic elites, resulting in loose connections among these entities. With the Chinese revolution on the brink of collapse, Sun decided to form the First United Front with the CCP in 1923, marking the onset of the second phase of KMT party-building. Under the guidance of the Comintern, Sun embarked on a transformation of the KMT by borrowing the principles of Leninist party to strengthen its organization. Party reform initially achieved significant success in expanding KMT influence with the help of CCP members. I will now discuss these two distinct phases in turn.

The Birth of Elite Mobilization Infrastructure. During Sun's early leadership, the principle of party building in various revolutionary organizations can

---

[5] See Yang (2012) on the debate among KMT elites concerning the First United Front.
[6] For example, Sun revoked the KMT membership of Ma Zhiyou, Feng Su, and Xie Zhi.
[7] Li Dazhao, Tan Pingshan, and Yu Shude are three KMT Central Committee members who were CCP members. Mao Zedong, Lin Boqu, Qu Qiubai, Zhang Guotao, Han Lingfu, Yu Fangzhou, and Shen Dingyi were the alternate members of the KMT Central Committee.
[8] For instance, Tan Pingshan was appointed Head of the Organization Department and Lin Boqu was appointed head of the Peasant Department.

be distilled to two overarching trends – the centralization of power and the emphasis on elites – that signify the rise of an elite mobilization infrastructure within the party.

First, Sun regarded himself as the "prophet" of the Chinese revolution; others could be enlightened only if following his guidance (Cui 2013). This elitist view inevitably resulted in Sun's distrust of even his close associates to faithfully carry out revolutionary tactics, leading to a tendency toward centralizing decision-making in revolutionary organizations. The centralization of power particularly manifested in decisions about party finance, largely because Sun was an effective fundraiser for these organizations. When the Chinese revolution suffered setbacks from suppression at the hands of regional warlords, Sun's natural inclination was further centralization of his power because he attributed these setbacks to other revolutionary elites who failed to carry out his vision. The Manifesto of the China Revolutionary Party (中华革命党), a KMT predecessor, even mandated unconditional obedience of party members to party leadership.

Second, Sun's elitist view engendered an elite mobilization infrastructure that recruited and coopted political and economic elites into the party. In the wake of the Qing Dynasty's downfall in 1911, Sun took proactive steps to strengthen the KMT's position in the new political landscape by recruiting prominent politicians from the newly established government and legislature into the party, thus positioning the party as a formidable competitor among the other political parties of the time. Many members of the first cabinet of the Republic of China were eventually persuaded to join the KMT, making it the largest party in the newly established National Legislature (Cui 2007). Similarly, local branches of the KMT sought to expand their influence by attracting local bureaucrats and traditional elites to their ranks.

The Fusion of an Elitist Party with Leninist Principles. The collapse of the Qing Dynasty created a political vacuum in China, plunging it into an era of warlordism during which the country was divided by military strongmen. Faced with the critical challenges that pushed the Chinese revolution to the brink of collapse, Sun made the fateful decision to embrace the Soviet Union, which led to the reform of the KMT and the establishment of the First United Front with the CCP in 1923. In exchange for this alliance, Sun received vital financial and military support from the Soviet Union, which proved instrumental in bolstering the revolutionary cause.

Prior to forming the First United Front, Sun had just initiated yet another party reform aiming to improve the KMT as early as 1922, focusing primarily on party organization at the elite level. Less than a year later, Sun embarked on a vastly different party reform in 1923 after he received financial and military assistance from the Soviet Union.[9] The 1924 reform marked a significant departure from any of Sun Yat-sen's earlier efforts to reorganize the KMT.

---

[9] L. Wang (2010) detailed the transition from the 1922 KMT reform aiming for improvement (改进) to the 1923 KMT reform aiming for reorganization (改组).

7.1 The KMT under a Dominant Leader (1921–1925)

To begin, the 1924 KMT reform institutionalized Leninist principles through a new party constitution. Sun invited Borodin, a Comintern agent, to participate in its drafting during the KMT's First Party Congress in 1924. Unsurprisingly, the 1924 KMT constitution was closely modeled after the one the Communist Party of the Soviet Union adopted at its Eighth Soviet Party Congress in 1919.[10] The two constitutions shared many similarities in terms of structure and content; in fact, some wording in the 1924 KMT Constitution was nearly identical to that of this model.

Importantly, the KMT emphasized building grassroots party organizations and establishing district party cells (区分部) for the purpose of mass mobilization. This reorganization was a significant departure from previous party building under Sun, whose attention gravitated toward building institutions to manage elites instead of rank-and-file party members. Sun's earlier reluctance to rely on the masses for the revolutionary endeavor derived from a pessimistic view regarding the untapped potential of the masses and their ability to be effectively mobilized for the revolution. Nonetheless, the May 4 Student Movement of 1919 rekindled Sun's interest in appealing to mass mobilization, primarily of Chinese youth. In the Manifesto of the First Party Congress of the KMT, Sun announced that the Chinese revolution could not succeed without the participation of workers and peasants.

Despite a shift toward appealing to the masses, the KMT remained a party relying primarily on an elite mobilization infrastructure for two reasons. First, Sun remained committed to his Three Principles of the People as a political philosophy superior to Communism (Q. Wang 2010; Cui 2013). He repeatedly made public speeches, signaling to both party members and outside observers that the intent behind KMT reform was not to make it a Communist party. The adoption of Soviet assistance was mainly intended to improve party discipline.

Second, the KMT delegated mass mobilization to CCP members, while senior KMT leaders remained closely connected with existing elites.[11] In essence, the core of KMT operation remained elite-centric, and mass mobilization was outsourced to the CCP. For example, approximately 90 percent of the leadership of KMT grassroots organizations was controlled by the CCP and KMT-Left factions (Q. Wang 2010). The CCP even prioritized establishing grassroots party organizations and mass mobilization under the banner of the KMT over their own.

---

[10] Note that the 1921 Constitution of the CCP also closely followed the 1919 Constitution of the Communist Party of the Soviet Union (CPSU). For studies of the similarities and differences among the 1919 CPSU, 1921 CCP, and 1924 KMT Constitutions, see, for example, L. Wang (2010), Q. Wang (2010), and Zhou (2018).

[11] For instance, several CCP members were appointed to take charge of the KMT's mass mobilization – Tan Pingshan as the head of the Organization Department and Lin Boqu as the head of the Peasant Department.

7.1.3 The Rebirth of the KMT as a Dominant Party

The 1924 KMT reform brought about a remarkable transformation of the organization, evident in substantial expansion in party membership and grassroots party organizations across China. Equally significant was the party's ability to gather systematic information about party operation, which stands as a crucial indicator of party bureaucratic capacity.

Before the 1923 party reform, internal KMT reports acknowledged the precarious state of the party organization, as party leaders possessing sporadic and conflicting information regarding party membership (Cui 2007: 571–574). Although Sun claimed to have over 200,000 members on the eve of the 1924 Party Congress (Cui 2007: 572), an internal KMT report indicated that the majority of party members were inactive.[12] In one report by the KMT Statistics Bureau, party membership, excluding overseas members, amounted to only 50,000 prior to the 1924 Party Reform (Tsuchida 2002: 87). Another party report suggested that the KMT had 60,080 party members domestically and 33,530 members overseas.[13]

Following the First Party Congress in 1924, the KMT organization began to gather more comprehensive and systematic data on party membership. Figure 7.1 shows a steep increase in KMT membership after the 1924 reform. Similar to the CCP, the May 30 Labor Movement of 1925 became the catalyst for expansion of the KMT as its membership soared to 175,335 domestic members in 1925, a 300 percent increase from 1924; by May 1926 the size of its membership had almost doubled to 317,178. By May 1926, mere months later, its domestic membership further expanded to 425,612.

Another indicator of the KMT's promising party reform is the rise of non-elites among its rank-and-file members. A membership report suggests that by October 1926 those with worker origins constituted 30 percent while intellectuals (i.e., students, teachers, journalists) accounted for 36.2 percent (Tsuchida 2002: 95). In addition, those from rural areas accounted for 7.5 percent, and members of the military represented only 4.83 percent of total party membership. The distribution of party membership across social classes demonstrated the KMT's success in integrating mass mobilization with its initial elite-centric mobilization infrastructure.

The expansion of grassroots party organizations was another hallmark of the KMT's transformation after the 1924 reform. Prior to 1924, it had established

---

[12] "第一次全国代表大会前之组织工作（民国十三年前）[Organizational Work Prepared for the First National Representative Conference (Pre-1924)]" in *Zhong guo guo min dang dang wu fa zhan shi liao: zu zhi gong zuo (Chinese Kuomintang Party Affairs: Organizational Work)* (1993 V1: 4).

[13] The total number was calculated based on the report in "第一次全国代表大会前之组织工作（民国十三年前）[Organizational Work Prepared for the First National Representative Conference (Pre-1924)]" in *Zhong guo guo min dang dang wu fa zhan shi liao: zu zhi gong zuo (Chinese Kuomintang Party Affairs: Organizational Work)*, (1993 V1: 10–47).

7.1 The KMT under a Dominant Leader (1921–1925)

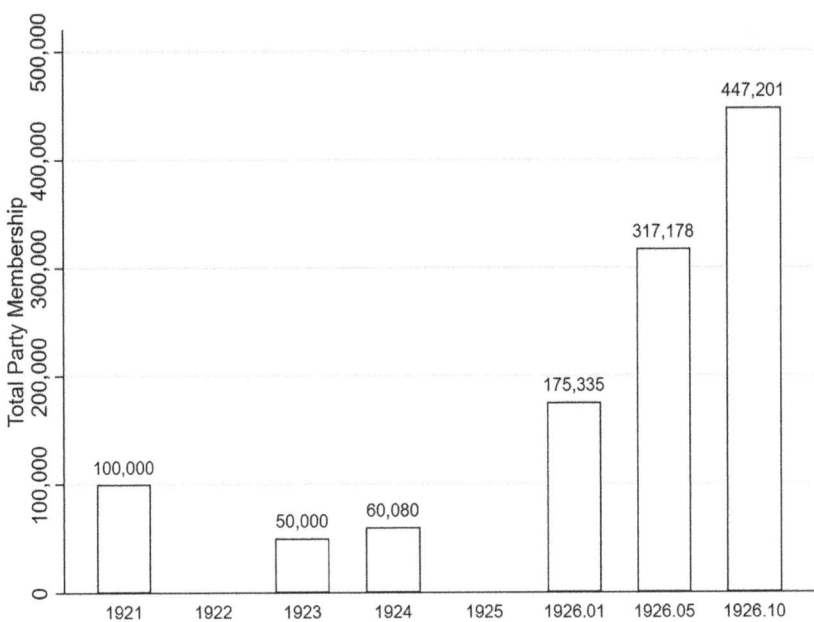

FIGURE 7.1 KMT membership (1924–1926)
Note: See Appendix A for the sources of KMT party membership data. The total number reported in this figure includes both rank-and-file and military members but excludes overseas members.

few provincial (省党部) and county party committees (县党部), and its internal party organization reported data for only 103 district party cells (区分部).[14] By May 1926, party committees had been established in twenty provinces with the exception of four in the periphery (Heilongjiang, Tibet, Qinghai, and Xinjiang);[15] furthermore, the KMT established 3,388 district party cells and 271 county party committees by May 1926.[16] In total the KMT's grassroots party organization covered 90 percent of provinces and 25 percent of counties (Q. Wang 2010). By comparison, the CCP established 1,730 district party cells and 295 county party committees in 1926. In essence, the KMT beat the CCP

---

[14] Calculated based on the provincial reports in "第一次全国代表大会前之组织工作（民国十三年前）[Organizational Work Prepared for the First National Representative Conference (Pre-1924)]" in *Zhong guo guo min dang dang wu fa zhan shi liao: zu zhi gong zuo* (*Chinese Kuomintang Party Affairs: Organizational Work*) (1993 VI: 10–17).

[15] Calculated based on the provincial reports in "第三次全国代表大会前之组织工作（民国十五年一月–十八年三月）[Organizational Work Prepared for the Third National Representative Conference (January 1926–March 1929)]" in *Zhong guo guo min dang dang wu fa zhan shi liao: zu zhi gong zuo* (*Chinese Kuomintang Party Affairs: Organizational Work*) (1993 VI: 88–92).

[16] See Appendix A for data source.

at its own game by 1926, attracting greater party membership with better organizational capacity at the grassroots level.

7.2 THE AGE OF AMBITION & LEADERSHIP CONTESTATION (1925–1937)

Under Sun's dominant leadership, the KMT experienced a remarkable transformation within a span of two years, becoming an emerging contender poised to dominate the political scene. The First United Front appeared to combine the best of both worlds for the KMT: Ready access to vital economic resources through the elite mobilization infrastructure and broad appeal from the general population via mass mobilization apparatus.

Beneath the success of the First United Front lurked a growing discontent within the party, fueled by the inherent incongruence between these two forms of mobilization infrastructure. The sudden death of Sun finally ruptured the delicate balance of power among KMT elites, sparking intense contestation in the battle for succession during the next two decades. Not only did the elite power struggle revert the KMT to an exclusively elite mobilization infrastructure, but the relatively equal balance of power also prevented KMT elites from overcoming the collective action problem by pursuing coherent party-building strategies.

A close look at the dynamics of elite power struggles within the KMT reveals three key observations. First, succession is always the Achilles heel for parties with a dominant leader. The sudden death of Sun resulted in an unrelenting KMT elite power struggle and even led to a series of intraparty armed conflicts. Second, when party elites enjoy a relatively equal balance of power, power sharing is not necessarily a stable equilibrium largely because they view intraparty competition as a zero-sum game. The constant reconfiguration of strategic alliances among KMT elites during their power struggle serve as a stark reminder that in the realm of politics one has no permanent friends or enemies. Third, although party elites employed various tactics to gain the upper hand in their power struggles, shifts in the balance of power and resolution of the stalemate in the power struggle are often driven by contingent events. Chiang's ascent and power consolidation within the KMT can be attributed to a series of unexpected events among his rivals.

This section further reveals the detrimental impact of elite power contestation on the development of party mobilization infrastructure. Factional politics and intraparty conflicts generated incoherent party-building strategies. Much like the CCP's experience under contested leadership, KMT elites pursued party-building strategies that prioritized their personal empowerment at the expense of the overall strength of the party. During Chiang Kai-shek's initial ascent, he emphasized party expansion within the military while impeding the growth of rank-and-file party members in the government bureaucracy, where his rivals wielded greater influence. The disparity in party building resulted

7.2 The Age of Leadership Contestation (1925–1937)

in a fragile party organization with uneven quality in resource mobilization, planting the seeds of its collapse a decade later.

Before delving into the discussion of the KMT elite power struggle, I should clarify the factional affiliation within the KMT during this period. Although factional politics is a hallmark of KMT politics, identifying KMT elites' factional affiliation is challenging for three reasons. First, allegiance among KMT elites evolved over time. Second, factional identities often cut across functional areas (e.g., party, government, and military systems), territorial control (e.g., Guangxi Gui faction, Sichuan Liu faction, and Shanxi Yan Qishan faction), and the relationships with Sun (i.e., his son and other close associates). Third, within a larger faction there encompass several smaller circles of closely knitted party elites.[17]

At the risk of oversimplifying factional identity within the KMT, I define KMT factions along two dimensions: ideological orientation and territorial control. First, the KMT comprised two factions based on ideological orientation. The accommodation of the CCP in the First United Front in 1924 created a deep division among KMT elites, who sorted themselves into the KMT-Left faction and the KMT-Right faction. The KMT-Left faction endorsed Sun's policy shift and considered the CCP an ally, but the KMT-Right faction opposed Sun's policy shift and regarded the CCP incompatible with its Three Principles of the People.

Second, other KMT factions emerged based on local strongmen's territorial control, allowing them to build their own patronage network and amass enormous resources.[18] Specifically, the KMT assimilated and coopted warlords for the party during the Northern Expedition in the late 1920s. Although these individuals later held nominal party positions, they often defied KMT leadership and at times even challenged Chiang through an extraparty network. These regional strongmen had amassed significant military and financial resources, offering them de facto power in the elite power struggle.

7.2.1 The Quagmire of Unrelenting Elite Contestation

Ironically, the factional struggle initially benefited Chiang Kai-shek for his rise but also undermined his domination when he later became the preeminent party leader in 1938. An outsider looking in during the initial succession battle after Sun's death in 1925, Chiang took advantage of the ideological division between the KMT-Left faction and KMT-Right faction, opportunistically building alliances with one faction at the expense of the other in the following decade. Consequently, the KMT experienced a continuous cycle of forming and dissolving elite alliances, highlighting the ongoing power struggle among its members.

---

[17] See Cui (2013), Eastman (1984), and Jin (2009).
[18] See the discussion of factions in Chi (1982).

The Formation of the Chiang–Wang Alliance. Sun's death in 1925 sparked a succession battle primarily involving Liao Zhongkai, Wang Ching-wei, and Hu Han-min. Liao and Wang were affiliated with the KMT-Left faction, and Hu belonged to the KMT-Right faction. Liao enjoyed widespread respect within the party, but Hu was considered the most qualified candidate to succeed Sun. The Liao–Hu stalemate led to the rise of Wang as a compromise to the situation.[19] As a member of the KMT-Left, Wang vowed to continue Sun's United Front policies after assuming the position of Chairman of the KMT Executive Committee and the Military Commission in July 1925.

Chiang Kai-shek was far from contention for party leadership initially because he was a military man without any experience in party affairs.[20] Nonetheless, the assassination of Liao Zhongkai in 1925 opened the door for Chiang, who exploited this opportunity by building an alliance with the KMT-Left faction to oust the KMT-Right faction from the KMT leadership circle. The KMT established a special commission led by Chiang Kai-shek, Wang Ching-wei, and Xu Zhongzhi to investigate Liao's assassination.[21] Through the process of investigation, Chiang aided Wang in sidelining Hu Han-min, who was briefly detained and later forced to leave China. In exchange for Chiang's support, Wang helped Chiang consolidate his power within the KMT Nationalist Army.[22] The Chiang–Wang alliance propelled Chiang to a prominent position within the party after the Second Party Congress in January 1926. He ascended to the influential No. 2 position within the KMT despite his lack of membership in the Central Committee just two years prior during the First Party Congress.

The Shift from the Chiang–Wang Alliance to the Chiang–Hu Alliance. The Chiang–Wang alliance was short-lived. Chiang soon contemplated distancing himself from this alliance because of perceived threats to his party and military power. First, the rising influence of the CCP and the KMT-Left faction within the KMT organization threatened Chiang's power within the party. The KMT-Left faction and the CCP accounted for 65 percent of the KMT Central Committee in 1926, while the KMT-Right faction dropped to 8.3 percent.

---

[19] Wang received support for his rise from Borodin of the Comintern.
[20] Chiang Kai-shek began his career in the military. By 1925 he had reached only the position of Commandant of the Whampoa Military Academy, which was established in 1924 with help from the Comintern and the Soviet Union (Yang 2012).
[21] The Comintern considered Chiang Kai-shek, the most reliable KMT military leader at the time. He was an early supporter of Sun's "Unifying with Russia and Accommodating Communism" as a tactic largely because he admired Soviet experience in building a highly disciplined military force. The Whampoa Military Academy mimicked the Soviet model and received substantial financial and military support from the Soviet Union. See Yang (2012) for a detailed discussion of the relationship between Chiang and the Comintern.
[22] Xu Zhongzhi, Chiang's superior, resigned as Minister of Military Affairs, and Chiang merged Xu's unit into the No. 1 Division of the KMT Nationalist Army, which consisted mainly of Chiang's proteges from Whampoa Military Academy.

7.2 The Age of Leadership Contestation (1925–1937)

Chiang's own faction accounted for only 10 percent of the KMT Central Committee.[23] In the Third Plenum of 1927, the KMT-Right faction continued to lose seats on the Central Committee, and Chiang was elected only as a standing member. Furthermore, the Plenum eliminated two party positions held by Chiang – Chairman of the Standing Committee of the Central Committee and Chairman of the Central Military Commission. Meanwhile, CCP members held leadership positions in many KMT local party branches.[24]

Second, a change in the Soviet Military Advisor to the KMT led to acrimony between Chiang and the Comintern in 1925.[25] The new advisor, Kuibyshev, opposed the KMT Northern Expedition because Stalin and other Soviet leaders feared that it could be a premature offence that weakens KMT's Nationalist Army. Chiang interpreted the lack of support as an indicator of an attempt by the Comintern and KMT-Left faction to undermine his control over the KMT Nationalist Army. Fearing a coup in the making, Chiang orchestrated the Zhongshanjian Incident on March 20, 1926, resulting in the expulsion of a significant number of CCP members from the KMT military forces.[26]

Sensing the rising anti-CCP sentiment within the KMT and the potential threat from an alliance between the KMT-Left faction and the CCP, Chiang decided to switch his alliance to the KMT-Right faction. Chiang initiated a bloody purge of CCP members on April 12, 1927, leading to the collapse of the First United Front. Chiang's anti-Communist purge deepened the division between the KMT-Left and KMT-Right factions. The KMT-Left faction, led by Wang, initially condemned the purge. The disagreement between Wang and Chiang led to the Ning–Han Split (宁汉分裂) in 1927, resulting in the establishment of two separate entities within the KMT: The Wuhan Nationalist Government led by Wang and the Nanjing Nationalist Government led by Chiang and Hu Han-min. Hu returned to the KMT leadership circle as the chairman of the KMT Central Committee (中央政治会议主席) and the acting chairman of the Nanjing Government.

The Ning-Han Split ended a few months later in August 1927 because both Chiang and Wang softened their stances. Wang became aware of the Comintern's plot to divide the KMT by supporting the CCP within the Wuhan government, so he had to adapt his stance and cut ties with the CCP. Meanwhile, Chiang's rapid rise sparked a coalition of KMT elites and regional military leaders to oust him, and he suffered a major military defeat in August

---

[23] The calculation of faction shares in the Central Committee is based on the author's database. See Figure 1.3 and Appendix B for more details.
[24] CCP members occupied seats on several provincial KMT Party Committees in Hunan, Hubei, and Jiangxi in 1924. By the time the KMT held the Second Party Congress in January 1926, more than eleven provinces and four major cities had established KMT local organizations with help from CCP members.
[25] The Comintern replaced Borodin, who was one of Chiang's main supporters, with Nikolay Kuibyshev as the Soviet Military Advisor to the KMT in October 1925.
[26] See Yang (2012) for further discussion.

1927. Eventually, Wang and Chiang reached a compromise and ended the Ning–Han Split, Wang agreeing to relocate the KMT government's capital to Nanjing and Chiang stepping down as commander in chief of the Northern Expedition. These compromises facilitated the establishment of a unified KMT Party Center and Government in Nanjing in August 1927.

The End of the Chiang–Hu Alliance and a "Civil War" among KMT Elites. The retreat by Chiang was ephemeral: He returned to the KMT leadership circle a few months later as the commander in chief for the KMT Nationalist Army on January 4, 1928. Hu Han-min sought to strengthen an alliance with Chiang to pursue Sun's vision of establishing a democratic government. By the end of 1928, Hu became the president of the Legislative Yuan, the highest legislative branch; Chiang remained the commander in chief of the KMT Nationalist Army. Meanwhile, Wang Ching-wei was forced to retreat from the KMT leadership circle because the CCP's radical insurgencies after 1927 increasingly discredited his earlier accommodationist approach.

Unfortunately, the Chiang–Hu alliance suffered from the same fate as the Chiang–Wang alliance. Hu, in an effort to curb Chiang's influence derived from his control over the KMT Nationalist Army, sought to institutionalize a party-state relationship by granting more power to the party over the government and military.[27] Chiang, on the other hand, resisted these changes while trying to accumulate power within the party. The conflict between Hu and Chiang led to the house arrest of Hu Han-min on February 28, 1931, resulting in an anti-Chiang coalition that established an alternative KMT National Government in Guangzhou (i.e., the Ning-Yue split 宁粤分裂). This coalition declared war against Chiang, and their military expedition was halted only after the Japanese invaded Northern China on September 18, 1931. As a compromise, Chiang resigned from his party leadership position again, ending the imminent civil war among the KMT factions. Wang Ching-wei and Hu Han-min remained at odds because of their previous ideological differences, so Sun Ke, the son of Sun Yat-sen, became the president of the Executive Yuan in charge of the government.

The newly established KMT government under the leadership of Sun Ke proved to be ineffective in its functioning. Sun had not developed a sufficient patronage network inside the Party or government, nor did he command the prestige like his father within the party; furthermore, Sun received no endorsements from most KMT senior elites, especially not from Chiang, Hu, and Wang. The lack of support effectively paralyzed Sun's government; for example, Soong Tse-ven, Minister of Finance, submitted his resignation to Sun's government, effectively undercutting its fiscal capacity (Coble 1986; Li 2011). In addition, Chiang Kai-shek, Wang Ching-wei, and Hu Han-min refused to travel to Nanjing to take up their new posts. The absence of these three men

---

[27] For Hu's tactics, see Cui (2013), Li (2011), and Q. Wang (2010).

in Nanjing crippled the operation of the KMT Central Committee, resulting in the resignation of Sun's cabinet a few months later.

Another Failed Attempt to Institutionalize Power Sharing. In a bid to mitigate the ongoing political turmoil amidst Japanese aggression and CCP insurgencies, KMT elites sought to establish a "truce" through the institutionalization of a power-sharing arrangement. The First Plenum of the Fourth Party Congress of the KMT in December 1931 delineated the specific scope and boundaries of power among Chiang, Wang, and Hu, providing a framework for their respective roles within the party. Specifically, all three were elected to the Standing Committee of the KMT Central Committee, and they rotated the position of Standing Committee Chairman. The KMT undertook a reorganization of the national government and legislatures, implementing a prohibition on joint leadership appointments by military officials within these institutions to curb Chiang's power. Wang was appointed President of the Executive Yuan, and Chiang assumed the role of Chairman of the National Military Council, maintaining his authority over the military system.

Nevertheless, de jure institutions for power sharing do not last when it is not aligned with the de facto power among KMT elites. Despite the power-sharing arrangement, Chiang's stronger de facto power over Hu and Wang left him dissatisfied with the constraints imposed upon him. Consequently, Chiang gradually and strategically sought opportunities to tilt the balance of power in his favor, aiming to consolidate his position within the KMT.

Chiang Kai-shek's stronger de facto power was firmly established through his control over substantial financial resources and the KMT Nationalist Army. Notably, his influence extended over Shanghai, Jiangsu, and Zhejiang, which were among the wealthiest regions in China. The rapid modernization of the Chinese economy had fostered a class of influential industrialists and bankers, particularly the influential financial guilds in Ningbo and Zhejiang. Recognizing the concerns of capitalists regarding labor mobilization in urban areas, Chiang provided political support by suppressing labor movements led by the CCP, thus securing financial resources from the capitalists to finance his military campaign and further enhancing his military strength (Coble 1986).

Hu Han-min remained skeptical about power-sharing arrangements because of his profound distrust of Chiang and Wang, stemming from their previous acts of betrayal. Hu later moved to Guangdong and attempted to build a coalition with local military strongmen in Guangdong and Guangxi to challenge Chiang's leadership in the KMT. These challenges culminated in several brief military confrontations with Chiang's forces.[28] Despite Hu's open challenge to the Nanjing government, Chiang did not directly confront Hu primarily because he wanted to preserve the de jure power-sharing arrangement. Hu was even appointed to various leadership positions within the KMT during this period.

---

[28] The Fujian incident by the No. 19 Army in 1933; the Two-Guang Incident by General Chen Jitang in Guangdong and Li Zhongren in Guangxi in 1936.

Wang Ching-wei, by contrast, adhered to the power sharing arrangement while attempting to expand his patronage network within the government. Because of Hu's refusal to participate in the power-sharing arrangement, Wang Ching-wei became Chiang's primary collaborator. As the Premier of the KMT government, Wang Ching-wei wielded power primarily through his de jure control over the executive branch; however, he faced challenges in building a robust patronage network because he lacked the leverage of military power to provide protection and secure the support of business elites (Cui 2013).

With the escalation of Japanese aggression and the looming threat of war, Chiang's influential position as the chair of the military commission exerted significant control over the decision-making processes within both the government and the party. The shadow cast by the impending Sino-Japanese conflict played a pivotal role in strengthening Chiang's position in the power balance with Wang. In light of the escalating tensions, Wang chose to adopt a compromise approach in addressing Japanese aggression, aiming to avert a military confrontation that could further bolster Chiang's power.

7.2.2 Party Building under the Shadow of Elite Contestation

The decade-long relentless elite conflict within the KMT inevitably hindered the party's efforts to build an effective elite mobilization infrastructure. During this period, KMT party-building strategies were primarily driven by the strategic maneuvers by contenders to party leadership positions. Chiang Kai-shek's opportunistic alliance with the leaders of the KMT-Left and the KMT-Right factions became the impetus in wavering party-building strategies. Furthermore, his firm control over the military incentivized him to introduce extraparty resources in intraparty competition. Meanwhile, Hu and Wang responded to Chiang's ascent by placing emphasis on reforming national party and government institutions to establish a power-sharing framework. Failing to curtail Chiang's rising power, they then sought to mobilize both intraparty and extraparty resources to counter his influence. Similar to the CCP, the power struggle among KMT elites led to radical changes in the recruitment, training, and expulsion of party membership.

Beyond conflicts over party-building strategies due to leadership contestation at the top, the KMT faced a strong headwind when attempting to build elite mobilization infrastructure outside its established stronghold. Regional strongmen resisted the efforts by the KMT to expand the party in their territories, fearing the loss of their autonomy due to the presence of KMT party organizations. The resistance was exacerbated when some KMT elites sought to address internal conflicts by leveraging external resources, such as enlisting the support of regional military leaders, in a bid to consolidate their positions within the party.

Chiang Kai-shek: Party Building for his Patronage Network. Of the KMT leaders, Chiang had the most consequential impact on KMT's party-building

7.2 The Age of Leadership Contestation (1925–1937)

strategies, which centered on three areas: (1) the abandonment of mass mobilization designated by the 1924 Party Reform, (2) the prioritization of party expansion into the military over rank-and-file members, and (3) the creation of patronage organizations within and alongside the KMT.

Despite the dramatic success the First United Front brought to the party, Chiang's steering the KMT away from mass mobilization originated in his fear of the rising influence of the CCP and the KMT-Left within the party. The KMT embarked on a series of party reorganization strategies that essentially aborted its previous efforts in building any capacity for mass mobilization. In particular, Chiang initiated a campaign in the name of "party-purification" (清党), which aimed to completely eradicate the CCP influence from the KMT. For instance, Chiang proposed "The Resolution to Organize Party Affairs"[29] in May 1926 after the Zhongshanjian Incident, and it was approved by the Second Plenum of Second Party Congress of the KMT. The Resolution effectively marginalized CCP members in its ranks by removing their leadership positions and limiting their roles on national and local party committees within KMT organization, as Chiang feared a military coup supported by the CCP and the Comintern was brewing.

Chiang did not see the changes in party regulations as a sufficient measure to eradicate the Communist influence, so he ordered the overhaul of the KMT organization after the infamous April 12 incident in 1927, during which thousands of CCP members were arrested or murdered. To screen out CCP members and sympathizers, the KMT dissolved all existing local party committees, reselected local party leaders, and reregistered the party members over the next two years.

Finally, Chiang decisively undermined the KMT's potential to become a mass party by dismantling its mass mobilization apparatus. During the Fourth Plenum of the Second Party Congress in February 1928, he abolished all five party departments dedicated to mass mobilization (e.g., peasants, workers, merchants, youth, and women) and replaced them with a single new entity: the Department of Mass Training (训练部).[30] Effectively, the KMT changed its attitudes toward the masses from *mobilizing* them to *controlling* them.[31] By April 1929, Chiang became the head of the KMT Organization Department, further extending his de jure power over party-building strategies in the KMT.

Another hallmark of Chiang's impact on KMT organization was his prioritization of party expansion into the military over rank-and-file members.

---

[29] "整理党务案 [Proposal to Organize Party Affairs]" in *Zhong guo guo min dang li ci quan guo dai biao da hui ji zhong yang quan hui wen xian hui bian (The compendium of China's KMT National Party Congress and Central Committee documents)* (2012 V4: 38–47).

[30] "改善中央党部组织案 [Proposal to Improve the Party Central Organization]" in *Zhong guo guo min dang li ci quan guo dai biao da hui ji zhong yang quan hui wen xian hui bian (The compendium of China's KMT National Party Congress and Central Committee documents)* (2012 V4: 32–37).

[31] Q. Wang (2010) and Cui (2013) have detailed discussion of the implications of these maneuvers.

In contrast to the CCP, Chiang's emphasis on expanding the KMT's presence within the military was not primarily driven by the desire to control the armed forces. Instead, it served as a counterweight strategy to patronage networks being developed by his rivals among the rank-and-file members. Chiang implemented a policy of mass recruitment in the military in 1928, which involved loosening the recruitment criteria with the aim of building his own patronage network and solidifying his control over the KMT. Meanwhile, Chiang advocated for stricter recruitment criteria for rank-and-file party members during the KMT's Third Party Congress.[32]

The final move by Chiang was the creation of several party factions that were fully committed to his leadership. The emergence of these patronage factions, such as Lixing She (力行社, also known as the Blue Shirt Society) and the Central Club (中央俱乐部, also known as the CC Faction), posed a further challenge to creating an effective and coherent elite mobilization infrastructure. These factions directly or covertly competed with the party in terms of recruitment, diverting attention and resources away from the party's goals. As a result, the unity and coherence of the KMT's party-building endeavors were undermined by the emergence of these parallel organizations.[33]

Hu Han-min: From Institutionalization Builder to Party Divider. Hu's influence in party building in the KMT can be divided into two stages. During the initial period from 1928 to 1931, Hu attempted to strengthen the KMT organization to facilitate power-sharing among elites holding leadership positions in the party, the state, and the military. Failing to use de jure institutions to constrain Chiang, Hu undermined the party by coalescing with regional warlords in Guangxi to challenge Chiang militarily in the second period, 1931–1936 until his death. Hu's refusal to participate in the day-to-day operations of the KMT discredited its efforts to build a cohesive elite mobilization infrastructure.

At first, Hu strove to build a strong party and create institutions in order to constrain Chiang's rising power, stemming from his control of the military. The top priority for Hu was to draft a constitution specifying both the distribution and boundary of power among the party, the government, and the military. Following Sun Yat-sen's blueprint, Hu helped draft "An Outline of Political Affairs" (训政纲领), which was approved at the Third Party Congress of the KMT in March 1929.[34] This outline legitimized the KMT as the only ruling party of China with the KMT National Party Congress playing a leadership

---

[32] "中国国民党总章 [The Chinese Kuomintang Bylaws]" in *Zhong guo guo min dang li ci quan guo dai biao da hui ji zhong yang quan hui wen xian hui bian (The compendium of China's KMT National Party Congress and Central Committee documents)* (2012 V5: 43–62).

[33] See Eastman (1972), Cui (2013), and Q. Wang (2010) for a discussion of these factions.

[34] "确定训政时期党政府人民行使政权治权之分际及方略案 [On the Plan Resolving Power-Sharing between the Party, Government, and the People during the Xunzheng Period]" in *Zhong guo guo min dang li ci quan guo dai biao da hui ji zhong yang quan hui wen xian hui bian (The compendium of China's KMT National Party Congress and Central Committee documents)* (2012 V4: 311–314).

role in civilian government. The highest decision-making body of the KMT – the Central Committee – was supposed to lead both the national government and the military.

Hu Han-min's endeavor to centralize power within the party, encompassing both the state and the military, stemmed not only from upholding Sun Yat-sen's legacy but also from an aspiration to establish institutional checks on Chiang's burgeoning military authority. Hence, Hu prioritized "rule by party" (党治) over "rule by military" (军治) for the centralization of power. Despite the emergence of an institution created to bestow upon the party greater de jure power over the military, the de facto power remained in the hands of those who controlled the guns. Hu continued to press for party institutions designed to check military power, inevitably resulting in a conflict with Chiang, which in turn led to Hu's brief house arrest in 1931 after their disagreement over the drafting of a constitution in which de jure power would be shifted to the government and away from the party.

The house arrest experience created a lasting impact on Hu. Although he was elected to the KMT Central Committee and appointed to various leadership positions later upon his release from house arrest, he refused to be involved with the KMT Nationalist government. Failing to create institutional checks and balances to confront Chiang, Hu sought external resources, forming an anti-Chiang coalition with military strongmen in Guangxi. Hu established a rival government and even founded an alternative party organization known as the "New Kuomintang" (Chen 2003; Cui 2013). In effect, Hu became an outsider trying to split the party as a way to undermine Chiang's influence.

Wang Ching-wei: Accepting the Terms of Cooptation. In contrast to Hu Han-min, Wang Ching-wei chose to stay in the power-sharing arrangement with Chiang but relied on both intraparty and extraparty resources to build his own personal power. The desire to maintain power sharing led Wang to miss an important opportunity to pursue the mass mobilization infrastructure that could have potentially strengthened his power. In 1928, the Reorganization Faction (改组派) emerged, comprising some KMT-Left elites who had faced defeat by Chiang and the KMT-Right during the anti-Communist purge in 1927. This faction sparked an intense discourse within the party regarding issues of class representation and the significance of mass mobilization. Chen Gongbo, a prominent figure in the Reorganization Faction, advocated for the KMT to represent peasants, workers, and the petty bourgeoisie, with a proposed membership distribution of 50 percent, 30 percent, and 20 percent respectively (Q. Wang 2010: 156–157). Nonetheless, Chen criticized the CCP's class struggle approach, arguing that capitalists should be allowed to join the party as long as they supported the revolution. Wang did not wholeheartedly support this faction, however. The assassination of Wang Leping, a key leader of this faction in 1930, effectively ended any move to shift party building in the KMT toward the mass-centric principle.

The falling out between Chiang and Hu in 1931 gave Wang an opportunity to return to the KMT leadership circle. Hoping to counter Chiang from within, Wang agreed to serve as the Premier of the KMT government. Wang was occupied by dealing with foreign affairs, especially Japanese aggression, and spent little time with party affairs. Hence, Wang's influence on KMT party building receded.

Resistance from Regional Strongmen in Party Expansion. Despite its success in the North Expedition military campaign and the establishment of the Nanjing Nationalist Government in 1928, the KMT did not achieve complete dominance as a ruling party. By 1929 the Nanjing Government held effective control over only 8 percent of the territories and 20 percent of the population in China. The majority of these territories remained under the control of regional strongmen, who aligned themselves with the KMT in exchange for political autonomy.

The regional strongmen, while submitting to KMT rule, were reluctant to allow the expansion of KMT party organization in their territories, fearing a loss of control. Complicating matters further, the KMT's elite power struggle led to alliances between military strongmen and figures such as Hu Han-Min and Wang Ching-wei at times,[35] further disincentivizing them from expanding the party in their territory. Moreover, the party's strategies centered around urban areas neglected the mobilization of rural populations, rendering the KMT susceptible during the Sino-Japanese War.

7.2.3 Leadership Contestation and Conflicting Party-Building Outcomes

The 1927 anti-Communist purge marked a turning point in KMT party building, leading to a permanent shift in the trajectory of KMT party organization. In the aftermath of the purge, KMT elites embarked on diverse strategies to mold the party organization in line with their own interests. To assess the direct impact of the KMT elite conflict on the development of party mobilization infrastructure, this analysis focuses on four key aspects: (1) overall party membership, (2) composition of KMT membership, (3) geographic distribution of party membership, and (4) functionality of grassroots party organizations.

An examination of these dimensions reveals a consistent trend: The power struggle among KMT elites deepened internal divisions within the party, incentivizing them to expand their own patronage networks. Subsequently, the development of personal patronage networks led to the assimilation of diverse

---

[35] For instance, Hu formed an anti-Chiang coalition with regional strongmen in Guangdong and Guangxi after 1931. Meanwhile, Wang attempted to challenge Chiang militarily through his alliance with regional warlords such as Zhang Fagui and Yan Xishan in Northern China. They even established an alternative KMT National Government in Peking.

7.2 *The Age of Leadership Contestation (1925–1937)*

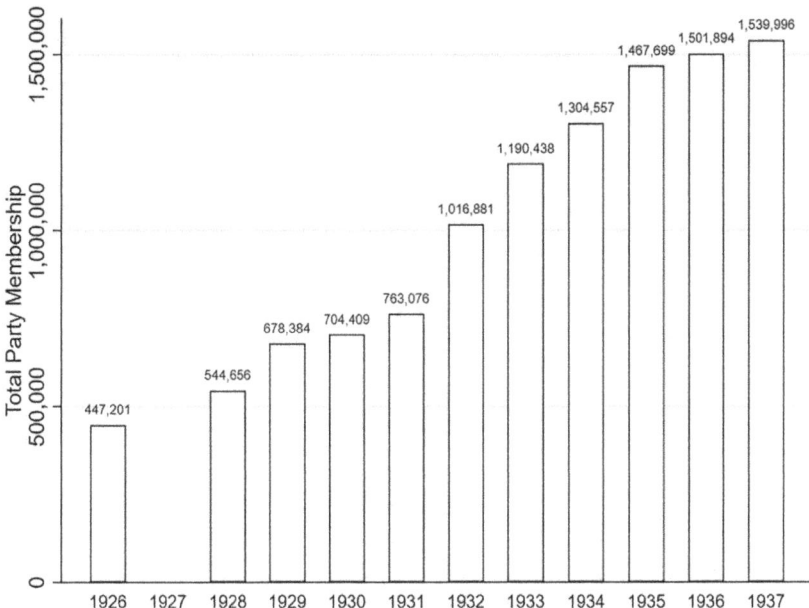

FIGURE 7.2 KMT membership (1926–1937)
Note: See Appendix A for the sources of KMT membership. The total number reported in this figure includes both rank-and-file and military members but excludes overseas members.

political, economic, and bureaucratic elites at the national and local levels into the party, perpetuating elite conflicts. Importantly, the KMT abandoned mass mobilization and became increasingly reliant on elites.

Total Party Membership. During the tumultuous events surrounding the 1927 anti-Communist purge, the KMT achieved only modest gains during the height of the succession battle between 1928 and 1932. However, KMT membership expansion experienced a surge when a truce was reached among KMT elites and the Chiang–Wang alliance was formed, following the breakdown of the Chiang–Hu alliance in 1932. During this period total KMT membership witnessed rapid growth, reaching 1.54 million on the eve of the Sino-Japanese War in 1937 (Figure 7.2).

Occupational Background of Party Members. The KMT party that emerged after the 1927 anti-Communist purge cannot be more different from its pre-purge counterpart in terms of its organization and structure. Despite growing membership, the KMT party after 1927 was anything but the revolutionary party that Sun envisioned it would be after the 1924 Party Reform. Closer examination of the occupational background of KMT members reveals profound changes within the party in two significant aspects: the share of rank-and-file party members vis-à-vis military party members and the occupation backgrounds of rank-and-file party members.

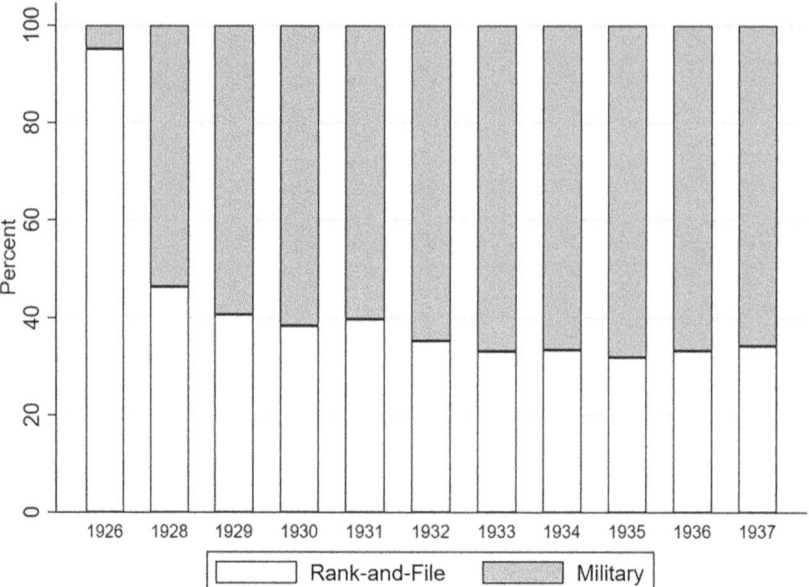

FIGURE 7.3 KMT rank-and-file and military membership (1926–1935)
Note: See Table A.3 in Appendix A for data sources. The total number reported in this figure includes both rank-and-file and military members but excludes overseas members.

To begin with, the KMT's rapidly expanding party membership was primarily fueled by the influx of military personnel. Following the events of 1927, Chiang aimed to bolster his position in the party by expanding the party within the military, which he commanded with firm control. As shown in Figure 7.3, the share of military personnel in KMT membership amounted only to 4.83 percent in 1926. In 1928, however, the share of military personnel jumped more than tenfold from 1926 – growing from 21,589 to 292,428 – and accounted for 53.69 percent of KMT membership. In subsequent years, KMT membership expansion in the military continued, and its share reached as much as 68.11 percent in 1935. Notably, KMT membership recruitment among the military resulted in an increase in quantity but not in quality. In many instances, entire military units were mandated to join the KMT, sometimes even without the knowledge of low-ranking service personnel. These KMT "members" had little idea of its ideology, let alone loyalty to the party.

By contrast, rank-and-file party membership experienced a 42 percent decline in 1928, attributable to the arrest, purge, and even the murder of numerous KMT members affiliated with or sympathetic to the CCP. From 1928 to 1931, a period marked by intense power struggles among KMT elites, rank-and-file party membership remained stagnant. The recruitment of

7.2 The Age of Leadership Contestation (1925–1937)

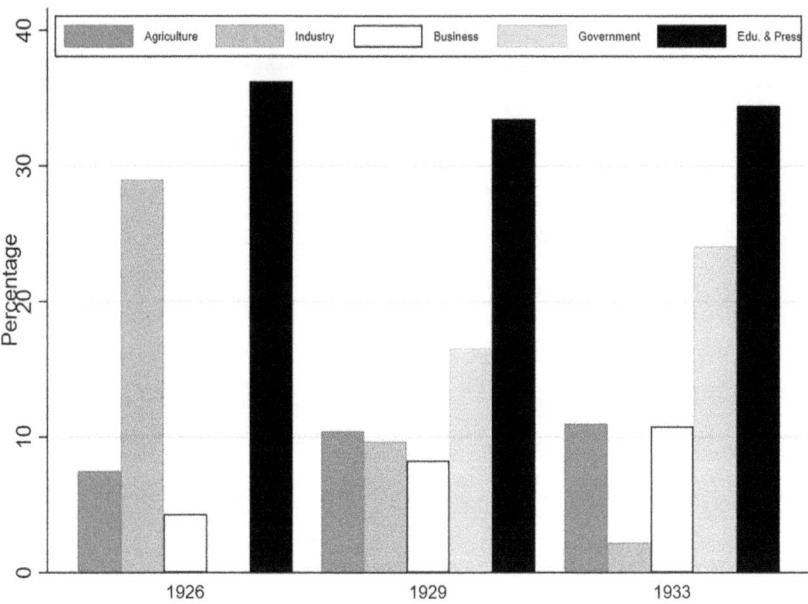

FIGURE 7.4 Occupational backgrounds of KMT rank-and-file members (1926–1933)
Note: See Table A.4 in Appendix A for data sources.

rank-and-file members grew only after 1932, when KMT elites attempted to institutionalize power sharing, but it was consistently outpaced by the recruitment of military personnel.

Crucially, not only did rank-and-file party members grow more slowly after 1927, but newly recruited members also came from a very different background. These shifts pointed to a fundamental return toward an elite-centered mobilization infrastructure within the party following the anti-Communist purge in 1927 (Figure 7.4). Prior to the purge, 72.7 percent of rank-and-file members comprised workers, students, intellectuals, and peasants, reflecting the mass mobilization strategy emphasized in the 1924 Party Reform under the First United Front. After the 1927 purge, a noticeable decline occurred in the representation of workers, accompanied by a sharp increase in party members with occupations in business and government. These changes suggest that the KMT prioritized elite-centric mobilization efforts while seeking to eradicate the influence of the CCP.

These changes marked the ultimate dilution of the revolutionary spirit of the KMT. First, most new party members were no longer the committed revolutionaries who joined the party because of their ideological conviction. Even KMT internal reports acknowledged that members recruited after the purge were primarily opportunistic individuals aiming to advance their individual well-being by tapping into the resources controlled by the KMT (Q. Wang 2010). Second, although the KMT had expanded its membership in rural areas,

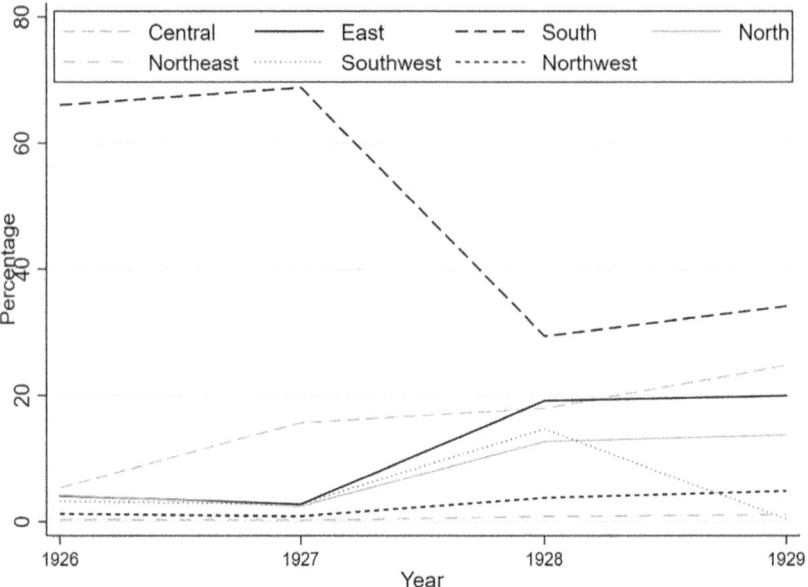

FIGURE 7.5 Geographic concentration of KMT rank-and-file members (1926–1929)
Note: Data source is from Cui (2013: 477). East includes Jiangsu, Zhejiang, Anhui, Nanjing, and Shanghai; Northeast includes Liaoning, Jilin, Heilongjiang, and Fengtian; Central includes Hubei, Hunan, Hankou, and Jiangxi; North includes Hebei, Henan, Shandong, Peking, Tianjin, and Qingdao; South includes Fujian, Guangdong, Guangxi, and Guangzhou; Southwest includes Sichuan, Yunnan, Guizhou; Northwest includes Shanxi, Shaanxi, Gansu, Ningxia, Qinghai, Rehe, Chahar, and Jinyuan.

its rural members were typically local elites with leadership positions and party apparatus, both at the county level.[36] Hence, KMT rural members distinctly differed from those of the CCP, which pursued tenants and poor peasants.

Geographic Distribution of Party Membership. The downstream effect from the KMT elite power struggle also manifested in the geographic distribution of rank-and-file membership (Figure 7.5). This reflects not only the competition among KMT elites to establish concentrated patronage networks in specific regions but also resistance from regional strongmen.

Before the First United Front collapsed, KMT membership was concentrated in South China because KMT headquarters was located in Guangdong. Combined with three other provinces (Guangxi, Hubei, and Hunan) that were the hotbeds for the Chinese revolution, these four provinces accounted for 85.1 percent of total KMT membership.

---

[36] "共产国际执行委员会远东局使团关于对广州政治关系和党派关系调查结果的报告 [Comintern Far East Bureau Report on Faction Relations and Party Relations in Guangzhou]" September 12, 1926, in *Lian gong (bu), gong chan guo ji yu zhong guo guo min ge ming yun dong (1926–1927) (Soviet, Comintern, and Chinese National Revolution (1926–1927))* (2002, V3: 482)

7.2 The Age of Leadership Contestation (1925–1937)

After 1927, attempts by KMT elites to establish their own patronage network at the expense of their intraparty rivals led to major shifts in geographic concentration of KMT membership. For instance, Chiang's endeavor to consolidate his own patronage network and undermine the power of his rivals resulted in a notable surge in party membership in East China, while causing a significant decline in Guangdong and Guangxi provinces because of the anti-Communist purge after 1927. KMT membership in East China (Jiangsu, Zhejiang, Anhui, Nanjing, and Shanghai) rose from 4.1 percent in 1926 to 19.94 percent in 1929; meanwhile, party membership in Southern and Southwest China (Guangdong and Guangxi), where the opposition government was established by Wang during the Ning–Han Split, suffered major losses, declining from 66.02 percent in 1926 to only 34.15 percent in 1929.[37]

In subsequent years Wang Ching-wei attempted to establish a patronage network within his Wuhan government, resulting in a significant increase in party membership in central China with the share rising from 5.36 percent to 24.76 percent. Conversely, the warlord in Guangxi, who had previously allied with Hu Han-min against Chiang, suppressed KMT party building efforts in the region. As a result, the membership from Guangxi plummeted from 30.2 percent in 1926 to a mere 1.9 percent in 1933. Similarly, the Northwest region under the control of General Zhang Zuolin also registered slow growth in KMT membership throughout the entire period.

Dysfunctional Grassroots Party Organizations. The KMT's fragility in mass mobilization becomes apparent when examining both the quantity and quality of its grassroots party organizations. Their expansion experienced a significant slowdown after 1928, coinciding with the party's shift away from mass mobilization efforts. By 1927 the KMT had established 451 county party committees, a number that increased to 634 by 1930. Following this peak, the number of county party committees wavered and even declined, ultimately covering only around 337 counties in 1937 (Figure 7.6). In contrast, the CCP maintained 387 county party committees in 1935. In other words, the KMT had not done a better job penetrating rural China than the CCP during this period despite its control of more territories and domination of the CCP politically and militarily.

The stagnation in the growth of KMT grassroots party organizations, however, tells only part of the story. Clearly, many of these organizations were not functioning effectively: internal KMT reports identified two main factors contributing to the dysfunctionality of local party affairs. First, the anti-Communist purge removed many KMT local leaders at the provincial and county levels, creating a political vacuum in local party leadership. Second, factional competition to fill local party leadership positions undermined cooperation among local party elites. Specifically, members of KMT factions attempted to marginalize rivals from other factions in the name of party cleansing (Q. Wang 2010).

---

[37] See Q. Wang (2010: 145–146) on the impact of party membership reregistration on Guangdong and southern China.

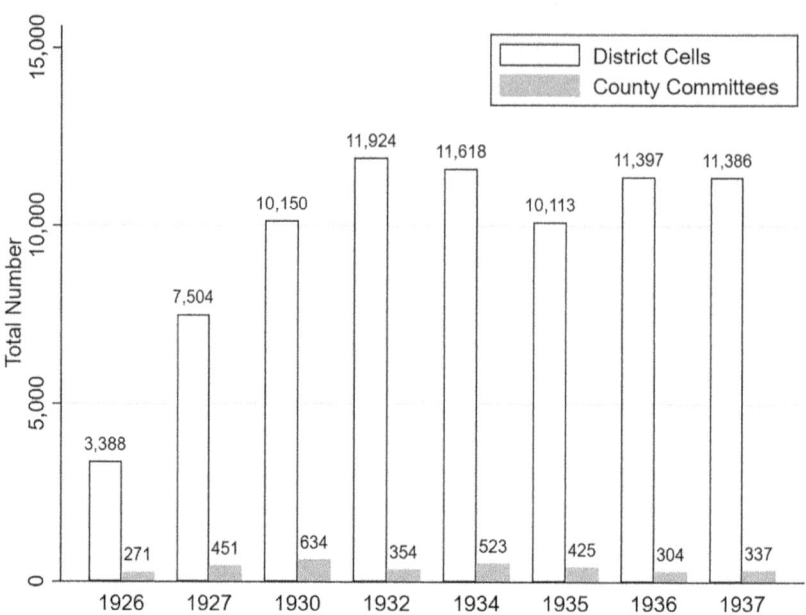

FIGURE 7.6 KMT grassroots county party committees and district cells (1926–1937)
Note: See Appendix A for the data sources of KMT grassroots party organizations. The total number reported in this figure excludes overseas branches.

In sum, the KMT reverted to an elite mobilization infrastructure after 1927 with a fragile party organization despite growing membership. The cracks in its foundation were largely the result of the intense power struggle among KMT elites, which eroded party cohesion and undermined party-building strategies. A crucial factor in the KMT's subsequent decline after the Sino-Japanese War can be traced back to its failure to effectively penetrate rural China. This failure to gain a foothold in rural areas planted the seeds of further deterioration for the party.

7.3 QUASI-DOMINANT LEADER & PARTY REFORM (1938–1945)

Despite Chiang Kai-shek's towering de facto power over Wang Ching-wei and Hu Han-min after 1931, he could not entirely eradicate their threats to his leadership position because of the formal power-sharing arrangement; however, two unforeseen events ultimately paved the way for him to assert his de jure dominance in party affairs: Wang's withdrawal from leadership and Hu's untimely death.

Chiang's successful consolidation of power elevated him to the position of preeminent leader within the party. With diminished threats from internal

7.3 Quasi-Dominant Leader & Party Reform (1938–1945)

rivals, Chiang adopted a new approach to building the party, aiming to transform it into a more disciplined organization to facilitate wartime mobilization. Chiang's party reforms encountered little resistance from KMT elites, but regional strongmen remained defiant toward his reform efforts. In addition, Chiang's party reform did not deviate from the elite mobilization infrastructure despite his intention to enhance the KMT's mass mobilization capacity.

On the surface party reform appeared highly successful after achieving rapid growth in party membership and grassroots organizations, particularly following Chiang's renewed emphasis on establishing mass mobilization capacity after 1939. Beneath this success the KMT remained a party deeply entrenched in an elite mobilization infrastructure, heavily reliant on the cooperation of regional strongmen and local elites for policy implementation. Furthermore, KMT party members were loosely connected to the party organization. The lack of infrastructure for mass mobilization capacity became an impediment later when the power of those elites, upon which the KMT relied, was weakened during the Japanese invasion as shown by its failures in grain extraction in Chapter 4.

7.3.1 Chiang Kai-shek as a Quasi-Dominant Party Leader

Chiang, as the military commission chair, effectively dominated the decision-making process in both the government and the party after 1931 because of the increasing Japanese aggression and prolong warfare with the CCP. He was, however, cautious not to completely marginalize Hu and Wang, because his earlier efforts prompted KMT elites to coalesce with regional warlords and mount a challenge against him.

The Exit of Wang and Hu from KMT Leadership Contestation. Although Wang Ching-wei lacked the political capital to challenge Chiang's leadership directly, he remained a significant presence within the party, effectively limiting Chiang's monopoly on power. Unfortunately, Wang's position was significantly weakened after he was seriously wounded in an assassination attempt on November 1, 1935.[38] To recover from the injury, Wang was forced to resign from his positions as the President of the Executive Yuan and Minister of Foreign Affairs.

Two weeks after the assassination attempt, Chiang consolidated his power during the Fifth Party Congress of the KMT, monopolizing leadership positions

---

[38] As the head of the executive branch, Wang was in charge of negotiating with the Japanese government. In part because he held a pessimistic view of the ability of the KMT to resist a Japanese invasion, he tried to negotiate a settlement with the Japanese to reduce casualties. Nonetheless, the anti-Japanese sentiment across China led to widespread condemnation of the KMT's soft stance on the Japanese invasion. Sun Fengming, a KMT soldier, attempted to assassinate KMT leaders during the Sixth Plenum of the Fourth Party Congress of the KMT. He had planned to assassinate Chiang Kai-shek; however, Chiang did not attend this meeting, so Sun decided to assassinate Wang instead.

across the party, the government, and the military. Wang was elected chairman of the KMT Central Committee at this meeting, but he had to travel abroad to recover from his injuries. During the next two years, Wang and Chiang found themselves at odds over policies regarding Japanese invasions, as Wang attempting to negotiate a settlement with the Japanese. Eventually, Wang established a puppet government in opposition to the Chiang-led KMT during the tumultuous period of the Sino-Japanese War. This maneuver effectively expelled him from KMT leadership circle, diminishing his influence within the party.

Tragically, Hu Han-min's fate was even worse compared to that of Wang Ching-wei. Just six months after the assassination attempt on Wang, Hu died unexpectedly following a cerebral hemorrhage while playing chess at home on May 12, 1936. Hu's anti-Chiang coalition quickly collapsed after Chen Jitang and Li Zongren, two military strongmen in Guangdong and Guangxi, surrendered to Chiang. The fall of Hu meant that the KMT-Right faction no longer had a de facto leader coordinating its efforts to challenge Chiang; thus, its influence vanished overnight.

Chiang's Challenges in De Jure Power Consolidation. By the end of 1936, Chiang became the preeminent KMT leader, and few KMT elites could challenge his party leadership position. In April 1938, Chiang was formally elected Director General of the KMT (总裁), formally establishing his legitimacy as the second-generation leader after Sun Yat-sen. Despite becoming the preeminent leader of the party, Chiang did not achieve the same de facto domination within the KMT as Mao had within the CCP. The challenges Chiang faced stemmed mainly from two sources: defiance from regional strongmen and factional struggle within his own inner circle.

The persistent power of regional strongmen can be attributed to the legacy of the Northern Expedition (1925–1928), a key phase in the KMT's endeavor to unify China. During this period Chiang adopted a strategy of cooptation, assimilating some regional military strongmen into the KMT's Nationalist Army in return for their support. Consequently, many of these strongmen were appointed as chairmen of KMT Provincial Committees across different provinces (Table 7.1). This arrangement granted them significant political autonomy and allowed them to maintain their own fiscal and military resources, which became the leverage for their defiance of Chiang.

Furthermore, Chiang encountered difficulties in reconciling the diverse factions within the party. Although no KMT factions openly opposed Chiang's leadership, power struggles among party elites persisted, including some within Chiang's own inner circle.[39] From 1935 to 1945, the KMT Central Committees consisted primarily of a dominant yet fragmented Chiang faction and a large number of smaller factions unable to ally and challenge Chiang. Chiang's faction accounted for less than 40 percent of the Central Committee,

---

[39] See Cui (2013), Eastman (1974), and Q. Wang (2010).

7.3 Quasi-Dominant Leader & Party Reform (1938–1945)

TABLE 7.1 *Military background of KMT provincial party committee chairmen (1928–1949)*

Province	Number of people		Number of years in office	
	Nonmilitary	Military	Nonmilitary	Military
Jiangsu	3	4	8	14
Zhejiang	3	7	4	18
Anhui	1	12	1	21
Jiangxi	1	6	1	21
Hubei	2	10	2	20
Hunan	0	8	0	22
Sichuan	0	6	0	22
Fujian	0	6	0	22
Guangdong	3	6	8	13
Guangxi	0	5	0	22
Yunnan	0	2	0	22
Guizhou	1	7	7	14
Hebei	0	10	0	22
Shandong	1	7	2	20
Henan	0	9	0	22
Shanxi	1	3	2	20
Shaanxi	1	7	4	18
Gansu	1	7	2	20
Ningxia	0	2	0	22
Qinghai	0	3	0	22
Total	18	127	41	397

Note: Data are based on Table 7-8 in Q. Wang (2010: 219).

but other factions amounted to more than 50 percent (Figure 1.3). In addition, the radical expansion of the KMT Central Committee – from 60 seats (full and alternate) in 1929 to 312 seats by 1945 – suggests that Chiang faced a daunting task of mitigating elite conflict and maintaining cohesion.

Chiang's leadership, although seemingly dominant, was in fact quasi-dominant; other KMT party elites held their own sources of de facto power, and their political survival was not entirely contingent on the KMT's fate. Section 7.3.2 shows how the leverage exerted by these elites posed a significant challenge to Chiang's endeavors to reform the party into a more disciplined and cohesive organization.

7.3.2 Party Building under a Quasi-Dominant Party Leader

After Chiang secured the institutionalization of his supreme position within the party, he recognized the importance of building a stronger party organization. Consequently, Chiang instigated several initiatives aiming to transform the KMT into a more effective and disciplined organization. In response to the need for wartime mobilization, he undertook efforts to rejuvenate the KMT's mass mobilization infrastructure. Simultaneously, he aimed to strengthen party discipline and ideological orientation by attracting enthusiastic Chinese youth; however, the implementation of these reforms varied and ultimately fell short of fully transforming the party largely because of the quasi-dominant nature of Chiang's leadership.

To begin, Chiang sought to emulate Sun's approach by using personal charisma and authority as effective tools to bolster party discipline. Under his guidance, the 1938 Emergent Party Congress issued a resolution to elevate his leadership status within the KMT.[40] The resolution stipulated that the KMT leadership position would hold the same prestige as Sun Yat-sen did. By signaling his preeminent position within the party, this resolution aimed to diminish factional conflicts and renew Sun's ideology, fostering elite cohesion under a strong party leader. Nonetheless, Chiang's attempt to invoke normative appeal among party members was bound to fail because he lacked the widely respected prestige and revolutionary experience that Sun possessed.

Chiang also revisited the idea of mass mobilization, aiming to improve the effectiveness of party organization during the War. This was a sharp departure from Chiang's previous skepticism of mass mobilization for fear of CCP infiltration. After a decade-long effort, Chiang believed that he had effectively eradicated the influence of the KMT-Left faction and the CCP within the party; thereby the imperative to strengthen the organization of the KMT outweighed those concerns. Chiang appointed a new head of the KMT Organization Department – Zhu Jiahua – who took steps to improve the party's connection with the masses (Li 2013). For instance, Zhu promoted the recruitment of nonelites and intellectuals into the party; he also emphasized the KMT's party building in rural areas to strengthen the coverage of grassroots party branches. Following the Fifth Plenum of the Fifth Party Congress in 1939, the KMT mandated local party branches to intensify party recruitment in rural areas.[41]

---

[40] For KMT justification to establish the director general position to institutionalize Chiang's leadership, see "改进党务并调整党政关系之原则 [The Principle of Improving Party Affairs and Adjusting Party-State Relations]" in *Zhong guo guo min dang li ci quan guo dai biao da hui ji zhong yang quan hui wen xian hui bian (The compendium of China's KMT National Party Congress and Central Committee documents)* (2012 V14: 178–180). For the final version of the institutionalization in the bylaws, see "修改总章案 [Resolution to Revise Party Bylaws]" in *Zhong guo guo min dang li ci quan guo dai biao da hui ji zhong yang quan hui wen xian hui bian(The compendium of China's KMT National Party Congress and Central Committee documents)* (2012, V14: 291–294).

[41] "整顿党务之要点 [Key Issues in the Reorganization of Party Affairs]" in *Zhong guo guo min dang li ci quan guo dai biao da hui ji zhong yang quan hui wen xian hui bian (The compendium of China's KMT National Party Congress and Central Committee documents)* (2012 V15: 148–158).

7.3 Quasi-Dominant Leader & Party Reform (1938–1945)

Despite the KMT's effort to strengthen mass mobilization capacity, the reliance on elites remained the core of its mobilization infrastructure. The "New County Institution"[42] (新县制) initiative exemplified the stark contrast between the KMT's and the CCP's approaches to mass mobilization: The KMT emphasized institutionally integrating party structures into local governments, while the CCP relied on mobilized compliance to engage rural households. For instance, the KMT issued a resolution in March 1938, aiming to strengthen the collaboration between the party and local governments.[43] In an effort to ensure that party branches gained control of the local government, the party mandated the recruitment of local elites, such as the head of the *baojia*, into the party (Xin 1991). During the following years, the KMT continued to press for collaboration between the local party branches and the government. In contrast, KMT resolutions did little to strengthen grassroots party organizations to penetrate civil society, nor did they emphasize building a bond between party members and peasants.

Recognizing his party-building efforts were yielding lackluster results due to KMT bureaucracy and local resistance, Chiang was compelled to seek alternative strategies to revitalize the KMT organization. To this end, Chiang permitted the establishment of a new political organization (Three Principles of the People Youth League, 三民主义青年团) specifically targeting Chinese youth and aiming to rejuvenate the revolutionary spirit of the KMT. This strategy mirrored Sun's early efforts in party building during the 1910s when he also created new parties rather than reforming existing ones. The new organization served dual purposes: first, to compete with the CCP in attracting Chinese youth to join the KMT and second, to rejuvenate the KMT, which was dominated by aging elites in existing party organizations.

The creation of the Three Principles of the People Youth League again generated tension with the KMT. In theory, its aim was to serve as the pipeline supplying disciplined and ideological youth to the KMT. In practice, however, the blurred line between the KMT and the Youth League undermined any such plan. First, the Youth League set the age limit of 16–38 for its members; however, before the Sino-Japanese War, 80 percent of KMT members were under the age of thirty-nine. Hence recruitment led to bitter fights among cadres in the Youth League and the KMT from national to local levels (Cui 2013; Q. Wang 2010). By 1940 Chiang had to intervene and reduce the age limit of Youth League members to 18–25 and that of the KMT to twenty-five and above.

To make the matters worse, some KMT elites considered the Three Principles of the People Youth League part of the KMT organization, but Youth League

---

[42] For the evolution of the "New County Institution," see Xin (1991).
[43] "关于改进党务与调整党政关系案 [Resolution on Improving Party Affairs and Adjusting Party-State Relations]" in *Zhong guo guo min dang li ci quan guo dai biao da hui ji zhong yang quan hui wen xian hui bian (The compendium of China's KMT National Party Congress and Central Committee documents)* (2012 V14: 378–401).

members considered themselves an independent organization. The confusion stemmed from the disconnect between the de jure objective of the Youth League and its de facto operation. In theory the Youth League was meant to prepare them for eventual admission into the KMT upon reaching the age limit. In practice the Youth League had operations in personnel management and finance independent of the KMT to avoid the influence of existing KMT factions like the CC Clique,[44] which controlled party affairs. Hence, members of the Youth League often challenged directives from the KMT while the party continued to try to intervene in its operations. Eventually, the conflicts between the KMT and the Youth League forced Chiang to abolish the latter and merge it with the KMT in 1947.

7.3.3 Rapid Party Expansion without Connecting the Masses

Following Chiang's consolidation of power, the KMT experienced seemingly remarkable expansion in both party membership and grassroots organizations from 1937 to 1945. Despite this growth, the KMT was far from a genuine mass party because the grassroots party organizations were still primarily controlled by political and economic elites who failed to serve as a liaison to the masses. Furthermore, Chiang's attempts to foster discipline and loyalty within the party did not yield the desired results.

Total Party Membership. The KMT initially suffered a blow from the chaotic retreat to Southwest China after the loss of Nanjing to the Japanese invasion. Not only did the party achieve merely tepid growth from 1937 to 1939 despite the 1938 KMT resolution calling for party expansion, but the rank-and-file membership actually declined from 633,086 in 1938 to 471,227 in 1939 (Figure 7.7). Only after the KMT settled the provisional wartime capital in Chongqing did it achieve rapid growth in party membership again. KMT rank-and-file party members achieved exponential growth beginning in 1940, doubling its size from 1,652,209 in 1939 to 3,977,178 in 1940. By 1945 the KMT registered 6.88 million party members.

The rapid expansion came after the KMT Organization Department mandated recruitment quotas to local party branches.[45] The quota system forced local party organizations to prioritize quantity over quality in recruitment as a KMT internal report revealed.[46] For instance, most local branches failed to

---

[44] The CC Clique refers to brothers Chen Guofu and Chen Lifu, Chiang's close allies who had been in charge of KMT affairs since 1926. See Fan (1994).
[45] The KMT Organization Department designed detailed quotas for each province based on its characteristics, such as population density, economic development, education level, and previous party development in 1940. See Q. Wang (2010).
[46] "八中全会中央组织部工作报告 [Report on Central Organization Work by the Eighth Plenum]" in *Zhong guo guo min dang dang wu fa zhan shi liao: zu zhi gong zuo (Chinese Kuomintang Party Affairs: Organizational Work)* (1993, V2: 401–402).

7.3 Quasi-Dominant Leader & Party Reform (1938–1945)

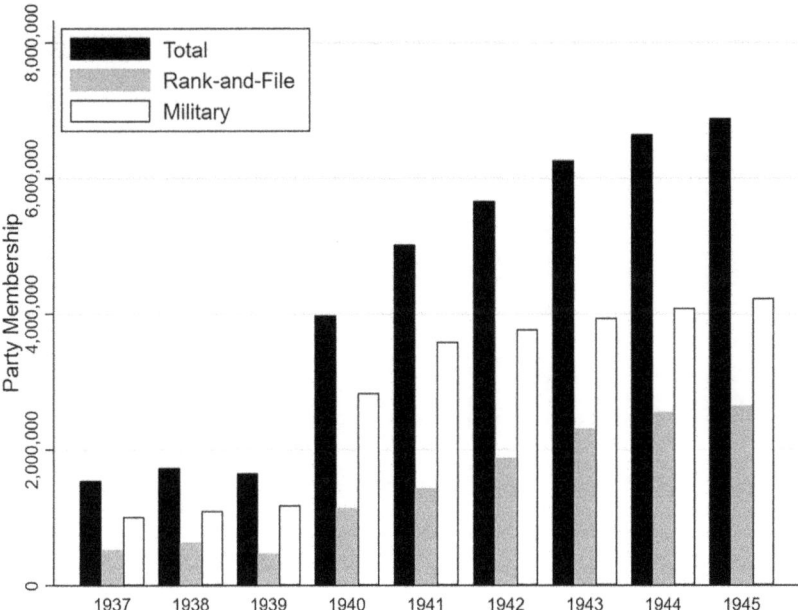

FIGURE 7.7 KMT membership (1937–1945)
Note: See Table A.3 in Appendix A for data sources. The total number reported in this figure includes both rank-and-file and military members but excludes overseas members.

achieve the recruitment quotas issued by the KMT Organization Department at the beginning. After receiving a reprimand from the Party Center, local branches had to intensify their party recruitment efforts sacrificing the quality of new recruits. In some instances, local branches even falsified party recruitment numbers to satisfy higher-level officials.

Notably, before Chiang reached preeminent status within the party, he prioritized party expansion in the military and hindered rank-and-file membership expansion. After Chiang emerged as the dominant party leader, party expansion became more balanced between the military and rank-and-file members. Between 1940 and 1945 the annual growth rate of rank-and-file party members surpassed that of military party members with the former increasing by an average of 39.33 percent per year while the latter increased by 30.59 percent.

Occupational Background of Party Members. Upon closer examination, the characteristics of rank-and-file party members reveals that the KMT failed to cultivate a mass mobilization infrastructure comparable to that of the CCP. For instance, the surge of rural KMT members was anything but peasants. Most new party members in rural China were local elites, including heads of the *baojia*, members of the gentry, and – in some instances – schoolteachers (Tsuchida 2002).

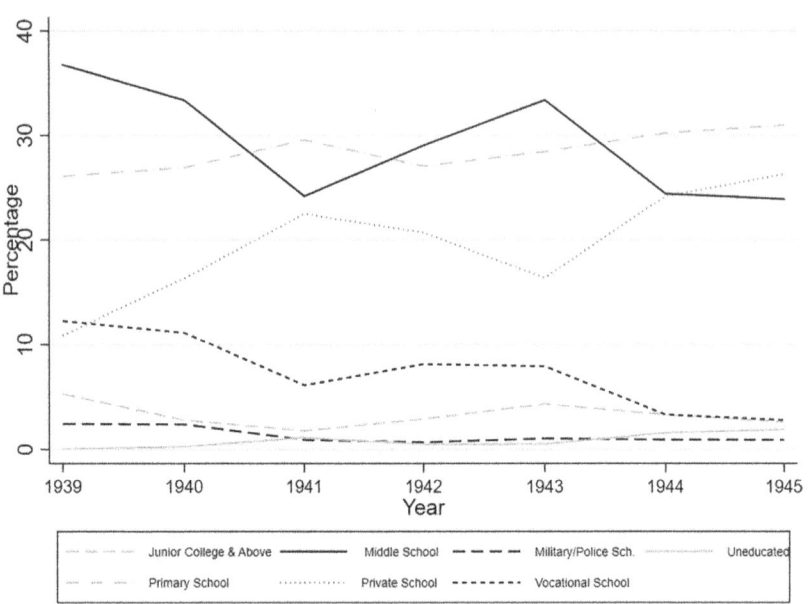

FIGURE 7.8 Education of newly recruited KMT rank-and-file members (1939–1945)
Note: Data are based on table 15-6 in Cui (2013: 870).

In fact, an investigation into the level of education of newly recruited party members revealed that the KMT's rural expansion failed to attract peasants. In rural China during this era, most peasants were uneducated and illiterate, but rural elites had received education in private schools (私塾) or primary schools (小学). If rural recruitment primarily attracted peasants, the uneducated new party members should have increased significantly. Nevertheless, share of uneducated new party members rose only slightly from 0.06 percent in 1939 to 1.9 percent in 1945; by contrast, shares of newly recruited KMT members with private or primary school education rose from 1939 to 1945, suggesting an influx of rural elites (Figure 7.8).

Finally, the share of party members in business and government steadily increased from 1933 to 1947 (Figure 7.9). Meanwhile, party members with worker backgrounds never recovered the status they had achieved prior to the anti-Communist purge. The overall characteristics of KMT members suggests that it still embodied an elite mobilization infrastructure with limited capacity to mobilize the masses.

Similarly, Chiang's efforts to strengthen the KMT's mass mobilization capacity through the creation of the Three Principles of the People Youth League were met with a somewhat elitist composition. In 1940 the majority of Youth League members were students (13.7 percent), party and government employees (63.5 percent), and education-sector employees (11 percent) while peasants and workers made up less than 2 percent of its membership (Q. Wang 2010).

7.3 Quasi-Dominant Leader & Party Reform (1938–1945)

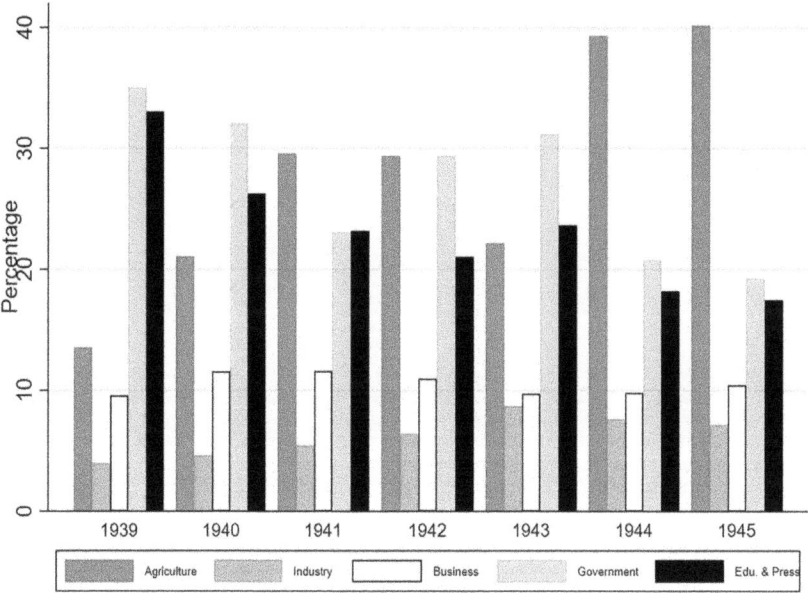

FIGURE 7.9 Occupational backgrounds of KMT rank-and-file members (1939–1945)
Note: See Table A.4 in Appendix A for data sources.

Grassroots Party Organizations. The KMT achieved some success in expanding grassroots party branches – at least by the numbers (Figure 7.10). By the onset of the Sino-Japanese War, the KMT had established county party commissions in only 337 counties, even fewer than the CCP that controlled a much smaller territory. By 1945, however, the KMT had established county party commissions in 1,954 counties. Furthermore, grassroots party cells expanded from 7,407 in 1939 to 58,936 in 1945.

The expansion of KMT grassroots party branches, however, masked the weakness in operation. KMT internal reports often revealed problematic operations in its grassroots organizations. For instance, many local party branches existed in name only because they did not hold regular meetings to connect party members. Second, Chiang's reform to enhance party-government fusion at the county level largely failed. Hence, competent party cadres either preferred to occupy positions at the higher level of party organizations or in the government, leaving incompetent party members holding leadership positions at the county level.

The weakness of KMT's bureaucratic capacity is evidence in a striking contradiction – the number of cadres responsible for managing party affairs continued to decline despite the growth in party membership. Before party expansion, the KMT had approximately 36,000 cadres in the party affairs system; however, by 1944, this number puzzlingly fell to 25,000 (Q. Wang 2010). In essence, the KMT failed to significantly enhance its capacity for managing party affairs.

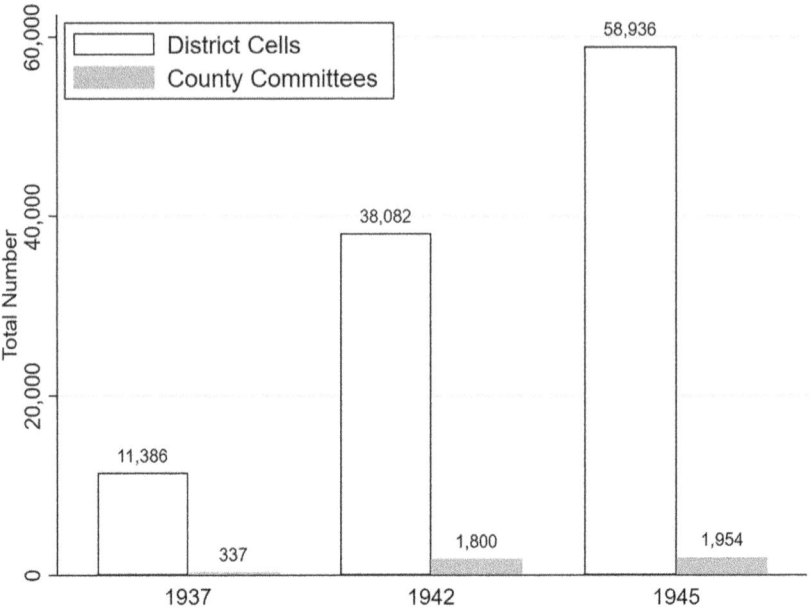

FIGURE 7.10 KMT grassroots county party committees and district cells (1937–1945)
Note: See Table A.1 in Appendix A for data sources.

7.4 SUMMARY

If Sun Yat-sen had not died suddenly in 1925, could the KMT have succeeded in transforming itself into a strong party by instilling Leninist principles into its elite mobilization infrastructure? Perhaps, but significant obstacles stand in the way of this alternative pathway for three reasons.

First, although Sun aimed to ingrain Leninist principles to transform the KMT organization without shifting its ideological orientation, its elite-centric principle of mobilization was fundamentally incongruent with the mass mobilization infrastructure under Communism. The KMT-Right faction was correct after all: it forestalled potential identity crisis within the KMT when the First United Front allowed CCP members to join the KMT while keeping their CCP membership.

Second, the elite mobilization infrastructure within the KMT fostered a constant power struggle among its elites, which is detrimental to building an effective and united party. Intraparty conflicts not only motivate party elites to prioritize the development of patronage networks over party cohesion but also incentivize them to seek external support, such as regional military strongmen when their internal resources proved inadequate. This phenomenon highlights why parties with an elite mobilization infrastructure are more prone to factional conflicts compared to parties with a mass mobilization infrastructure.

7.4 Summary

Finally, despite being an elite party beset by internal power struggles, the KMT was not as weak as many might suspect. Although the total number of KMT members and grassroots organizations could be inflated, the KMT unquestionably dominated the CCP prior to the Sino-Japanese War because of its comparative advantages in accessing financial resources to fund party and government operations; however, even with a large party membership, the KMT remained deeply rooted in an elite mobilization infrastructure. The party's fate was intricately linked to the strength of its elites; however, when economic elites faced setbacks during wartime, the party's comparative advantage became a liability, jeopardizing its vitality (see Chapter 4).

8

The Legacies of Party Building in China and Beyond

Revolutions are transformative moments leaving long-lasting impacts. Even those unsuccessful revolutions unleash shockwaves across society over time. Among the legacies of the revolutionary experience, one enduring impact lies in the governance style and party-building strategies of its survivors. After all, revolutionaries have no blueprint to guide their struggle for power; even when such a plan exists, they still must improvise to respond to an array of unforeseen and unique circumstances. Hence, the unique learning experiences are destined to leave a lasting imprint on surviving party elites, who often cling to past strategies that contributed to their victory while eschewing those that proved fruitless. For the losers of a revolutionary struggle, bitter defeat may present the opportunity for them to embark on a new path to revive the party.

One cannot help but pondering how the CCP's early revolutionary experience contributed to its tendency to employ volatile political campaigns while maintaining its resilience during numerous tumultuous events after 1949.[1] In the decades that followed, the CCP frequently embraced the revolutionary style of governing, transforming the Chinese society by dismantling the traditional elite power structure and employing mass mobilization to implement unpopular policies. This style of governing created a series of upheavals in the political system and shattered the social fabric, yet the CCP seems like a cat with nine lives, navigating through a myriad of political and economic disasters after 1949 and remaining the poster child for the authoritarian resilience that many dictators emulate with envy.

---

[1] Zhang and Liu (2019) are among the few who attempt to establish this link. They focus on the divergence in economic growth in Jiangsu and Zhejiang, arguing that the variation in revolutionary struggles in these two provinces generates different impacts on central–local relations.

8.1 The CCP: Victim of Its Own Success

Meanwhile, KMT elites sought to draw lessons from their defeat in mainland China, adopting distinct approaches in the post-war party-building and state-building strategies in Taiwan. They seemed to grasp the essence of building a strong political party – the need of a dominant party leader. Chiang finally became a truly dominant leader after the KMT retreated to Taiwan. The leadership domination mitigated elite conflict, allowing the KMT to embark on significant party reform from 1950 to 1952. The KMT established a centralized and authoritarian regime in Taiwan, laying the groundwork for its subsequent economic development and political transformation and becoming one of East Asia's economic miracles. The KMT continued to achieve considerable elite cohesion, dominating local elections during its authoritarian rule for over thirty years. Despite such progress, KMT domination deteriorated after Taiwan's democratization in late 1980s, suggesting the limitation of KMT party reform.

In the remainder of this chapter, I first illuminate the legacies of CCP and KMT party-building experiences on their subsequent governing approaches in mainland China and Taiwan, respectively. I then take stock of the critical insights derived from the party-building experiences of the CCP and the KMT, discussing the major takeaways for understanding the organizational development by revolutionary parties more broadly.

8.1 THE CCP: VICTIM OF ITS OWN SUCCESS

The CCP treats its revolutionary history as sacred for good reason. The party underscores the survival of the Long March, the liberation of China from Japanese occupation, and the triumph over the KMT as compelling evidence of its mandate from the Chinese people, thereby legitimizing its monopoly in the political system after 1949. The party staunchly safeguards the narratives of its revolutionary history, fervently repudiating any contention that might potentially tarnish the luster of its revolutionary legacy.

The CCP revolutionary experience is not limited to buttressing regime legitimacy because it left a profound impact on its leaders' understanding of the key ingredients that bind the party together to overcome external adversities. For one, the party's revival under Mao's dominant leadership fueled a predisposition toward the veneration of a strong leader and the preservation of party unity at all costs. Party elites tolerated – and even endorsed – the emergence of the personality cult surrounding Mao after 1949, which ultimately precipitated a sequence of calamitous policies. In addition, the success of mobilized compliance for grain extraction acted as a beacon guiding the CCP to seek compliance with unpopular policies, resulting in a turn toward political campaigns and mass mobilization as an expedient means of policy implementation. Traces of treasuring dominant party leadership and mobilized compliance can be found in the tumultuous political events and the surprising durability exhibited by the CCP post-1949.

8.1.1 The Tragic Legacy of Dominant Leadership

Mao Zedong was universally revered as the paramount leader in post-1949 China. Few had the audacity to challenge his authority, and those who even attempted to question his decisions suffered dearly. Mao was lionized as the savior of the new China, whose visionary strategies and tactical prowess rescued the CCP from the precipice. As demonstrated in the preceding chapters, the emergence of Mao as the dominant party leader was indeed a consequential factor in the CCP's escaping the trap of the elite power struggle that had weakened the party organization. Hence, the glorification of Mao was not without merit.

The downside of cultivating a dominant leader during the revolutionary struggle, however, is that the dominant leader is there to stay after the revolutionary movement seized the state power. The dividends of a dominant leader can metamorphose into a detrimental element for the new regime. This transformation occurs because the triumph of revolutionary movements gives birth to a dominant ruling party with little viable domestic opposition. In the absence of external threats, dominant leaders may face fewer constraints and prioritize their own retention of power, potentially at the expense of the party's well-being. Dominant leaders consolidate their power by establishing a coercive apparatus and promoting a personality cult, thereby reducing the utility of a strong party to those leaders. Even if dominant leaders maintain their interest in a resilient authoritarian party, the very presence of such figures may not prove beneficial for organizations in the long run. Studies in organizational behavior have demonstrated that an overly dominant leadership suppresses cooperative behaviors among team members and fosters a bandwagon effect in collective decision-making (Judge, Piccolo, and Kosalka 2009; Kakkar and Sivanathan 2022). Mao Zedong and Joseph Stalin were two such leaders who stood above the party and even initiated purges and campaigns that rocked their party organizations (Dikötter 2019; Torigian 2022).

One need to look no further than Chinese society during the Maoist era to comprehend the tragedy of dominant leadership. Chinese society endured unrelenting upheaval and calamitous events ranging from the Great Leap Forward to the Cultural Revolution, and these political campaigns claimed innumerable lives while simultaneously ripping the social fabric and crippling both party and governmental organizations at times. Despite these policy catastrophes, Mao's dominance remained largely unscathed; if anything, his supreme stature was further fortified as whoever dared to express dissent were marginalized and died during various political campaigns. Ultimately, Mao became a lonely and blind emperor, detached from and oblivious to unfolding realities.

The tendency to venerate a dominant party leader did not dissipate with Mao's death in 1976. Although Deng Xiaoping recognized the peril of a dominant party leader and advocated for collective leadership among party leaders after 1978 (Manion 1993), China's political system continued to display a

8.1 The CCP: Victim of Its Own Success

propensity toward the cultivation of a dominant leader. Deng himself, despite retiring from party and governmental positions in the 1980s, was a dominant figure who wielded ultimate authority over key party and government decisions (Shih 2022; Vogel 2011). Subsequent CCP Party General Secretaries have strived to establish a commanding leadership within the party. Indeed, some scholars question the degree to which Chinese elite politics truly underwent an institutionalization of power sharing after the Maoist era, arguing that prestige and personal power remain at the heart of elite politics (Fewsmith 2022; Gilley 2003; Pei 2006; Torigian 2022). The resurgence of Xi Jinping as a dominant leader and his dismantling of the CCP's collective leadership serve as testaments to the enduring impact of the successful revolutionary experience in which a strongman, venerated as a towering figure, continues to cast a long shadow over contemporary Chinese politics.

8.1.2 Mobilized Compliance as an Obstacle to Institutionalization of Policymaking and Implementation

The CCP achieved remarkable success in resource mobilization during the Sino-Japanese War by capitalizing on its mobilization infrastructure for grain extraction. Importantly, grassroots party organizations employed the tactics of mobilized compliance, which entailed rallying ordinary citizens to become the agents of the party and manipulating the tension in policy implementation away from the party. Consequently, the CCP overcame the challenges in assessment and enforcement of grain levies, two substantial hurdles in any form of tax collection in an environment characterized by weak institutions and insufficient bureaucratic capability. The core principle of mobilized compliance – manipulating tension within society to achieve policy compliance – has subsequently been applied in various policy realms. The primacy of mobilized compliance created a double-edged sword for CCP leaders in post-1949 policy implementation. On one hand, it proved to be an effective and convenient tool, allowing the party to achieve desirable outcomes from unpopular policies while mitigating resentment toward the central leadership. On the other hand, the continuous reliance on mobilized compliance also became a lasting hindrance to the institutionalization and implementation of policymaking.

To understand the lasting impact of mobilized compliance as an obstacle to the institutionalization of policy implementation in China, the political and economic environments that the CCP confronted in the 1950s during the early stage of state building must first be considered. When the People's Republic of China (PRC) was founded in 1949, the CCP inherited an economy devastated by a half-century of protracted warfares. In addition, the outbreak of the Korean War and the aspiration for rapid industrialization fueled mounting pressure on the CCP to revive the economy and extract fiscal revenue. Moreover, the acute challenge of reconstructing bureaucratic capabilities loomed large, given that the Party lacked the human and financial resources required to fully staff government bureaucracies at every level while robust party organizations had yet to develop in urban China. Last, the CCP encountered a skeptical urban populace, among which it had yet to firmly establish trust and allegiance. The political and economic landscape presented a significant challenge to policy compliance at a time when the CCP could ill afford missteps.

The CCP initially attempted to follow the typical practices of state building by drafting constitutions, creating state and party bureaucracies, and enacting laws and regulations; furthermore, the CCP maintained some continuity in government bureaucracy and economic planning by retaining some elements and human resources of the bureaucratic infrastructure left behind by the KMT (Kirby 1990). The Party also tried to jumpstart state building by emulating the Soviet model of government bureaucracies and economic policymaking (Bernstein and Li 2010). After all, the CCP had little experience managing an urban economy, promoting industrial policies, and governing a territory of such vast size prior to 1949. Nevertheless, the Party quickly realized that the KMT bureaucratic infrastructure was inherently incongruent with the CCP's mass mobilization infrastructure and that the Soviet paradigm was out of sync with the Chinese context.

The desire for rapid policy outcomes led CCP leaders to return to an instrument in the "toolbox" of successful governance during the Sino-Japanese War – mobilized compliance – by favoring campaign-style policy implementation over the more gradual process of institution building. The application of mobilized compliance was not exclusive to this period of state building. The following discussion illustrates the ubiquity of the principle of mobilized compliance in policy implementation ranging from urban taxation to rural governance in post-1949 China.

Urban Tax Collection in the 1950s. Tax collection in urban China in the early 1950s epitomizes the challenges of policy implementation and the rationale for reverting to mobilized compliance as the remedy. In a detailed study, Chen (2005) documented a debate on the strategies of urban tax collection in the distinct approaches adopted in Shanghai and Tianjin, two of the most developed industrial and commercial hubs in China at the time. Specifically, the CCP confronted an urgent need to generate fiscal revenue from urban China when the potential of rural taxation had reached its maximum potential before alienating the peasantry; however, the party faced equivalent, if not greater, challenges in assessing and enforcing urban taxation as a result of its weak bureaucratic capacity in managing an urban economy. Unsurprisingly, the CCP initially chose to retain many employees from the KMT's taxation and economic departments, particularly in major cities (Chen 2005; Kirby 1990).

In the face of mounting fiscal pressure, Bo Yibo, who was the Minister of Finance at the time, mandated the implementation of "democratic assessment" meetings in which business owners were convened to report their business

8.1 The CCP: Victim of Its Own Success

incomes for urban tax collection. These meetings resembled the very same democratic assessment that had taken place in rural China for grain levies during the Sino-Japanese War. This decision was deeply influenced by Bo's prior experiences in the Jin-Ji-Lu-Yu base area, where mobilized compliance played a prominent role in rural grain extraction. Major cities across northern and northeastern China, including Tianjin, quickly responded to Bo's call. Notably, these democratic assessment meetings were not limited to private factory and shop owners; they also involved workers and employees, fostering an atmosphere of collective pressure for tax assessment and compliance.

Meanwhile, Gu Zhun, a CCP cadre who simultaneously held the directorships of both the Finance and Tax Bureaus in Shanghai, advocated for an institution-building approach to urban taxation by employing bureaucratic methodologies in tax assessment and enforcement. Gu's perspective was shaped primarily by his experience as an accounting expert in the 1930s prior to joining the CCP. Once the CCP took control of Shanghai, Gu observed that approximately 2,000 private firms accounted for over 60 percent of the city's tax revenues and that these firms maintained remarkable, systematic bookkeeping practices. Thus, he endeavored to implement a series of strategies to enhance the bureaucratic efficiency of the Shanghai Tax Bureau. His objective was to tax these major firms through well-defined rules and equitable practices, thereby enhancing the tax morale of large and small business owners across Shanghai through examples.

Given that the CCP established a centralized fiscal system post-1949, Bo found himself unable to accommodate Gu's resistance to his democratic assessment approach to urban taxation, especially considering that Shanghai was one of the largest tax bases. Faced with persistent pressure from Bo, Gu acquiesced to the implementation of the democratic assessment in Shanghai in March 1950; however, his compliance was marked by a noticeable reluctance, resulting in an execution that lacked full commitment and enthusiasm. The use of democratic assessment ignited a significant backlash from business owners in Shanghai, leading to a collapse in tax collection and a surge in bankruptcies in subsequent months. This bleak reality eventually compelled party elites to align with Gu,[2] reverting to the Shanghai model that Gu championed. His strategy was proven successful, when the tax revenue quotas set by the Central Government from 1950 to 1952 were met.

Nonetheless, Gu's defiance of Bo came at a significant political cost, sowing the seeds of his later purge during the ensuing Three-Anti and Five-Anti Political Campaigns in late 1952. Gu was labeled a "counterrevolutionary," stripped of all his government and party positions in 1952. These two campaigns, originally conceived to combat corruption within government and business sectors, not only significantly destroyed private business across China

---

[2] According to Chen (2005), Gu was endorsed by Mao Zedong, Chen Yun, and Chen Yi, the mayor of Shanghai.

but also marked the end of Gu's Shanghai model for China's urban taxation during Mao's Era.

The Shadow of Mobilized Compliance. The use of mobilized compliance is not exclusive to urban taxation; indeed, this principle was frequently invoked in myriad strategies for policy compliance when the CCP aimed to achieve concrete results from unpopular policies in the ensuing years.

In rural China, for instance, the CCP continued to deploy the principle of mobilized compliance to tackle issues in policy implementation, such as rural taxation and land reform. When the CCP intensified rural extraction to feed urban industrialization in the 1950s, the dynamics in which team leaders served dual roles as enforcers and supervisors of grain procurement fostered a zero-sum environment among various production teams to facilitate household compliance (Oi 1989). The CCP engaged in moral mobilization during the land reform campaign from 1950 to 1952 as an integral tactic for state building (Javed 2022). During this land reform campaign, the CCP orchestrated a series of mass gatherings, enabling the public to act as "self-righteous, incorruptible judges," and resorted to violence against traditional rural elites. This land reform consequently shattered the traditional power hierarchy in rural China, creating an essential power vacuum that the CCP was subsequently able to fill.

The use of mobilized compliance reached its climax during the tumultuous periods of the Great Leap Forward and the Cultural Revolution. Both political campaigns instigated conflicts among ordinary citizens under the banner of class struggle, which became a distinguishing feature of mass mobilization for compliance. To achieve demanding and often unrealistic policy objectives – whether fulfilling excessive grain quotas or identifying a requisite number of "rightists" in a work unit or locality – Chinese citizens were frequently thrust into a zero-sum game for their own wellbeing. Survival and safety were predicated on a willingness to expose and assail others, fostering an environment of mistrust and tension that persisted throughout these historical events.

Although the post-1980 market reforms significantly moderated the CCP's reliance on mobilized compliance and political campaigns to achieve policy compliance, traces of this approach still linger. For example, local officials in China have deployed what can be called "relational repression" to suppress and demobilize protesters, indicating that the legacy of mobilized compliance continues to influence contemporary governance technique (Deng and O'Brien 2013). Specifically, the friends and relatives of potential protesters and activists are encouraged to employ their social ties to discourage protests entirely. This approach reflects a subtle and personalized application of power, tapping into the intimate social fabric to exert influence and maintain order. More recently, the principle of mobilized compliance manifested itself in the Chinese government's Zero-COVID policy from 2020 to 2022. To ensure adherence to stringent quarantine measures, the government created a zero-sum game, such that one person's noncompliance could inconvenience others. For instance, entire villages or neighborhoods were subjected to indiscriminate quarantine measures following the discovery of a single positive COVID case. This blanket approach serves to heighten citizens' vigilance, fostering a shared responsibility to abide by the guidelines set forth by local governments.

Overall, the reliance on the principle of mobilized compliance yields mixed results, from rapid policy achievements to catastrophic outcomes. Regardless of policy results, a unique advantage of employing mobilized compliance in policy implementation is that it enables both the party and the central government to sidestep accountability for the coercive nature and unfavorable consequences of policy implementation. It accomplishes this by shifting the tension of policy implementation from the state–society interaction to the relations among the citizens themselves.

8.2 THE KMT: OLD WINE IN A NEW BOTTLE

The afterlife of the KMT in Taiwan provides a unique perspective to examine the influence of unsuccessful revolutionary experiences. Defeat in the Civil War of 1946–1949 did not signify the end of the KMT. Retreating to Taiwan, an island off the coast of Fujian province, the KMT found a new lease on life. The eruption of the Korean War in June 1950, followed by the immediate intervention of the United States, provided the KMT with the crucial security protection it needed to shield itself from the potential assault of the CCP's People's Liberation Army. This strategic alignment allowed the KMT to reposition and reestablish itself, defying what seemed like its inevitable demise.

The bitter loss at the hands of the CCP compelled KMT leaders to contemplate new avenues for reviving both the party and its governance strategies. Chiang, in his own personal reflection, conceded that the CCP's superior organizational prowess played a crucial role in the KMT's loss of China (Dickson 1993; Eastman 1981). Consequently, party reform emerged as a pressing priority on Chiang's agenda, becoming a central initiative in the reconstruction and revitalization of both the state and the party in Taiwan.

Aiming at emulating the CCP's capacity for party discipline and mobilization, two major themes emerged in the KMT's reform and governance style in Taiwan. For one, Chiang recognized that factional conflicts had debilitated the KMT's pre-1949 party-building efforts, leading to a dysfunctional party organization. Consequently, Chiang sought to marginalize previous intraparty rivals, ultimately solidifying himself as a genuine and uncontested party leader. In addition, the KMT undertook a comprehensive revamping of party organization, aiming to construct a disciplined Leninist party aligned with Sun Yat-sen's vision during the First United Front in 1924. The purpose of this dual approach was to forge a unified and resolute party that could rise from the ashes of defeat, embodying the strength and unity that had previously eluded it.

These reforms initially came to fruition, transforming the KMT into an organization far more effective than its predecessor in mainland China. Dominating local elections and monopolizing the national political arena, the

KMT emerged as the preeminent authoritarian ruling party in Taiwan, maintaining control for over three decades. Importantly, the KMT's approach to policymaking evolved from a pre-1949 period marked by chaotic and disastrous mismanagement of the economy – largely stemming from internal factional conflicts – to a post-1949 era characterized by a reliance on the expertise and discernment of bureaucrats. Subsequently, Taiwan carried out numerous successful rural and industrial reforms and blossomed into one of East Asia's economic miracles.[3]

Nonetheless, the KMT's attempt to emulate the CCP fell short of capturing one true essence, namely the construction of a mass mobilization infrastructure that would penetrate society and achieve policy compliance through grassroots party organizations. The KMT continued to lean on its elite mobilization infrastructure, enticing local elites into the party by establishing a clientelist patronage machine to infiltrate Taiwanese society (Bosco 1992; Rigger 1999). Inevitably this machine politics approach encountered robust competition following Taiwan's democratization in the late 1980s, leading to the loss of the KMT's once unchallenged monopoly within the political system (Greene 2007; Cheng 1989).

8.2.1 Cultivation of a Dominant Leadership

The absence of elite cohesion and ceaseless internal strife posed considerable obstacles for the KMT throughout the Republican Era. Despite Chiang's strenuous efforts to consolidate his position after ascending to the role of the party's paramount leader in 1935, he continually faced resistance from KMT elites, including some in his own faction. These party elites and regional strongmen wielded considerable de facto power stemming from their control over military, territorial, governmental, and party resources. Thus, Chiang was confronted by these elites with substantial leverage to defy his commands, thereby perpetuating a complex web of internal conflict that hobbled the party's unity and effectiveness.[4]

The retreat to Taiwan dramatically altered the balance of power among KMT elites, presenting Chiang with a unique opportunity to fortify his control after the exit of his intraparty rivals. To begin, regional strongmen lost territorial control in mainland China, depleting their leverage against Chiang. In addition, some KMT and military elites met various fates: Some perished on the battlefield; others were captured or surrendered to the CCP. Furthermore, several key KMT figures chose exile to the West rather than relocate to Taiwan, driven by fear of an impending military assault from the CCP in the early months of 1950.[5] This confluence of events cleared the obstacles for

---

[3] See Kuo and Myers (2012) and Haggard (1990, 2018).
[4] See Chapter 7 for a discussion of these KMT elites.
[5] Li Zhongren, Soong Tse-ven, and Kung Hsiang-hsi were exiled to the United States.

8.2 The KMT: Old Wine in a New Bottle

Chiang to assert a level of authority that had previously eluded him, reshaping the power dynamics within the party and setting the stage for a new phase in its evolution.

Witnessing Mao's domination within the CCP and Sun's prestige in the early days of the KMT, Chiang perceived the cultivation of his personal authority as an essential means to reform the party with an aim of mitigating factional conflict and enhancing party discipline (Ren 2008: 76–88). The formation of the Central Reform Committee (中央改造委员会, CSC hereafter) in August 1950 formally institutionalized the consolidation of Chiang's power within the party. The CSC served as the core leadership for planning party and government transitions in Taiwan,[6] standing above all party, government, and military organizations and answering only to Chiang, who remained the Director General.[7]

All sixteen CSC members were handpicked by Chiang, who trusted them as loyal and competent associates.[8] Importantly, the CSC relegated Chiang's political rivals to the Central Advisory Committee, an honorary body without any de facto power to make party and government decisions. Effectively, Chiang deprived his opponents of the power in the new party and government apparatus in Taiwan; furthermore, the creation of CSC significantly reduced the number of core KMT ruling elites to a 16-member body, a sharp contrast to the previous KMT Central Standing Committee and Central Executive Committee in mainland China, which comprise 50 and 223 members, respectively.

The 1950–1952 party reform may be Chiang's greatest achievement as leader of the KMT (Myers and Lin 2007: 7–8). The establishment of the CSC fostered a close-knit leadership circle whose members demonstrated loyalty to Chiang without the ambition-seeking personal power that might provoke conflicting strategies in party-building. In reciprocation for their allegiance, Chiang bestowed upon CSC members the autonomy to craft and carry out party and government policies. This arrangement not only strengthened Chiang's leadership but also laid the foundation for a rise in bureaucratic professionalism within Taiwan's governance, marrying political fidelity with an emphasis on expertise and effective administration. The interplay between these factors contributed to a more harmonious and efficient political landscape, a remarkable departure from the KMT's constant elite power struggle that crippled the party and government organizations in mainland China during the Republican Era.

Over the subsequent two decades, Chiang maintained his dominant position until his death in 1975. Capitalizing on his father's legacy, Chiang Ching-kuo ascended to leadership of the KMT. The elder Chiang had assiduously prepared his son for this role, having entrusted him with numerous party and government positions both in mainland China and Taiwan. This deliberate

---

[6] See Myers and Lin (2007) for the formation and operation of the CSC.
[7] See Dickson (1993: 66) for the organizational structure of the CSC.
[8] See Myers and Lin (2007: 5) for the full list of CSC members.

grooming process facilitated a smooth transition of power, ensuring continuity in leadership while imbuing the younger Chiang with the experience and acumen needed to guide the party's future. Despite being an indisputable party leader, Chiang Ching-kuo eventually abolished the ban on opposition parties in 1986. This seminal act effectively dismantled the institutional barriers to multiparty competition within Taiwan's political system, laying the groundwork for the subsequent democratization.

8.2.2 Grassroots Party Building with Elite-Centric Characteristics

During most of the Republican Era, the KMT prioritized elite mobilization, consciously distancing itself from the CCP by abandoning party apparatuses for mass mobilization in 1927. The KMT's deficiency in mass mobilization capacity impaired its ability to mobilize financial resources from rural China during the Sino-Japanese War, leading to pronounced inequities and widespread resentment stemming from its regressive grain extraction. In addition, the KMT's assimilation of national and local elites proved to be a perilous strategy. Although these elites acted as effective conduits enabling the KMT to exert its influence, they were opportunistic individuals without ideological commitment. These ambitious individuals viewed their affiliation with the KMT more as a convenient avenue for accessing state resources for personal gain, not genuine adherence to the party's revolutionary ideology. Consequently, the KMT remained a loosely organized and undisciplined party, plagued by pervasive corruption.

The loss of China forced KMT leaders to recognize the essential importance of mass mobilization and party discipline (Ren 2008: 89). To this end, Chiang Kai-shek initiated a party reform from 1950 to 1952, directed at the creation of a Leninist party reminiscent of Sun Yat-sen's objective in the creation of the First United Front in 1924. Under Chiang's dominant leadership, the KMT embarked on a series of cohesive party-building strategies over the next two decades, aiming to fortify party discipline and expand mass mobilization capacity.

The Agenda of the 1950–1952 Party Reform. Upon establishing the CSC in July 1950, the committee promptly embarked on its duties, delineating six core missions. This was a decisive act that signaled a commitment to the transformation of the party, framing the key challenges and opportunities that lay ahead. Below are the six primary missions of the CSC.[9]

1. Make the KMT a revolutionary–democratic party.
2. Broaden the social base by recruiting peasants, workers, youth, intellectuals, and capitalists.
3. Adopt democratic centralism as the organizing principle.

---

[9] See Dickson (1993) and Myers and Lin (2007) for the details of the party reform.

8.2 The KMT: Old Wine in a New Bottle

4. Designate party cells as the basis of grassroots organization units.
5. Institutionalize party decisions through the party committee and formal procedure.
6. Reaffirm Sun Yat-sen's Three Principles of the People as the KMT ideology.

These objectives reflected Chiang's commitment to break with the past by strengthening party discipline and organizational cohesion. Specifically, the CSC acknowledged that even a large membership was inadequate for deep societal penetration because grassroots party structures were the missing links vital to transforming an expansive but loosely connected membership into a potent political entity. This realization came as a costly lesson from the Republican Era, whereas the KMT's considerably larger membership proved less effective in mass mobilization compared to the CCP's smaller but more cohesive membership base. In a bid to amplify grassroots party building, the KMT instituted a sweeping mandate for the formation of party cells within every stratum of Taiwanese society. Beyond mere establishment, the reform delineated specific protocols for the operation of these party cells, mandating regular gatherings and instructive sessions for party members. This structured approach to integration highlights a determined effort to deepen the party's roots and coherence across the societal spectrum. This move was a significant departure from pre-1949 party building, whereas the KMT was accustomed to focusing on building institutions to mitigate elite conflicts at the national level.

Simultaneously, the KMT emphasized the induction of peasants and workers into the party rather than exclusively absorbing public employees and military personnel. This strategic choice drew from pre-1949 lessons as the KMT recognized the former group was more conducive to penetrating the society than the latter. A 1951 KMT report on its organizational structure exemplified the emphasis on recruiting peasants and workers (Ren 2008: 190). The report disaggregated the composition of the newly inducted party members, workers and peasants constituting 38 percent, contrasted with a mere 14.4 percent from the ranks of public employees. In addition, indigenous Taiwanese constituted an impressive 58.6 percent of the new recruits. Instead of lauding this progress, however, the KMT Party Center harbored a sense of dissatisfaction with the modest expansion in the worker and peasant segments. Its response underscored a driving aspiration for further recruitment from nonelites, reflecting a nuanced understanding of the party's strategic needs and a commitment to more fully representing the laboring classes.

One should note that KMT leaders found that party reforms could not furnish immediate relief with mounting pressure to rejuvenate the economy and integrate further into Taiwanese society. Thus, the KMT maintained an elite-centric mobilization infrastructure even as party reform entailed a focus on building a mass mobilization capacity. For instance, the KMT reverted to indirect rule by incorporating societal elites and constructed a clientelist machine as a shortcut to penetrate Taiwanese society. Initially, these reforms significantly improved the organizational effectiveness of the KMT; however, the continued reliance on indirect rule and clientelism underscores a fundamental and unheeded lesson from the KMT's defeat on the mainland. The failure to create a genuine mass mobilization infrastructure reveals a lingering vulnerability and a seeming inability to fully grasp the underlying reasons for its previous failures.

Party Membership Recruitment from Indigenous and Migrated Population. By the end of the reform in 1952, the KMT had amassed 281,974 party members and 34,476 party cells in Taiwan. The share of party members in Taiwan's population amounted to 3.5 percent, far exceeding the 0.9 percent during its height in mainland China in 1948. KMT party membership steadily increased in subsequent years, doubling to 564,784 in 1958 (Ren 2008: 191–192).

The remarkable growth in KMT party membership and party cells concealed a significant proportion of the party membership with origins in the migrated mainland population who retreated to Taiwan along with the KMT after 1948.[10] The disparity can be reflected in party membership from several KMT party branches. Broadly speaking, the KMT party membership in Taiwan comprised two main branches: one was the Special Branch (特种党部) and the Professional Branch (职业党部); and the other, the Taiwan Provincial Branch (台湾省党部). The Special Branch consisted largely of KMT members in the military, state-owned enterprises, and government-sponsored civil society; and the Professional Branch was made up of KMT members within the party organizations. Primarily, the members populating the Special and Professional branches were individuals who had migrated from mainland China following the defeat of the KMT. Only the Taiwan Provincial Branch predominantly comprised regular party members recruited from among ordinary Taiwanese citizens. Although party membership in the Taiwan Provincial Branch nearly doubled its size from 115,865 in 1952 to 220,965 in 1958, its share remained less than half the total KMT membership in Taiwan (Ren 2008). In other words, the KMT's membership initiative saw greater triumph in attracting the population that had migrated from mainland China as opposed to the indigenous populace of Taiwan.

Importantly, the overall share of peasants and workers in the Taiwan Provincial Branch stubbornly hovered around 30 percent from 1952 to 1960, and public employees and industrialist–merchants declined only from 57.20 percent to 50.12 percent during the same period (Ren 2008). These trends indicate that even among the party members from the indigenous Taiwanese population, the KMT remained a largely elite-centric party similar to its predecessor in mainland China prior to the retreat.

---

[10] An estimated 2,000,000 mainlanders migrated to Taiwan after the defeat of the KMT.

8.2 The KMT: Old Wine in a New Bottle

Societal Penetration through Clientelism. The languid increase in party membership among the indigenous Taiwanese population insinuated a challenging landscape for the KMT, which faced an urgent necessity to amplify its mass mobilization capacity. This urgency was particularly acute in vital areas of policy implementation, encompassing local elections, land reform, and industrialization. Faced with these immediate needs, the KMT had to simultaneously adopt indirect rule by assimilating local elites into its ranks. This approach bore a marked resemblance to its previous party-building strategies, reflecting a pragmatic adaptation to the challenges of the time.

Initially, most of the CSC local committees included highly educated party cadres who had migrated from mainland China, reflecting an inherent elite tendency in party building (Ren 2008: 111–114). In the years following the party reform, public employees, rather than peasants and workers, dominated various levels of party leadership throughout the period from 1957 to 1962. Even when the KMT emphasized the recruitment of new members from rural areas, the Party Center mandated local party branches to pay special attention to doctors and agricultural experts as well as other rural elites because the Party viewed them as the potential power brokers, who could facilitate the KMT's policy implementation (Ren 2008: 198–199).

After the KMT encountered a slow growth in rural party membership in Taiwan, closer attention was paid to the Peasant Associations (农会, PAs hereafter) as an alternative venue to penetrate rural areas. PAs had been developed in Taiwan over a century. Because of the dominant role played by PAs in coordinating agricultural production, they had a robust connection with rural households in Taiwan. In an effort to prevent potential opposition to mobilizing PAs to challenge KMT rule, the KMT reformed them and established linkage between PAs and the Party. For instance, KMT grassroots party organizations encouraged peasants to join their local PAs while recruiting activists in PAs to become party members. The KMT party membership share in PAs rose from 4.5 percent in 1954 to 7.4 percent in 1969; moreover, the KMT membership share in PA leadership was even higher, accounting for close to 70~90 percent of county and township PA leadership in 1957 (Ren 2008: 220–227). The penetration into PAs proved to be an effective strategy for the KMT to implement rural reform. For instance, the PAs played a crucial role in enhancing the KMT's campaign to revive the rural economy, contributing to the later economic transformation in Taiwan (Looney 2020).

Building a clientelist machine through local elections was another important strategy the KMT used to penetrate the Taiwanese society and control the masses. Taiwan had experimented with the limited election of local assemblies since colonialization by the Japanese. After the KMT arrived in Taiwan, it promoted local elections to serve as a strategy for self-governance and to ease tensions after the massacre of numerous Taiwanese in an incident that occurred on February 28, 1948. To ensure its domination in these local elections, the KMT supported the development of local factions in various townships and villages, building an extensive clientelism and patronage machine. Coupled with the KMT's Emergency Laws that limited space for opposition parties, the KMT ensured party mobilization through election.

8.3 DOMINANT LEADER, MOBILIZATION INFRASTRUCTURE, AND CONTINGENCIES

The reversal of fortunes of the CCP and the KMT during the Republican Era were indeed a momentous historical event. But what if Mao Zedong had remained marginalized in the CCP leadership circle, never consolidating his power prior to the Sino-Japanese War? And what if the skirmish between China and Japan had not turned into a full-scale interstate war? The answer is simple: The course of Chinese history would have been entirely different.

As demonstrated in preceding chapters, if Mao had not consolidated his power within the CCP prior to the Sino-Japanese War, the party would likely have been unable to transform its mobilization infrastructure that in turn successfully facilitated grain extraction. Instead, an unrelenting intraparty elite struggle would have plunged the CCP into self-defeating party-building strategies, mirroring the disastrous experience of the Jiangxi Soviet in the early 1930s. Stated bluntly, the CCP would have been unable to capitalize on the political vacuum left by the Sino-Japanese War had it failed to pivot to building a mass mobilization infrastructure in rural China. Eventually, the party would have succumbed to the fiscal shock that followed the KMT's withdrawal of financial support in 1941, obliviated in an "early death" of just another revolutionary party.

Likewise, the Sino-Japanese War was indeed a pivotal moment in Chinese history – not only did the war create a political vacuum for the CCP to fill as the conventional wisdom suggested, but it also decimated the comparative advantage of the KMT's elite mobilization infrastructure; otherwise, Mao's power consolidation alone would have been insufficient to alter the fate of the CCP because the KMT would have still maintained the resources needed to suppress or even eradicate the CCP outright. Even Mao credited the Japanese invasion for CCP's revival, claiming that the regeneration of the CCP would not have occurred without the political opportunity presented by the Japanese invasion (Mao 1991, V8:201). The impact of the war on the reversal of fortune of these two parties fundamentally hinged on the shifting comparative advantage from KMT's elite mobilization infrastructure over the CCP's mass mobilization infrastructure.

What-if thought experiments offer counterfactuals to underscore the essential foundations necessary for resilient revolutionary parties prior to the capture of state power, namely leadership domination and resource mobilization. Concurrently, contingent events must not be dismissed as mere random noise outside systematic analysis. Instead, they are consequential in disrupting the equilibria of intraparty balance of power and comparative advantages of party

8.3 Final Reflection

mobilization infrastructure, which in turn sculpt the strategic behaviors of political actors and the destiny of revolutionary organizations.

In the end, we must recognize that revolutions unfold in turbulent times, when the power dynamics both within and between political organizations are subject to ceaseless flux and transformation. Revolutionary parties often operate in an environment with weak formal institutions regulating the distribution of power in the political sphere. Any power-sharing arrangements within and between political entities are plagued by the credibility crisis in this type of environment.

Acutely aware of the delicacy in the balance of power equilibrium in this unstable environment, party elites are reluctant to cooperate wholeheartedly and commit to power sharing. Party elites under contested leadership find overcoming the collective action problem behind party-building strategies challenging even when facing external existential threats. The obstacle to cooperation is that individual political survival often trumps the survival of the party. The rise of a dominant leader mitigates the collective action problem among party elites because party leadership domination diminishes concern that party-building strategies will be exploited to enhance the personal power of their intraparty rivals at their own expense. A dominant leader is unlikely to tolerate such expansion of power among subordinates. Consequently, party elites find unity in their pursuit of coherent strategies, working collectively to fortify the party against external threats.

The evolution of party strength held by the CCP and the KMT during the pre-1949 era is a telling example for the critical role of dominant party leadership. After all, the narrative propagated by the CCP carries a measure of truth. The emergence of Mao as a dominant party leader unquestionably revived the CCP; however, his rise as the catalyst for the CCP's revival cannot be attributed solely to his charisma, visionary tactics, or revolutionary strategies. More importantly, his consolidation of power effectively quelled the intraparty elite conflicts that had previously wreaked havoc within the party. The demise of the KMT, by contrast, reveals an Achilles heel of dominant party leadership. The sudden departure of a dominant leader often leads to intense power contestation among party elites, spelling the downfall of the party. Precisely because of the relatively equal balance of power among KMT elites, the power-sharing arrangement among them repeatedly broke down even when the KMT faced existential threats stemming from the CCP insurrection and the Japanese invasion. Although Chiang Kai-shek solidified his position only after Wang Ching-wei and Hu Han-min were forced to exit the succession battle; regional strongmen remained defiant to Chiang, undermining the effectiveness of the party.

Apart from dominant party leadership, the effectiveness of party mobilization infrastructure for resource mobilization is another indisputable source of the strength of revolutionary parties. Although initial resource endowment could shape organizational form and revolutionary tactics, revolutionary organizations must explore a wide range of strategies in response to unexpected fiscal demand or supply shocks during the course of revolutionary movements. Consequently, the nature of party mobilization infrastructure, coupled with the nature of the fiscal shocks, delineates the constraints and opportunities that revolutionary organizations encounter in their attempts to address these financial challenges.

The crucial role of resource mobilization elucidates reasons that the KMT held dominance over the CCP from 1927 to 1937 despite internal strife among its party elites. The KMT's elite mobilization infrastructure, notwithstanding its mixed quality, allowed for immediate access to an array of state resources and taxation derived from urban economic activities. Conversely, the CCP's mass mobilization infrastructure met with difficulties in extracting resources from the populace during its infancy. Thus, the contrasting effectiveness in resource mobilization largely defined the relative strength of these two parties during this period. CCP failures in the Jiangxi Soviet base era exemplify the roots of its organizational fragility at the time: Intense elite power struggle, conflictual party-building strategies, and ineffective extractive capacity.

Can other revolutionary parties follow the CCP's ascent as a blueprint to succeed in their struggle for political power? Some rebel organizations with transformative goals imitated the pre-1949 CCP model of intensive and extensive governance (Stewart 2021), yet many of these faithful followers of the CCP model, such as FRETILIN in East Timor and Hezbollah in Lebanon, did not successfully seize state power despite surviving the repression from external rivals. After all, challenging state power is far different from capturing it.

The challenges to truly replicating the CCP's success reveal that stubborn balance of power among party elites hinders the rise of a dominant leader. The emergence of dominant leaders does not always occur because of "event-making men." They may instead be "eventful men" (Hook 1945). The wits, endowed resources, and personality traits are undeniable factors contributing to the rising power of these strong men and women. Their path to the pinnacle of power, nonetheless, often benefited from the downfalls of their rivals, followed by events that had little to do with their own doing. This is hardly a surprise because the relative equal balance of power among party elites is likely to result in stalemates, and these self-reinforcing equilibria can be broken only by exogenous and surprising turns of events.

By the same token, constructing an effective mobilization infrastructure for resource mobilization is a punishing journey for any political organization. The urgency of resource mobilization amid revolutionary struggle often tempts the organization with relatively easy access to windfall revenues, such as foreign support and natural resources. This access inadvertently weakens party elites' incentives to build a penetrating mobilization infrastructure from the ground up. Furthermore, the effectiveness of a revolutionary party's mobilization infrastructure for resource mobilization is relative to its rivals' mobilization infrastructure. The crucial role of contingencies does not imply that

8.3 Final Reflection

they are the predominant causes of the rise and fall of revolutionary parties. Instead, dominant leadership and resource mobilization remain the building blocks of resilient revolutionary parties, with contingencies acting as the final forces that tip the scales.

Finally, replicating the CCP's success also hinges on party–military relations, an aspect that I have not yet explored in this book. Strengthening party control over the armed forces involves more than merely assimilating generals and soldiers into the party, an attempt at which the KMT under Chiang Kai-shek had tried and failed. The "guardianship dilemma" presents an acute challenge to any revolutionary party because party elites whose source of power stems from the control of the coercive apparatus are reluctant to "kiss the ring" because they could have the ability to opt out of the party, as exemplified by Zhang Guotao's defiance to the CCP Party Center during the Long March. The third pillar of strength for revolutionary parties – the development and control of coercive capacity – merits further exploration in subsequent studies.

Appendices

Appendix A: Data on Party Membership and Organizations

I constructed a panel dataset on CCP and KMT membership and grassroots organizations from 1921 to 1945 from a variety of sources.

CCP Membership. The majority of CCP membership data come from *Zhong guo gong chan dang dang nei tong ji zi liao hui bian (1921–2000)* (*The Compendium of Chinese Communist Party Statistics (1921–2000)*). When there are multiple monthly data points within a single year, I always report the last monthly data point in that year.

Some yearly data come from different sources. The 1924 datum is the sum of party membership from different regional branches' reports in pp. 256–281 in *Zhong gong zhong yang wen jian xuan ji* (*CCP Party Center Selected Documents*) (1989, V1). The data of 1925 and 1926 are from *Zhong guo gong chan dang zu zhi shi zi liao* (*The Compendium of the Chinese Community Party Organizational History*) (2000, V1: 39). The data of 1927, 1929, and 1931 are from *Zhong guo gong chan dang zu zhi shi zi liao* (The *Compendium of the Chinese Community Party Organizational History*) (2000, V2: 68). The 1928 datum is from Yang and Yang (1988: 236).

CCP County Party Committee and Party Cell. The data was constructed by the author based on provincial party organization history (组织史资料) in the following twenty-nine provinces: Anhui, Beijing, Chongqing, Fujian, Gansu, Guangdong, Guangxi, Guizhou, Hainan, Hebei, Heilongjiang, Henan, Hubei, Hunan, Jiangsu, Jiangxi, Jilin, Liaoning, Neimenggu, Ningxia, Shaanxi, Shandong, Shanghai, Shanxi, Sichuan, Tianjin, Yunnan, and Zhejiang.

KMT Membership. The majority of KMT membership data come from Tables 11-1 and 13-1 in Q. Wang (2010), which were obtained from *Zhong guo guo min dang dang wu fa zhan shi liao: zu zhi gong zuo* (*Chinese Kuomintang Party Affairs: Organizational Work*) (1993, V1). I excluded overseas KMT membership in total domestic membership. The 1921 and 1924 data are from page 3 of the same source above. The 1923 and 1926 data are from Tsuchida (2002: 82). The 1928 datum is from Cui (2007, V1: 574).

KMT County Party Committee and Party Cell. The data was constructed by the author based on *Zhong guo guo min dang dang wu fa zhan shi liao: zu zhi gong zuo* (*Chinese Kuomintang Party Affairs: Organizational Work*) (1993, V1 & V2).

TABLE A.1 *CCP and KMT party membership and grassroots organizations*

	CCP			KMT		
Year	Total domestic membership	County party committee (Xianwei)	Party cell (Zhibu)	Total domestic membership	County party committee	District cell (Qufenbu)
	(1)	(2)	(3)	(4)	(5)	(6)
1921	57	5	0	10,000		
1922	195	21	0			
1923	420	55	0	50,000		
1924	386	69	1	60,080		
1925	3,164	461	8			
1926	18,526	1,730	35	447,201	271	3,388
1927	17,650	3,232	295		451	7,504
1928	22,500	1,855	453	544,656		
1929	69,319	1,556	426	678,384		
1930	122,318	1,571	480	704,409	634	10,150
1931	124,617	1,217	456	763,076	585	
1932		1,168	453	1,016,881	354	11,924
1933	300,000	977	433	1,190,438		
1934	411,000	828	434	1,304,557	523	11,618
1935		660	387	1,467,699	425	10,113
1936		384	364	1,501,894	304	11,397
1937	40,000	617	519	1,539,996	337	11,386
1938	90,000	913	787	1,731,231		
1939	500,000	1,464	981	1,652,209		7,407
1940	800,000	4,794	1,100	3,977,178		17,817
1941	763,000	2,221	1,089	5,021,697		
1942	736,000	2,712	931	5,658,352	1,800	38,082
1943		2,387	888	6,261,748		
1944	853,000	6,023	913	6,642,801		
1945	1,211,000	12,869	1,276	6,880,187	1,954	58,936

Note: Author's dataset. See discussion above for data source.

Appendix A: Sources of Party Data

TABLE A.2 *CCP party membership class backgrounds (%)*

Year	Intellectuals	Workers	Peasants	Data Source
1922		11		*CCP Party Center Selected Documents* (1989, V1:47)
1923	61	39		*CCP Party Center Selected Documents* (1989, V1:167–168)
1926.11	27	60	12	*CCP Party Center Selected Documents* (1989, V2:504)
1927.3	19	51	19	*The Compendium of Chinese Communist Party Organizational History* (2000, V1:11)

TABLE A.3 *KMT rank-and-file and military membership*

Year	Total domestic membership	Rank-and-file members	Military members	Share of rank-and-file in total members (%)	Share of military in total members (%)
1926	447,201	425,612	21,589	95.2	4.8
1928	544,656	252,228	292,428	46.3	53.7
1929	678,384	276,028	402,356	40.7	59.3
1930	704,409	270,467	433,942	38.4	61.6
1931	763,076	303,353	459,723	39.8	60.2
1932	1,016,881	358,351	658,530	35.2	64.8
1933	1,190,438	394,086	796,352	33.1	66.9
1934	1,304,557	435,618	868,939	33.4	66.6
1935	1,467,699	468,014	999,685	31.9	68.1
1936	1,501,894	498,956	1,002,938	33.2	66.8
1937	1,539,996	526,977	1,013,019	34.2	65.8
1938	1,731,231	633,086	1,098,145	36.6	63.4
1941	5,021,697	1,431,281	3,590,416	28.5	71.5
1942	5,658,352	1,883,826	3,774,526	33.3	66.7
1943	6,261,748	2,315,084	3,946,664	37.0	63.0
1944	6,642,801	2,555,279	4,087,522	38.5	61.5
1945	6,880,187	2,648,169	4,232,018	38.5	61.5

Note: Author's dataset. See discussion above for data source.

TABLE A.4 *KMT party membership occupational background (%)*

Year	Agriculture	Industry	Business	Government	Education and press
1926	7.50	29.00	4.30		36.20
1929	10.43	9.67	8.27	16.54	33.44
1933	10.98	2.21	10.78	24.05	34.40
1939	13.54	3.96	9.58	35.01	33.02
1940	21.06	4.64	11.57	32.05	26.22
1941	29.58	5.47	11.61	23.06	23.15
1942	29.38	6.42	10.98	29.37	21.01
1943	22.17	8.72	9.74	31.19	23.63
1944	39.33	7.64	9.82	20.78	18.19
1945	40.17	7.17	10.46	19.25	17.47
1947	23.34	10.82	10.03	21.55	24.48

Note: The data were obtained from Tsuchida (2002).

Appendix B: Coding for CCP and KMT Central Committee

B.1 CCP CENTRAL COMMITTEE CLASS BACKGROUND CODING

I obtained the list of CCP Central Committee members from the *CCP News* website (中国共产党新闻网), which is available through the following link: http://cpc.people.com.cn/GB/64162/139962/index.html (accessed on July 19, 2021).

The coding of the social class backgrounds of CCP Central Committee members was based on the family background of the individual. I mainly relied on autobiographies available on Baidu Baike (百度百科) to identify their family background and cross-examine the information from Wikipedia. Notably, this coding scheme followed the classification of social class used by the CCP after 1949. The post-1949 classification of social class in the PRC was often determined by a family's economic background prior to 1949, rather than the occupation held by the individual at the time (Davis 2000).

Notably, some family backgrounds of CCP CC members were missing in the sources above (70 of 171 CC members do not have family background information). Hence, I relied on the occupation of the individual when they joined the CCP as the proxy for family social class background. This strategy stems from the stagnant social mobility in the Chinese society prior to 1949; thus a CCP member's occupational background and family background were mostly identical. This is particularly true for CCP members from rural areas. However, the occupation and family background could be different for the early cohort of CCP members who joined the CCP in the 1920s and later became CCP party elites. Specifically, many early CCP members were students and teachers in the secondary or higher education sectors when they joined the party, and they came from a variety of family backgrounds. Hence, the use of occupation data may overcount CC members in the intellectual class undercount CC members in the peasant and worker classes.

Here are the definitions of family social class classification:
Intellectuals: Students, teachers, writers, artists, journalists.
Workers: Workers and laborers in traditional and modern industries.
Peasants: Tenant peasants, poor peasants, middle peasants, rich peasants.
Military: Soldiers in any military units.
Other: Landlords, business owners, businessmen, government employees.

B.2 KMT CENTRAL COMMITTEE MEMBERSHIP FACTION CODING

I obtained the list of KMT Central Committee members from Wikipedia, which is available through the following link: https://zh.wikipedia.org/wiki/%E4%B8%AD%E5%9C%8B%E5%9C%8B%E6%B0%91%E9%BB%A8%E4%B8%AD%E5%A4%AE%E5%A7%94%E5%93%A1%E6%9C%83 (accessed on July 15, 2021).

For KMT faction coding, I relied on autobiographies available on Baidu Baike (百度百科) to identify the factions of KMT CC members and cross-examine the information from Wikipedia. The coding follows the rules below:

1) If these autobiographies indicate the specific faction that the individual belonged to, then code the faction classification accordingly;
2) If specific faction information is unavailable, then the faction classification is based on the individual's support to a specific faction during factional conflicts among Chiang, KMT–Left, KMT–Right, and Regional Warlord.
3) If the information on steps 1–2 is unavailable, then the faction classification is based on career advancement of the individual endorsed by specific faction leaders;
4) If information on steps 1–3 is unavailable, then the faction classification was coded as "KMT–Other."

Notably, KMT had many different factions, including smaller ones within Chiang's own faction (Q. Wang 2018). For the purpose of this book, I am mainly interested in factions that support or oppose Chiang. Hence, I coded these smaller factions within the major faction defined below:

CCP Faction: CCP members who were able to join the KMT under the agreement of the First United Front (1924–1927).

Chiang Faction: Followers of Chiang Kai-shek, including those who belong to the CC (Central Club) Clique (中央俱乐部) run by the Chen Kuo-fu and Chen Li-fu Brothers, the Blue Shirts Society (蓝衣社), the "Green-White" corps (青白团), the "Three Youth Corps" (三民主义青年团), and Whampoa Military Academy Faction (黄埔军校派).

Appendix B: Coding of CCP and KMT Central Committee 213

KMT–Left Faction: Followers of Wang Ching-wei and members of KMT Reform and Reorganization Faction (改组派).

KMT–Right Faction: Followers of Hu Han-min and members of KMT Western Hill Meeting Faction (西山会议派).

Regional Warlord Factions: Regional warlords in Guangdong (粤系), Guangxi (桂系), Shanxi (晋系), Hunan (湘系), Yunan (滇系), Northeast Military Faction (东北军系), Military Faction (川康系), and Northwest Military Faction (西北军系). Regional warlords functioned as independent factions in their own right, rather than as a cohesive military coalition of factions

Other: KMT members who did not belong to any of the factions above.

The coding yielded similar results to Q. Wang (2010, Table 14-1) that traced the changes of seat share among KMT factions during the 5th and 6th Party Congress. For example, Q. Wang (2010) indicates that the shares of the Chiang faction (based on my definition above) were 45% and 40.7% in the 5th and 6th KMT CC, respectively. My data indicated the seat share of Chiang's faction were 43.3% and 42.8% in the 5th and 6th KMT CC, respectively.

Appendix C: Data on Fiscal Revenue (1937–1945)

C.1 ITEMIZED CCP AND KMT WARTIME FISCAL REVENUES

Locating systematic data on CCP finances during the pre-1949 era has been a challenging task for several reasons. First, the CCP base areas were administratively and fiscally decentralized because of the blockage by the Japanese occupation and KMT troops. Second, CCP bureaucracies were not well trained for recordkeeping because they lacked professional training and experience. Therefore, my data collection relied on several volumes of finance and economic records of the most prominent CCP base areas, including the Shaan-Gan-Ning, where the CCP Party Center was located during the war. These volumes provide detailed records of CCP's economic production, fiscal revenue, and spending in the base areas. Specifically, I constructed a panel data of comprehensive fiscal revenues in two CCP major base bases – Shaan-Gan-Ning and Jin-Sui – relying on two compendiums of economic and finance archives detailed below. I then supplemented the data with other sources for missing data in grain extraction.

Meanwhile, I obtained most of the KMT finance data in several government and party publications and archives. One important source came from Arthur Young, who served as an economic adviser in the U.S. Department of State from 1922 to 1928. He later became the financial adviser to the KMT government and to the Central Bank of China from 1929 to 1946. As a result, he obtained detailed records of KMT finance statistics during the Republican Era based on KMT government records. Specifically, Young (1965) offers detailed finance data for the KMT central government. In addition, I obtained the data for KMT's grain extraction from Chang (1958), Eastman (1984), and Hao (2008).

To provide a comprehensive picture of government finance by the CCP and the KMT, I reorganized the data in three major ways. First, I include grain levies in kind in total government revenue. Grain levies in kind was a major form

Appendix C: Data on Fiscal Revenue (1937–1945)

of direct fiscal extraction by the CCP and the KMT governments during the war, but the data were not typically included in the reports of itemized fiscal revenue by both parties. Second, I include monetary expansion in government total revenues, thus providing a complete picture of how CCP and KMT government financed the government and the military during the war. Notably, KMT government was not the only one that employed monetary expansion policies for wartime finance. Several CCP base areas issued their own currencies and prohibited the circulation of the KMT currency (*fabi*) during the war. Consequently, this strategy functioned much like a monetary expansion, effectively aiding in the financing of both the government and its military operations. Third, the CCP border governments had engaged in opium production and trade within two of its base areas (i.e., Shaan-Gan-Ning and Jin-Sui). As elucidated in Chapter 4, the advent of opium production emerged as an apt financial solution, bridging the revenue gap after the KMT ceased its monetary support in late 1940. The financial records in party archives often used codenames (e.g., 特产 [special product], 药品变价 [medicine price]) to disguise the nature of the revenue from these sources. Figure 4.2 reported the sources of the opium data.

After collecting these data, I standardized them to enable a comparison between the CCP and the KMT, given the differing currency units used in these reports. The process of standardization entails converting fiscal revenue into grain units by using the grain prices for any given year in each base area and in the KMT controlled territories. In what follows, I first report itemized CCP and KMT revenues in their original currency unit. I then present the data in grain unit (*shi* 石). Notably, the conversion into grain unit accounts for hyperinflation in both KMT and CCP controlled territories during the war.

TABLE C.1 *Shaan-Gan-Ning itemized fiscal revenue (in local currency)*

Year	Currency (货币单位)	Grain (Shi) (公粮实征(石))	Grain (粮食)	Tax exchange for labor in salt transportation. (公盐代金)	Forfeiture (没收款)	Tax exchange for labor in cloth production (寒衣代金)	Fines (罚款)	Tax on merchandise (货物税)	Salt tax (盐税)	Trade (贸易)
1939	法币	52,251								
1940	法币	97,354			95,480		18,962	658,213		
1941	边币	201,617		7,009,000		427,705	285,695	1,964,133		
1942	边币	165,369	6,002,000	355,557,000				7,871,254		
1943	边币	184,123		90,435,926				67,811,000	20,295,000	3,000,000
1944	券币	160,000		45,793,291				480,584,076	89,429,804	
1945	券币	124,000		80,503,716				114,370,052	25,329,778	
								322,014,863	177,108,175	

Year	Currency (货币单位)	Salt Rev. (盐业收入)	Rev. from opium (特产)	Rev. from public enterprises (公营企业收入)	Rev. from Public Assets (公产收入)	Bank borrowing (银行借款)	Bonds (公债)	Monetary supply in Guang hua juan (光华券发行)	Monetary supply in bian bi (边币发行)	Monetary supply in liu tong juan (流通券发行)
1939	法币							217,925		
1940	法币							2,794,565		
1941	边币	1,220,000	139,623,000	427,390	5,017		4,050,939	1,237,275	23,023,350	1,213,080
1942	边币		1,306,958,533						91,026,835	4,553,842
1943	边币		135,388,778	183,854,391		1,111,502,030				81,533,675
1944	券币		757,995,348	225,410,404						228,373,328
1945	券币									629,968,474

216

Year	Currency (货币单位)	Misc. rev. (其它收入)	Others External financial support (协款)
1939	法币	141,457	7,933,315
1940	法币	681,169	10,538,585
1941	边币	-4,908,757	
1942	边币	75,167,000	
1943	边币	122,498,852	
1944	券币	3,644,199	
1945	券币	48,302,230	

Notes on data sources:

1) The original revenue data are from *Kang ri zhan zheng shi qi shaan gan ning bian qu cai zheng jing ji shi liao zhai bian* (*Shaan-Gan-Ning Border Region Finance and Economic Selective Historical Record During the Sino-Japanese War*) (1981, V6: 40–42, 43–44, 45–48, 57–62, 65–68, 77–81, 81–83).
2) The grain collection data are from *Kang ri zhan zheng shi qi shaan gan ning bian qu cai zheng jing ji shi liao zhai bian* (*Shaan-Gan-Ning Border Region Finance and Economic Selective Historical Record During the Sino-Japanese War*) (1981, V6: 152).
3) The opium revenue was based on *Kang ri zhan zheng shi qi shaan gan ning bian qu cai zheng jing ji shi liao zhai bian* (*Shaan-Gan-Ning Border Region Finance and Economic Selective Historical Record During the Sino-Japanese War*) (1981, V6: 425–427).
4) Data error: The original revenue from 'business revenue' [营业收入], which is a code name for opium revenue, in 1943 should be 1,306,958,532.94 instead of 306,958,532.94. The errors were discovered through the percentage and actual value discrepancies.
5) Data on monetary expansion are from *Kang ri zhan zheng shi qi shaan gan ning bian qu cai zheng jing ji shi liao zhai bian* (*Shaan-Gan-Ning Border Region Finance and Economic Selective Historical Record During the Sino-Japanese War*) (1981 V5: 120–12, 135–136, 142–146, 392–395).
6) Misc. Rev. includes all the other revenues reported in the yearly reviews but not included in the categories here.

TABLE C.2 *Shaan-Gan-Ning itemized fiscal revenue (in grain* (shi))

			Direct taxation					Indirect taxation				Economic production		
Year	Grain price in local currency (粮食价格)	Grain (Shi) (公粮实征 (石))	Grain transportation. (粮食)	Tax exchange for labor in salt (公盐代金)	Forfeiture (没收款)	Tax exchange for labor in cloth production (寒衣代金)	Fines (罚款)	Tax on merchandise (货物税)	Salt Tax (盐税)	Trade (贸易)	Salt revenue (盐业收入)	Revenue from opium (特产)	Revenue from public enterprises (公营企业收入)	Revenue from Public Assets (公产收入)
1939	39.50	52,251		0	2,417		480	16,664						
1940	64.00	97,354		0		6,683	4,464	30,690						
1941	317.00	201,617		22,110				24,830						
1942	1,655.00	165,369	3,627	0				40,973	33,747	1,813	737	84,364	6,678	78
1943	9,317.00	184,123		9,707				51,581	9,599			134,647		
1944	1,179.20	160,000		38,834				96,990	21,480			114,814	155,915	
1945	4,708.50	124,000		17,098				68,390	37,615			160,984	47,873	

	Monetary Expansion			Others		
Year	Bank borrowing (银行借款)	Bonds (公债)	Monetary supply in Guang hua juan (货币发行)	Misc. rev. (其它收入)	KMT financial support (协款)	Total
1939			5,517	3,581	200,843	281,754
1940			43,665	10,643	164,665	364,921
1941		12,779	72,629	-15,485		318,481
1942			55,001	45,418		431,050
1943	119,298		175,021	13,148		697,124
1944			193,668	3,090		784,791
1945			133,794	10,259		600,012

Notes on data sources:

1) The exchange rates are based on the grain prices reported in *Kang ri zhan zheng shi qi shaan gan ning bian qu cai zheng jing ji shi liao zhai bian* (*Shaan-Gan-Ning Border Region Finance and Economic Selective Historical Record During the Sino-Japanese War*) (1981, V6: 90).

2) I converted all the monetary expansion into *bianbi* first, then converted them into grain units.

TABLE C.3 *Shaan-Gan-Ning itemized fiscal revenue as share of total revenue*

Year	Direct taxation (%)	Indirect taxation (%)	Economic production (%)	Monetary expansion (%)	Others (%)
1939	19.6	5.9	0.0	2.0	72.6
1940	29.7	8.4	1.9	12.0	48.0
1941	70.2	7.8	0.0	26.8	-4.9
1942	39.2	17.8	19.7	12.8	10.5
1943	27.8	8.8	19.3	42.2	1.9
1944	25.3	15.1	34.5	24.7	0.4
1945	23.5	17.7	34.8	22.3	1.7

Note: The calculation is based on Table C.2.

TABLE C.4 *Jin-Sui itemized fiscal revenue (in local currency)*

		Direct taxation					
Year	Currency (货币单位)	Grain extraction (Shi) (公粮(石))	Tax exchange for grain extraction (Shi) (公粮变款)	Land tax (田赋)	Individual donation (捐金)	Apportionment (借摊款)	Fines (没收罚金)
1940	农币	89,817		198,776	3,698,841	862,196	429,226
1941	农币	212,758	9,377,048	500,000			
1942	农币	207,604	16,318,167	2,677,008			
1943	农币	161,587	68,367,283	16,680,000			
1944	农币	220,857	108,144,514				
1945	农币	215,313	284,384,990				3,654,903

		Indirect Taxation	Economic Production	Monetary Expansion		Others
Year	Currency (货币单位)	Tax on merchandise (货物税)	Revenue from opium (药品变价)	Bank borrowing (银行贸易投资)	Bonds (公债)	Misc. rev. (其它收入)
1940	农币	72,384	207,166	2,735,509		710,005
1941	农币	9,051,117	13,180,510	8,203,925		659,511
1942	农币	6,788,229	18,165,632	3,933,456		18,789,112
1943	农币	15,690,068	792,607,764		36,000,000	0
1944	农币	9,754,823	908,190,320	80,404,980		29,934,083
1945	农币	106,861,320	876,691,707	265,834,032		264,579,419

Notes on data sources:
1) The original revenue data are from *Jin sui bian qu cai zheng shi zhi liao xuan bian* (Jin-Sui Border Region Finance and Economic Selective Historical Record) (1986, V2: 609–611).
2) Misc. Rev. includes all the other revenues reported in the yearly revenues but not included in the categories here.

TABLE C.5 *Jin-Sui itemized fiscal revenue (in grain (shi))*

Year	Grain price in local currency (粮食价格)	Grain extraction (Shi) (公粮(石))	Tax exchange for grain extraction (Shi) (公粮变款)	Direct taxation			
				Land tax (田赋)	Individual donation (献金)	Apportionment (借摊款)	Fines (没收罚金)
1940	80	89,817		2,485	46,236	10,777	5,365
1941	1275	212,758	7,355	392			
1942	1623	207,604	10,053	1,649			
1943	4348	161,587	15,725	3,836			537
1944	6800	220,857	15,904				
1945	6800	215,313	41,821				

	Indirect Taxation		Economic Production	Monetary Expansion		Others	
Year	Tax on merchandise (货物税)	Revenue from opium (药品变价)	Bank borrowing (银行贸易投资)	Bonds (公债)	Misc. rev. (其它收入)	Total
1940	905	2,590	34,194		8,875	192,368
1941	7,099	10,338	6,434		517	244,376
1942	4,182	11,192	2,423		11,576	237,104
1943	3,609	182,302	0	8,280	0	375,340
1944	1,435	133,557	11,824		4,402	384,114
1945	15,715	128,925	39,093		38,909	440,868

Notes on data sources:

1) The exchange rates from local currency to grain unit are based on *Jin sui bian qu cai zheng shi zhi liao xuan bian* (*Jin-Sui Border Region Finance and Economic Selective Historical Record*) (1986, V2: 38, 103, 461, 473, 604). I first calculated the exchange rates between grain and various currencies based on CCP's own conversion rate reported in these tables (e.g., *fabi, nongbi, baiyangbi*). I then converted the prices to *nongbi* based on the exchange rates among these different currencies.

TABLE C.6 *Jin-Sui itemized fiscal revenue as share of total revenue*

Year	Direct taxation (%)	Indirect taxation (%)	Economic production (%)	Monetary expansion (%)	Others (%)
1940	80.4	0.5	1.3	17.8	4.6
1941	90.2	2.9	4.2	2.6	0.2
1942	92.5	1.8	4.7	1.0	4.9
1943	48.3	1.0	48.6	0.0	0.0
1944	61.8	0.4	34.8	3.1	1.1
1945	58.3	3.6	29.2	8.9	8.8

Note: The calculation is based on Table C.5.

TABLE C.7 *KMT central government itemized fiscal revenue (in millions of fabi)*

	Direct taxation						Indirect taxation			
Year	Income Tax	Excess profit tax	Business tax	Special business tax	Land tax excluding tax in kind	Tax in kind through grain collection	Customs	Salt monopoly & Subtax	Consolidated tax	Others
1939	27						33	61	22	27
1940	44	25					38	80	46	33
1941	80	70					15	296	121	84
1942	198	291	610		516	2,556	160	1,180	309	899
1943	765	884	1,785	57	4,014	6,326	377	3,025	657	3,750
1944	1,194	1,189	3,032	45	3,392	26,261	493	14,529	2,046	8,431
1945	2,120	1,833	7,318	11	6,326	60,000	3,321	53,506	23,144	4,672
						280,000				

	Economic Production		Monetary Expansion				
Year	Public enterprises and properties	Sale of internal bonds	Sale of external bonds	Bank loans	Income on unissued bonds	Misc. Rev.	Total
1939	7	25		2,311		237	2,750
1940	28	8		3,834		1,288	5,424
1941	22	127		9,443	270	362	13,446
1942	102	155	208	20,082	675	1,216	32,927
1943	99	3,871	15	40,857	635	2,560	89,612
1944	202	1,647	342	140,091	606	5,592	242,831
1945	6,247	62,727	92	1,043,257	2	51,861	1,546,437

Notes on data sources:
1) KMT fiscal data derive from Table 2 in Young (1965: 14).
2) Others in "Indirect Taxation" include monopolies of cigarettes, matches, sugar, wine and tobacco, stamps, minerals, and wartime consumption.
3) Misc. Rev. includes other nonborrowed incomes and balance of previous year.

Appendix C: Data on Fiscal Revenue (1937–1945)

TABLE C.8 *KMT itemized fiscal revenue as share of total revenue*

Year	Direct taxation (%)	Indirect taxation (%)	Economic production (%)	Monetary expansion (%)	Misc. rev. (%)
1939	1.0	5.2	0.3	84.9	8.6
1940	1.3	3.6	0.5	70.8	23.7
1941	20.1	3.8	0.2	73.2	2.7
1942	24.1	7.7	0.3	64.1	3.7
1943	37.7	8.7	0.1	50.6	2.9
1944	28.4	10.5	0.1	58.8	2.3
1945	19.2	5.5	0.4	71.5	3.4

Note: The calculation is based on Table C.7.

C.2 CCP AND KMT GRAIN EXTRACTION

TABLE C.9 *Degree of grain extraction by the CCP and KMT*

Year	KMT	CCP		
	Central Gov. (%)	Shaan-Gan-Ning (%)	Jin-Sui (%)	Jin-Cha-Ji (%)
1941	4.00	13.85	21.00	15.72
1942	8.67	11.14	17.40	14.29
1943	10.39	10.16	19.61	10.52
1944	6.30	8.83	19.35	9.35
1945	3.73	7.75	21.00	9.35
Yearly Average	6.62	10.35	19.67	11.85

Data source:
1) 1941–1944 KMT grain data is from Chang (1958: 144), and 1945 data is from Eastman (1984: 60). The grain extraction data included levy (征实), borrowing (征借), and mandatory procurement (征购) of grain and rice by the KMT central government.
2) Shaan-Gan-Ning data are from *Kang ri zhan zheng shi qi shaan gan ning bian qu cai zheng jing ji shi liao zhai bian* (*Shaan-Gan-Ning Border Region Finance and Economic Selective Historical Record During the Sino-Japanese War*) (1981, V6: 152).
3) Jin-Sui 1941 data are from *Jin sui bian qu cai zheng shi zhi liao xuan bian* [*Jin-Sui Border Region Finance and Economic Selective Historical Record*] (1986, V2: 497, 499, 501, 503, 510).
4) The Jin-Cha-Ji grain data is from Wei, Xing, and Fu (1984, V4: 545).

C.3 DATA ON DISTRIBUTION OF GRAIN BURDEN

TABLE C.10 *Distribution of grain burden across classes of rural resident (1941–1945)*

Year	CCP base	Landlord	Rich peasants	Middle peasants	Poor peasants	Data source
1942	Jin-Cha-Ji	21.8	17.0	9.8	3.8	Wei, Xing, and Fu (1984, V4:733)
1943		21.8	29.7	9.8	3.8	Wei, Xing, and Fu (1984, V4:504), Jizhong district.
1944		22.8	18.5	19.0	11.6	Wei, Xing, and Fu (1984, V4:525–529). The reported numbers are based on a representative sample of some individuals.
1941	Jin-Sui	37.5	27.6	22.0	13.8	*Jin sui bian qu cai zheng shi zhi liao xuan bian* (Jin-Sui Border Region Finance and Economic Selective Historical Record) (1986, V2: 497). The reported numbers are based on data from 9 counties.
1942		29.4	41.0	22.0	7.2	*Jin sui bian qu cai zheng shi zhi liao xuan bian* (Jin-Sui Border Region Finance and Economic Selective Historical Record) (1986, V2: 499). The reported numbers are based on data from two villages.
1943		48.6	33.9	20.2	8.0	*Jin sui bian qu cai zheng shi zhi liao xuan bian* (Jin-Sui Border Region Finance and Economic Selective Historical Record) (1986, V2: 501). The reported numbers are based on averages of three counties.

TABLE C.10 (continued)

Year	CCP base	Landlord	Rich peasants	Middle peasants	Poor peasants	Data source
1944		39.3	32.7	20.3	8.0	Jin sui bian qu cai zheng shi zhi liao xuan bian (Jin-Sui Border Region Finance and Economic Selective Historical Record) (1986, V2: 503). The reported numbers are based on the averages of eight counties).
1945		40.0	33.2	18.2	10.7	Jin sui bian qu cai zheng shi zhi liao xuan bian (Jin-Sui Border Region Finance and Economic Selective Historical Record) (1986, V2: 509–510). The reported numbers are based on averages of seven counties.
1941	Shaan-Gan-Ning	30.0	23.5	14.5	8.5	Kang ri zhan zheng shi qi shaan gan ning bian qu cai zheng jing ji shi liao zhai bian (Shaan-Gan-Ning Border Region Finance and Economic Selective Historical Record During the Sino-Japanese War) (1981, V6: 153–154)
1942		25.6	19.6	12.0	8.7	Hong se dang an: yan'an shi qi wen xian dang an hui bian (The Red Archive: Selected Documents and Archives in the Yan'an Period) (2013, V8: 194–195). The reported numbers are based on averages of two districts.

(continued)

228 Appendix C: Data on Fiscal Revenue (1937–1945)

TABLE C.10 (continued)

Year	CCP base	Landlord	Rich peasants	Middle peasants	Poor peasants	Data source
1943		22.6	13.5	8.1	2.1	Kang ri zhan zheng shi qi shaan gan ning bian qu cai zheng jing ji shi liao zhai bian (Shaan-Gan-Ning Border Region Finance and Economic Selective Historical Record During the Sino-Japanese War) (1981, V6: 147).
1944		36.5	18.9	11.4	4.9	Kang ri zhan zheng shi qi shaan gan ning bian qu cai zheng jing ji shi liao zhai bian (Shaan-Gan-Ning Border Region Finance and Economic Selective Historical Record During the Sino-Japanese War) (1981, V6: 162).
1945		39.0	21.7	12.7	7.4	Hong se dang an: yan'an shi qi wen xian dang an hui bian (The Red Archive: Selected Documents and Archives in the Yan'an Period) (2013, V9: 339). The reported numbers are based on averaging the numbers from two districts.
1941	Shandong	30.5	28.7	12.2	7.9	Shan dong ge ming gen ju di cai zheng shi liao xuan bian (The Selected Archives of Shandong Revolutionary Base Area Finance) (1985, V4: 205). The reported numbers are based on the average of five districts.
1942		30.2	28.9	12.1	8.7	
1943		28.9	22.4	9.6	3.7	
1944		26.1	20.3	8.5	3.1	
1945		24.5	18.3	8.4	1.9	

Note: The numbers represent the percentage of total grain levies contributed by each class of rural residents. The total may not sum to 100% due to some figures being averages of multiple districts within the base area.

Appendix D: Regression Analysis in Chapter 4

TABLE D.1 *Regression analysis of CCP grain extraction and party size (1940–1945)*

	Total grain levies (log)					
	Base area level analysis				County-level analysis	
	(1)	(2)	(3)	(4)	(5)	(6)
Party membership size (Log)	0.539*** (0.189)	0.567*** (0.230)	0.486** (0.250)	0.533** (0.222)	0.641** (0.148)	0.089* (0.048)
Indirect tax (Log)	0.119*** (0.056)	0.222*** (0.068)		0.054 (0.097)		
Opium revenue (Log)	−0.087*** (0.026)	−0.057 (0.031)		−0.068** (0.031)		
Borrowing (Log)	−0.096 (0.095)	0.001 (0.099)		0.064 (0.121)		
Population (Log)		−0.382 (0.233)				0.037 (0.120)
Percent of CCP government establishment		0.537 (2.236)				8.773*** (0.247)
Percent KMT government establishment		−3.160 (2.966)				0.002 (0.159)
Percent Japanese government establishment		−1.002 (1.467)				−0.267 (0.297)
Time trend	YES	YES	YES	YES	YES	YES
Base FE	NO	NO	YES	YES	NO	NO
Year FE	NO	NO	YES	YES	YES	YES
County FE	NO	NO	NO	NO	YES	YES
Observations	18	18	18	18	2,595	2,595

Note: Standard errors are reported in parentheses for base level analysis. Bootstrap standard errors are reported in parentheses for county-level analysis.
* Significant at 0.1 level.
** Significant at 0.05 level.
*** Significant at 0.01 level.

TABLE D.2 *Regression analysis of KMT grain extraction and party size (1941–1945)*

	Total grain levies (log)			
	Provincial level analysis		County-level analysis	
	(1)	(2)	(3)	(4)
Party membership size (Log)	0.330	0.057	0.325**	0.069
	(0.234)	(0.145)	(0.169)	(0.088)
Indirect tax (Log)	−1.209	0.213		
	(1.003)	(0.731)		
Other revenue (Log)	0.723	0.796		
	(0.547)	(0.522)		
Borrowing (Log)	−1.737	−2.108**		
	(1.363)	(1.330)		
Population (Log)	0.971***	0.442		0.147
	(0.368)	(0.302)		(0.181)
CCP government establishment				−0.452
				(0.577)
KMT government establishment				8.507***
				(1.546)
Japanese government establishment				−0.263
				(0.358)
Time trend	YES	YES	YES	YES
Province FE	NO	YES	NO	NO
Year FE	NO	YES	YES	YES
County FE	NO	NO	YES	YES
Observations	95	95	2,595	2,595

Note: Bootstrap standard errors are reported in parentheses.
* Significant at 0.1 level.
** Significant at 0.05 level.
*** Significant at 0.01 level.

Appendix D: Regression Analysis in Chapter 4

TABLE D.3 *Regression analysis of CCP grain extraction and party size (controlling for informal institution)*

	Total grain levies (log)	
	Base area level analysis	County-level analysis
	(1)	(2)
Party membership size (Log)	0.622***	0.087*
	(0.240)	(0.047)
Indirect tax (Log)	0.252**	
	(0.081)	
Opium revenue (Log)	−0.027	
	(0.038)	
Borrowing (Log)	−0.030	
	(0.101)	
Population (Log)	−0.373**	0.024***
	(0.242)	(0.117)
CCP government establishment	−0.989	8.656***
	(2.504)	(0.276)
KMT government establishment	−4.940	−0.004
	(3.239)	(0.158)
Japanese government establishment	−1.559	−0.302
	(1.530)	(0.292)
County head from same county	2.853	0.373
	(1.991)	(0.258)
Party secretary from same county	−0.655	0.034
	(2.456)	(0.274)
Time trend	YES	YES
Base FE	NO	NO
Year FE	NO	YES
County FE	NO	YES
Observations	18	2,595

Note: Standard errors are reported in parentheses.
* Significant at 0.1 level.
** Significant at 0.05 level.
*** Significant at 0.01 level.

References

Acemoglu, Daron, Simon Johnson, and James A. Robinson. 2002. "Reversal of Fortune: Geography and Institutions in the Making of the Modern World Income Distribution." *The Quarterly Journal of Economics* 117: 1231–94.

Aminzade, Ronald R., Jack A. Goldstone, Doug McAdam, Elizabeth J. Perry, William H. Sewell, Sidney Tarrow, and Charles Tilley. 2001. *Silence and Voice in the Study of Contentious Politics, Cambridge Studies in Contentious Politics*. Cambridge: Cambridge University Press.

Anria, Santiago, and Jennifer Cyr. 2017. "Inside Revolutionary Parties: Coalition-Building and Maintenance in Reformist Bolivia." *Comparative Political Studies* 50: 1255–87.

Atkinson, Anthony B., and Thomas Piketty, eds. 2007. *Top Incomes over the Twentieth Century: A Contrast between Continental European and English-Speaking Countries*. Oxford: Oxford University Press.

Averill, Stephen C. 2006. *Revolution in the Highlands: China's Jinggangshan Base Area*. Lanham: Rowman & Littlefield.

Bartels, Larry M. 1998. "Electoral Continuity and Change, 1868–1996." *Electoral Studies* 17: 301–26.

Bates, Robert H., and Da-Hsiang D. Lien. 1985. "A Note on Taxation, Development, and Representative Government." *Politics & Society* 14: 53–70.

Beissinger, Mark R. 2002. *Nationalist Mobilization and the Collapse of the Soviet State, Cambridge Studies in Comparative Politics*. Cambridge: Cambridge University Press.

Beramendi, Pablo, Mark Dincecco, and Melissa Rogers. 2019. "Intra-Elite Competition and Long-Run Fiscal Development." *The Journal of Politics* 81: 49–65.

Bernstein, Thomas P., and Hua-Yu Li. 2010. *China Learns from the Soviet Union, 1949-Present, The Harvard Cold War Studies Book Series*. Lanham: Lexington Books.

Besley, Timothy, and Torsten Persson. 2013. "Chapter 2 - Taxation and Development." In *Handbook of Public Economics*, eds. Alan J. Auerbach, Raj Chetty, Martin Feldstein and Emmanuel Saez. Vol. 5. Amsterdam: Elsevier. 51–110.

2009. "The Origins of State Capacity: Property Rights, Taxation, and Politics." *American Economic Review* 99: 1218–44.

Bianco, Lucien. 1971. *Origins of the Chinese Revolution, 1915–1949*. Stanford, CA: Stanford University Press.

2001. *Peasants without the Party: Grass-Roots Movements in Twentieth-Century China*, Armonk, NY: M.E. Sharpe.

Birch, Sarah, Ursula Daxecker, and Kristine Höglund. 2020. "Electoral Violence: An Introduction." *Journal of Peace Research* 57: 3–14.

Blaydes, Lisa. 2010. *Elections and Distributive Politics in Mubarak's Egypt*. New York: Cambridge University Press.

Boecking, Felix. 2017. *No Great Wall: Trade, Tariffs and Nationalism in Republican China, 1927–1945*. Cambridge, MA: Harvard University Press.

Bosco, Joseph. 1992. "Taiwan Factions: Guanxi, Patronage, and the State in Local Politics." *Ethnology* 31: 157–83.

Boucek, Françoise. 2009. "Rethinking Factionalism: Typologies, Intra-Party Dynamics and Three Faces of Factionalism." *Party Politics* 15: 455–85.

Braun, Otto. 1982. *A Comintern Agent in China 1932–1939*. Stanford, CA: Stanford University Press.

Breslawski, Jori, and Colin Tucker. 2022. "Ideological Motives and Taxation by Armed Groups." *Conflict Management and Peace Science* 39: 333–50.

Brewer, John. 1990. *The Sinews of Power: War, Money, and the English State, 1688–1783*. Cambridge, MA: Harvard University Press.

Brownlee, Jason. 2007. *Authoritarianism in an Age of Democratization*. New York: Cambridge University Press.

Cai zheng bu hai guan zong shui wu si shu bian. 1943. *Shi nian lai zhi hai guan [The Customs of the Past Decade]*. Chongqing: Zhong yang xin tuo ju yin zhi chu.

Cai zheng bu cai zheng nian jian bian zuan chu. 1935. "*Cai zheng nian jian [Financial Statistical Yearbook]*." Nanjing: Cai zheng bu cai zheng nian jian bian zuan chu.

Campbell Angus, Philip E. Converse, Warren E. Miller, and Donald E. Stokes 1964. *The American Voter*. Chicago: University of Chicago.

Carmines, Edward G., and Nicholas J. D'Amico. 2015. "The New Look in Political Ideology Research." *Annual Review of Political Science* 18: 205–16.

Chang, Kia-Ngau. 1958. *The Inflationary Spiral: The Experience in China 1939–1950*. Cambridge, MA: The MIT Press.

Chang, Lianting, ed. 2015. *Shandong Dang Shi Zi Liao Wen Ku [Shandong Party History Selective Documents]*. Jinan: Shandong ren min chu ban she.

Chen, Hongmin. 2003. "Cong 'hu hanmin lai wang han dian gao' kan 'xin guo min dang' zai bei fang de huo dong (1932–1936) [Study of 'New KMT's' Activities in Northern China Based on Hu Hanmin's Telegraphs and Mails]." *Anhui shi xue* (6): 34–40.

Chen, Yun. 1982 [1935]. "(Yi) Zun Yi Zheng Zhi Ju Kuo Da Hui Yi [(Second) Zunyi Enlarged Politburo Conference]." *Zhong gong dang shi zi liao* (6): 1–12.

Chen, Yung-fa. 1986. *Making Revolution: The Communist Movement in Eastern and Central China, 1937–1945*. Berkeley: University of California Press.

1990. *Yan'an de yin ying [The Shadow of Yan'an]*. Taipei: Zhong yang yan jiu yuan jin dai shi yan jiu suo.

2005. "Zhong gong jian guo chu qi de gong shang shui shou: yi tian jin he shang hai wei zhong xin [Chinese Taxation of the Urban Private Sector in the Early 1950s:

An Examination of Tianjin and Shanghai]." *Zhong Yang yan jiu yuan jin dai shi yan jiu suo ji kan*. 48: 137–187.

1998. *Zhongguo gong chan ge ming qi shi nian [Seventy Year's of Chinese Communist Revolution]*. Taipei: Lian jing chu ban shi ye gong si.

Cheng, Tun-Jen. 1989. "Democratizing the Quasi-Leninist Regime in Taiwan." *World Politics* 41: 471–99.

Cheng, Zhongyuan. 2006. *Zhang wentian zhuan [Biography of Zhang Wentian]*. 2nd ed. Beijing: Dang dai zhong guo chu ban she.

Chi, Hsi-sheng. 1982. *Nationalist China at War: Military Defeats and Political Collapse, 1937–45*. Ann Arbor: University of Michigan Press.

Coble, Parks M. 2023. *The Collapse of Nationalist China: How Chiang Kai-Shek Lost China's Civil War*. Cambridge: Cambridge University Press.

1986. *The Shanghai Capitalists and the Nationalist Government, 1927–1937*. 2nd Cambridge, MA: Harvard University Press.

Collier, Paul. 2000. "Rebellion as a Quasi-Criminal Activity." *Journal of Conflict Resolution* 44: 839–53.

Collier, Paul, and Anke Hoeffler. 2004. "Greed and Grievance in Civil War." *Oxford Economic Papers* 56: 563–95.

Connell, Dan. 2001. "Inside the EPLF: The Origins of the 'People's Party' and Its Role in the Liberation of Eritrea." *Review of African Political Economy* 28: 345–64.

Converse, Philip E. 1964. "The Nature of Belief Systems in Mass Publics." In *Ideology and Discontent*, ed. Apter DE. New York: Free Press. 206–61.

Cox, Gary W. 2015. "Electoral Rules, Mobilization, and Turnout." *Annual Review of Political Science* 18: 49–68.

Cui, Zhiqing, ed. 2007. *Guo min dang zheng zhi yu she hui jie guo zhi yan bian (1905–1949) [Evolution of Kuomintang's Political and Social Structure (1905–1949)]*. Vols. 3. Beijing: She hui ke xue wen xian chu ban she.

ed. 2013. *Guo min dang jie gou shi lun (1905–1949) [Study on Kuomintang's Structure (1905–1949)]*. Beijing: Zhong hua shu ju.

Dai, Xiangqing, and Huilan Luo. 1994. *Ab Tuan Yu Fu tian shi bian shi mo [The Ab-League and the Development of Futian Incident]*. Henan: Henan ren min chu ban she.

Davis, Deborah S. 2000. "Social Class Transformation in Urban China: Training, Hiring, and Promoting Urban Professionals and Managers after 1949." *Modern China* 26: 251–75.

de la Calle, Luis, and Ignacio Sánchez-Cuenca. 2013. "Killing and Voting in the Basque Country: An Exploration of the Electoral Link between Eta and Its Political Branch." *Terrorism and Political Violence* 25: 94–112.

de Zeeuw, Jeroen, ed. 2008. *From Soldiers to Politicians: Transforming Rebel Movements after Civil War*. Boulder: Lynne Rienner Publishers.

Deng, Yanhua, and Kevin J. O'Brien. 2013. "Relational Repression in China: Using Social Ties to Demobilize Protesters." *The China Quarterly* 215: 533–52.

Dewan, Torun, and Francesco Squintani. 2016. "In Defense of Factions." *American Journal of Political Science* 60: 860–81.

Dickson, Bruce J. 1993. "The Lessons of Defeat: The Reorganization of the Kuomintang on Taiwan, 1950–52." *The China Quarterly* 133: 56–84.

Dikötter, Frank. 2019. *How to Be a Dictator: The Cult of Personality in the Twentieth Century*. New York: Bloomsbury Publishing.

Dimitrov, Georgi. 1972. *Selected Works in Three Volumes*. Bulgaria: Sofia Press.
Dimitrov, Martin K. 2022. *Dictatorship and Information: Authoritarian Regime Resilience in Communist Europe and China*. Oxford: Oxford University Press.
Dincecco, Mark. 2009. "Fiscal Centralization, Limited Government, and Public Revenues in Europe, 1650–1913." *The Journal of Economic History* 69: 48–103.
  2011. *Political Transformations and Public Finances: Europe, 1650–1913*. Cambridge: Cambridge University Press.
  2017. *State Capacity and Economic Development: Present and Past*. Cambridge: Cambridge University Press.
Dorris, Carl E. 1976. "Peasant Mobilization in North China and the Origins of Yenan Communism." *The China Quarterly* 68: 697–719.
Duara, Prasenjit. 1988. *Culture, Power, and the State: Rural North China, 1900–1942*. Stanford, CA: Stanford University Press.
Duiker, William J. 2000. *Ho Chi Minh*. 1st ed. New York: Hyperion.
Duverger, Maurice. 1954. *Political Parties, Their Organization and Activity in the Modern State*. London, New York: Methuen; Wiley.
Eastman, Lloyd E. 1974. *The Abortive Revolution: China Under Nationalist Rule, 1927–1937*. Cambridge, MA: Harvard University Press.
  1972. "Fascism in Kuomintang China: The Blue Shirts." *The China Quarterly* 49: 1–31.
  1991. *The Nationalist Era in China, 1927–1949*. Cambridge: Cambridge University Press.
  1984. *Seeds of Destruction: Nationalist China in War and Revolution, 1937–1949*. Stanford, CA: Stanford University Press.
  1981. "Who Lost China? Chiang Kai-Shek Testifies." *The China Quarterly* 88: 658–68.
Egorov, Georgy, and Konstantin Sonin. 2011. "Dictators and Their Viziers: Endogenizing the Loyalty-Competence Trade-Off." *Journal of the European Economic Association* 9: 903–30.
Eisenstadt, S. N. 1978. *Revolution and the Transformation of Societies: A Comparative Study of Civilizations*. New York: Free Press.
Ellis, Stephen. 1999. *The Mask of Anarchy: The Destruction of Liberia and the Religious Dimension of an African Civil War*. New York: New York University Press.
Ertman, Thomas. 1997. *Birth of the Leviathan: Building States and Regimes in Medieval and Early Modern Europe*: Cambridge: Cambridge University Press.
Esherick, Joseph. 2022. *Accidental Holy Land: The Communist Revolution in Northwest China*. Berkeley: University of California Press.
Esherick, Joseph W. 2022. *China in Revolution: History Lessons*. Maryland: Rowman & Littlefield.
  1995. "Ten Theses on the Chinese Revolution." *Modern China* 21: 45–76.
Etcheson, Craig. 1984. *The Rise and Demise of Democratic Kampuchea*, Westview Special Studies on South and Southeast Asia. Boulder, CO: Westview.
Etzioni, Amitai. 1975. *A Comparative Analysis of Complex Organizations: On Power, Involvement, and Their Correlates*. New York: Free Press.
Fainsod, Merle. 1963. *How Russia Is Ruled*. Cambridge, MA: Harvard University Press.

Fairbank, John K., and Albert Feuerwerker, eds. 1986. *The Cambridge History of China: Volume 13: Republican China 1912–1949*, eds. Fairbank John K. and Feuerwerker Albert. Vol. 13. The Cambridge History of China. Cambridge: Cambridge University Press.
Fan, Xiaofang. 1994. *Jiang jia tian xia chen jia dang [Chiang's World, Chens' Party]*. Taipei: Zhou zhi wen hua shi ye gu fen you xian gong si.
Fei, Ran. 1944. "Shu gong ping di yi yu de liang di yi [Lost in Equity While Winning Grain Extraction]." *Xinhua Ribao [Xinhua Daily]*, July, 31.
Fernandez, Raquel, and Dani Rodrik. 1991. "Resistance to Reform: Status Quo Bias in the Presence of Individual- Specific Uncertainty." *The American Economic Review* 81: 1146–55.
Fewsmith, Joseph. 2022. *Forging Leninism in China*. Cambridge: Cambridge University Press.
  1985. *Party, State, and Local Elites in Republican China: Merchant Organizations and Politics in Shanghai, 1890–1930*. Honolulu: University of Hawaii Press.
  2021. *Rethinking Chinese Politics*. Cambridge: Cambridge University Press.
Fisher, Justin, and Todd A. Eisenstadt. 2004. "Introduction: Comparative Party Finance: What Is to Be Done?." *Party Politics* 10: 619–26.
Friedrich, Carl J., and Zbigniew Brzezinski. 1965. *Totalitarian Dictatorship and Autocracy*. 2nd ed. Cambridge: Harvard University Press.
Galbiati, Fernando. 1985. *P'eng P'ai and the Hai-Lu-Feng Soviet*. Stanford: Stanford University Press.
Gandhi, Jennifer 2008. *Political Institutions under Dictatorship*. New York: Cambridge University Press.
Gao, Hua. 2000. *Hong tai yang shi zheng yangs sheng qi lai de: Yan'an zheng feng de lai long qu mai (How the Red Sun Rose: The Origins of Yan'an Rectification)*. Hong Kong: The Chinese University Press.
  1999. "'Su Ab Tuan' shi jian de li shi kao cha [A Historical Investigation of the Ab-League Purge]." *Er shi yi shi ji [The Twenty-first Century]* 54: 60–70.
Garfias, Francisco. 2018. "Elite Competition and State Capacity Development: Theory and Evidence from Post-Revolutionary Mexico." *American Political Science Review* 112: 339–57.
Geddes, Barbara. 1999. "What Do We Know about Democratization after Twenty Years?" *Annual Review of Political Science* 2: 115–44.
Geddes, Barbara, Joseph Wright, and Erica Frantz. 2018. *How Dictatorships Work: Power, Personalization, and Collapse*. New York: Cambridge University Press.
Gerring, John, and Strom C. Thacker. 2008. *A Centripetal Theory of Democratic Governance*. Cambridge: Cambridge University Press.
Gilley, Bruce. 2003. "China's Changing of the Guard: The Limits of Authoritarian Resilience." *Journal of Democracy* 14: 18–26.
Gillin, Donald G. 1964. "'Peasant Nationalism' in the History of Chinese Communism." *The Journal of Asian Studies* 23: 269–89.
Giustozzi, Antonio. 2022. *The Taliban at War: 2001–2021*. Oxford, England: Oxford University Press.
Goldstone, Jack A. 1980. "Theories of Revolution: The Third Generation." *World Politics* 32: 425–53.
  2001. "Toward a Fourth Generation of Revolutionary Theory." *Annual Review of Political Science* 4: 139–87.

Goodwin, Jeff. 2001. *No Other Way Out: States and Revolutionary Movements, 1945–1991*. New York: Cambridge University Press.
Gould, Roger V. 1995. *Insurgent Identities: Class, Community, and Protest in Paris from 1848 to the Commune*. Chicago: University of Chicago Press.
Greene, Kenneth F. 2007. *Why Dominant Parties Lose: Mexico's Democratization in Comparative Perspective*. New York: Cambridge University Press.
Grzymala-Busse, Anna Maria. 2002. *Redeeming the Communist Past: The Regeneration of Communist Parties in East Central Europe*. New York: Cambridge University Press.
Gunther, Richard, and Larry Diamond. 2003. "Species of Political Parties: A New Typology." *Party Politics* 9: 167–99.
Guo, Dehong. 2014. *Wang ming nian pu* [*Wang Ming Chronology*]. Beijing: She hui ke xue wen xian chu ban she.
Gurr, Ted R. 1970. *Why Men Rebel*. Princeton, N.J.: Princeton University Press.
Hafner-Burton, Emilie M., Susan D. Hyde, and Ryan S. Jablonski. 2013. "When Do Governments Resort to Election Violence?" *British Journal of Political Science* 44: 149–79.
Haggard, Stephan. 2018. *Developmental States*. Cambridge: Cambridge University Press.
Haggard, Stephan, and Robert R. Kaufman. 1990. *The Political Economy of Inflation and Stabilization in Middle-Income Countries*, Policy, Research, and External Affairs Working Papers. Washington, DC (1818 H St., NW, Washington 20433): Country Economics Dept., World Bank.
Hale, Henry E. 2006. *Why Not Parties in Russia? Democracy, Federalism, and the State*. New York: Cambridge University Press.
Hardin, Russell. 1982. *Collective Action*. Baltimore: Johns Hopkins University Press.
Hao, Yinxia. 2013. "Kang zhan shi qi guo gong liang dang liang zheng zhi du xiang shi xing yan jiu [Similarities of Food Politics of the KMT and the CCP in the Period of Anti-Japanese War]." *Bai ji wen li xue yuan xue bao* 33: 17–22.
 2009. "Kang zhan shi qi guo min zheng fu tian fu zheng shi zhong de li yi ji tuan guan xi [The Interaction of Various Interest Groups in the Implementation of Land Tax in Kind by the National Government During the Period of Anti-Japanese War]." *Nan jing shi fan da xue xue bao* (6): 49–54.
 2008. "Kang zhan shi qi guo min zheng fu tian fu zheng shi zhi du zhi yan jiu [Study on the Policy of 'Land Tax in Kind' of National Government during the Anti-Japanese War]." Ph.D. Dissertation. Central China Normal University.
Hartford, J. Kathleen. 1980 "Step by Step: Reform, Resistance, and Revolution in Chin-Ch'a-Chi Border Region." Ph.D. Dissertation, Stanford University.
Hochschild, Jennifer, and Traci Burch. 2007. "Contingent Public Policies and Racial Hierarchy: Lessons from Immigration and Census Policies." In *Political Contingency: Studying the Unexpected, the Accidental, and the Unforeseen*, eds. Shapiro Ian and Bedi Sonu,. New York: NYU Press.
Hofheinz, Roy. 1977. *The Broken Wave: The Chinese Communist Peasant Movement, 1922–1928*. Cambridge, MA: Harvard University Press.
Honaker, James, Gary King, and Matthew Blackwell. 2011. "Amelia II: A Program for Missing Data." *Journal of Statistical Software* 45: 1–47.
Hong se dang an – Yan'an shi qi wen xian dang an hui bian bian wei hui, ed. 2013. *Hong se dang an: Yan'an shi qi wen xian dang an hui bian* [*The Red Archive: Selected Documents and Archives in the Yan'an Period*]. Vol. 8. Xi'an: Shanxi ren min chu ban she.

Hong se dang an – Yan'an shi qi wen xian dang an hui bian bian wei hui, ed. 2013. *Hong se dang an: Yan'an shi qi wen xian dang an hui bian* [*The Red Archive: Selected Documents and Archives in the Yan'an Period*]. Vol. 9. Xi'an: Shanxi ren min chu ban she.
Hook, Sidney. 1945. *The Hero in History, a Study in Limitation and Possibility*. London: Secker & Warburg.
Horgan, John. 2009. *Walking Away from Terrorism: Accounts of Disengagement from Radical and Extremist Movements*. New York: Routledge.
Hou, Kunhong. 2000. *Kang zhan shi qi de zhong yang cai zheng yu di fang cai zheng* [*Financial Arrangements Between the Central and Local Governments during the Sino-Japanese War, 1937–1945*]. Taipei: Guo shi guan.
Huang, Daoxuan. 2024. *Tie shui liu: Zhan shi zhong gong ge ming xi tong de yun zuo, 1937–1945* [*Flowing Steel: Operating Systems of the Chinese Communist Party During Wartime, 1937–1945*]. Hong Kong: The Chinese University of Hong Kong Press.
  2011. *Zhang li he xian jie: Zhong yang su qu de ge ming, 1933–1934* [*Tension and Limits: Revolution of the Central Soviet Area, 1933–1934*]. Beijing: She hui ke xue wen xian chu ban she.
Hunter, Wendy. 2010. *The Transformation of the Workers' Party in Brazil, 1989–2009*. New York: Cambridge University Press.
Huntington, Samuel P. 1968. *Political Order in Changing Societies*. New Haven: Yale University Press.
Huỳnh, Kim Khánh. 1982. *Vietnamese Communism, 1925–1945*. Ithaca: Cornell University Press.
Invernizzi, Giovanna M. 2023. "Antagonistic Cooperation: Factional Competition in the Shadow of Elections." *American Journal of Political Science* 67: 426–39.
Ishiyama, John. 2016. "Introduction to the Special Issue 'from Bullets to Ballots: The Transformation of Rebel Groups into Political Parties.'" *Democratization* 23: 969–71.
Ishiyama, John, and Anna Batta. 2011. "Swords into Plowshares: The Organizational Transformation of Rebel Groups into Political Parties." *Communist and Post-Communist Studies* 44: 369–79.
Iyob, Ruth. 1995. *The Eritrean Struggle for Independence: Domination, Resistance, Nationalism, 1941–1993*. New York: Cambridge University Press.
Jackson, Henry F. 1977. *The Fln in Algeria: Party Development in a Revolutionary Society*. Westport, Conn: Greenwood Press.
Javed, Jeffrey A. 2022. *Righteous Revolutionaries: Morality, Mobilization, and Violence in the Making of the Chinese State*. Ann Arbor: University of Michigan Press.
Jenkins, J. Craig. 1983. "Resource Mobilization Theory and the Study of Social Movements." *Annual Review of Sociology* 9: 527–53.
Jiangxi sheng dang an guan and zhong gong jiang xi sheng wei dang xiao dang shi jiao yan shi, eds. 1982. *Zhong yang ge ming gen ju di shi liao xuan bian* [*the Selection of Central Party Revolutionary Base Historical Documents*]. Nanchang: Jiangxi ren min chu ban she.
Jiangxi sheng shui wu ju, Fujian sheng shui wu ju, Jiangxi dang an guan, and Fujian dang an guan, eds. 1985. *Zhong yang ge ming gen ju di gong shang shui shou shi liao xuan bian, 1929.1–1934.2* [*Selected Documents on Industry, Commerce, and Taxation in the Party Central Revolutionary Base Areas 1929.1–1934.2*]. Sanming: Fujian ren min chu ban she.

Jin Sui bian qu cai zheng jing ji shi bian xie zu. 1986. *Jin sui bian qu cai zheng shi zi liao xuan bian [Jin-Sui Border Region Finance and Economic Selective Historical Record]*. Taiyuan: Shan xi ren ming chu ban she.

Jin, Yilin. 2009. *Guo min dang gao ceng de pai xi zheng zhi: Jiang jie shi "zui gao ling xiu" di wei shi ru he que li de [Factional Politics among KMT Elites: The Emergence of Chiang Kai-Shek's Paramount Leader Status]*. Beijing: She hui ke xue chu ban she.

Johnson, Chalmers. 1962. *Peasant Nationalism and Communist Power: The Emergence of Revolutionary China 1937–1945*. Stanford, CA: Stanford University Press.

1977. "Peasant Nationalism Revisited: The Biography of a Book." *The China Quarterly* 72: 766–85.

1966. *Revolutionary Change*, Basic Studies in Politics. Boston: Little, Brown.

Jones, Philip E. 2003. *The Pakistan People's Party: Rise to Power*. Karachi: Oxford University Press.

Judge, Timothy A., Ronald F. Piccolo, and Tomek Kosalka. 2009. "The Bright and Dark Sides of Leader Traits: A Review and Theoretical Extension of the Leader Trait Paradigm." *The Leadership Quarterly* 20: 855–75.

Jun shi ke xue yuan jun shi li shi yan jiu bu zhu., ed. 2000. *Zhong guo ren min jie fang jun quan shi [The Complete History of Chinese People's Liberation Army]*. Vol. 3–4. Beijing: Jun shi ke xue chu ban she.

Kakkar, Hemant, and Niro Sivanathan. 2022. "The Impact of Leader Dominance on Employees' Zero-Sum Mindset and Helping Behavior." *Journal of Applied Psychology* 107: 1706–24.

Kalyvas, Stathis N. 2007. "Book Review: Weinstein, JM (2007). Inside Rebellion: The Politics of Insurgent Violence. Cambridge, UK: Cambridge University Press." *Comparative Political Studies* 40: 1146–51.

Kalyvas, Stathis N. 1996. *The Rise of Christian Democracy in Europe*. Ithaca, NY: Cornell University Press.

Kataoka, Tetsuya. 1974. *Resistance and Revolution in China: The Communists and the Second United Front*. Berkeley: University of California Press.

Keefer, Philip. 2007. "Clientelism, Credibility, and the Policy Choices of Young Democracies." *American Journal of Political Science* 51: 804–21.

Key, V. O. 1949. *Southern Politics in State and Nation*. 1st ed. New York: A. A. Knopf.

Kirby, William C. 1990. "Continuity and Change in Modern China: Economic Planning on the Mainland and on Taiwan, 1943–1958." *The Australian Journal of Chinese Affairs* 24: 121–41.

Kirchler, Erich. 2007. *The Economic Psychology of Tax Behaviour*. Cambridge: Cambridge University Press.

Kirchler, Erich, Erik Hoelzl, and Ingrid Wahl. 2008. "Enforced Versus Voluntary Tax Compliance: The 'Slippery Slope' Framework." *Journal of Economic Psychology* 29: 210–25.

Kitschelt, Herbert, and Steven Wilkinson. 2007. *Patrons, Clients, and Policies: Patterns of Democratic Accountability and Political Competition*. New York: Cambridge University Press.

Koss, Daniel. 2018. *Where the Party Rules: The Rank and File of China's Communist State*. New York, NY: Cambridge University Press.

Kotkin, Stephen. 2017. *Stalin, Vol. II: Waiting for Hitler, 1929–1941*. UK: Penguin.

Kuo, Tai-Chün, and Ramon Hawley Myers. 2012. *Taiwan's Economic Transformation: Leadership, Property Rights and Institutional Change 1949–1965*. London; New York: Routledge.
Lachapelle, Jean, Steven Levitsky, Lucan A. Way, and Adam E. Casey. 2020. "Social Revolution and Authoritarian Durability." *World Politics* 72: 557–600.
Lebas, Adrienne. 2011. *From Protest to Parties: Party-Building and Democratization in Africa*. Oxford; New York: Oxford University Press.
  2013. "Violence and Urban Order in Nairobi, Kenya and Lagos, Nigeria." *Studies In Comparative International Development* 48: 240–62.
Levi, Margaret. 1989. *Of Rule and Revenue*. Berkeley: University of California Press.
  2006. "Why We Need a New Theory of Government." *Perspectives on Politics* 4: 5–19.
Levitsky, Steven, James Loxton, Brandon Van Dyck, and Jorge I. Domínguez, eds. 2016. *Challenges of Party-Building in Latin America*. Cambridge: Cambridge University Press.
Levitsky, Steven, and Lucan Way. 2022. *Revolution and Dictatorship: The Violent Origins of Durable Authoritarianism* Princeton, NJ: Princeton University Press.
Levitsky, Steven, and Mauricio Zavaleta. 2016. "Why No Party-Building in Peru?" In *Challenges of Party-Building in Latin America*, eds. Levitsky Steven, Loxton James, Van Dyck Brandon and Domínguez Jorge I. New York: Cambridge University Press 412–39.
Levitsky, Steven R., and Lucan A. Way. 2012. "Beyond Patronage: Violent Struggle, Ruling Party Cohesion, and Authoritarian Durability." *Perspectives on Politics* 10: 869–89.
Li, Huaiyin. 2018. "Ji zhong hua di fang zhu yi yu jin dai guo jia jian she [Localism Centralization and Modern State Building: Revisit Warlord Politics under Peking Government in Republican China]." *Jing dai shi yan jiu* (5): 67–84.
Li, Jiao. 2015. "Zheng liang hua bian yu ming zhu jian zheng: Kang zhan chu qi shaan gan ning bian qu zhi li fang shi de bian ge [Grain Extraction, Revolt and Democratic Governing: The Evolution of Governing Style in Shaan Gan Ning Border Region During the Early Phase of Anti-Japanese War]." *Dang shi yan jiu yu jiao xue* (241): 34–42.
Li, Jia, and Joseph Wright. 2023. "How Personalist Parties Undermine State Capacity in Democracies." *Comparative Political Studies* 56: 2030–65.
Li, Rui. 2020. "Gong chan guo ji dui zhong guo gong chan dang de jing ji yuan zhu yan jiu [Thesis on Comintern's Financial Assistance to the Chinese Communist Party]." MA. Thesis. Heilongjiang University,.
Li, Yurong. 2017. "Cong jin ru shanxi dao li zhu hua bei: Ba lu jun de liang xiang chou cuo yu ju shi cai zheng 1937–1940 [From Entering Shaanxi to Consolidating in Northern China- the No. 8 Route Army's Finance 1937–1940)]." *Kang ri zhan zheng yan jiu* (4) : 81–98.
Li, Yunhan. 1987. *Cong rong gong dao qing dang [From Accommodating to Purging the CCP]* Taipei: Ji ren shu ju.
Li, Yang. 2011. "Hu han min yu jiang jie shi de dang quan yu jun quan zhi zheng [The Struggle of Party State and Military State between Hu Hanmin and Chiang Kai-Shek]." *Kai fang shi dai* (9): 84–103.
Li, Yunhan, ed. 1993. *Zhong guo guo min dang dang wu fa zhan shi liao: Zu zhi gong zuo [Chinese Kuomintang Party Affairs: Organizational Work]*. Taipei: Zhong guo guo min dang zhong yang wei yuan hui dang shi wei yuan hui.

Lin, May-li. 2005. *Xi yang shui zhi zai jin dai zhong guo de fa zhan* [*The Evolution of Western Taxation System in Republican China*]. Taipei, Taiwan: Institute of Modern History, Academia Sinica.

Liu, Dayu. 2013. "Zhu jia ye yu zhang shi guo min dang de dang wu zheng dun [Zhu Jiaye and Wartime KMT Party Reorganization]." *Min guo dang an* (1): 117–24.

Looney, Kristen E. 2020. *Mobilizing for Development: The Modernization of Rural East Asia*. Ithaca, NY: Cornell University Press.

Loxton, James. 2021. *Conservative Party-Building in Latin America: Authoritarian Inheritance and Counterrevolutionary Struggle*. New York, NY: Oxford University Press.

Lü, Xiaobo. 2025. "Mobilized Compliance: When Do Political Parties Facilitate Wartime Fiscal Extraction?" University of Texas at Austin Working Paper.

Luo, Yuanzheng, ed. 2005. *Zhong hua min guo shi lu wen xian tong ji (Yi)* [*Records of Republic of China: Archives and Statistics (1)*]. Changchun: Jilin ren min chu ban she.

Lupu, Noam. 2016. *Party Brands in Crisis: Partisanship, Brand Dilution, and the Breakdown of Political Parties in Latin America*. Cambridge: Cambridge University Press.

Luttmer, Erzo F. P., and Monica Singhal. 2014. "Tax Morale." *Journal of Economic Perspectives* 28: 149–68.

Lyons, Terrence. 2016. "From Victorious Rebels to Strong Authoritarian Parties: Prospects for Post-War Democratization." *Democratization* 23: 1026–41.

Ma, Debin, and Jared Rubin. 2019. "The Paradox of Power: Principal-Agent Problems and Administrative Capacity in Imperial China (and Other Absolutist Regimes)." *Journal of Comparative Economics* 47: 277–94.

Madison, James. 1787. "Federalist 10." *The Federalist Papers* 22: 1787–88.

Magagna, Victor V. 1991. *Communities of Grain: Rural Rebellion in Comparative Perspective*. Ithaca: Cornell University Press.

Magaloni, Beatriz. 2008. "Credible Power-Sharing and the Longevity of Authoritarian Rule." *Comparative Political Studies* 41: 715–41.

  2006. *Voting for Autocracy: Hegemonic Party Survival and Its Demise in Mexico*. Cambridge; New York: Cambridge University Press.

Mainwaring, Scott, and Timothy Scully. 2003. *Christian Democracy in Latin America: Electoral Competition and Regime Conflicts*. Stanford, Calif.: Stanford University Press.

Malloy, James M. 1970. *Bolivia: The Uncompleted Revolution*. Pittsburgh: University of Pittsburgh Press.

Mampilly, Zachariah, and Shalaka Thakur. 2025. "Rebel Taxation as Extortion or a Technology of Governance? Telling the Difference in India's Northeast." *Comparative Political Studies*. 58:462–93. https://journals.sagepub.com/doi/full/10.1177/00104140241237472.

Manion, Melanie. 1993. *Retirement of Revolutionaries in China: Public Policies, Social Norms, Private Interests*. Princeton, N.J.: Princeton University Press.

Mann, Michael. 1984. "The Autonomous Power of the State: Its Origins, Mechanisms and Results." *European Journal of Sociology / Archives Européennes de Sociologie / Europäisches Archiv für Soziologie* 25: 185–213.

Manning, Carrie. 2007. "Party-Building on the Heels of War: El Salvador, Bosnia, Kosovo and Mozambique." *Democratization* 14: 253–72.

Mansfield, David. 2017. *Understanding Control and Influence: What Opium Poppy and Tax Reveal About the Writ of the Afghan State*: Afghanistan Research and Evaluation Unit.

Mao, Zedong. 1991. *Mao Ze Dong Xuan Ji [Mao's Selective Essays]*. Vol. 1. Beijing: Remin chu ban she.

1991. *Mao Ze Dong Xuan Ji [Mao's Selective Essays]*. Vol. 4. Beijing: Re min chu ban she.

1991. *Mao Ze Dong Xuan Ji [Mao's Selective Essays]*. Vol. 8. Beijing: Re min chu ban she.

Marbach, Moritz. 2021. "Choosing Imputation Models." *Political Analysis* 30: 597–605.

Marr, David G. 2013. *Vietnam State, War, and Revolution (1945–1946)*. Berkeley: University of California Press.

Mayhew, David R. 2007. "Events as Causes: The Case of American Politics." In *Political Contingency: Studying the Unexpected, the Accidental, and the Unforeseen*, eds. Shapiro Ian and Bedi Sonu. New York: NYU Press.

McAdam, Doug, John McCarthy, D, and Mayer N. Zald. 1996. "Introduction: Opportunities, Mobilizing Structures, and Framing Processes – toward a Synthetic, Comparative Perspective on Social Movements." In *Comparative Perspectives on Social Movements*, eds. McAdam Doug, John McCarthy, D and Mayer N. Zald. New York: Cambridge University Press.

Meisner, Maurice J. 1967. *Li Ta-Chao and the Origins of Chinese Marxism, Harvard East Asian Series,*. Cambridge: Harvard University Press.

Meng, Anne. 2020. *Constraining Dictatorship: From Personalized Rule to Institutionalized Regimes*. Cambridge: Cambridge University Press.

Meng, Anne, Jack Paine, and Robert Powell. 2023. "Authoritarian Power Sharing: Concepts, Mechanisms, and Strategies." *Annual Review of Political Science* 26:153–73.

Michels, Robert. 1915. *Political Parties; a Sociological Study of the Oligarchical Tendencies of Modern Democracy*. New York: Hearst's International Library Co.

Miller, Michael K. 2020. "The Autocratic Ruling Parties Dataset: Origins, Durability, and Death." *Journal of Conflict Resolution* 64: 756–82.

Mitchell, Christopher. 1977. *The Legacy of Populism in Bolivia: From the MNR to Military Rule*. New York: Praeger.

Mitter, Rana. 2020. *China's Good War: How World War II Is Shaping a New Nationalism*. Cambridge, MA: Harvard University Press.

Moore, Barrington. 1966. *Social Origins of Dictatorship and Democracy; Lord and Peasant in the Making of the Modern World*. Boston: Beacon Press.

Myers, Ramon H., and Hsiao-ting Lin. 2007. *Breaking with the Past: The Kuomintang Central Reform Committee on Taiwan, 1950–52*. Stanford, CA: Hoover Institution Press.

North, Douglass C., and Barry R. Weingast. 1989. "Constitutions and Commitment: The Evolution of Institutional Governing Public Choice in Seventeenth-Century England." *The Journal of Economic History* 49: 803–32.

North, Robert C. 1963. *Moscow and Chinese Communists*. 2nd ed. Stanford, CA: Stanford University Press.

Oi, Jean C. 1989. "Market Reforms and Corruption in Rural China." *Studies in Comparative Communism* 22: 221–33.

Olson, Mancur. 1993. "Dictatorship, Democracy, and Development." *American Political Science Review* 87: 567–76.
Oppenheim, Ben, Abbey Steele, Juan F. Vargas, and Michael Weintraub. 2015. "True Believers, Deserters, and Traitors: Who Leaves Insurgent Groups and Why." *The Journal of Conflict Resolution* 59: 794–823.
Opper, Marc. 2020. *People's Wars in China, Malaya, and Vietnam*. Ann Arbor: University of Michigan Press.
Paige, Jeffery M. 1975. *Agrarian Revolution: Social Movements and Export Agriculture in the Underdeveloped World*. New York: Free Press.
Parsa, Misagh. 2000. *States, Ideologies, and Social Revolutions: A Comparative Analysis of Iran, Nicaragua, and the Philippines*. New York: Cambridge University Press.
Pei, Minxin. 2006. *China's Trapped Transition: The Limits of Developmental Autocracy*. Cambridge, MA: Harvard University Press.
Peng, Zhen. 1981[1941]. *Guan yu jin cha ji bian qu dang de gong zuo he ju ti zheng ce bao gao* [*A Report Concerning Party Work and Policy*] Beijing: Zhong gong zhong yang dang xiao chu ban she.
Pepinsky, Thomas. 2007. "Autocracy, Elections, and Fiscal Policy: Evidence from Malaysia." *Studies In Comparative International Development* 42: 136–63.
  2009. *Economic Crises and the Breakdown of Authoritarian Regimes: Indonesia and Malaysia in Comparative Perspective*. New York, NY: Cambridge University Press.
Pepper, Suzanne. 1999. *Civil War in China: The Political Struggle 1945–1949*. Lanham, Md.; Oxford: Rowman & Littlefield Publishers.
  2004. "The Political Odyssey of an Intellectual Construct: Peasant Nationalism and the Study of China's Revolutionary History: A Review Essay." *The Journal of Asian Studies* 63: 105–25.
Perry, Elizabeth J. 1980. *Rebels and Revolutionaries in North China, 1845–1945*. Stanford, CA: Stanford University Press.
Persico, Nicola, José C. R. Pueblita, and Dan Silverman. 2011. "Factions and Political Competition." *Journal of Political Economy* 119: 242–88.
Plaut, Martin. 2016. *Understanding Eritrea: Inside Africa's Most Repressive State*. Oxford: Oxford University Press.
Pool, David. 2001. *From Guerrillas to Government: The Eritrean People's Liberation Front, Eastern African Studies*. Athens: Ohio University Press.
Powell, Robert. 2021. "Power Sharing with Weak Institutions." University of California, Berkeley Working Paper.
Quandt, William B. 1969. *Revolution and Political Leadership: Algeria, 1954–1968*. Cambridge: MIT Press.
Queralt, Didac. 2019. "War, International Finance, and Fiscal Capacity in the Long Run." *International Organization* 73: 713–53.
Remick, Elizabeth J. 2002. "The Significance of Variation in Local States: The Case of Twentieth Century China." *Comparative Politics* 34: 399–418.
Ren, Yude. 2008. *Xiang xia zha gen: Zhong guo guo min dang yu Taiwan di fang zheng zhi de fa zhan (1949–1960)* [*Rooting Down: The Evolution of KMT and Local Politics in Taiwan (1949–1960)*]. Taipei: Dao xiang chu ban she.
Reno, William. 2011. *Warfare in Independent Africa, New Approaches to African History*. New York: Cambridge University Press.
Reuter, Ora John. 2017. *The Origins of Dominant Parties: Building Authoritarian Institutions in Post-Soviet Russia*. New York: Cambridge University Press.

Revkin, Mara, and Ahmad Mhidi. 2016. "Quitting Isis." *Foreign Affairs*, January 10, 2016.
Revkin, Mara Redlich. 2020. "What Explains Taxation by Resource-Rich Rebels? Evidence from the Islamic State in Syria." *The Journal of Politics* 82: 757–64.
Riedl, Rachel Beatty. 2014. *Authoritarian Origins of Democratic Party Systems in Africa*. Cambridge: Cambridge University Press.
Rigby, T. H. 1968. *Communist Party Membership in the U.S.S.R. (1917–1967)*. Princeton: Princeton University Press.
Rigger, Shelley. 1999. *Politics in Taiwan: Voting for Democracy*. London; New York: Routledge.
Robnett, Belinda. 1997. *How Long? How Long?: African-American Women in the Struggle for Civil Rights*. New York: Oxford University Press.
Ross, Michael L. 2004. "Does Taxation Lead to Representation?" *British Journal of Political Science* 34: 229–49.
Ruiting, Guo, ed. 2002. *Zhong guo gong chan dang dang nei tong ji zi liao hui bian (1921–2000) [The Compendium of Chinese Communist Party Statistics (1921–2000)]*. Beijing, China: Zhong gong zhong yang zu zhi bu xin xi guan li zhong xin.
Saich, Tony. 2021. *From Rebel to Ruler: One Hundred Years of the Chinese Communist Party*. Cambridge, MA: The Belknap Press of Harvard University Press.
  1994. "Introduction: The Chinese Communist Party and the Anti-Japanese War Base Areas." *The China Quarterly* 140:1000–1006.
  1991. *The Origins of the First United Front in China: The Role of Sneevliet (Alias Maring)*. 2 Vols. Leiden: Brill.
Saich, Tony, and Bingzhang Yang. 1996. *The Rise to Power of the Chinese Communist Party: Documents and Analysis*. Armonk, NY: M.E. Sharpe.
Sartori, Giovanni. 1976. *Parties and Party Systems: A Framework for Analysis*. Cambridge Eng.; New York: Cambridge University Press.
Scarrow, Susan E. 2004. "Explaining Political Finance Reforms: Competition and Context." *Party Politics* 10: 653–75.
  1999. "Parties and the Expansion of Direct Democracy: Who Benefits?." *Party Politics* 5: 341–62.
Scheidel, Walter. 2018. *The Great Leveler: Violence and the History of Inequality from the Stone Age to the Twenty-First Century*. Princeton: Princeton University Press.
Schenoni, Luis L. 2021. "Bringing War Back in: Victory and State Formation in Latin America." *American Journal of Political Science* 65:405–21.
Scheve, Kenneth, and David Stasavage. 2010. "The Conscription of Wealth: Mass Warfare and the Demand for Progressive Taxation." *International Organization* 64: 529–61.
Schurmann, Franz. 1966. *Ideology and Organization in Communist China*. Berkeley: University of California Press.
Scott, James C. 1998. *Seeing Like a State: How Certain Schemes to Improve the Human Condition Have Failed*. New Haven: Yale University Press.
Selbin, Eric. 1993. *Modern Latin American Revolutions*. Boulder, CO: Westview Press.
Selden, Mark. 1995. "Yan'an Communism Reconsidered." *Modern China* 21: 8–44.
  1971. *The Yenan Way in Revolutionary China*. Cambridge: Harvard University Press.
Shaan gan ning bian qu caiki zheng jing ji shi bian xie zu. 1981. *Kang ri zhan zheng shi qi shaan gan ning bian qu cai zheng jing ji shi liao zhai bian [Shaan-Gan-Ning Border Region Finance and Economic Selective Historical Record During the Sino-Japanese War]*. Vol. 1-10. Xi'an, China: Shaanxi ren min chu ban she.

Shandong cai zheng yan jiu shuo, ed. 1985. *Shandong ge min gen ju di cai zheng shi liao xuan bian [the Selected Archives of Shandong Revolutionary Base Area Finance]*. Vol. 1-6. Shandong, China: Shandong cai zheng yan jiu shuo.
Sheng, Renxue, ed. 1985. *Zhang guo tao nian pu ji yan lun [Chronology and Speeches by Zhang Guotao]*. Beijing: Jie fang ju chu ban she.
Shih, Victor C. 2022. *Coalitions of the Weak, Cambridge Studies in Comparative Politics*. Cambridge: Cambridge University Press.
Shively, W. Phillips. 1972. "Party Identification, Party Choice, and Voting Stability: The Weimar Case." *The American Political Science Review* 66: 1203–25.
Siddiqui, Niloufer A. 2022. *Under the Gun: Political Parties and Violence in Pakistan*. Cambridge: Cambridge University Press.
Sierra, Raúl Sánchez de la. 2020. "On the Origins of the State: Stationary Bandits and Taxation in Eastern Congo." *Journal of Political Economy* 128: 32–74.
Skocpol, Theda. 1979. *States and Social Revolutions: A Comparative Analysis of France, Russia, and China*. Cambridge: Cambridge University Press.
Slater, Dan. 2003. "Iron Cage in an Iron Fist: Authoritarian Institutions and the Personalization of Power in Malaysia." *Comparative Politics* 36: 81–101.
  2010. *Ordering Power: Contentious Politics and Authoritarian Leviathans in Southeast Asia*. Cambridge: Cambridge University Press.
Smith, Benjamin. 2005. "Life of the Party: The Origins of Regime Breakdown and Persistence under Single-Party Rule." *World Politics* 57: 421–51.
Staniland, Paul. 2014. *Networks of Rebellion: Explaining Insurgent Cohesion and Collapse*. Ithaca: Cornell University Press.
Stasavage, David. 2016. "Representation and Consent: Why They Arose in Europe and Not Elsewhere." *Annual Review of Political Science* 19: 145–62.
  2011. *States of Credit: Size, Power, and the Development of European Polities*. Princeton, N.J.: Princeton University Press.
Stekhoven, Daniel. J., and Peter. Bühlmann. 2012. "MissForest—Non-Parametric Missing Value Imputation for Mixed-Type Data." *Bioinformatics* 28: 112–8.
Stewart, Megan A. 2021. *Governing for Revolution: Social Transformation in Civil War*. Cambridge: Cambridge University Press.
Stokes, Gale. 1993. *The Walls Came Tumbling Down: The Collapse of Communism in Eastern Europe*. New York; Oxford: Oxford University Press.
Strauss, Julia C. 1998. *Strong Institutions in Weak Polities: State Building in Republican China, 1927–1940*. Oxford, New York: Oxford University Press.
Sun, Jianwei. 2019. "'Dao su qu ti kuan': Su qu wei shang hai zhong gong zhong yang yun shu huang jing zhi kao cha – Yi gan dong bei, Zhong yang suqu wei Zhong xing ['Withdrawing Funding from Soviet Base': A Study of Transferring Gold from Soviet Area to Shanghai Party Center-Focusing on Northeast Jiangxi and Central Soviet Area]." *Su qu yan jiu* (2): 30–40.
Sun, Yanling. 2015. "Kang ri shi qi guo min zheng fu wei zhong gong jun dui ti gong jun fei shu er kao [The Amount of Military Expenditure Provided by the National Government for the CCP Army During the Anti-Japanese War]." *Jun shi li shi* (2): 10–15.
Suny, Ronald. 1993. *The Revenge of the Past: Nationalism, Revolution, and the Collapse of the Soviet Union*. Stanford, CA: Stanford University Press.
  1998. *The Soviet Experiment: Russia, the Ussr, and the Successor States*. New York: Oxford University Press.

Svolik, Milan W. 2012. *The Politics of Authoritarian Rule.* Cambridge University Press.
  2009. "Power Sharing and Leadership Dynamics in Authoritarian Regimes." *American Journal of Political Science* 53: 477–94.
Tavits, Margit. 2013. *Post-Communist Democracies and Party Organization.* Cambridge: Cambridge University Press.
Teiwes, Frederick C. 1994. *Formation of the Maoist Leadership*, Research Notes and Studies No. 10. London: Contemporary China Institute, University of London.
Thachil, Tariq. 2014. *Elite Parties, Poor Voters: How Social Services Win Votes in India.* Cambridge: Cambridge University Press.
Thaxton, Ralph. 1983. *China Turned Rightside Up: Revolutionary Legitimacy in the Peasant World.* New Haven: Yale University Press.
The No. 2 National Archive, ed. 2012. Zhong guo guo mind dang li ci quan guo dai biao da hui ji zhong yang quan hui wen xian hui bian [*The Compendium of China's Kmt National Party Congress and Central Committee Documents*]. Vol. 4. Beijing: Jiu zhou chu ban she.
Tilly, Charles. 1990. *Coercion, Capital, and European States, AD 990–1990.* Cambridge, MA: B. Blackwell.
  1978. *From Mobilization to Revolution.* Reading, Mass.: Addison-Wesley Pub. Co.
Timmons, Jeffrey F. 2010. "Taxation and Representation in Recent History." *The Journal of Politics* 72: 191–208.
Torigian, Joseph. 2022. *Prestige, Manipulation, and Coercion: Elite Power Struggles in the Soviet Union and China after Stalin and Mao.* New Haven: Yale University Press.
Trimberger, Ellen Kay. 1978. *Revolution from Above: Military Bureaucrats and Development in Japan, Turkey, Egypt, and Peru.* New Brunswick, N.J.: Transaction Books.
Tsai, Lily L. 2007. *Accountability without Democracy: Solidary Groups and Public Goods Provision in Rural China.* New York, NY: Cambridge University Press.
Tsuchida, Akio. 2002. "Kang zhan shi qi zhong guo guo min dang dang yuan fen de te zheng he yan bian [The Evolution of KMT Party Member Characteristics During Wartime]." *Min guo yan jiu* (060: 82–102.
Van de Ven, Hans J. 1992. *From Friend to Comrade: The Founding of the Chinese Communist Party, 1920–1927.* Berkeley: University of California Press.
Van Dyck, Brandon. 2017. "The Paradox of Adversity: The Contrasting Fates of Latin America's New Left Parties." *Comparative Politics* 49: 169–89.
Van Vugt, Johannes P. 1991. *Democratic Organization for Social Change: Latin American Christian Base Communities and Literacy Campaigns.* New York: Bergin & Garvey.
Vladimirov, P. P. 1975. *The Vladimirov Diaries: Yenan, China, 1942–1945.* 1st ed. Garden City, NY: Doubleday.
Vogel, Ezra F. 2011. *Deng Xiaoping and the Transformation of China.* Cambridge: Harvard University Press.
Vu, Tuong. 2016. *Vietnam's Communist Revolution: The Power and Limits of Ideology.* Cambridge: Cambridge University Press.
Wan, Ning. 2005. "'Zhong guo qing gong': Su lian yuan zhu Zhong guo kang zhan de shuang cong ce lue ['Prioritizing the KMT over the CCP': The Dual Strategy by Soviet Aid to China During the Anti-Japanese War]." *Hubei xing zhen xue yuan yuan bao* (6): 70–74.

Wang, Jianhua. 2018. "Qun zhong lu xian ru he lian cheng de: Ji yu shaan gan ning bian qu zheng liang dong yuan de guan cha shi jiao [How Does Mass Line Come into Being? —Based on the Grain Collection Mobilization of Shaanxi-Gansu-Ningxia Border Region Government]." *Si chuan da xue xue bao* 214: 29–40.
 2017. "Zhong Yang Gen Ju Di De Cai Zheng Dong Yuan [Fiscal Mobilization in Central Soviet Base Area]." *Dong nan xue shi* (5): 62–72.
Wang, Liangqing. 2010. *Gai zhao de dan sheng [The Birth of Reorganization]*. Gaoxiong, Taiwan: Fu wen chu ban she.
Wang, Qisheng. 2010. *Dang yuan, dang quan yu dang zheng: 1924–1949 nian Zhong guo guo min dang de zu zhi xing tai [Comrades, Control and Contention of the Kuomintang, 1924–1949]*. Beijing: Hua wen chu ban she.
Wang, Shengze. 2018. "Fu jian bai qu dang zu zhi de jing fei wen ti yan jiu [A Study of Party Finance of Party Organizations in Fujian Border Region]." *Su qu yan jiu* (4): 21–34.
Wang, Yuhua. 2022. *The Rise and Fall of Imperial China: The Social Origins of State Development*. Princeton, NJ: Princeton University Press.
Wei, Xiahai, Xing, Guang and Fu, Shangwei eds. 1984. *Kang ri zhan zheng shi ji jin cha ji bia qu cai zheng jing ji shi zi liao xuan bian [Jin Cha Ji Border Region Finance and Economic Selective Historical Record During the Sino-Japanese War]*. Tianjing, China: Nankai da xue chu ban she.
Weinstein, Jeremy M. 2006. *Inside Rebellion: The Politics of Insurgent Violence*. Cambridge: Cambridge University Press.
Wickham-Crowley, Timothy P. 1992. *Guerrillas and Revolution in Latin America: A Comparative Study of Insurgents and Regimes since 1956*. Princeton, N.J.: Princeton University Press.
Wolf, Eric R. 1969. *Peasant Wars of the Twentieth Century*. 1st ed. New York: Harper & Row.
Wou, Odoric Y. K. 1994. *Mobilizing the Masses: Building Revolution in Henan*. Stanford, CA: Stanford University Press.
Wu, Ai. 2013a. "Da zhuan ze: Zhong gong zai 1936 nian (Er) [The Major Turning Point: the CCP in 1936 (II)]." *Jiang huai wen shi* (5): 30–57.
 2013b. "Da zhuan ze: Zhong gong zai 1936 nian (San) [The Major Turning Point: the CCP in 1936 (III)]." *Jiang huai wen shi* (6): 45–63.
Xiao, Hongjin. 2010. "Lun kang zhan shi qi si chuan tian fu 'San Zheng' [On Three Methods of Extraction of Land Tax in Sichuan During the Anti-Japanese War]." MA Thesis. Sichuan Normal University.
Xie, Jianping, and Pingsheng Xiao. 2019. "Zhong yang su qu shi qi zheng fu cai zheng yu suan de chao zhi yu kong zhi [Over Expenditure and Control of Government Budget During the Period of the Central Soviet Area]." *Gan nan shi fan da xue bao* (1): 18–24.
Xin, Ping. 1991. "Lun xin xian zhi [On New County System]." *Kang ri zhan zheng yan jiu* (2): 182–211.
Xu, Yi, ed. 1982. *Zhong yang ge ming gen ju di cai zheng jing ji shi chang bian [The Compendium of Economic and Financial History in the Central Revolutionary Base Area]*. Vols. 2. Beijing: Ren min chu ban she.
Yang, Kuisong. 1991. "'Li san lu xian' de xing cheng ji Zhong gong Zhong yang yu gong chan guo ji he yuan dong ju de zheng lu [The Formation of 'Lisan Line' and Debates among CCP Party Center, Comintern and Far-east Bureau]." *Jing dai shi yan jiu* (1): 196–220.

2006. *Xi'an shi bian xin tan: Zhang xue liang yu zhong gong guan xi zhi mi* [A New Perspective on the Xi'an Incident: The Mysterious Relationship between Zhang Xueliang and the CCP]. Nanjing: Jiangsu ren min chu ban she.

2009. "Xin zhong guo tu gan bei jing xia de di zhu fu nong wen ti [The Issue of Landlord and Rich Peasant under New China's Land Reform]." www.yangkuisong.net/ztlw/sjyj/000285.htm.

2012. *Yang kuisong zhu zuo ji: ge ming* [Publications of Yang Kuisong: Revolution]. Vol. 3. Guilin Shi: Guangxi shi fan da xue chu ban she.

2011. "Zheng zhi du li de qian ti: You guan gong chan guo ji dui Zhong gong cai zheng yuan zhu wen ti de li shi kao chao [The Precondition for Political Independent: An Historical Investigation of Issues Concerning Comintern Financial Support to the CCP]." In *Du shi qiu shi: Zhong guo xian dai shi du shi li ji* [Notes on China Contemporary History]. Hanzhou: Zhejiang da xue chu ban she.

Yang, Yunruo, and Kuisong Yang. 1986. "1928–1943 nian jian gong chan guo ji he zhong guo ge ming guan xi de ruogan yan jiu ke ti [Research on the Relationship between Comintern and Chinese Revolution 1928–1944]." *Jiao xu yu yan jiu* (1): 39–43.

Ye, Zuolong. 2011. *Peng pai yu hai lu feng geng ju di* [Peng Pai and Hailufeng Base]. Beijing: Zhong gong zhong yang dang xiao chu ban she.

Yin, Hongqun. 2017. "Kang ri zhan zheng shi ji tian fu zheng shi yu xin sheng quan de que li [Land Tax Grain Levies and New Gentry Power during the Anti-Japanese War]." *Nanjing she hui ke xue* (12): 131–36.

Young, Arthur N. 1947. *China's Economic and Financial Reconstruction*. New York. https://search.worldcat.org/title/5082977.

  1971. *China's Nation-Building Effort, 1927–1937; the Financial and Economic Record*. Stanford, CA: Hoover Institution Press.

  1963. *China and the helping hand, 1937–1945*. Cambridge, MA: Harvard University Press.

  1965. *China's Wartime Finance and Inflation, 1937–1945*. Cambridge, MA: Harvard University Press.

Yu, Boliu. 1995. *Zhong yang su qu jing ji shi* [Economic History of the Central Soviet Region]. Nanchang: Jian gxi ren min chu ban she.

Zhang, Haiyan. 2014. "'Hua xian shi bian' ji qi shan hou gong zuo su lun [A Study of 'Huan County Incident' and Its Resolution]." *Zhong gong dang shi yan jiu* (9): 101–08.

Zhang, Hongsheng, and Haibing Zhou. 2012. "Hui yi wo de fu qing zhang wen tian (Shang) [Remembering My Father Zhang Wentian (I)]." *Jiang huai wen shi* (5): 68–84.

Zhang, Jiakang. 2013. "Zun yi hui yi qian hou de zhang wen tian he mao ze dong [Zhang Wentian and Mao Zedong: Before and after Zunyi Conference]." *Dang shi zhong heng*. (8): 54–58.

Zhang, Kan, and Changchun Xu. 1999. *Zhong yang su qu cai zheng jing ji shi* [History of Economy and Finance in the Central Soviet Region]. Xiamen: Xiamen da xue chu ban she.

Zhang, Qi, and Mingxing Liu. 2019. *Revolutionary Legacy, Power Structure, and Grassroots Capitalism under the Red Flag in China*. Cambridge: Cambridge University Press.

Zhang, Taisu. 2023. *The Ideological Foundations of Qing Taxation: Belief Systems, Politics, and Institutions*. Cambridge: Cambridge University Press.

Zhang, Yufa. 2001. *Zhong hua min guo shi gao* [*The History of Republic of China*]. 2nd ed. Taipei, Taiwan: Linking Books.

Zhao, Shenghui. 1987. *Zhong guo gong chan dang zu zhi shi gang yao* [*An Outline of the Chinese Communist Party Organization History*]. Vol. 1. Anhui: Anhui ren min chu ban she.

Zhong gong Hebei sheng wei zu zhi bu, Zhong gong Hebei sheng wei dang shi zi liao zheng ji bian shen wei yuan hui, Hebei sheng dang an ju. 1990. *Zhongguo gong chan dang hebei sheng zu zhi shi zi liao: 1922–1987* [*The CCP Hebei Province Party Organization History Documents: 1922–1987*]. Shijiazhuang: Hebei ren min chu ban she.

Zhong gong Shanxi Sheng wei zu zhi bu, Zhong gong Shanxi Sheng wei dang shi yan jiu shi, Shanxi Sheng dang an guan, ed. 1994. *Zhongguo Gong Chan Dang Shanxi Sheng Zu Zhi Shi Zi Liao* [*CCP Shaanxi Provincial Party History Documents*]. Xi'an: Shanxi ren min chu ban she.

Zhong gong zhong yang dang shi zi liao zheng ji wei yuan hui, Zhong gong zhong yang dang shi yan jiu shi bian. 1982. *Zhong gong dang shi zi liao* [*Historical Documents of Chinese Communist Party Center*]. Vol. 6. Beijing: Zhong gong zhong yang dang xiao chu ban she.

Zhong gong zhong yang zu zhi bu, Zhong gong zhong yang dang shi yan jiu shi, Zhong yang dang an guan. 2000. *Zhong guo gong chan dang zu zhi shi zi liao* [*The Compendium of Chinese Communist Party Organizational History*]. Vol. 1. Beijing: Zhong gong dang shi chu ban she.

Zhong yang dang an guan, Hubei sheng dang an guan, Hunan sheng dang an guan. 1985. *Xiang E xi su qu ge ming li shi wen jian hui ji* [*The Compendium of Historical Revolution Documents in the Xiang-Er-Xi Soviet Area*]. Vols. 4. Changsha: Hubei ren min chu ban she chu ban.

Zhong gong zhong yang dang shi di yi yan jiu bu, ed. 2002. *Gong chan guoji, lian gong(bu) yu zhong guo ge min wen xian zi liao xian ji, 1927–1931* [*The Selected Volume of Comintern and Chinese Revolution Archives*]. Vol. 1. Beijing: Zhong yang wen xian chu ban she.

Zhong hua ren min gong he guo cai zheng bu hui. "Zhongguo nong min fu dan shi" bian ji wei yuan. 1994. *Zhong guo nong min fu dan shi* [*The History of Peasant's Burden in China*]. Vol. 3. Beijing: Zhong guo cai zheng jing ji chu ban she.

Zhong yang dang an guan. 1989. *Zhong gong zhong yang wen jian xuan ji* [*CCP Party Center Selected Documents*]. Vols. 15. Beijing: Zhong gong zhong yang dang xiao chu ban she.

Zhou, Xiaohui. 2018. "'Yi er wei shi' bei jing xia guo gong liang dang zhao qi dang zheng jian she ji qi bi jiao yan jiu [A Comparison of Early CCP and KMT Party Manifesto Drafting in the Context of 'Learning from the Soviet']." *Dang shi yu wen xian yan jiu* (1): 76–83.

Zhou, Zhuwen. 2014. "'Bu pa na, jiu pa luan': Yi zhong gong liang zheng shou de tong yi lei jin shui qu jing ['No Afraid of Collection, but Afraid of Disorder': The Evolution of Consolidated Tax through Grain Extraction in Northen Hebei]." *Kang ri zhan zheng yan jiu*. (3): 43–56.

———. 2012. "Feng bi de cun zhuang: 1940–1944 jin xi bei jiu guo gong liang zhi zheng shou [Isolated Villages: The Collection of Saving-the-Country Grain in Northwest Shanxi]." *Kang ri zhan zheng yan jiu* (1): 53–62.

2023. *Hua bei kang ri geng ju di jiu guo gong liang yan jiu* [A Study of Grain Levies in Northern China Base Area]. Beijing: She hui ke xue wen xian chu ban she.

Zhu, Hong. 2007. "Da ge min shiqi sulian he gongchan guoji dui guogong liangdang jingji yuanzhi zhi bijiao [the Comparison of Financial Aid from the Comintern and the Soviet to the KMT and the CCP During Chinese Revolution]." *Dang de wen xian* (2): 52–57.

Zhu, Yuxiang. 1963. "Kang ri zhan zheng shi qi guo min dang zheng fu de tian fu zheng shi yu liang shi zheng gou [KMT Government's Land Tax in Kind and Grain Procurement During the Anti-Japanese War]." *Shang dong da xue xue bao* (1): 79–96.

Ziblatt, Daniel. 2017. *Conservative Parties and the Birth of Democracy*. New York: Cambridge University Press.

Index

Afwerki, Isaias, 10, 40
Algeria
   National Liberation Front in, 10, 35, 42
   nationalism in, 35
   Provisional Government of the Algerian Republic, 44
   revolutionary organizations in, 11
authoritarian regimes, 23
   autocracies and, political parties in, 22–24
   dominant political parties in, 24–25

Bella, Ben, 42, 44
bellicist theory of state formation, 27, 51
Bharatiya Janata Party (India), 36–37
Blue Shirt Society. *See* Lixing She (Blue Shirt Society)
Bo Gu, 139–40, 144
Bo Yibo, 192–93
Bolivia
   Movement for Socialism in, 37
   revolutionary movements in, 37
   Revolutionary Nationalist Movement, 8, 10, 37
Boumédiène, Houari, 42, 44
Braun, Otto, 139

Cai Hesen, 121–22
CC Faction. *See* Central Club (CC Faction)
CCP. *See* Chinese Communist Party (CCP)
Central Club (CC Faction), 168
Chen Duxiu, 61, 110
   First United Front and, 113
   mass mobilization infrastructure under, 111–13, 114

   during ascension to power, 111
   Comintern and, 112–13
   loss of leadership, 112–13
Chen Gongbo, 169
Chen Jiongming, 58
Chen Jitang, 178
Chiang Ching-kuo, 197–98
Chiang Kai-shek, 3, 21, 68. *See also* Kuomintang (KMT)
   arrest of, 75
   Comintern and, 162–63
   consolidation of power by, 110, 178–79
   alliance with Hu Han-min, 162–65
   alliance with Wang Ching-wei, 162
   internal civil war as result of, 164–65
   economic elites and, 69, 161–66
   land tax policies under, 83
   mass mobilization under, 180–81
   military career of, 162
   party reforms under, 176–85, 198–200
   party-building under, 166–70
      through patronage networks, 166–68
      as quasi-dominant leader, 179–82
   power-sharing under, 165–66
   purge of CCP members under, 112, 163
   as quasi-dominant leader, 176–85, 196–98
   party-building under, 179–82
   power consolidation under, 178–79
   Sun Yat-sen as influence on, 180
   suppression of labor movements, 69
   Three Principles of the People League and, 181–82
   Zhongshanjian Incident and, 163

China. *See also* methodological approach, to Republican-era China; *specific topics*
  authoritarian regime in, 3
  Civil War in (1946–1949), 1, 195
  inflation in, 77
Chinese Communist Party (CCP). *See also* First United Front; grain extraction, infrastructure for; grain levies; methodological approach, to Republican-era China; mobilized compliance, infrastructure for, in CCP; *specific topics*
  Comintern financial support of, 57–58, 59, 62, 63, 66
  constitution of, 157
  contingent events for, 20–21
  dominant leadership in, 40, 138–44
    historical legacy of, 190–91, 202–5
  extractive capacity of
    expropriation limits and, 67
    revenue sources and, 63–67, 79, 100
    during Sino-Japanese War, 77–81, 100
    Soviet base areas, 62–67
    taxation policies, 63–64, 66–67, 80
  grain burden distribution schemes by, 101–2
    progressive, 102
  Kuomintang and
    defeated of, 1–4
    Second United Front and, 76
  membership of, 89
    declines in, 1
    from 1921–1949, 2
    purge of, 112
  opium revenue for, 80, 81
  party-building in, 16–19
    under Chen Duxiu, 113–16
    during elite contestation (1927–1935), 124–30
    under Mao Zedong, 144–48
  prewar resource mobilization by (1921–1937)
    expropriation as instrument of, 67
    extractive capacity and, 55–56
    organizational structure, 55–56
    party institutionalization, 55–56
    party longevity, 55–56
    summary of, 73–74
    theoretical approach to, 55–56
  Red Army and, 64–66
    expansion of, 65
  reversal of fortune for, 1–4, 12
    contingent events for, 20–21
    degree of elite power struggle and, 16–19

  methodological approach to, 16–21
  party strength as element in, 19–20
  party-building as element of, 16–19
  resource mobilization and, 19–20
  revolutionary legacy of, 189–95
  in Shaan-Gan-Ning area, 79–81
  Sino-Japanese War and, 16, 21, 137–38
    extractive capacity during, 77–81, 86–107
    response to fiscal shock during, 96
  Yan'an Rectification Campaign, 20, 138, 144, 147–48, 149, 151
  Zunyi Conference, 139–40, 145
Chinese Revolution (1911), 12
Chinese Revolutionary Party. *See* Zhonghua Gemin Dang (Chinese Revolutionary Party)
Christian Democratic Party (Italy), 24
Civil War (1946–1949), in China, 1, 195
clientelism, 201–2
Comintern (Communist International)
  Chen Duxiu and, 112–13
  Chiang Kai-shek and, 162
  Chinese Communist Party supported by, 57–58, 59, 62, 63, 66
  Kuomintang supported by, 59–61
  Mao Zedong and, 139, 143, 144
  mass mobilization infrastructure of CCP influenced by, 111, 120–24
    under Chen Duxiu, 112–13
    Returned Student Faction and, 120
  Qu Qiubai and, 124–25
communism. *See* Chinese Communist Party (CCP); Indochinese Communist Party (ICP); Soviet Union; *specific topics*
Communist International. *See* Comintern (Communist International)
compliance theory, 33. *See also* mobilized compliance, infrastructure for, in CCP
Congress Party (India), 8
contracting-out parties, 24–25
Cuba, authoritarian regime in, 3
Cultural Revolution, 190, 194

Deng Xiaoping, 190–91
dominant leaders, dominant leadership and. *See also* quasi-dominant leaders, Chiang Kai-shek as; *specific people*
  in Chinese Communist Party, 40
    historical legacy of, 190–91, 202–5
  in Kuomintang, 153–60
    historical legacy of, 196–98, 202–5
  regime type and, 40

Index

dominant political parties, in authoritarian regimes, 3
domination, political
  conceptual approach to, 4–12
  contingencies for, 10–12
  equilibrium outcomes for, 10–12
  of revolutionary parties
    definition of, 4–5
    dominant party leaders in, 6–7
    origins of, 4
    in political revolutions, 5
    power-sharing by, 6–7
    in social revolutions, 5
  theoretical approach to, 4–12

East Timor, 204
ELF. *See* Eritrean Liberation Front (ELF)
elites, political
  in Chinese Communist Party, mass mobilization infrastructure and, 119–35
  in Kuomintang, 58–61, 68–69
  Mao Zedong supported by, 138
  resource mobilization of, 8, 9
  in revolutionary parties
    balance of power and, 39–43
    incentives for, 34–43
    party-building in, 39–43
    power consolidation among, 42–43
    power sharing among, 41–42
EPLF. *See* Eritrean People's Liberation Front (EPLF)
Eritrea, authoritarian regime in, 3
Eritrean Liberation Front (ELF), 3, 40
Eritrean People's Liberation Front (EPLF), 43
Etzioni, Amitai, 33
extractive capacity. *See also* grain extraction, infrastructure for
  of Chinese Communist Party, 62–67
    expropriation limits and, 67
    mobilized compliance infrastructure and, 86–95
    prewar resource mobilization and, 55–56
    revenue sources and, 63–67, 79, 100
    taxation policies, 63–64, 66–67, 80
  of Kuomintang, 67–73
    through elite mobilization, 68–69
    during Sino-Japanese War, 76–78
    taxation policies, 60–61, 70, 71–72
    transformation of, 70–72
    urban bias in, 71–73
  resource mobilization and, theoretical approach to, 45–51
  of revolutionary parties, 33–34, 49–51

factionalism, 24
failed states, after regime collapse, 3
First United Front, 57, 58–59, 79, 111, 152, 195, 198
  Chen Duxiu and, 112
  collapse of, 112, 121
  formation of, 153, 155, 156
  mass mobilization infrastructure of CCP and, 111–12, 116–17
  power struggle within, 160
FLN. *See* National Liberation Front (FLN)
Four Major Mobilization Campaign, 88
FRETILIN, in East Timor, 204
From Mobilization to Revolution (Tilly), 33
From Rebel to Ruler (Saich), 52
FSLN. *See* Sandinista National Liberation Front (FSLN)

GPRA. *See* Provisional Government of the Algerian Republic (GPRA)
grain burden distribution schemes
  by Chinese Communist Party, 101–2
    progressive scheme by, 102
    across rural classes, 102–3
    during Sino-Japanese War, 101, 102
    zero-sum game within the village, 92–93
  by Kuomintang, 101–2
    regressive scheme by, 101–2
    across rural classes, 102–3
    during Sino-Japanese War, 101, 102
grain extraction, infrastructure for. *See also* mobilized compliance, infrastructure for, in CCP
  by Chinese Communist Party, 96–108
    areas of, 97–98
    degree of extraction, 97–98
    impact of grassroots party, 89–95, 103–7
    scale of government and, 106
  informal institutions in, 106–7
  in Jin-Cha-Ji area, 97–98, 102–3
  in Jin-Sui area, 97–98, 102–3
  by Kuomintang, 81–86, 96–108
    under Chiang Kai-shek, 83–84
    degree of extraction, 97–98
    impact of grassroots party, 103–7
    through indirect rule, 83–84
    through land tax centralization, 82–83, 84–86
    liability of elite mobilization, 81–86
    scale of government and, 106
  as revenue source, 100
  reversed causality and, 106–7
  in Shaan-Gan-Nin area, 97–98, 102–3

grain levies. *See also* mobilized compliance, infrastructure for, in CCP
  by Chinese Communist Party, 86–95
    coercive tactics, 88, 90, 93–94
    contribution to government revenue, 98–101
    democratic assessment of, 91–92
    diffusion of mobilized compliance, 94–95
    expansion of, 87–89
    grain burden distribution schemes, 92–93
    local elites and, 90
    statistical analysis of, 105
    village as unit for, 90–91
  as fiscal extraction, 100
  by Kuomintang
    contribution to government revenue, 98–101
    statistical analysis of, 105
Great Leap Forward, 190, 194
Gu Yinfen, 70–71
Gu Zhun, 193–94
guardianship dilemma, 205

Ha Huy Tap, 45
Hezbollah, in Lebanon, 204
hierarchical mass parties, 24–25
Ho Chi Minh. *See* Nguyen Ai Quoc (Ho Chi Minh)
Hu Han-min, 17–18, 21, 162–65, 176. *See also* Kuomintang (KMT)
  anti-Chiang coalitions, 170
  loss of leadership, 177–78
  New Kuomintang and, 169
  party-building under, 168–69
  on power-sharing arrangements, 165
  Sun Yat-sen as influence on, 168–69
Hungarian Communist Party, 41
Hungary, revolutionary parties in, 41

ICP. *See* Indochinese Communist Party (ICP)
ideology, party
  political mobilization and, 9
  of revolutionary parties
    accommodationist approach to, 37
    as constraining/sorting device, 34–37
    ideological sources of, 31
    for incoherent parties, 35
    mobilization infrastructure and, 36
    resource mobilization and, 36
incoherent revolutionary parties, 35
incorporation, as power accumulation strategy, 6–7
independence parties, revolutionary parties and, 52–53

India
  Bharatiya Janata Party in, 36–37
  Congress Party in, 8
Indochinese Communist Party (ICP), 2, 10, 44–45. *See also* Nguyen Ai Quoc (Ho Chi Minh)
Institutional Revolutionary Party (Mexico), 36
iron law of oligarchy, 42–43
Italy, Christian Democratic Party in, 24

Japan. *See also* Sino-Japanese War
  Wang Ching-wei negotiations with, 177
Jin-Cha-Ji area, grain extraction in, 97–98, 102–3
Jin-Sui area, 80–81
  grain extraction in, 97–98, 102–3
  mobilized compliance in, 86–95
  opium revenue, 81

Key, V. O., 24
Khider, Mohammed, 42
Kirov, Sergei, 11
KMT. *See* Kuomintang (KMT)
Korean War, 195
Kuibyshev, Nikolay, 163
Kung Hsiang-hsi, 69
Kuomintang (KMT). *See also* First United Front; grain extraction, infrastructure for; Hu Han-min; methodological approach, to Republican-era China; Wang Ching-wei; *specific topics*
  baojia system, 68–69
  Chinese Communist Party and
    defeat by, 1–4
    as organizational influence, 195–96
    Second United Front and, 76
  clientelism and, 201–2
  collapse of, 1
  Comintern support of, 59–61
  composition of Central Committee, 18
  conceptual approach to, 152–53
  as revolutionary organization, 152
  constitution of, 157
  contestation of leadership within, 161–66
  dominant leadership in, 153–60
  historical legacy of, 196–98, 202–5
  extractive capacity of, 67–73
    through elite mobilization, 68–69
    during Sino-Japanese War, 76–78
    taxation policies, 70, 71–72
    transformation of, 70–72
    urban bias in, 71–73
  factions within, 154–55, 161
    ideological orientation of, 161

Reorganization Faction, 169
territorial control of, 161
grain burden distribution schemes by, 101–2
regressive, 101–2
grain levies by
  contribution to government revenue, 98–101
  statistical analysis of, 105
Manifesto of the China Revolutionary Party, 156
May 4 Student Movement and, 154, 157
membership from 1921–1949, 2
mobilization infrastructures for
  under Chiang Kai-shek, 69, 83–84
  historical legacy of, 202–5
  through indirect rule, 83–86
  through land tax centralization, 82–83, 84–86
Nanjing Nationalist Government and, 61, 68
Northern Expedition and, 70–71, 161, 170, 178
party membership in, 159, 171–75
  educational background of, 184
  expansion of, 158–60, 170, 182–85
  geographic distribution of, 158–60, 174–75
  indigenous peoples in, 200
  military members, 172
  from 1926–1937, 171
  from 1937–1945, 183
  occupational background of, 171–74, 183–84, 185
  party cells and committees, 158–60, 176, 186
  rank-and-file members, 172, 173
  recruitment for, 200
party organization
  through grassroots approaches, 158–60, 175–76, 185
  through party reforms, 3, 167, 198–99
  weaknesses in, 152
party reforms, 158–60, 176–85
  through organizational changes, 3, 167, 198–99
party-building by
  under Chiang Kai-shek, 166–70, 198–202
  conflicting outcomes, 170–76
  historical legacy of, 198–202
  under Hu Han-min, 168–69
  through patronage networks, 166–68
power struggles within, 160–76
  civil war as result of, 164–65
  among elites, 161–66

power-sharing in, 165–66
predecessors of, 56
prewar resource mobilization by (1921–1937)
  distribution of customs revenue, 72–73
  elite mobilization, 58–61
  extractive capacity of, 67–73
  fiscal foundations for, 70–72
  summary of, 73–74
  theoretical approach to, 55–56
provincial party committee chairmen (from 1928–1949), 179
during Qing Dynasty, role in collapse of, 154
reversal of fortune for, 1–4, 12
  contingent events for, 20–21
  methodological approach to, 16–21
  party strength as element in, 19–20
  resource mobilization and, 19–20
revolutionary legacy of, 195–202
Shanghai Massacre, 61
Sino-Japanese War and, 19–20, 21, 152, 185
  extractive capacity during, 76–78, 81–86
  response to fiscal shock during, 85
  as successor to earlier revolutionary organizations, 154
Sun Yat-sen and, 21, 58, 111, 154–55
in Taiwan, 200
Three Principles of the People League, 181–82
Whampoa Military Academy and, 58–59
Zhang Guotao defection to, 142

Le Hong Phong, 45
Lebanon, Hezbollah in, 204
Lenin, Vladimir, 156–57, 186
Li Dazhao, 111
Li Lisan, 45, 121–22
  leadership of CCP under, 127
  rejection of, 129–30
Li Weihan, 121, 122
Li Zongren, 178
Liao Zhongkai, 155, 162
Liu Lantao, 93
Liu Shaoqi, 122
Lixing She (Blue Shirt Society), 168
Lominadze, Besso, 121
Long March, 139–42
Luo Zhanglong, 122

Madison, James, 24
Malayan Communist Party, 41
Manifesto of the China Revolutionary Party, 156

Mao Zedong, 3, 17–18
  Comintern and, 139, 143, 144
  consolidation of power for, 110, 137–44, 151, 202
    among party elites, 138
  dominant leadership of, 40, 190
  Long March and, 140–42
  party-building strategies under, 144–48
    during power struggles, 147–48
  Red Army and, 64–65, 123–24
  rural mobilization infrastructure under, 148–51
    CCP membership and, 148, 149–51
    party cells/committees in, 150
  Wang Ming and, 138
    Comintern and, 144
    power struggles between, 142–44, 147–48
  Yan'an Rectification Campaign, 20, 138, 144, 147–49, 151
  Zhang Guotao and, 138
    power struggles between, 140–42, 145–46
  Zunyi Conference and, 139–40, 145
Maring. See Sneevliet, Henk (Maring)
Marx, Karl, 113–14
Marxism, Sinification of, 144
mass mobilization infrastructure, of CCP, from 1921–1934
  under Chen Duxiu, 111–14, 120
    ascension to power, 111
    Comintern and, 112–13
    loss of leadership, 124–25, 136
  collapse of, 119–35
  Comintern influences on, 111, 120–24
    under Chen Duxiu, 112–13
    Returned Student Faction and, 120
  Communist revolution and, 111–19
  contradictions in, 130–35
  First United Front and, 111–12, 116–17
  Marx and, 113–14
  methodological approach to, 24–25, 110
  origins of, 111–13
    Comintern influence in, 111
  party elites in, 119–35
    rise and fall of, 122–24
  party leadership in, 120–24
    turnovers in, 120–22, 125–30
  party membership, 117, 132
    party cells, 118, 119, 132, 150
    transformation of, 133–35
  party-building through, 113–16
    discriminatory strategies for, 124–30
    internal reports on, 115
  rich peasant policies in, 127–29
  in social movements, 3
  Soviet Union as influence on, 113–16, 125–29
    Party Manifesto, 113
    through worker support, 126–27
  summary of, 135–36
  theoretical approach to, 109–10
  weaknesses of, 130–35
    lack of grassroots organization, 131–33
  worker-centric mobilization, 116–19, 135
    grassroots party cells, 118–19, 150
    through party membership, 117–19, 133–35, 150
mass mobilization infrastructure, of KMT
  under Chiang Kai-shek, 180–81
  elite-centric, 155–57
    formation of, 155–56
    Leninist principles in, 156–57, 186
    methodological approach to, 110
May 4 Student Movement, 154, 157
methodological approach, to Republican-era China, 12–30
  on collapse of Kuomintang, 25–27
  conflict-centric view, 23
  data sources in, 15–16
  mass mobilization and, 24–25
  party-building and, 22–24
    in authoritarian regimes, 23
    in totalitarian regimes, 23
  power sharing studies, 22–24
  research design, 12–16
    case selection in, 12–13
    intraparty elite balance of power in, 13–14
    key variables, 13–15
    mixed methods approach, 13
    mobilization infrastructure in, 15
    party-building strategies, 14
    resource mobilization capacity in, 15
  resource endowment and, 25
  resource mobilization and, 24–25, 27
    in research design, 15
  on rise of communism, 25–27
  Sino-Japanese War in, 25–27
Mexico, Institutional Revolutionary Party, 36
Mif, Pavel, 122, 144
MNR. See Revolutionary Nationalist Movement (MNR)
mobilization, political. See also Chinese Communist Party (CCP); Kuomintang (KMT); mobilized compliance, infrastructure for, in CCP
  conceptual approach to, 4–12

Index

contingencies for, 10–12
equilibrium outcomes for, 10–12
mobilized compliance, 20
party ideology and, 9
through party-building, 9
resource mobilization, 7–10
  of elites, 8, 9
  financial resources, 7
  human resources, 7
  for social movements, 7
  state capacity as influence on, 7
theoretical approach to, 4–12
mobilization infrastructures, for financial resource. *See also* mass mobilization infrastructure, of CCP; mass mobilization infrastructure, of KMT; rural mobilization infrastructure, of CCP
for Kuomintang
  under Chiang Kai-shek, 83–84
  historical legacy of, 202–5
  through indirect rule, 83–86
  through land tax centralization, 82–83, 84–86
  liability of, 81–86
mobilized compliance, infrastructure for, in CCP
  compensation effect of, 89–95
  extractive capacity, 86–95
  ineffectiveness of bureaucratic capacity, 87–89
  Four Major Mobilization Campaign, 88
  grain levies and, 86–95
    coercive tactics, 88, 90, 93–94
    democratic assessment of, 91–92
    diffusion of mobilized compliance, 94–95
    expansion of, 87–89
    grain burden distribution schemes within a village, 92–93
    local elites and, 90
    village as unit for, 90–91
  historical legacy of, 191–95
  institutionalization of, 191–95
  in Jin-Sui area, 86–95
  monetary policies and, 86
  of peasants, 91–92, 201
  in Shaan-Gan-Ning area, 94–95
  during Sino-Japanese War, 96
  voluntary, 89
Movement for Socialism, in Bolivia, 37

Nanjing Nationalist Government, 61, 68
National Liberation Front (FLN), 10, 35, 42
nationalism, in Algeria, 35
Neumann, Heinz, 121
New Kuomintang party, 169
Nguyen Ai Quoc (Ho Chi Minh), 10, 40, 44–45
Nicaragua, Sandinista National Liberation Front in, 8
Northern Expedition, 70–71, 161, 170, 178

oligarchy. *See* iron law of oligarchy
opium production, Chinese Communist Party revenue from, 80, 81

party ideology. *See* ideology, party
party leadership. *See also* Chinese Communist Party (CCP); Kuomintang (KMT)
  in mass mobilization infrastructure of CCP, 120–24
  turnovers in leadership, 120–22, 125–30
party-building
  under Chiang Kai-shek, 166–70
  through patronage networks, 166–68
  as quasi-dominant leader, 179–82
  in Chinese Communist Party, 16–19
  under Mao Zedong, 144–48
  mass mobilization infrastructure and, 113–16, 124–30, 147–48
  under Hu Han-min, 168–69
by Kuomintang
  under Chiang Kai-shek, 166–70, 179–82
  conflicting outcomes, 170–76
  historical legacy of, 198–202
  under Hu Han-min, 168–69
  through patronage networks, 166–68
methodological approach to, 22–24
  in authoritarian regimes, 23
  in totalitarian regimes, 23
political mobilization through, 9
in revolutionary parties, 34–43, 188–89
  elite incentives in, 39–43
  intraparty power struggles as element of, 41
patronage networks
  Chiang Kai-shek and, 166–68
  Wang Ching-wei and, 175
peasant populations, mobilization of
  mass mobilization infrastructure in, 127–29
  through mobilized compliance, 91–92, 201
People's Republic of China (PRC)
  Cultural Revolution in, 190
  formation of, 191–92
  Great Leap Forward and, 190
  mobilized compliance in, 194
  tax collection in, 192–94
political domination. *See* domination, political
political elites. *See* elites, political

political mobilization. *See* mobilization, political
political parties. *See also* party-building;
        revolutionary parties
    in autocracies, 24
    contracting-out, 24–25
    hierarchical mass parties, 24–25
    ideology of, 9
    mobilization of, through party-building, 9
    religious organizations and, 48
    in totalitarian regimes, 24
political party strength
    of Chinese Communist Party, 19–20
    dynamic model of, 50
    of Kuomintang, 19–20
power, consolidation of. *See also* power
        accumulation strategies; power-sharing
    by Chiang Kai-shek, 110, 178–79
    by Chinese Communist Party, 16–19
    in Kuomintang, 16–19
    by Mao Zedong, 110, 137–44, 151, 202
        among party elites, 138
    methodological approach to, 22–24
    in revolutionary parties, 42–43
power accumulation strategies
    incorporation as, 6–7
    state substitution as, 6–7
power-sharing
    Hu Han-min on, 165
    in Kuomintang, 165–66
    by revolutionary parties, 6–7
    Wang Ching-wei on, 165, 169–70
PRC. *See* People's Republic of China (PRC)
Provisional Government of the Algerian
        Republic (GPRA), 44

Qing Dynasty, 12
    Kuomintang role in collapse of, 154, 156–57
Qu Qiubai, 45, 120, 121, 122
    Comintern and, 124–25
quasi-dominant leaders, Chiang Kai-shek as,
        176–85, 196–98
    party-building under, 179–82
    power consolidation under, 178–79

Red Army
    Chinese Communist Party and, 64–66
    expansion of, 65
    Mao Zedong and, 64–65, 123, 124
religious organizations, political parties and, 48
Ren Bishi, 122, 143
Reorganization Faction, 169
resource mobilization. *See also* Chinese
        Communist Party (CCP); Kuomintang
(KMT); revolutionary parties;
        specific topics
    extractive capacity and, 61–73
        theoretical approach to, 61–62
    methodological approach to, 15, 24–25, 27
        in research design, 15
    of political elites, 8, 9
    political mobilization and, 7–10
        of elites, 8, 9
        financial resources, 7
        human resources, 7
        for social movements, 7
        state capacity as influence on, 7
    in revolutionary parties, 32–34
Revolutionary Nationalist Movement (MNR),
        8, 10, 37
revolutionary organizations. *See also specific
        topics*
    in Algeria, 11
    in Vietnam, 11
revolutionary parties. *See also* Chinese
        Communist Party (CCP);
        Kuomintang (KMT)
    balance of power in, 39–43
        intraparty struggles, 41
        power sharing, 41–42
    in Bolivia, 37
    domination leadership in, 45–51
    endogenous/exogenous interactions in, 31–32
    in Hungary, 41
    ideological sources of, 31
        accommodationist approach to, 37
        as constraining/sorting device, 34–37
        incoherent, 35
        mobilization infrastructure and, 36
    independence parties and, 52–53
    party elites
        balance of power and, 39–43
        incentives for, 34–43
        for party-building, 39–43
        power consolidation among, 42–43
        power sharing among, 41–42
    party mobilization infrastructure, 43–45
        comparative advantages of, 46–48
        equilibria of, 44, 49–51
        mobilized compliance, 47
    party-building in, 32, 34–43
        elite incentives in, 39–43
        historical legacy of, 188–89
        intraparty power struggles as element of, 41
    political domination of
        definition of revolutionary parties, 4–5
        dominant party leaders, 6–7

Index

origins of, 4
  in political revolutions, 5
  power-sharing by, 6–7
  in social revolutions, 5
  psychological sources of, 31
  resource mobilization in, 32–34
    bureaucratic capacity and, 33–34
    challenges in, 45–46
    compliance theory for, 33
    extractive capacity and, 33–34, 49–51
    fiscal, 45–46
    leadership domination to, 45–51
    party ideology and, 36
    social networks and, 31–32
    strength of, 32
    dynamic model of, 50
    taxation models and, 46
    theoretical approach to, 31–32
    summary of, 51–54
revolutions, political, structural perspective of, 11
rural mobilization infrastructure, of CCP
  under Mao Zedong, 148–51
    CCP membership and, 148, 149–51
    party cells/committees in, 150
  theoretical approach to, 137–38

Saich, Tony, 52
Sandinista National Liberation Front (FSLN), 8
Second United Front, 76
Shaan-Gan-Ning area
  grain extraction in, 97–98
  mobilized compliance in, 94–95
Shanghai Massacre, 61
Sino-Japanese War, 1–2, 10
  Chiang Kai-shek during, 21
  Chinese Communist Party expansion during, 16, 21, 137–38
  resource mobilization and, 75–76
  data for grain extraction infrastructure during, 103–4
  extractive capacity during, 76–81
  of Kuomintang, 76–77
  grain burden distribution schemes during, 101, 102
  Kuomintang and, 19–20, 21, 152, 185
    extractive capacity during, 76–78
    extractive capacity of, 76–77
    fiscal shocks for, 76–77
    resource mobilization and, 75–76
  mobilized compliance infrastructure during, 96
  resource mobilization during, 75–76
Sneevliet, Henk (Maring), 111
social movements

mass mobilization and, 3
resource mobilization for, 7
Soong Tse-ven, 60, 69, 70–71, 164–65
Soviet Union
  Ho Chi Minh trained in, 44–45
  Kuomintang supported by, 1–2
  mass mobilization infrastructure of CCP influenced by, 113–16, 125–29
    Party Manifesto, 113
    through worker support, 126–27
Stalin, Joseph, 11, 190
state building. *See* state formation, bellicist theory of
state capacity, resource mobilization influenced by, 7
state formation, bellicist theory of, 27, 51
state substitution, as power accumulation strategy, 6–7
Su Zhaozheng, 121
Sun Fengming, 177
Sun Ke, 164–65
Sun Yat-sen, 17–18, 21, 58, 111, 122, 195. *See also* First United Front; Kuomintang (KMT)
  Chiang Kai-shek influenced by, 180
  death of, 160
  dominant leadership of, 154–55
    alliance with Chinese Communist Party, 154–55
    alliance with Soviet Union, 154
    Comintern and, 155
  elite-centric mass mobilization under, 155–57
  formation of, 155–56
  Leninist principles in, 156–57, 186
  Hu Han-min influenced by, 168–69
  May 4 Student Movement and, 154, 157
  reform of Kuomintang under, 158–60
  Three Principles of the People, 152–53, 154, 157

Taiwan, Kuomintang in, 200
taxation mechanisms and models
  for Kuomintang, land tax centralization, 82–83, 84–86
  in People's Republic of China, 192–94
  Three Principles of the People, 152–53, 154, 157
  Three Principles of the People Youth League, 181–82
  through patronage networks, in KMT, 166–68
Tilly, Charles, 33
totalitarian regimes, political parties in, 24
Tran Phu, 45

Vietnam
  authoritarian regime in, 3
  dominant leadership in, 40
  Indochinese Communist Party in, 2, 10
voluntary compliance infrastructure, 89

Wang Ching-wei, 17–18, 21, 112, 162, 164, 176
  loss of leadership, 177–78
  negotiations with Japanese, 177
  patronage networks and, 175
  on power-sharing, 165, 169–70
Wang Kequan, 122
Wang Ming, 20, 65, 122
  Mao Zedong and, 138
    Comintern and, 144
    power struggles between, 142–44, 147–48
Whampoa Military Academy, 58–59, 162

Xi Jinping, 191
Xiang Zhongfa, 121, 122, 123–24
Xu Zhongzhi, 162

Yan Xishan, 82, 170
Yan'an Rectification Campaign, 20, 138, 144, 147–48, 149, 151
Yang Hucheng, 21
Yuan Shikai, 154

Zeng Xing, 155
Zhang Fagui, 170
Zhang Guotao, 20, 111, 205
  defection to KMT, 142
  Mao Zedong and, 138
    power struggles between, 140–42, 145–46
  Zhou Enlai and, 142
Zhang Hao, 145–46
Zhang Wentian, 139–40
Zhang Xueliang, 21, 75
Zhang Zuolin, 175
Zhonghua Gemin Dang (Chinese Revolutionary Party), 56
Zhou Enlai, 121–22, 124, 139–40, 142
Zhu De, 123, 124, 139–40
Zhu Jiahua, 180
Zunyi Conference, 139–40, 145

For EU product safety concerns, contact us at Calle de José Abascal, 56–1º,
28003 Madrid, Spain or eugpsr@cambridge.org.